MEDIATING INDIANNESS

AMERICAN INDIAN STUDIES SERIES

Gordon Henry, *Series Editor*

Bawaajimo: A Dialect of Dreams in Anishinaabe Language and Literature, Margaret Noodin 978-1-61186-105-1

Centering Anishinaabeg Studies: Understanding the World through Stories, edited by Jill Doerfler, Niigaanwewidam James Sinclair, and Heidi Kiiwetinepinesiik Stark 978-1-61186-067-2

Document of Expectations, Devon Abbott Mihesuah 978-1-61186-011-5

Dragonfly Dance, Denise K. Lajimodiere 978-0-87013-982-6

Facing the Future: The Indian Child Welfare Act at 30, edited by Matthew L. M. Fletcher, Wenona T. Singel, and Kathryn E. Fort 978-0-87013-860-7

Follow the Blackbirds, Gwen Nell Westerman 978-1-61186-092-4

The Indian Who Bombed Berlin and Other Stories, Ralph Salisbury 978-0-87013-847-8

Masculindians: Conversations about Indigenous Manhood, edited by Sam McKegney 978-1-61186-129-7

Mediating Indianness, edited by Cathy Covell Waegner 978-1-61186-151-8

The Murder of Joe White: Ojibwe Leadership and Colonialism in Wisconsin, Erik M. Redix 978-1-61186-145-7

National Monuments, Heid E. Erdrich 978-0-87013-848-5

Ogimawkwe Mitigwaki (*Queen of the Woods*), Simon Pokagon 978-0-87013-987-1

Ottawa Stories from the Springs: anishinaabe dibaadjimowinan wodi gaa binjibaamigak wodi mookodjiwong e zhinikaadek, translated and edited by Howard Webkamigad 978-1-61186-138-9

Plain of Jars and Other Stories, Geary Hobson 978-0-87013-998-7

Sacred Wilderness, Susan Power 978-1-61186-111-2

Seeing Red—Hollywood's Pixeled Skins: American Indians and Film, edited by LeAnne Howe, Harvey Markowitz, and Denise K. Cummings 978-1-61186-081-8

Shedding Skins: Four Sioux Poets, edited by Adrian C. Louis 978-0-87013-823-2

Stories through Theories/Theories through Stories: North American Indian Writing, Storytelling, and Critique, edited by Gordon D. Henry Jr., Nieves Pascual Soler, and Silvia Martinez-Falquina 978-0-87013-841-6

That Guy Wolf Dancing, Elizabeth Cook-Lynn 978-1-61186-139-9

Those Who Belong: Identity, Family, Blood, and Citizenship among the White Earth Anishinaabeg, Jill Doerfler 978-1-61186-169-3

Visualities: Perspectives on Contemporary American Indian Film and Art, edited by Denise K. Cummings 978-0-87013-999-4

Writing Home: Indigenous Narratives of Resistance, Michael D. Wilson 978-0-87013-818-8

MEDIATING INDIANNESS

Edited by Cathy Covell Waegner

Michigan State University Press
East Lansing

⊗The paper used in this publication meets the minimum requirements of ANSI/NISO Z39.48-1992 (R 1997) (Permanence of Paper).

Michigan State University Press
East Lansing, Michigan 48823-5245

Printed and bound in the United States of America.

21 20 19 18 17 16 15 1 2 3 4 5 6 7 8 9 10

Library of Congress Control Number: 2014954453
ISBN: 978-1-61186-151-8 (pbk.)
ISBN: 978-1-60917-436-1 (ebook: PDF)
ISBN: 978-1-62895-045-8 (ebook: ePub)
ISBN: 978-1-62896-045-7 (ebook: Kindle)

Book design by Scribe Inc. (www.scribenet.com)
Cover design by Shaun Allshouse, www.shaunallshouse.com
Cover image is Indigenous Indices of Refraction, Brussels 2012 ©2012 Kimberly Blaeser, and is used with permission.

green press INITIATIVE Michigan State University Press is a member of the Green Press Initiative and is committed to developing and encouraging ecologically responsible publishing practices. For more information about the Green Press Initiative and the use of recycled paper in book publishing, please visit www.greenpressinitiative.org.

Visit Michigan State University Press at www.msupress.org

For Gerald Vizenor

Ever teasing, ever transgressing,
consummate storier
—Chris LaLonde

rock gestures copper
words shimmer in shifting light–
new mediations
—Kimberly Blaeser

Contents

Preface

The photograph on the cover of this volume, taken by photographer-poet Kimberly Blaeser, is titled "Indigenous Indices of Refraction, Brussels 2012." Amid the neatly lined-up Belgian figurines in a souvenir shop—the yeoman, ministers, cooks, market-sellers, aristocrats, and toy soldiers boasting Belgian flags against a backdrop of fans made of famed Flemish lace—we see a young woman gazing through the collectibles at two quite different doppelgänger images of herself, one close up and directly inquiring, the other more distanced, formally portrait-like. Possibly referencing both the pioneering fifteenth-century Flemish paintings that encoded the "other side" of the scene on the canvas in convex-mirror reflection, and the Irwin Brothers' studio century-old photograph of Mabel Mahseet, a Comanche woman who boldly frees herself from the interior frame of the picture,[1] Blaeser presents—we presume—an intricate transcultural view of "Indianness."

But where is the Indigenousness, beyond association with an earlier picture? Does it lie with the young woman foregrounded in the picture and her contrasting images? With the ostensibly darker-skinned man reflected in the mirror? Is it perhaps the inexplicable profile-shadow in the center of the back frame? If we look very carefully on the lower left of one of the interior frames, we see the photographer—is her mediating (camera) eye the source of the "Indigenous indices"? And what is meant here by "indices"—measurements? taxonomy? layers of indirectness? "Measurements" and "taxonomy" call up ambivalent associations of membership in the Dawes Commission rolls of tribal members, determining who was to receive "allotments" at the beginning of the twentieth century or, very recently, who is entitled to monetary compensation from the federal government. Indices as "layers of indirectness," as multiple refractions, does more justice to the postmodern Native, with his or her palimpsests of inherited and selected identity, each layer deepening and slightly transforming.

As the articles in this volume reveal, Indianness can be as complex and elusive as the Indigeneity of this photograph. Or it can be as stereotypical as the typically Belgian dolls and stand-up tin soldiers with their toy cannons. As indicated in the "Notes on Contributors" at the end of this volume, Kimberly Blaeser is Anishinaabe and an enrolled—as well as engagé—member of the Minnesota Chippewa Tribe, having grown up on the White Earth Reservation in northwestern Minnesota; she is now a professor of English at the University of Wisconsin–Milwaukee. Furthermore, as her name reveals and as she tells her readers in a well-known poem called "Family Tree,"[2] she is also of German descent. Part of the elaborate network of her given and chosen affiliations was presented at the "Crow Commons" performance by five scholars, reproduced in Part 4 of this volume, at the MESEA (Multi-Ethnic Studies: Europe and the Americas) biennial conference in Barcelona, Spain, where the contributors to the volume met in June 2012 to develop the "Mediating Indianness" project.

The unusual project team combines (Native) American and European (German, British, Romanian) scholars, an interdisciplinary group of both senior and junior academics from the fields of cultural and literary studies, anthropology, rhetoric, and creative writing. The initial findings were presented in a four-panel format at the MESEA conference, the overall conference theme being "Media and Mediated Performances of Ethnicity." The goal of the "Mediating Indianness" project was to offer fresh insights into interpretation of pertinent cultural and historical phenomena, drawing transnationally and academically creatively on resources and scholarship from both sides of the Atlantic. Not irrelevantly, we considered subtitling this volume "Transatlantic Refractions."

Indeed, the title of the project and this volume was chosen with care. The selection of such a potentially essentialist term as "Indianness"[3] is deliberate and indeed points to the complex *construction* of ethnicity as filtered through media, despite frequent assertions of "authenticity." From William "Buffalo Bill" Cody's claim, extravagantly advertised on both sides of the Atlantic, that he was staging "true-to-life" scenes from Indian life in his Wild West shows (1872–1908) to contemporary Native hip-hopper Quese IMC's announcement that in his engagé songs he tells his people's "own history" and draws on their *true* culture,[4] media of all types have served to promote disparate agendas claiming legitimacy. In this project we present a broad range of media instruments, such as print, film, stage play, ritual dance performance, music, recorded interviews, orality/alphabetization, photography, rhetoric of treaty-making (and-breaking), and virtual networking; as the volume's contributors show, these instruments have been used in exploitative, informative, educative, sustaining, protesting, and/or entertaining ways to negotiate Native American identities and images.[5] We do not shy away from the issue of evaluation, and how it is only tangential to medial[6] artificiality, in offering explanations of why, for instance, the multimedia blitz of Eric Gansworth's 2010 experimental play *Re-Creation Story* is perceived as conveying viable and valuable Indianness.

"Conveying" is a common lexical item in the word field of "*mediating*," along with "transmitting," "conducting," and "imparting," as well as the semantically more intrusive "filtering," "distilling," "screening," and "intervening." All of these processes play a role in our discussions. We place far less emphasis on the reconciliation involved in a key meaning of "mediating," however: the arbitration, intercession, or settlement a "mediator" can strive for between two disagreeing parties suggests resolution. This is probably too pat for most artistic and cultural-theoretical discourse, in which the constant dialogizing interchange is vital. Granted, arbitration has proved important for the present legal negotiation of compensation for American Indian land. If we return to the seminal MELUS interview with Gerald Vizenor in 1981,[7] however, we recall that he, now a grandmaster of Native American studies, stated his self-understanding as a Native author and scholar succinctly: "I'm an upsetter."[8] He aimed to upend the mediation of Indianness that had resulted in fixed stereotyping; in a strong objection that has become a meme echoing throughout Native American studies ever since, he memorably proclaimed: "[Natives Americans are] invented and we're invented from traditional static standards and we are stuck in coins and words like artifacts."[9]

The active mediation that can expose the construction of this stereotyping, can stir up processes to pry Native Americans from those standardized coins, is the strategy of the Native artists and writers dealt with in this volume, as well as, on a metalevel, the tactic of the scholar-contributors presenting their analyses. To capture the element of "upset," we can stress the concept of "refracting," which the cover photo depicts so richly. Refraction is a distortion. It appears frequently in academic debates on translation,[10] since the translator must constantly make choices based on sociocultural contexts that necessarily "distort" the source text. In medical treatises, the refractive power of the eye is examined, underpinning the figurative refraction of perception in general. With their investigations of wave behavior, physicists potentially supply colorful terms for cultural studies with articles on the "negative index of refraction" or even "negative refraction metamaterials."[11] We seem to move far beyond physics into the realm of metaphor when considering that refraction causes not only *mirages* but also *rainbows*—I refer to these images later in discussing

Gerald Vizenor's relevant poem "Crow Commonage," the final contribution to our volume. Robert Stam, one of the scholars instrumental in the (re)discovery of Mikhail Bakhtin's dialogics and its integration into cinematic and ethnic studies, reminds us of the complexity and multiplicity of levels of refraction in cultural mediation in this reading of one of Bakhtin's insights: "Rather than the direct reflection of the real, or even a refraction of the real, artistic discourse constitutes a refraction of a refraction, that is, a mediated version of an already textualized and discursivized socio-ideological world."[12]

Part 1 of this volume, titled "Transethnicity/Transculturality and Protest in Historical Contexts," focuses on some of the complicated refractions of cultural processes from early nineteenth-century appropriation and self-construction to postmodern mediation of historical events. Billy J. Stratton's contribution, "'You Have Liberty to Return to Your Own Country': Tecumseh, Myth, and the Rhetoric of Native Sovereignty," sets the tenor of our volume with its scrutiny of historical Native protest in word and deed in connection with notions of sovereignty and linked with transcultural, performative, and "cultural capital" concerns in various media. Stratton pleads for a decolonializing consideration of the Shawnee leader's speeches and the myriad representations of this organizer of a large Native confederacy, a ripping away of the layers of vested-interest assessments and "imperial nostalgia"[13] that have instrumentalized the defiant Tecumseh as everything from a formidable but deservedly conquerable enemy to one of the patrons, as it were, of a shopping mall. Tecumseh, along with the female figure of Pocahontas, has been immortalized in determining tableaux in the U.S. Capitol's *Frieze of American History* as Native Americans subsumed into the annals of American history shaped as "Manifest Destiny." A careful investigation of the historical contexts of Tecumseh's speeches, praised by contemporary listeners as commanding, reveals his clever rhetorical and political strategies (such as transculturally refracting the American government's arguments in order to apply them eloquently to the Native Americans' situation) intended to further pan-Indigenous objection to the developing policies of early nineteenth-century expansion, which led to the brutal Indian removals. Supported by postulates from postmodern theorists such as Jacques Derrida and Roland Barthes as well as by Gerald Vizenor's committed philosophy and configuration of Native studies semiotics, Stratton demonstrates how the cultural capital of Tecumseh's leadership and rhetorical performances has been appropriated, and he eloquently calls for a renewing valuation of Tecumseh's powerful (speech) acts:

> Despite the force of colonial negation, deracination, and suppression, the words and ideas attributed to Tecumseh break through the imposed silences that artistic representations such as *The Death of Tecumseh* and *The Dying Tecumseh* represent. This function allows for the articulation of conceptions of Native sovereignty that actively question the legitimacy of hegemonic discourse, while serving as powerful inspiration for contemporary Native American and Indigenous scholars and activists in the ongoing contest over the meaning of the past and the challenge of the future.[14]

The volume continues with a remarkable example of ethnic self-invention in the nineteenth century: the autobiographical account of the African American slave cum Native prince Okah Tubbee. In her article "'IndiVisible' Identities: Mediating Native American and African American Encounters and Transethnic Identity," Sonja Georgi presents *A Thrilling Sketch of the Life of Okah Tubbee* (1848, 1852)[15] in the context of theory on transethnic affiliation and mixed-race autobiography, in which the narrative itself is often biracial with a white editor and an ethnic "subject," and in this case with the additional editing by Tubbee's Native wife. Denying tricksterism, the slave Warner McCary, apparently of African American and white ancestry, claimed that he had been captured from the Choctaw by whites as a young child, which he proved by suddenly being able to speak Choctaw when he first met Native Americans. He became a musician billed on stage as a "Negro Indian . . . the greatest wonder of the age,"[16] as well as a doctor/medicine man, and he vociferously espoused the cause of the Natives threatened by removal. Tracing the many twists and refractions in Tubbee's diverse career, Georgi shrewdly mediates his autobiographical account as a valuable achievement by this "free mover" in the antebellum times of severe ethnic restriction, reading "the allegedly invented tale of a runaway slave and charlatan as a narrative of transethnic agency."[17]

Tubbee's self-agency has a certain correspondence to the Native participants in Buffalo Bill's wildly popular Wild West shows who, despite being squeezed into egregious stereotypes in the arena, found ways to exercise a measure of performative self-empowerment in what Cathy Covell Waegner calls the "transcultural crack" ("'Buffalo Bill Takes a Scalp': Mediated Transculturality on Both Sides of the Atlantic with William F. Cody's Wild West, from Show to Hollywood and YouTube"). In one of the earliest motion picture sequences (1894), a Buffalo Bill "Show Indian" looks at the camera/audience and brandishes his knife, cutting through an invisible wall between performers onstage and camera, which substitutes for the live spectators—a moment of choice, of empowerment, of "giving the crowd a thrill" as the Show Indian protagonist puts it in James Welch's historical novel *The Heartsong of Charging Elk*.[18] For an ethnic performer playing for a largely white audience, opening up this transcultural crack can permit the entry of enthusiasm, critique, irony, or protest. Applying Wolfgang Welsch's theory of transculturality, along with updates by Günter Lenz and others, Waegner offers as a pragmatic analytical tool five modes of *mediated transculturality*, which emerge from the grandiose historical Wild West shows as well as from four works depicting it and from present-day revivals. On a metalevel, the *reception* of the Wild West mediation, especially in Internet platforms, runs a full spectrum ranging from naively approving to highly critical.

Native literature, with its emphasis on tricksters and deconstruction of imposed stereotypes, has long lent itself to postmodern impulses. In his contribution "Native Postmodern? Re-mediating History in the Fiction of Stephen Graham Jones and D. L. Birchfield," A. Robert Lee offers a dazzling survey of the Native postmodern, focusing on the recent and so far undervalued fiction of Jones and Birchfield, in particular the ways it refracts and reorients their respective tribal pasts, Blackfeet and Choctaw, linking them to European postmodern stimuli: "Far from some baroque dance, the texts at issue give consequential new bearings, full of transperspective and so willing to reach beyond, even travesty, inherited boundaries of chronology or place. . . . Trickster, that wily stalwart of Native tradition, is given leave to join at the creative interface with Bakhtinian dialogics, Eco's 'open' text, or the semiotics of simulation/dissimulation argued for by Baudrillard."[19] Jones's novel *Ledfeather* (2008) polyvocally intertwines two tribal eras, those of the contemporary Browning-Glacier Blackfeet reservation and the Starvation Winter of 1883–84, whereas Choctaw D. L. Birchfield's *Field of Honor* (2004) metafictionally zigzags through the colonial steps from Indian removal to Vietnam, giving the narrative, as Lee tells us, the shape of an elaborate board-game, encoding a re-cultivated historical past into "inerasable tribal presence."[20]

Lee has also written an expert review of *Blue Ravens: Historical Novel* (2014), the stunning new work by Gerald Vizenor. In the early review titled "Flight Times in Gerald Vizenor's *Blue Ravens:* White Earth Mediating History," Lee places the novel, which embeds a carefully researched geographical and historical "zeitgeist" panorama of the World War I era with surprising connections, in the contexts of Vizenor's canon, of modernism with its call for creative upsetting, and of postmodern writing with "Native signature."[21] In less than a decade after the last Show Indians had returned from their final Wild West performances in Europe, young Natives—including Vizenor's relatives from the White Earth Reservation—were once more crossing the Atlantic, projecting images of Indianness in Europe, this time in the brutal trench warfare of the Great War in Europe. Basile Beaulieu, the storier-narrator, and his quasi-twin brother, Aloysius, a visual artist, are immediately commanded to serve as scouts, on the stereotypical assumption that Natives are natural trackers. Wearing war paint, these gentle and artistic brothers are indeed strategically effective scouts on the front, yet reform the cliché into engaged but grotesque protest, becoming "a native presence in the folly and deadly chaos of the war . . . [with] mutable comic face[s] in the rain" and gore of the combat.[22] Their return to White Earth becomes untenable—"The native soldiers who were once the military occupiers [on the Rhine in Koblenz, Germany] had returned to the ironic situation of the occupied on a federal reservation,"[23] and the brothers again journey to Europe, to Paris, to join in the international movement of modernism. Aloysius's enormous, shimmering blue ravens with protective wings, expressive claws, and totemic eyes fly off the artist's and the novelist's paper and soar creatively through the transatlantic landscape.

Part 2 of this volume is titled "(Trans)Media Literacy, Youth Cultures, and Nation." From her hands-on work with helping to develop the "Four Worlds Curriculum" for the Cherokee Nation's educational programs, Ellen Cushman can adeptly demonstrate how the Cherokee syllabary rejects the European-centered paradigm of knowledge based on the Western alphabet. In Cushman's article, "**ᏣᎳᎩ ᏗᎪᏪᎵ** Cherokee Writing: Mediating Traditions, Codifying Nation," we are introduced to Sequoyah's system of writing, which was developed in the 1820s and encoded the Cherokee vernacular and logic, undermining the colonial project of Western literacy for the Native Americans. Cushman places her inquiry within the theoretical framework provided by Walter D. Mignolo, an Argentinian semiotician and cultural anthropologist, especially his work on "decolonial rhetoric," including "epistemic de-linking" and other acts of "epistemic disobedience." The contemporary Cherokee educational programs mediate not only from syllabary to alphabet but also from *material* semiotic forms to syllabary and alphabet: "This curriculum translates the knowledge presented in a selection of our wampum belts into English and Cherokee and is organized around Cherokee historical time and physical location,"[24] thus strengthening the Cherokee sense of diachronic and synchronic nationhood.

In his learned essay called "'We Can Tell Our Own History, We Can

Tell Our Own Future': Quese IMC, Culture Shock Camp, and an Indigenous Hip-Hop Movement," Chris LaLonde vividly shows how the lively Native hip-hop scene has adopted and refracted the African American rap strategies, injecting twenty-first-century flavor into the notion of Indigenous Nations: "Given the subversive and communal nature of hip-hop . . . , it makes sense that young Native artists would turn to it as a vehicle for expression and resistance."[25] Like many youthful hip-hop artists belonging to ethnicities and language groups around the globe, Quese IMC raps largely in "first-person singular," fusing highly personal lyrics with ethnic protest and calls for tolerance and constructive action through (postmodern) elements of complex intertextuality (hip-hop "sampling"), "flow, layering, and rupture."[26] He eloquently objects to being stereotyped by audiences and other MCs: "and it pisses me off / when I get on a stage and MC battle/ and I am ready with punch lines / and the guy just babbles / making fun of my origin, my being / and my blood's racing / dissing my culture / telling me to go back to the reservation / calling me a drunk savage and everything that's degrading / dancing around like a cartoon *indian* / while the crowd's hooraying / cheering like idiots / and I'm tired of it being okay for you to make fun of my people."[27] Ceremonial drumming and traditional chanting root Quese IMC's rapping in Pawnee and Seminole cultures, and simultaneously serve the cause of pan-Indigeneity.

Quese IMC's strategies are intricate, but his messages to his generally youthful audiences are clear. In contrast, Christine Plicht skillfully shows us why cinemagoers continue to be baffled yet fascinated by Jim Jarmusch's experimental film *Dead Man*, in which a Romantic poetry-reciting Native named "Nobody" defies all received notions of "alterity." Applying the definitions of alterity developed by Emmanuel Lévinas, Jeffrey T. Nealon, Michael Taussig, and Dan Zahavi, Plicht demonstrates, with her article "Jim Jarmusch's *Dead Man* Revisited: Still Thwarting All Cultural and Cinematic Notions of Alterity," how the director's cinematic devices work against the grain to challenge the viewer's film literacy. The young town on the edge of the frontier is presented as a corroded and corrupt wasteland; the upright easterner named William Blake both slowly dies throughout the movie and becomes a war-painted outlaw, unwittingly guided by Nobody's Anglo-Indigenous spirituality; communication fails on all levels. The haunting, minimalistic soundtrack consists in the electric guitar twangs of the Canadian rock musician Neil Young, who affiliates with Native Americanness, subjectively responding to the film sequences. Plicht contrasts this unconventional soundtrack with those of *Dances with Wolves* and *The New World*, convincing us that the multifarious confusion of the *Dead Man* spectator is productive: "The film illustrates the possible deconstruction of all relations and simultaneously asks the viewer to engage in a constant reconstruction."[28]

In "Mediating the Native Gaze: The American Indian Youth's Cinematic Presence in Chris Eyre's Films," Ludmila Martanovschi turns to a leading Native filmmaker to examine the ways his movies present the perspective of and on his youthful protagonists. Not unlike the first-person learner in an ethnic bildungsroman, the young characters are depicted as forging an adolescent sense of self in connection to their family, peers, and mentors, and in negotiation, often under incapacitating circumstances, with standard media images of both teenagerism and Nativeness. The fathers tend to be particularly problematic, immersed in their own insecurities or deep-set anger at past and present injustices, looking askance at their offspring or absenting themselves entirely. Martanovschi references not only recent scholarship on Indigenous film but also Eyre's interview statements in Neil Diamond's ambitious and award-winning documentary on the Hollywood Indian, ironically titled *Reel Injun* (2009); Chris Eyre calls on media producers to deconstruct received stereotypes and thus do justice to viable and dynamically changing contemporary Native identities.[29] This is certainly Eyre's own agenda in the otherwise diverse films Martanovschi analyzes, pioneering *Smoke Signals* (1998), unsettling *Skins* (2002), and the more easily digestible, made-for television movie *The Edge of America* (2003). She assures us that "[the youthful protagonists'] finally healthy way of looking at the world and at their own tribal nations is posited as the promise of the Native perspective's continuance into the future."[30]

In her essay "Refraction and Helio-tropes: Native Photography and Visions of Light," Kimberly Blaeser adroitly places her work, and that of other Native photographers, notably Victor Masayesva, within a transmedia and transgeneric nexus of photography, text/poetry, and ceremony. The color choice and striking lighting can have celebratory or protesting, even political, force enhanced by the aesthetics. The unexpected juxtapositions, such as a bright green convertible parked at the base of an abandoned cliff dwelling in Masayesva's "Green Mobile" and the sharply outlined shadow of a young woman superimposed on ancient sandstone ruins in Blaeser's "Ephemeral Habitation at Cavate," [31] reverberate with associations of reclaimed time and cultural energy. "Ephemeral Habitation at Cavate" is a profoundly synesthetic "picto-poem," a full poem interlacing with the photo, reinforced by the "mottled wall" background of a weather-worn cliff dwelling and the further textual stratum of "DO NOT COPY," like a twenty-first-century petroglyph;[32] to select one component that supports a leitmotif of this volume, we can stress the tilted female shadow figure that leans into and onto—and thus personally recovers—the texture of her possible past. The poem describes the shadow angle as "slant and thin," a tenuous but nonetheless powerful refraction recalling Emily Dickinson's poetic dictum to "tell it slant";[33] surely this is what Blaeser accomplishes in mediating her own and other lyrical Native photographs.

In the center of the volume we have placed a creative "Interlude," which refers self-reflexively to the experiences of the MESEA conference from which the *Mediating Indianness* volume arose. Evelina Zuni Lucero has produced "RefleXions: A Creative Essay," in which the double meaning of "reflections" as both thoughts and mirrorings demonstrates the linking of the conference themes and her personal reactions with historical transatlantic movements. Bravely autobiographical and complexly metaphorical, Lucero does not exempt herself as a cell-phoning, multilingual academic from the distorting, often misguided and violent cultural processes that the giant bronze statue of Christopher Columbus reigning on his high column near the port of Barcelona represents for her. She repeatedly emphasizes the unknown factor "X" graphically in her text, a factor needed to make exploding energy productive, a factor she and presumably her fellow panelists have touched base with as they return, somewhat "transformed," to their domestic spheres.[34] Jane Haladay's poem, spiked with Catalan and Spanish phrases, titled "Festa de Sant Joan: June 23, 2012, Barcelona, Spain," employs the theme of explosion in different ways, referring not only to the fireworks of the "Sant Joan" holiday celebration but also to the explosion from the narrowness of the Old World that led to the colonization and exploitation of the supposedly "uninhabited" and "new" one across the Atlantic. Like Lucero, Haladay views herself as a MESEA conference participant in the context of these historical processes with a constructive twist, Haladay's being that she and her MESEA colleagues of different ethnicities and nationalities join forces to establish new spaces for scholarly research and creative work: "my friend the Pueblo writer / and me, the white teacher / from North Carolina. / We mediate together / the streets' tight and ordered beauty / recognizing how too much compression / leads to sinister expansion / to a giddy blind desire / for the spaces and philosophies / long inhabited by others."[35]

Part 3 of *Mediating Indianness*, "Performance, Gender, and Cultural Capital," develops the gender angle of Blaeser's picto-poem within the contexts of performed ritual or onstage enactment and "marketable" but largely intangible resources. Anthropologist Sally McBeth valuably presents extensive personal observation, interviews, and immediate images casting light on a vibrant Native tradition in which women play a major role: "'The Bear Is Our Protector': Metaphor and Mediation in the Northern Ute (Nuche)

Bear Dance." This spring social dance, probably well over 1,000 years old, arises from the mythic encounter between a she-bear and a male Ute hunter: "Members of my interview sample have told me the dance is in imitation of the bear as it steps forward and backward at a standing tree, sharpening its claws for the coming hunt. Altogether, they say, this dance creates a rhythm that quickens the flow of blood in the body and renews a zest for life."[36] In addition to dance, the fertility celebration involves music, consecration practices, game-playing, and joking. The four days of the Bear Dance are "woman's choice"—but the powerful "Cat Man" and the male MC assure a strong measure of masculine control. As one of McBeth's photos clearly shows, the traditional music arising from wood rasps and bone instruments is now electronically transmitted by a microphone and a "boom box" with loudspeakers, and the use of new media such as Facebook and cell phones to advertise the celebration opens it up to twenty-first-century "viral communicative" transformations, refracting the Bear Dance on four levels of mediation[37] from "symbolic metaphor in ritual" to Ute "cultural capital" and serving to telescope eminent anthropologist Clifford Geertz's distinction between the emic (insider) and etic (outsider).

The Native all-around media artist Eric Gansworth has fully embraced an abundance of "new media" high jinks in his onstage narratives, including multiple functional reproductions of the Haudenosaunee Creation story in his 2008 experimental work *Re-Creation Story: A Play*, as Nicholle Dragone thoroughly demonstrates in her article "Eric Gansworth's Theatrical Productions: 'Indianness' Mediated through the Juxtaposition of Cultural Capital and Performance." The cultural and economic *value* of Native "products," such as oral tales, the elaborate Tuscarora beadwork "whimsies," dance regalia, the "Red Card" issued by the Haudenosaunee Confederacy, and even "Indianness" itself, rises in Gansworth's plays when the protagonists' personal negotiations are encoded in the exchanges and performances. In a moving example, the young woman named Fiction Tunny in Gansworth's *Smoke Dancing: A Novel* (2004) creates a strikingly individual and high-tech ceremonial dress of black velvet on which macabre purple beadwork roses both cover up and simultaneously expose the raised bruises that cover her body from her father's beatings. Fiction Tunny has ingeniously enlarged the hospital photographs taken of her bruises to model patterns for the telling roses.

In his chapter titled "Eric Gansworth's *Re-Creation Story*: Mediation and Remediation," John Purdy stresses the self-referentiality of Gansworth's functions as playwright, character, and—in *Home Fires and Reservation Roads: A Performance* (2011)—actor. An early interviewer of Gansworth and one of the first to support Gansworth's work academically, Purdy authoritatively presents the creative strategies generating the Onondaga novelist/playwright's work:

> [Eric Gansworth] has always been a media shifter whose visual art plays the chorus to his verbal arts. With his paintings and writings, Gansworth creates two forms of *mediation* as he situates between his vision and his audience: One mediation is visual and thus visceral and immediate; the other is verbal and thus cerebral and long-lived. However, while in the act of creating and performing, he may be engaged in a re-mediation: a reclamation of older narratives—personal and communal—that becomes a retelling of self, a re-creation story.[38]

Dragone has already pointed out the effect of Gansworth pressing the "return button" in *Re-Creation Story*, each replay being one with intentionally modulated differences: "By the end of [the repeated presentations of the Creation], the re-creation of Gansworth's own identity as a Haudenosaunee man has been mediated through the *overlaying* of retellings" [my emphasis].[39] Both Dragone and Purdy show how Gansworth's canon as a whole reflects an "overlaying" of echoing motifs, stories, and techniques that become his idio-cultural capital.

"Mobile Indians: Capitalism, the Performance of Mobility, and the Mediation of Place in Minda Martin's Documentary *Free Land*"—this is the title of Kerstin Schmidt's essay; processing an independent documentary film with an eye to visualization theory, Schmidt points out the fragility of (Native) women's movement within the dialectic of restriction and rootlessness. Minda Martin's experimental *Free Land* (2010) autobiographically recounts a young woman's quest to understand the sources of poverty and homelessness that define her family's history. Through diaries, telegraphed letters, maps, charts, photographs, interviews with the Dawes Commission, "found" film footage, and creative writing, the filmmaker multimedially reconstructs her ancestors' life paths, while at the same time altering and manipulating these media documents by coloring, racking focus, and posterization. The soundwork of the film is also meticulously forged, including "ghost voices" of her maternal ancestors. The documentary is a biting critique of capitalism and of the received idea that failure in economic performance should be assessed as individual, not systemic. As in Eric Gansworth's canon, the image of the rearview window, which simultaneously looks forward and backward, in which the present and the past overlap, serves as an image of current artistic use of past cultural capital. Schmidt's treatment of gender in this chapter does not exclusively focus on the women in Martin's family; she ends with a rearview analysis of the filmmaker's father's deeply lined face as a visual map of both his and his daughter's convoluted paths.

During the MESEA conference in Barcelona, the presentation of the "Mediating Indianness" project was concluded with a performance called "'Crow Commons': Creative Correspondences and Virtual Affiliations." This exposition of virtual exchanges was developed and staged by Native American studies scholars Kimberly Blaeser, Jane Haladay, Gordon Henry, Molly McGlennen, and Jesse Peters.[40] As the following comment by outgoing MESEA president Dorothea Fischer-Hornung manifests, the "Crow Commons" proved to be a particularly successful experiment in academic discourse:

> Attending the "Crows Commons" was one of the most profound moments in over a decade of organizing MESEA conferences. To be a part of the creative process amongst a "commons" of Native American authors and Native Studies scholars moved me deeply—both intellectually and emotionally. What remains is the honesty, the respect, the community, and—above all—the work.[41]

Robert Stam and Ella Shohat, who were keynote speakers at the conference and are the authors of—among a plethora of other publications—*Race in Translation: Culture Wars in the Postcolonial Atlantic* (2012), support Fischer-Hornung's assessment and her prospect of continued community and respect as well as *work* in academic and committed praxis applications and exchange:

> An exercise in Anishinaabe and Native Studies choral authorship, the four-part "Mediating Indianness" panel was for many attendees the highpoint of the 2012 MESEA Conference. The high-flying "Crow Commons" subpanel, for example, gave dynamic expression and lively form to what is often an abstract ideal—the commons. Framed by the playful drumming of Gordon Henry, the "Crow Commons" consisted of artfully interwoven poems, citations, and reflexions, some tragic and some wryly humorous. Playing every possible change on the avian theme—"strutting crows," "soaring spirits," scholarly "migrations," "roostings," and improvisational "winging it"—the performance modelled an inspiringly vibrant and dialogic alternative to academic protocols that too often form exercises in scholarly "enclosure" and a competitive search for "distinction." Books like *Mediating Indianness* open the way to a productive dialogue

> between the indigenous commons and the non-indigenous radical commons (itself partially inspired by the Indian as "exemplar of liberty") of movements like Occupy and Copyleft. *Mediating Indianness*, in this sense, forms a key moment in this long-deferred conversation.[42]

The name Gerald Vizenor was frequently invoked in the "Crow Commons" performance and its written version (in Part 4 of this volume); indeed, the entire volume is laced with references to his work and concepts. We are honored that he has written a response, an "Envoy." It consists in an affecting and witty original poem called "Crow Commonage" and a recovered, precious Ojibwe dream song. The inveterate trickster Vizenor smuggles the imagined blue ravens from his new novel into the crow commonage, since the "common crows" are "blued by sundown," becoming "blue shimmers alight in the white pine"; the raven-crows might be merely fleeting glimpses of "trace and transience," perhaps evanescent mirages, but with strong creative powers in their ability to spontaneously "change on the wing." These shape-shifting raven-crows are "translations," Vizenor tells us, or, drawing on the terminology of our cover photograph with which I began this preface, images of *refractions* in dialogic interchanges among scholars and cultures that enable the participants, corresponding to Vizenor's rainbow-like raven-crows, to "touch the distance."[43] Gerald Vizenor's "Envoy" includes an autobiographical note of astonishment that through his military service in Japan, he gained access to haiku as an expressive art form and obtained a fresh view on his Native "cultural capital":

> How ironic that my service as a soldier would lead to a literary association of haiku, and an overture to the natural motion of *anishinaabe* dream songs. Truly, haiku and imagistic poetry enhanced my perception and experience of *anishinaabe* dream songs, and my consideration of natural reason, comparative philosophies, and native survivance.[44]

As the contributions in this volume confirm, the processes of mediation can indeed take unexpected, indirect, and fruitfully unsettling paths.

ADDENDUM ON RECENT SCHOLARSHIP

Although, to our knowledge, our study combines disparate "media instruments" and examines the process of "mediating" in connection with Native

American studies concerns in ways not repeated in other volumes, this addendum to the preface offers some of the recent scholarship relating to relevant mediation. Most of these books are referenced in more detail in our articles.

Visualities: Perspectives on Contemporary American Indian Film and Art (2011), edited by Denise K. Cummings, gathers a pantheon of leading scholars to investigate a spectrum of (sub)genres within Indigenous art and film, always emphasizing the ethical perspective. No doubt she is correct in claiming that "the visual has become a primary means of mediating identities,"[45] particularly considering the ever deepening academic discourse on perception and "gaze"; indeed, her volume builds upon a specification of the "visual" in the term "visuality," which encodes hegemonies in its meaning: "visuality concerns the field of vision as a site of power and social control."[46] Dean Rader expands his contribution in Cummings's volume[47] into a fruitfully conceived and beautifully illustrated book *Engaged Resistance: American Indian Art, Literature, and Film from Alcatraz to the NMAI* (2011), which moves beyond the usual three genres mentioned in his title to the protest site of Alcatraz and the National Museum of the American Indian as syncretic and material sites of aesthetic and culturally political production.

A notably valuable and scholarly study of Native theater is Birgit Däwes's *Native North American Theater in a Global Age: Sites of Identity Construction and Transdifference* (2007). Her claims that the "spectator's gaze is always infused . . . with the historicized practice of colonial surveillance" and that "metatheatrical . . . strategies are used . . . to disturb the linear gaze" fit in meaningfully with the discussion in this volume of Eric Gansworth's experimental and mediational tactics to reorient that gaze.[48] To stress the "dialogic, relative, and processual"[49] positioning of Self and Other within the plays and in the performative situation itself, Däwes draws on Helmbrecht Breinig and Klaus Lösch's well-developed and still attractive theory of *transdifference* as propagated in *Multiculturalism in Contemporary Societies: Perspectives on Difference and Transdifference* (2002).

X-Marks: Native Signatures of Assent (2010), by Scott Richard Lyons, is a fascinating cultural-historical study based on the implications and extensions of the "X" with which Native leaders were compelled to sign so many infamous treaties; he attempts to answer his central question, "Is it possible today to envision the survival of indigenous identity, culture, and nationalization in a nonessentialistic manner?,"[50] by exposing the functions of contemporary "X-marks." I could well imagine viewing these Xs as a complex mode of mediation.

The form of mediation that appears to reign in current scholarship is that of film. Michelle Raheja has made great strides in developing a differentiated theory of Indigenous film in her *Reservation Reelism: Redfacing, Visual Sovereignty, and Representations of Native Americans in Film* (2010). Her concept of "redfacing," which moves beyond the use of coppery makeup for film actors to those actors' role as "human shields to absorb, deflect, redirect, and placate the fantasies projected in these 'celluloid Indians' by the dominant culture,"[51] can enrich the study of "mediating Indianness." Furthermore, Lee Schweninger, in *Imagic Moments: Indigenous North American Film* (2013), productively applies Gerald Vizenor's usage of "imagic moments," "survivance," and "absence/presence" to analyses of "(mis)representations" in selected Indigenous films after carefully considering the vexed discourse about which films can be placed in that category.[52]

A creatively didactic approach making Indigenous film studies accessible to students and the nonexpert public is adopted by the colorful volume *Seeing Red—Hollywood's Pixeled Skins: American Indians and Film* (2012), with its introduction cleverly structured as a film script by the editors LeAnne Howe, Harvey Markowitz, and Denise K. Cummings, and with its treasure trove of bibliographical resources. The contributions in the form of "reviews" of films containing Native Americans refreshingly stress the irony or humor in viewing the stereotypes and (mis)representations. The engaged volume edited by M. Elise Marubbio and Eric L. Buffalohead, *Native Americans on Film: Conversations, Teaching, and Theory* (2013), emphasizes the pedagogical benefits of placing "Native-centered" films on the syllabus, but not without involving the students in the current discourse on multifarious Indigenous film strategies. The editors wisely prioritize the rich and revealing, and often contradictory, stances of the filmmakers themselves rather than reduce the worldviews and communities to monolithic Nativeness contained in one overarching theory of Indigenous film.

German scholar Eva Gruber's excellent study of humor as a key strategy in Native Americans' negotiation and performance of their "Indianness" remains to be mentioned: *Humor in Contemporary Native North American Literature: Reimagining Nativeness* (2008). Gruber's work and the books mentioned above are a mere sampling of relevant English-language scholarship produced on both sides of the Atlantic. The burgeoning of such publications attests to sustainable forms of Native American resistance and presence, the examination of which, to use Native filmmaker Beverly R. Singer's still apt phrase, "wip[es]" the artificially distorting "war paint off the lens"[53] and investigates forms of deliberate refraction and creative mediation.

NOTES

1. The photograph, taken in the late nineteenth or early twentieth century and archived in the Western History Collections of the University of Oklahoma Libraries, is reproduced in Kimberly Blaeser, "Refraction and Helio-tropes: Native Photography and Visions of Light" in this volume.
2. The poem was included in Kimberly Blaeser, *Apprenticed to Justice* (Cambridge, UK: Salt Publishing, 2007).
3. Jodi A. Byrd's new, impressive study of American empire-building, *The Transit of Empire: Indigenous Critiques of Colonialism* (Minneapolis: University of Minnesota Press, 2011), strikingly utilizes the term "Indianness" in the negative sense of institutionalized perceptions of Native Americans that further the agenda of "U.S. settler imperialism" (xv). We operate more heuristically with the term, which for us can include a spectrum of functions covering the full range from imposed to self-determined.
4. Radio interview, 23 September 2011, http://www.blogtalkradio.com/nativetrailblazers/2011/09/23/native-hip-hop-artist—quese-imc-on-native-trailblazers.
5. As far as we can tell, no other publication combines these disparate "media instruments" and explicitly the process of "mediating" in connection with Native American studies. The addendum to this preface offers some of the recent scholarship relating to relevant mediation.
6. This fitting adjective appears ever more frequently in Continental European scholarship, and is included in, for example, book titles in English; in keeping with this volume's transatlantic shading, we will occasionally employ "transmedial."
7. Neal Bowers and Charles L. P. Silet, "An Interview with Gerald Vizenor," *MELUS* 8.1 (1981): 41–49.
8. Ibid., 45.
9. Ibid., 47.
10. For instance, David Katan, "Mediating the Point of Refraction and Playing with the Perlocutionary Effect: A Translator's Choice?," in *Cultural Studies: Interdisciplinarity and Translation*, ed. Stefan Herbrechter (Amsterdam: Rodopi, 2002), 177–195.
11. C. G. Parazzoli et al., "Experimental Verification and Simulation of Negative Index of Refraction Using Snell's Law," *Physical Review Letters* 90 (2003): n.p.; George V. Eleftheriades and Keith G. Balmain, eds., *Negative-Refraction Metamaterials* (Hoboken, NJ: John Wiley, 2005).
12. Robert Stam, "Bakhtin, Polyphony; and Ethnic/Racial Representation," in *Unspeakable Images: Ethnicity and the American Cinema*, ed. Lester D.

Friedman (Urbana: University of Illinois Press, 1991), 252. Stam's main mediation of Bakhtin's work is found in *Subversive Pleasures: Bakhtin, Cultural Criticism, and Film* (Baltimore: Johns Hopkins University Press, 1989).

13. Rosaldo Renato, *Culture and Truth: The Remaking of Social Analysis* (New York: Beacon Press, 1989).
14. Billy J. Stratton, "'You Have Liberty to Return to Your Own Country': Tecumseh, Myth, and the Rhetoric of Native Sovereignty," in this volume.
15. See Sonja Georgi, "'IndiVisible' Identities: Mediating Native American and African American Encounters and Transethnic Identity in *A Thrilling Sketch of the Life of Okah Tubbee*," in this volume, for exact titles of the various editions.
16. Quoted in ibid.
17. Ibid.
18. James Welch, *The Heartsong of Charging Elk: A Novel* (New York: Doubleday, 2000); published in the United Kingdom as *Heartsong* (Edinburgh: Canongate Books, 2001), 52; for more details about the early motion picture clip, see Cathy Waegner, "'Buffalo Bill Takes a Scalp': Mediated Transculturality on Both Sides of the Atlantic with William F. Cody's Wild West, from Show to Hollywood and YouTube," in this volume.
19. A. Robert Lee, "Native Postmodern? Re-mediating History in the Fiction of Stephen Graham Jones and D. L. Birchfield," in this volume.
20. Ibid.
21. A. Robert Lee, "Flight Times in Gerald Vizenor's *Blue Ravens:* White Earth Mediating History," in this volume.
22. Gerald Vizenor, *Blue Ravens: Historical Novel* (Middletown, CT: Wesleyan University Press, 2014), 130.
23. Ibid., 175.
24. Ellen Cushman, "ᏣᎳᎩ ᏗᎪᏪᎵ Cherokee Writing: Mediating Traditions, Codifying Nation," in this volume.
25. Chris LaLonde, "'We Can Tell Our Own History, We Can Tell Our Own Future': Quese IMC, Culture Shock Camp, and an Indigenous Hip-Hop Movement," in this volume.
26. Ibid.
27. Quese IMC, "I am my Ancestors," *The Betty Lena Project*, 2006, quoted in ibid.
28. Christine Plicht, "Jim Jarmusch's *Dead Man* Revisited: Still Thwarting All Cultural and Cinematic Notions of Alterity," in this volume.
29. Martanovschi incisively points out the young protagonists' discursive triumph over the "cowboys" who rudely take the boys' seats in the bus; the Native youths signify on "John Wayne's teeth" in a clever sing-chant. I cannot resist inserting an unsettling biographical experience here. When I visited

a remote village in the Sierra Madre de Oaxaca mountain range of Mexico in November 2013, an Indigenous girl was sitting at the checkout counter of a tiny store as its cashier; I noticed that she was immersed in watching a flickering black-and-white movie on an ancient TV. Looking more closely, I was quite shocked to see that she was captivated by a western from the 1950s in which the Natives were "red demons" and the Mexicans evil banditos, all soundly subdued by a triumphant John Wayne! This incident certainly reflected the resilience of mediated stereotypes and reinforced my belief in the importance of our "Mediating Indianness" project.

30. Ludmila Martanovschi, "Mediating the Native Gaze: The American Indian Youth's Cinematic Presence in Chris Eyre's Films," in this volume.
31. Figure 6 in Kimberly Blaeser, "Refraction and Helio-tropes: Native Photography and Visions of Light," in this volume.
32. Ibid.; the two quotations in this sentence are from Blaeser's picto-poem, figure 6.
33. The phrase "thin and slant" appears in Blaeser's picto-poem (ibid.); "Tell it slant" is Emily Dickinson's well-known phrasing from her unnamed poem, which begins "Tell all the Truth but tell it slant."
34. Evelina Zuni Lucero, "RefleXions: A Creative Essay," in this volume.
35. Jane Haladay, "Festa de Sant Joan: June 23, 2012, Barcelona, Spain," in this volume.
36. Sally McBeth, "'The Bear Is Our Protector': Metaphor and Mediation in the Northern Ute (Nuche) Bear Dance," in this volume.
37. See McBeth.
38. John Purdy, "Eric Gansworth's *Re-Creation Story*: Mediation and Remediation," in this volume.
39. Nicholle Dragone, "Eric Gansworth's Theatrical Productions: 'Indianness' Mediated through the Juxtaposition of Cultural Capital and Performance," in this volume.
40. Since Jesse Peters could not attend the MESEA conference in June 2012, Chris LaLonde kindly read Peters's texts.
41. Email from Dorothea Fischer-Hornung to Cathy Waegner, 16 March 2013.
42. Email from Robert Stam to Cathy Waegner, 23 March 2013; a more detailed version of the final point in the email comment can be found in Robert Stam and Ella Shohat, *Race in Translation: Culture Wars in the Postcolonial Atlantic* (New York: New York University Press, 2012): We "appreciate [Slavoj Žižek's] invocation of the 'commons,' a term increasingly used on the left to evoke shared noncommodified access to nature, open-source collaboration, and practices such as copyleft and creative commons. . . . The idea of 'the commons' animates the work of such diverse figures as Peter Linebaugh,

Naomi Klein, Arundhati Roy, Giuseppe Cocco, Vandana Shiva, Arturo Escobar, David Graeber, and Michael Hardt and Antonio Negri. Coming full circle, we would assert a further connection between the commons as conceived by the indigenous culture of the Red Atlantic (including Eva Morales) and the theory and praxis of the commons within the West itself (going back to the 'Charter of the Forest' section of the Magna Carta), all part of a multi-pronged struggle again all forms of 'enclosure,' including that of the 'intellectual commons'" (130).

43. All the quotations are from Gerald Vizenor, "'Envoy': Response to 'Crow Commons,'" in this volume.
44. Ibid., 307. How fitting it is that Gerald Vizenor's collection of haiku, *Favor of Crows: New and Collected Haiku*, was published in February 2014. The respective covers of *Favor of Crows* and the 2014 novel *Blue Ravens*, with the striking bird motifs created by Native artist Rick Bartow, seem to speak to each other, and we feel privileged to have had the opportunity to participate very modestly in the dialogue with our *Mediating Indianness* volume.
45. Denise K. Cummings, ed., *Visuality: Perspectives on Contemporary American Indian Film and Art* (East Lansing: Michigan State University Press, 2011), xiii.
46. Ibid., xiv.
47. Dean Rader, "Indigenous Semiotics and Shared Modernity," in ibid., 143–160.
48. Birgit Däwes, *Native North American Theater in a Global Age: Sites of Identity Construction and Transdifference* (Heidelberg: Universitätsverlag Winter 2007), 387.
49. Ibid., 385.
50. Scott Richard Lyons, *X-Marks: Native Signatures of Assent* (Minneapolis: University of Minnesota Press, 2010), 34.
51. Michelle Rahaja, *Reservation Reelism: Redfacing, Visual Sovereignty, and Representations of Native Americans in Film* (Lincoln: University of Nebraska Press, 2010), 11.
52. Lee Schweniger, *Imagic Moments: Indigenous North American Film* (Athens: University of Georgia Press, 2013), passim. Schweniger retrieves the felicitous term "imagic moments" from Gerald Vizenor, "Interimage Simulations: Fugitive Poses of Native American Indians," in *Multiculturalism in Contemporary Societies: Perspectives on Difference and Transdifference*, ed. Helmbrecht Breinig, Jürgen Gebhardt, and Klaus Lösch (Erlangen: Universitätsbund Erlangen-Nürnberg, 2002), 231. The other terms appear throughout Vizenor's corpus and are specifically documented in our articles.

53. Beverly R. Singer, *Wiping the War Paint Off the Lens: Native American Film and Video* (Minneapolis: University of Minnesota Press, 2001).

WORKS CITED

Blaeser, Kimberly. *Apprenticed to Justice*. Cambridge, UK: Salt Publishing, 2007.

Bowers, Neal, and Charles L. P. Silet, "An Interview with Gerald Vizenor," *MELUS* 8.1 (1981): 41–49.

Breinig, Helmbrecht, Jürgen Gebhardt, and Klaus Lösch, eds. *Multiculturalism in Contemporary Societies: Perspectives on Difference and Transdifference*, Erlangen: Universitätsbund Erlangen-Nürnberg, 2002.

Byrd, Jodi A. *The Transit of Empire: Indigenous Critiques of Colonialism*. Minneapolis: University of Minnesota Press, 2011.

Cummings, Denise K. ed. *Visuality: Perspectives on Contemporary American Indian Film and Art*. East Lansing: Michigan State University Press, 2011.

Däwes, Birgit. *Native North American Theater in a Global Age: Sites of Identity Construction and Transdifference*. Heidelberg: Universitätsverlag, Winter 2007.

Howe, LeAnne, Harvey Markowitz, and Denise K. Cummings, eds. *Seeing Red—Hollywood's Pixeled Skins: American Indians and Film*. East Lansing: Michigan State University Press, 2012.

Lyons, Scott Richard. *X-Marks: Native Signatures of Assent*. Minneapolis: University of Minnesota Press, 2010.

Marubbio, M. Elise, and Eric L. Buffalohead, *Native Americans on Film: Conversations, Teaching, and Theory*. Lexington: University Press of Kentucky, 2013.

Quese IMC, "I am my Ancestors," *The Betty Lena Project*, 2006.

———. Radio interview, 23 September 2011. Http://www.blogtalkradio.com/nativetrailblazers/2011/09/23/native-hip-hop-artist—quese-imc-on-native-trailblazers.

Rader, Dean. *Engaged Resistance: American Indian Art, Literature, and Film from Alcatraz to the NMAI*. Austin: University of Texas Press, 2011.

———. "Indigenous Semiotics and Shared Modernity." In Denise K. Cummings, ed., *Visuality: Perspectives on Contemporary American Indian Film and Art*, 143–160. East Lansing: Michigan State University Press, 2011.

Rahaja, Michelle. *Reservation Reelism: Redfacing, Visual Sovereignty, and Representations of Native Americans in Film*. Lincoln: University of Nebraska Press, 2010.

Rosaldo. *Culture and Truth: The Remaking of Social Analysis*. New York: Beacon Press, 1989.

Schweniger, Lee. *Imagic Moments: Indigenous North American Film*. Athens: University of Georgia Press, 2013.

Singer, Beverly R. *Wiping the War Paint Off the Lens: Native American Film and Video* Minneapolis: University of Minnesota Press, 2001.

Stam, Robert. "Bakhtin, Polyphony, and Ethnic/Racial Representation." In *Unspeakable Images: Ethnicity and the American Cinema*, ed. Lester D. Friedman, 251–276. Urbana: University of Illinois Press, 1991.

Stam, Robert and Ella Shohat. *Race in Translation: Culture Wars in the Postcolonial Atlantic*. New York: New York University Press, 2012.

Vizenor, Gerald. *Blue Ravens: Historical Novel*. Middletown, CT: Wesleyan University Press, 2014.

———. *Favor of Crows: New and Collected Haiku*. Middletown, CT: Wesleyan University Press, 2014.

———. "Interimage Simulations: Fugitive Poses of Native American Indians." In *Multiculturalism in Contemporary Societies: Perspectives on Difference and Transdifference*, ed. Helmbrecht Breinig, Jürgen Gebhardt, and Klaus Lösch, 229–247. Erlangen: Universitätsbund Erlangen-Nürnberg, 2002.

Welch, James. *The Heartsong of Charging Elk: A Novel*. New York: Doubleday, 2000.

PART ONE

Transethnicity/ Transculturality and Protest in Historical Contexts

"You Have Liberty to Return to Your Own Country"

Tecumseh, Myth, and the Rhetoric of Native Sovereignty

BILLY J. STRATTON

Two monumental artworks of the nineteenth century focusing on the death of the Shawnee leader Tecumseh tellingly reveal ways in which native American historical experience has been instrumentalized in the construction of national identity. Two decades after Tecumseh's death at the 1813 Battle of Moraviantown, the German artist Frederick Pettrich was commissioned to create a sculpture titled *The Dying Tecumseh*; this work was displayed in the U.S. Capitol in Washington, D.C., until 1916 and now resides in the collection of the Smithsonian American Art Museum. It is an imposing sculpture that offers an ostentatious representation of its subject, which, according to Bil Gilbert, "could be that of one of the champions of classical legend—an expiring Hector or Siegfried—who so engaged romantic artists of 19th-century Europe."[1] Positioned on the second floor of the museum in a space adorned by three of Thomas Moran's majestic landscape paintings, the sculpture depicting Tecumseh's death becomes a metaphor that signifies not only the tragic, yet inevitable, vanquishing of native American peoples but also the broader conquest of the North American wilderness. Tecumseh is also featured in a panel of the grand panorama of paintings rendered in the neoclassical style of simulated bas-relief that adorn the rotunda of the U.S. Capitol. Ambitiously titled *The Frieze of American History*,[2] this elaborate work includes panels depicting vital historical touchstones in North American history. Of the nineteen historical episodes that make up this series, nine of them concern colonial interactions

Figure 1. Pettrich's monumental sculpture (1856) presents Tecumseh as a classical dying hero amid the "untouched" American wilderness. (Courtesy of the Smithsonian American Art Museum, photo by Mary Tait)

with the native peoples of North America, including a particularly affecting work, *The Death of Tecumseh*. Although the tableau centers on a mounted American militiaman who has presumably just fired the fatal shot, set amid a scene of brutal hand-to-hand combat, one cannot help but admire the dignity of the fallen figure of Tecumseh supported by a fellow native warrior, and mourn for the man who was the architect of the most powerful pan-tribal confederacy in colonial history, eclipsing even that brought together in New England during the 1670s by the Pokanoket sachem Metacomet. It is, however, in the production of precisely the sort of mediating artistic representation of tragic Indianness found in these examples that Tecumseh's actions of protest have become appropriated and neutralized as both cultural capital and an indispensable component of the prevailing conception of American frontier history.

In the revisionist construction of the American historical narrative as exemplified by the Capitol frieze, such events and their results become a teleological origin and inevitability, rather than, as Maureen Konkle suggests, a "catastrophic" event in time that took place on Indian land.[3] The strong sense of narrative unity conveyed through the frieze panels acts to naturalize and substantiate the legacy of colonialism qua progress, while relegating

Figure 2. The Death of Tecumseh (fallen figure on the far right), U.S. Capitol Rotunda, 1878–1889. (Courtesy of the Architect of the Capitol office)

native people to a valiant, but doomed, past. Such images reduce native peoples and cultures to a totalizing monolith where the primary touchstone of particularity and difference is constituted in their relationship to colonial culture. Native people and history are thus rendered as fulfilling one of two dialectical positions: as noble or bloodthirsty savages—who either aided the endeavors of colonists or fought and resisted their relentless incursions. And while ironic simulations of cultural cooperation are presented in scenes of treaty-making in the frieze panels such as those featuring William Penn and the Lenape, as well as another depicting the agreement made between James Oglethorpe, the founder of the Georgia colony, and the Muskogee Creek near present-day Savannah, perhaps the most recognizable is the portrayal of the fable of Pocahontas interceding to spare John Smith from execution. Whereas such images may not constitute myths in and of themselves, as Roland Barthes has said, "myth is not defined by the object of its message, but by the way in which it utters this message."[4] In the case of *The Frieze of American History*, it is precisely in the way the constitutive stories have been incorporated into the master narrative of American history that allows them to function as alibis for discovery and conquest, while acting at the same time to deracinate and disembody native subjectivities from their own culturally relevant and specific lived experiences.

The native figures frozen in Pettrich's *The Dying Tecumseh* and *The Death of Tecumseh* continue to perpetuate distortions of native American culture and history in much the same way as the stark engravings and illustrations of *indian* savages that adorn the pages of nineteenth-century American frontier histories, or the 1956 film *The Searchers*, in which John Ford cast Navajo and non-native actors as Comanche warriors. Ford's casting represents just one example of the trivialization of ethnic and cultural difference perpetuated in Hollywood westerns. Andy Warhol's screen-print of Russell Means in his *American Indian Series* (1976), by contrast, disrupts such "terminal creeds"[5] by drawing attention to the artificiality and deceptiveness of American mythologization. Offering an alternative, as will be discussed in more detail, to a particular strain of American myth-making that renders colonial aggression as progress and native American resistance as tragic victimry, accounts of a number of Tecumseh's anticolonial speeches and public statements have been preserved in the historical record. As with the famous, if not apocryphal, words attributed to native leaders such as Logan, Seattle, and Chief Joseph, examples of native American oratory and their mediation, emendation, revision, and fictionalization by non-native writers and journalists have functioned to subvert and normalize the trauma of native frontier experience. This representational practice has worked to render native subjectivities as paragons of tragic remembrance in a way suggestive of Renato Rosaldo's concept of imperial nostalgia.[6] The efficacy of this farce is not simply a function of the deployment of the words of famous native leaders, however, but is only made possible by an American public's unwillingness to acknowledge the violent and traumatic nature of collective history. Thus, through figures such as Tecumseh, Logan, Seattle, and Chief Joseph, "native resistance was abstracted as a fugitive pose in national histories," to use the words of Gerald Vizenor, and imbued with meaning through the aesthetics of romantic victimry, tragedy, and nostalgia.[7] The functioning of this interpretive process is deconstructed in his work, as well as that of Rosaldo, who asserts in his description of imperial nostalgia that "the peculiarity of their yearning, of course, is that agents of colonialism long for the very forms of life they intentionally altered or destroyed . . . where people mourn the passing of what they themselves have transformed."[8]

As linguistic representations rather than muted imagistic simulations, examples of native American oratory are fraught with the indeterminacies of *différance* stemming from the inherent nature of such texts, and further exacerbated by the mediation of translation, transcription, and interpretation, as well as the unavoidable infelicities that attend the differences between oral and written texts. Despite these effects, however, native American oratory offers vital counterdiscourses that disrupt the stability of colonial narratives and bear witness to native American self-representation, conceptions of land, and efforts to resist invasion and defend territories in the face of colonial aggression and nation-building. When read ironically, and with a perceptive sense of natural reason, which necessitates an attention to what lies between the lines and within the silences, such stories can be freed from the tropes endemic to the literature of dominance and function instead as native stories of what Vizenor calls "survivance" with their assertions of "an active sense of presence over absence, deracination, and oblivion."[9] In the ideological struggle over the American past, writers and historians have sought to elide and neutralize enduring narratives of native survivance and to mediate Indianness through a process of historical and cultural deracination, which conspires to transform figures of anticolonial resistance into what Robert Warrior, in his review of Gordon Sayre's *The Indian Chief as Tragic Hero*, has described as "beloved heroes within early American literary texts."[10] Sayre addresses the place of Tecumseh in American literary history as it was constructed through a considerable outpouring of nineteenth-century literary texts centered upon his life and deeds. In the aftermath of Tecumseh's death, Sayre shows that his identity as a native American historical figure was reduced to little more than a function of the "men who built political or literary careers on their association with the Indian hero."[11] These signifying practices have inevitably resulted in the dis-identification of Tecumseh's words and being from relevant local histories and Shawnee tribal memories in the ambivalent colonial rhetoric of effacement.

In several popular stories that circulated in the years after Tecumseh's death at Moraviantown, for example, accounts of the unified native resistance to the ongoing colonial incursions that he helped to organize and lead following the American Revolution were most readily redefined through the all-too-common tropes of frontier revenge and racial hatred. The success of such efforts was aided by the public's unfamiliarity with native American culture and history, in which communal territorial control was most often obscured or erased within the fictive category of the *indian*, which Vizenor identifies as a "simulation and ruse of colonial dominance."[12] In the minds of most Americans of the early nineteenth century, native American people existed as the fearful creations of writers and journalists in the form of barbarous and savage creatures in captivity narratives and frontier adventure novels whereby cultural practices and tribal histories were concocted to support the Manichaean binaries of westward expansionism. In a narrative titled simply "Tecumseh," which first appeared in 1824, the legitimacy of Shawnee resistance is obfuscated through the substitution of a fictive story regarding the influence of the life and death of Tecumseh's purported father,[13] Onewequa.[14] The narrative conforms to the conventions of nineteenth-century melodrama and includes such episodes as an account of Onewequa's captivity and escape among the Creek, his romance and marriage to Tecumseh's supposed mother, Elohama, and his tragic death at the hands of "a party of men who had recently assisted in the massacre of an Indian settlement."[15] These fictional elements combine to form the basis of

Tecumseh's savagistic motivations of vengeance and retribution. That none of this seems to have any real historical basis is of no consequence since native people were denied an unmediated voice in the literary accounts produced at the time. Without the existence of an independent counter-discourse, the sensational account of Onewequa's death acted to reinforce the binary logic of colonial representation through the provocative question posed by Elohama, "Oh! my Onewequa, hast thou fallen thus, and is there none to avenge thee?"[16] With the child Tecumseh present as a silent witness held in her arms, Elohama exclaims:

> The arm of the warrior is broken since thou art laid low; but the young plant at my breast, who shall gather strength to crush thy destroyers. When thou hast past yon sky of storms, thou shalt see and converse with the Great Spirit amid his clouds. Then let thy petitions all rest on the name of Tecumseh. For him shalt thou ask the soul of the warrior and the strength of the mighty. Then shall he be as a whirlwind and a storm, that scatter desolation and death; as a fire spreading over the hill and valley, consuming the race of dark souls.[17]

The imagery employed in this scene recalls the melodramatic rhetoric of the vanishing *indian* that circulated in works such as J. M. Eastburn and Charles Sands's *Yamoyden: A Tale of the Wars of King Philip* (1820), James Fenimore Cooper's *The Last of the Mohicans* (1826), Dumont de Montigney's *Tecumseh: A Poem in Four Cantos* (1828), and John Augustus Stone's *Metamora; or, the Last of the Wampanoags* (1829). In all of these accounts, the *indian*, as with the wilderness, is undergoing a violent process of conquest and destruction under the force of the civilizing march of progress.

Following the description of Onewequa's dramatic death, the narrative resumes four years later with Elohama taking Tecumseh to visit the grave of his fallen but hitherto unknown father. In this scene the circuit of vengeance and retribution is made complete. When the identity of the grave is revealed to Tecumseh, along with a brief account of the circumstances of his father's death, he undergoes a transformation from *indian* child to "a ghastly ferocity."[18] Upon learning the "truth" of his father's fate, the narrative continues, "Tecumseh heard, and the livid glare of his eyes changed suddenly to flashes of lightning. 'Mother,' he exclaimed, 'give me my hatchet, and lead me to their villages, I will drink their blood; I will consume their race!'"[19] While such a visceral response may seem expected given the circumstances, the subtle elision of the rational motives of native warfare prompted by territorial invasion is made apparent through the strategic deployment of the motifs of *indian* savagery and cannibalism. The dissemination of such historical fictions acted to reduce, obscure, and trivialize the efforts undertaken by Tecumseh to organize communal and pan-tribal resistance as the result of an individualized, albeit dramatic, blood feud. The consequence of this epistemological shift is that the immediate motives of the confederated native resistance to colonial expansionism are effectively neutralized through the reinscription of frontier history as a chaotic and disordered struggle in which victimry and "exterminating hatred,"[20] rather than courage and justice, came to define the cycles of conflict that inevitably ensued.

In another story, "Sketches of Savage Life" (1836), the motive for Tecumseh's militarism is shifted from the death of his father to the ill treatment he is said to have endured as a young man at an unnamed borderland settlement. Tecumseh's character is also called into question in this account through the common cultural association with vice, for although he is described as "commanding in person," it is also claimed that from the age of twenty-three to twenty-six he was also "an inveterate drunkard and idler."[21] While Tecumseh is subjected to recurrent instances of abuse and insult, as the author reminds, these were merely "the usual contempt shown an Indian by the backwoodsmen" in which "the civilest expression used to him was 'Get out of the way, you Indian dog.'"[22] While unconscious at one of the border settlements after a bout of heavy drinking subsidized by money obtained from the sale of beaver and marten skins, "some mischievous fellows having previously drawn several stripes down his face and neck with black and green paint, and daubed his hair with turpentine, he was kicked out of the house."[23] This humiliating episode, which reinforces the stereotypes of native drunkenness and indolence, comes to a climax when Tecumseh is refused food at the home of a "backwoodsman," and then shot in the act of stealing chickens.[24] After fleeing back into the forest and regaining his senses Tecumseh reflects upon "the disgrace he had brought upon himself in the presence of the white man, and frequently before this time in the estimation of his own nation," vowing never again to drink alcohol, but also "that he would never forgive those who insulted him—that he declared war to the last day of his life against the Americans."[25]

It is no secret that the stereotype of the drunken *indian* has long been used to demean native American culture and to obfuscate the manner by which land theft in North America was orchestrated through treaties and other dubious but "legal" means. Even the words of Tecumseh's greatest British ally, General Isaac Brock, which appear in a letter to a British official describing Tecumseh, bear witness to the currency of these ideas: "from a life of dissipation he is not only become in every respect abstemious but has likewise prevailed on all his Nation, and many other Tribes, to follow his example."[26] Although such testimony might seem to confirm the veracity of Tecumseh's characterization in "Sketches of Savage Life," as James Laxer points out in *Tecumseh and Brock*, "Tecumseh's earlier 'life of dissipation' is a theme picked up by others who have written about the Shawnee chief. Significantly, it was a view not shared by Stephen Ruddell."[27] In fact, Ruddell, in his own memoir concerning his experiences with Tecumseh, claims just the opposite: "he rarely ever drank ardent spirits to excess—when inebriated he was widely different from other Indians—perfectly good humored and free from those savage ideas which distinguished his companions."[28] The dissemination of sordid narratives, rendered through the pathos of vice, vengeance, and savagism, acts to obscure and trivialize Tecumseh's actual motivations and those of his allies in defense of their political sovereignty and homelands.

Before obtaining my current position at the University of Denver, I taught at a university located in northwestern Ohio within traditional Shawnee territory. I often asked students about Tecumseh in the native American studies courses I taught there. Many indicated at least some level of familiarity, but when pressed about the significance of places such as Fallen Timbers and Fort Miamis in relation to Tecumseh's life, students rarely exhibited any detailed knowledge about these locations or their importance to the Shawnee people and Tecumseh's lived experience. Of course, these places were sites of significant instances of conflict between American and native forces in the late eighteenth and early nineteenth centuries. In Maumee, Ohio, at the Fallen Timbers Battlefield and Fort Miamis National Historic Site, an assortment of monuments memorializes and codifies the warfare of this period in the history of the former Northwest Territory. Included among them is Turkey Foot Rock, a landmark where, according to the official placard, "Chief Turkey Foot of the Ottawa Indians rallied his warriors during the battle." At the center of the park is a fifteen-foot bronze sculpture created by Bruce Saville depicting General Anthony Wayne, the commander of the American forces. Wayne is positioned in this memorial between and above two other figures, both anonymous, an *indian* warrior and a Kentucky militiaman. The narrative told through these figures reinforces the perspective found in "Sketches of Savage Life," in which the unified native resistance to colonial expansion led by Tecumseh is rendered as "the bloodthirsty vengeance of the Shawnees and other tribes, roused by the war spirit, which soon led them over the frontier."[29] With Wayne commanding the center position and being the only figure granted a named identity, a clear verdict on this conflict and its place in the myth of the American frontier is insinuated while also shaping the memory and diachronic identity of the past.

A nearby informational plaque reinforces the symbolic capital of Wayne's role in bringing "civilization" to the region, declaring that as a result of the Battle of Fallen Timbers, "the Indians surrendered their claims to most of Ohio. The treaty pacified the frontier for fifteen years and opened Ohio to peaceful settlement." Although the word "Indian" is found numerous times on the monument and supplementary informational panels, the term serves as little more than an empty signifier and simulation of the voided past of native people who are rendered silent in the legends of American historiography.

The mediation and cultural capital distortion of Fallen Timbers is made even more apparent on the other side of U.S. Highway 24, where a portion of the former battleground has been developed into an outdoor mall complex named The Shops at Fallen Timbers. In a way that is both different from and similar to the recirculation of the tropes of war in *The Dying Tecumseh* and *The Death of Tecumseh*—where the monument (re)presents as the shopping mall effaces through differing forms of appropriation—the effect on the public's (mis)understanding of Tecumseh as well as Shawnee and native American history is largely the same. Located within the confines of conventional American historiography and popular culture, Tecumseh's life and his untimely death as a beloved leader in the native American struggle against colonial expansionism are recast in such memorials as a romanticized national tragedy. As a consequence, his words and speeches advocating pan-Indian unity and national sovereignty function as spectral soliloquies in the rhetoric of disappearance, vanishing, and conquest. It is as though Tecumseh is assigned a new identity through the politics of nostalgic tragedy as a martyr, betrayed by the British, which allows him to be recuperated and claimed as one of America's own, bearing ironic witness to the manifest manners of providential frontier history and exceptionalist destiny.

As the primary aim of this chapter is to address the historical legitimacy to which systems of colonial representation lay claim, it is also important to consider the various ways in which the speeches of Tecumseh can function to challenge and disrupt mediations of Indianness in the associated discourses of American history and popular culture. In the pages to follow, I consider how the words of Tecumseh, as well as subsequent descriptions of them, can be seen as efforts to articulate claims of tribal sovereignty, while also serving as some of the earliest vehicles of decolonization. Using the Battle of Fallen Timbers (20 August 1794) and the Battle of Moraviantown (5 October 1813) as useful historical anchor points, we can trace the trajectory of Tecumseh's influence as the leader of Shawnee opposition to American encroachment in conjunction with his emergence as an

Figure 3. Two-cent postage stamp featuring the so-called General Anthony Wayne Memorial, erected in 1929 to commemorate the 1794 Battle of Fallen Timbers. (Courtesy of David Aeschliman, www.stamp-collecting-world.com)

influential and charismatic proponent of pan-tribal unity. As a participant in both battles and among the native American representatives who refused to sign the Treaty of Greenville of 1795, in which the Shawnee, Wyandot, Miami, and other native nations were compelled to cede large portions of their territories, Tecumseh demonstrated fidelity to his commitment to native national sovereignty and cultural preservation. In the testimony of those who witnessed Tecumseh's speeches in support of these causes, he is almost universally described as an exceedingly eloquent and commanding speaker, with one witness, John McDonald, a settler of the Ohio Territory, describing him as "one of the most dignified men I ever beheld."[30] General Brock is another contemporary who shared this view, writing of Tecumseh, "a more sagacious or a more gallant warrior does not, I believe, exist. He was the admiration of everyone who conversed with him."[31] Despite the praise and acknowledgment of Tecumseh's "distinguished character" and "dauntless spirit"[32] offered by American and British observers of the time, however, he nonetheless remained in the minds of many a "remarkable savage" who was given over to the "deeper penciling of ferocity and bloodthirstiness" commonly attributed to native people.[33]

To better appreciate Tecumseh's oratory and rhetorical practice, which has been celebrated in numerous history texts and literary anthologies, one must be attentive to the influence of a complex array of hermeneutic factors. Because Tecumseh was not in control of the manner by which his words and ideas were disseminated—outside the context of his oratorical performances—in their reiteration to American readers, details such as the audience, the context and occasion for the speeches, the linguistic capacity of interpreters, as well as the sources used for the transcriptions and translations all become critical areas of concern. That Tecumseh's words have been transcribed and reprinted for American audiences allows his ideas to endure in the American historical narrative. Such mediations, however, also expose Tecumseh's words to the effects of iterability, which Jacques Derrida defines as the ways in which written words can be disseminated beyond the original context of their performance, which is to say, the particular author, subject, and immediate audience of a given text.[34] Circumstances such as these demand a responsiveness to a multiplicity of rhetorical functions and strategies when considering Tecumseh's speeches, and not just those uttered by him but also those utilized by translators, editors, and journalists who sought to bring his words to the attention of a curious American public. Consequently, contemporary readers must be open to efforts to disentangle the persuasive linguistic strategies that are inextricably tied to the specific occasion and audience of Tecumseh's speeches from the perlocutionary effects and affects that his words produced on those who encountered them in the years following his death and through the context of Indian removal.

An instructive case in point demonstrating the complexity of meaning attached to Tecumseh's words and character relates to the way he was viewed in relation to his British allies. In an article appearing in the *American Weekly Messenger*, subtitled the "Character of Tecumseh," the anonymous author expresses a clear hesitancy to denounce Tecumseh for his efforts in rallying the native confederacy to resistance and for his alliance with the British, asking "whether this grand idea originated in his own, or his brother's mind, or was suggested by the British."[35] Tecumseh's younger brother, the reformed alcoholic Lalawithica, who became known as the prophet Tenskwatawa, advocated the rejection of Euro-American goods and influences, especially whisky, after experiencing a powerful vision. As an antecedent to the influence Wovoka would exert among the native peoples of the Northern plains in the late nineteenth century, Tenskwatawa encouraged a return to traditional ceremonial practice and belief. The messianic teachings advocated by Tenskwatawa provided the spiritual support for Tecumseh's efforts to oppose frontier expansion and reclaim Shawnee territory. For some American historians and scholars, however, as Alfred Cave has noted, the roles of

Tenskwatawa and Tecumseh within the conflict of this period have come to represent both sides of the savage native binary, "Noble Tecumseh, Vicious Tenskwatawa, the Good Indian and the Bad."[36]

For nineteenth-century American readers, as the "Character of Tecumseh" reminds, while Tecumseh was considered a savage in every respect, he was "the greatest perhaps since the days of Pontiac."[37] Such ambivalent rhetoric notwithstanding, Tecumseh was an *American* savage, and thus much preferable to the "British dogs"[38] who continued to represent a significant threat to vital national interests from their base in Canada. Contributing to the authority of such political and cultural distinctions, in accounts of a speech by Tecumseh given after learning of the planned retreat by General Henry Proctor at Malden on 18 August 1812, preserved in the reports of the British War Office and in an American congressional report, titled *Barbarities of the Enemy, Exposed* (1814), which later found its way into *Thatcher's Indian Biography* (1832), the British general is berated for his cowardice and duplicity.[39] With the adopted Wyandot/frontiersman Samuel Saunders serving as interpreter—a capacity he had also fulfilled with regard to the "Treaty with the Chippewa, Etc., 1808"[40]—commenting on the previous war with the Americans, Tecumseh affirmed the loyalty and support that the native people had shown toward the British. He states, "Listen! When the war was declared, our Father stood up and gave us the tomahawk, and told us he was now ready to strike the Americans; that he wanted our assistance; and that he certainly would get us our lands back, which the Americans had taken from us."[41] Tecumseh recalls past promises and allegiances, ones the Shawnee and other native people had honored, in contrast to Proctor's plans for retreat in the wake of Commodore Oliver Perry's defeat of the Royal British Navy in the Battle of Lake Erie. The historian John Sugden describes this event as "a defining engagement of the war" and notes that Proctor had tried to hide the news of this defeat from his native allies.[42] Tecumseh became livid when he learned of Proctor's plans, hurling insults that compared Proctor "to a fat dog, that carries its tail upon its back, but when affrighted, it drops it between its legs and runs off."[43] Degrading as this characterization was, especially since it was delivered in the presence of Proctor's own troops, the British general offered no defense for his actions, but only the promise that he was pulling back to rally his forces for a strategic defense against the Americans at the fork of the Thames.[44] In one of the many articles to appear in the years after Tecumseh's death, the nostalgic distinction between the Shawnee and the British is made obvious in an 1834 edition of the *American Railroad Journal*: "Had the dauntless spirit and quick weighted sagacity of the Indian warrior been shared by his British brother, it is probable that our troops, after a harassing march to Malden, would have met with a warmer reception than they experienced from a few bed ridden paralytics and a group of defenseless women and children."[45]

The decision made by Proctor recalled to Tecumseh and his Indian allies the bitter memories of a previous betrayal of native forces at the end of the Battle of Fallen Timbers in which the British refused them entry into Fort Miamis. The treachery of this act revealed the calculating pragmatism of British priorities, which were focused on defending and protecting their own colonial interests despite the staggering losses suffered by their native allies. In a speech attributed to Blue Jacket, a prominent Shawnee leader of the previous generation who advocated native neutrality in the months leading up to the outbreak of the War of 1812, an assembled native audience was reminded of these previous British betrayals: "They have often promised to help us, and at last, when we could not withstand the army that came against us, and went to the English for refuge, the English told us, 'I cannot let you in, you are painted too much, my children.' It was then we saw the British dealt treacherously with us."[46] As Sugden points out, the refusal to provide sanctuary at Fort Miamis was an incident that would not be forgotten, embittering Tecumseh and other natives for the next two decades.[47] Despite the appeals for neutrality expressed by Blue Jacket and other tribal elders who were becoming more accommodationist in their dealings with American officials, the continual incursions of Anglo explorers, miners, trappers, and settlers onto native American lands led Tecumseh and his younger nativist followers to view armed resistance as their last best hope for cultural preservation and continued political sovereignty. Whatever the failings of British officers such as Proctor, the relationship Tecumseh had previously forged with General Isaac Brock demonstrated a capacity, improbable as it may have been, for the two sides to work together for their mutual benefit. In contrast to Tecumseh's insulting characterization of Proctor, he was reported to have said to his men of Brock on the eve of the capture of Fort Detroit on 13 August 1812: "This is a man."[48]

The meaning of the war for Tecumseh and other native people of his generation's perspective, regardless of allies, and the spiritual significance that the land held to them, is made evident in Tecumseh's final words to Proctor in September 1813: "Our lives are in the hands of the Great Spirit. We are determined to defend our lands, and if it be his will, we wish to leave our bones upon them."[49] While expressions such as these would convey specific cultural meaning for Tecumseh, in the minds of American readers these ideas, and similar ones from other native leaders, would combine to form the basis of a nostalgic claiming of the memories of vanquished native

Figure 4. Heated confrontation between Tecumseh and William Henry Harrison, August 1810. (Nineteenth-century lithograph, one copy of which is located in the New York Public Library, digital ID 808986)

people, and in the process, transform them into indispensably tragic figures in American history. At the same time, such notions also worked to subtly bolster erstwhile Puritan conceptions of divine providence and exceptionalism, which were soon to be modernized by John L. O'Sullivan as "Manifest Destiny" in 1845.[50]

The predicament Tecumseh was forced to deal with regarding the retreat from Malden recalls his legendary meetings with William Henry Harrison, the governor of Indiana Territory, at Vincennes in 1810 and 1811. For Tecumseh and his native allies who were fighting to defend the ever-shrinking remnants of their homelands, the prospect of additional territorial losses represented nothing short of cultural obliteration. Tecumseh's speech to Proctor regarding the impending retreat of the British echoed the sentiments expressed in the series of meetings with Harrison in August 1810, in which the two were widely reported as nearly coming to blows. In a statement delivered to Harrison at their initial meeting on 12 August, Tecumseh opens with a summation of the concerns of the allied native groups of the Old Northwest and Great Lakes region as a protest to the cession of three million acres of land in Indiana Territory stipulated in the 1809 Treaty of Fort Wayne. Although the numerous inconsistencies apparent in the different versions of this speech have been noted by critics, as Robert Yagelski observes, "they all agree that Tecumseh steadfastly refused to accept the treaty."[51]

Tecumseh exploits and appropriates the conventional Western tropes of divine providence and exceptionalism in his remarks to assert the position of native peoples who were given little option but to stand in defense of their families, territory, and ways of life. Employing a rhetoric intended to advance an understanding of the significance of the treaty in the minds of native people, Tecumseh declines to ask Harrison to "tear the treaty," but instead inverts the positionality of native peoples by placing them in the privileged position of American citizens defending *their* homelands from invasion. Tecumseh's repudiation of what he considered the dishonest negotiations and the deceitful intentions of American officials, which were undertaken with illegitimate "government chiefs" who had no authority to make agreements or cede native lands, is both subtle and rhetorically incisive. Tecumseh makes his point by drawing a comparison between the Shawnee people and the American invaders, stating, "Sir, you have liberty to return to your own country. The being within communing with past ages, tells me, that once, nor until lately, there was no white man on this continent, that it then all belonged to red men, children of the same parents, placed on it by the Great Spirit that made them."[52] Tecumseh demonstrates extraordinary diplomatic restraint in laying out the grievances of the Shawnee people and their allies in this meeting, putting forth a line of reasoning grounded in a conception of territorial primacy and communal ownership: "The white people have no right to take the land from the Indians, because they had it first; it is theirs. They may sell, but all must join."[53] Tecumseh is especially careful in refraining from any threats of violence or insurrection in this meeting, although when Harrison reports back to government officials in Washington, he characterizes Tecumseh as "sufficiently insolent and his pretensions arrogant."[54]

After a week had passed without receiving any assurances in regard to the status of native lands, on 20 August Tecumseh again met with Harrison and reasserted his objections concerning the terms and conditions of the Fort Wayne treaty. His waning patience is evident in this encounter as his words become more demonstrative while drawing a comparison between British betrayals and American injustices, referencing the horrific massacre in February 1782 of ninety-six Christian Delaware by a Pennsylvania militia led by David Williamson at the Moravian mission town of Gnadenhutten, Ohio: "You recollect that the time the Delaware lived near the white people and satisfied with the promise of friendship and remained in security, yet one of their towns was surrounded and the men, women, and children murdered."[55] Terroristic assaults such as this, as well as the assassination of native leaders such as Cornstalk, Malunthy, and White Eyes, emboldened native resistance and contributed to the declining influence of accommodationist native leaders and a turn toward pan-Indian, nativist resistance.[56] While certainly not in agreement with Tecumseh's conclusions, Harrison could not deny the effectiveness in his allusion to American atrocities, noting in a report to the War Department, "every instance of injustice and injury which have been committed by our citizens upon Indians from the commencement of the revolutionary war . . . was brought forward and exaggerated."[57] Tecumseh, however, was resolute in the memory of such traumatic events and continued: "If the land is not restored to us you will soon see when we return to our homes how it will be settled."[58] Tecumseh makes it clear that the Shawnee and their allies will not only fight to reclaim their fraudulently ceded territory but also intend to exact retribution on "all those chiefs that sold the land."[59]

One of the difficulties with this speech, and the way it has been deployed to mediate Indianness in American frontier history, is that it is often presented as if emerging out of a social vacuum, without the necessary context of surrounding events. In fact, besides Tecumseh and Harrison, there were at least seventy-five other native representatives who were witnesses and participants in this meeting. Furthermore, Tecumseh's speech is routinely presented as a tragic soliloquy with no mention of Harrison's response, which was nonetheless translated into Shawnee, Potawatomi, and Miami, whereby he rejected Tecumseh's charges and "denied that his government had treated the Indians dishonestly and unjustly."[60] According to contemporaneous reports of this critical meeting, Tecumseh rose to speak "for some time with great vehemence and anger" and ended by calling Harrison a liar. In the words of an anonymous reporter in the *American Weekly Messenger* of August 1814, this pronouncement against Harrison demonstrated that Tecumseh was "equal to the insidious arts of diplomacy."[61] As Sugden notes, however, when the dust had settled, Tecumseh readily apologized for his conduct, "but both men sensed the inevitability of conflict."[62] Harrison agreed to convey Tecumseh's complaints to the president as the meeting came to a close, while expressing serious doubts that the conditions he insisted upon could be met. Tecumseh's legendary parting words articulated his profound frustration and served as an ominous portent of his and his people's future: "I hope the Great Spirit will put some sense into [President Madison's] head toinduce him to direct you to give up this land. It is true, he is so far off. He will not be injured in the war. He may still sit in his town, and drink his wine, whilst you and I will have to fight it out."[63] An account of these meetings that was published in 1821 redirects attention away from the vital territorial concerns at issue to a nostalgic and mythic emplotment of Tecumseh's life: "The council which the American general Harrison held with the Indians at Vincennes in 1811, affords an admirable instance of the sublimity which sometimes distinguished his eloquence."[64]

In the historical teleology that is fulfilled in *The Death of Tecumseh*, this meeting is interpreted as foreshadowing Tecumseh's eventual defeat and death, while propelling William Henry Harrison and Richard Johnson, the cavalry officer who claimed to have killed Tecumseh, to national prominence.[65] The account of Tecumseh's death provided by Thomas Rowland and published in 1813 signals a shift from a rhetoric of savagism and deracination to one of colonial nostalgia: "Tecumseh is certainly killed, I saw him with my eyes, it was the first time I had seen this celebrated chief. There was something so majestic, so dignified, and yet so mild in his countenance, as he lay stretched out on his back on the ground where a few minutes before he had rallied his men to the fight, that while gazing on him with admiration and pity, I forgot he was a savage."[66] But neither Tecumseh nor his death could be so easily forgotten as the lessons drawn from his life would continue to play a vital role in the consolidation of American national power through the nineteenth century, in which the so-called Indian problem would lead inexorably to the Indian Removal Act and the Trail of Tears, as well as the massacres at Sand Creek, the Marias River, and Wounded Knee. Given the accumulated burdens of these traumatic events in the decades after Tecumseh's death, it became incumbent upon American writers to redeem his image through public acts of nostalgic mourning that functioned as a trite form of national salvation. In this highly mediated rendition of American frontier history, Tecumseh is cast as a formidable yet tragic adversary, whose prowess as leader, orator, and military tactician led to his being described in one nineteenth-century account as "a stormy cloud, dark, terrible and mysterious on the horizon of American prosperity."[67] Characterizations such as these render the influence and legacy of Tecumseh's resistance as a reflection of the heroism and bravery of those who vanquished him. With Harrison and Johnson as the primary beneficiaries, Bil Gilbert observes that "for reasons of obvious self-interest the conquerors of Tecumseh eulogized him first as a 'red Hannibal-Napoleon' and then as a man of preternatural sagacity, courage and honor. Typically, the *Indiana Centinel*, published in Vincennes, editorialized: 'Every schoolboy in the Union now knows that Tecumseh was a great man. His greatness was his own, unassisted by science or education. As a statesman, warrior and patriot, we shall not look on his like again.'"[68]

For the self-affirming narrative of American frontier history to remain intact, no other characterization was possible. While Tecumseh's speeches have been cleverly sublimated within the narrative of victory culture, even here, in their heavily fraught and mediated forms, his voice, and those of other native people who fought to resist the onslaught of frontier expansionism, breaks through to challenge this selfsame colonial discourse. In Robert B. McAfee's 1816 account of the Vincennes meeting, Tecumseh's opposition to American colonial expansionism is made clear: "[The Shawnee leader] said, that 'the policy which the United States pursued, of purchasing lands from the Indians, he viewed as a mighty water, ready to overflow his people, and that the confederacy which he was forming among the tribes, to prevent any individual tribe from selling without the consent of the others, was the dam he was erecting to resist this mighty water.'"[69]

Some may be quick to dismiss Tecumseh's statements as the romanticized mediations of sympathetic white writers, but to do so threatens to erase and silence the native voice in what is already the nearly univocal narrative of American frontier history. Perhaps such commentators prefer the myth created by representations typified by *The Dying Tecumseh* and *The Death of Tecumseh,* which reduce Tecumseh and native people, in general, to instrumental signifiers in much the same way that Roland Barthes conceives the mythology of French imperialism in the reduction of the image of the saluting black soldier on the cover of the magazine *Paris-Match,* and analyzed in *Mythologies.* But as with the image of the uniformed black soldier, the colonial representations of Tecumseh are also susceptible to decolonial interpretations, "because myth is speech stolen and restored. Only, speech which is restored is no longer quite that which was stolen: when it was brought back, it was not put exactly in its place."[70] The reclamation of native historical figures such as Tecumseh from the status of instrumental colonial signifier demands a renewed approach to historical narrative and the positing of alternate lines of critical inquiry. Did Tecumseh utter *exactly* the words attributed to him in the innumerable speeches and meetings he held and attended during his time as a leader of native resistance in the first decade of the nineteenth century? Given the historical context and the weight of the evidence regarding this conflict, along with the nature of the unified native opposition to colonial encroachment, does it even matter? The undeniable fact that Tecumseh organized an unprecedented confederation, fought for decades to preserve Shawnee national sovereignty and territory, and met repeatedly with British and American military representatives to convey the reasons for his refusal to accept colonial policies speaks to the spirit, if not the substance, of such words. Where are those historians, one wonders, who question the "authenticity" of accounts of Harrison's and Proctor's words and speeches, calling into question the transcriptions that form the primary documents of American colonial history? Despite the force of colonial negation, deracination, and suppression, the words and ideas attributed to Tecumseh break through the imposed silences that artistic representations such as *The Death of Tecumseh* and *The Dying Tecumseh* represent. This function allows for the articulation of conceptions of native sovereignty that actively question the legitimacy of hegemonic discourse, while serving as powerful inspiration for contemporary native American and Indigenous scholars and activists in the ongoing contest over the meaning of the past and the challenge of the future.

NOTES

1. Gilbert, "The Dying Tecumseh"; Pettrich's sculpture took more than twenty more years to complete (modeled ca. 1837–1846, carved 1856).
2. The frieze is attributed to artists Constantino Brumidi (Italian Greek American), Filippo Costaggini (Italian), and Allyn Cox; Costaggini was responsible for *The Death of Tecumseh* tableau. The original conception of the frieze was painted from 1878 to 1889. http://www.aoc.gov/capitol-hill/murals/frieze-american-history.
3. Konkle, *Writing Indian Nations*, 2.
4. Barthes, *Mythologies*, 109.
5. See Vizenor, "Aesthetics of Survivance," in which he defines "terminal creeds" in negative contrast to the ways in which native American peoples address disharmony and imbalance. Vizenor also initiated the use of *indian*, lowercase and italicized, to indicate the "absence of real natives—the contrivance of the other in the course of dominance" (*Manifest Manners*, vii). He consistently writes native(s) in lowercase, and I follow that practice throughout this essay.
6. Rosaldo, *Culture and Truth*, passim.
7. Vizenor, *Fugitive Poses*, 145. For a broader discussion of the implications of colonial representation and its relation to native intellectual and political sovereignty, see 145–166.
8. Rosaldo, *Culture and Truth*, 69.
9. Vizenor, "Aesthetics of Survivance," 1.
10. Warrior, "The Role of Native American Voices in Rethinking Early American Literary Studies," 369.

11. Sayre, *The Indian Chief as Tragic Hero*, 270.
12. Vizenor, *Manifest Manners*, vii.
13. John Sugden, in *Tecumseh: A Life*, identifies Tecumseh's father, Pukeshinwau, and mother, Methoataaskee, being Shawnee of different clans (13). Sugden goes on to state that Tecumseh's father was killed in a battle at Point Pleasant during Lord Dunmore's War, in October 1774 (28). Other historians seem to be in agreement with these details. Bil Gilbert, using slightly different spellings, confirms these names in *God Gave Us This Country*, 6. Gilbert also attributes questions concerning the tribal identity of Pukeshinwa to stories spread by Tecumseh's brother, Tenskwatawa, intended as an affront to "white pride" (53).
14. "The Infant Tecumseh," 332. This story reached a wide audience through the nineteenth century, with one version being reprinted in the *Canadian Magazine and Literary Repository* 3 (July–December 1824): 137–139, and again as "Tecumseh" in *The North American, or Weekly Journal of Politics, Science & Literature* (9 June 1827): 28.
15. Ibid.
16. Ibid.
17. Ibid.
18. Ibid., 333.
19. Ibid.
20. Ibid., 332.
21. "Sketches of Savage Life," 204.
22. Ibid.
23. Ibid.
24. Ibid., 204–205.
25. Ibid., 204.
26. Quoted in Laxer, *Tecumseh and Brock*, 157.
27. Ibid. Stephen Rudell was a white settler who was taken captive and eventually adopted into Tecumseh's own family, becoming an adoptive brother. He fought in numerous campaigns with the Shawnee and later returned to his family, after which time he wrote a memoir entitled *Reminiscences of Tecumseh's Youth*. As Laxer notes, this manuscript is held in the collection of the Wisconsin Historical Society and was made available online in 2003.
28. Quoted in Laxer, *Tecumseh and Brock*, 157.
29. "Sketches of Savage Life," 204.
30. Quoted in Sugden, *Tecumseh*, 6–7.
31. Laxer, *Tecumseh and Brock*, 157.
32. "Speech of Tecumseh," 95.
33. "Tecumseh" (1834), 414.

34. Derrida, "Signature Event Context," 315–316.
35. "From Views of the Campaign of the North-Western Army," 8.
36. Cave, "The Shawnee Prophet, Tecumseh, and Tippecanoe," 637.
37. "From Views of the Campaign of the North-Western Army," 8.
38. See note 42.
39. Thatcher, *Indian Biography*, 2: 237.
40. This official name of the treaty with a dismissive "etc." is a subtle indicator of the government's view of native Americans as an indistinct and even insignificant group of cultural others.
41. *Barbarities of the Enemy*, 160.
42. Sugden, *Tecumseh*, 356–361.
43. "Speech of Tecumseh," 95.
44. Sugden, *Tecumseh*, 360.
45. "Tecumseh" (1834), 414.
46. Quoted in Sugden, *Tecumseh*, 132.
47. Ibid., 90.
48. Laxer, *Tecumseh and Brock*, 146.
49. "Speech of Tecumseh," 95.
50. See O'Sullivan, "Annexation," 5–10.
51. Yagelski, "A Rhetoric of Contact," 64.
52. Quoted in Sugden, *Tecumseh*, 134.
53. Quoted in ibid.
54. Ibid., 199.
55. Ibid., 97.
56. See Dowd, *A Spirited Resistance*, 75–79, 95.
57. Gilbert, *God Gave Us This Country*, 206.
58. Sugden, *Tecumseh*, 98.
59. Ibid.
60. Ibid., 201.
61. "From Views of the Campaign of the North-Western Army," 8.
62. Sugden, *Tecumseh*, 202.
63. Quoted in ibid.
64. "Tecumseh," (1821), 299.
65. After his military service, William Henry Harrison went on to serve as governor of Indiana Territory and U.S. congressman and senator representing Ohio, and was elected the ninth president of the United States in the election of 1840. Richard Johnson, already an experienced congressman and a prominent voice in support of the declaration of war on Great Britain in 1812, left Congress to command two regiments of Kentucky volunteers during the war. At its close, he returned a war hero and served as congressman and senator,

eventually becoming vice president of the United States during the administration of Martin Van Buren.

66. Rowland, "Copy of a letter from Maj. Tho. Rowland," 126.
67. "Tecumseh" (1827), 28.
68. Gilbert, "Dying Tecumseh."
69. McAfee, *History of the Late War*, 25–26.
70. Barthes, *Mythologies*, 125.

WORKS CITED

Barbarities of the Enemy, Exposed in a Report of the Committee of the House of Representatives of the United States, appointed to enquire into the spirit and manner in which the war has been waged by the enemy. And the Documents, Accompanying Said Report. Worcester, MA: Isaac Sturtevant, 1814.

Barthes, Roland. *Mythologies*. Trans. Annette Lavers. New York: Hill and Wang, 1984.

Cave, Alfred A. "The Shawnee Prophet, Tecumseh, and Tippecanoe: A Case Study of Historical Myth-Making." *Journal of the Early Republic* 22.4 (2002): 637–673.

Derrida, Jacques. "Signature Event Context." In *Margins of Philosophy*, 309–330. Chicago: University of Chicago Press, 1982.

Dowd, Gregory. *A Spirited Resistance: The North American Indian Struggle for Unity, 1745–1815*. Baltimore: Johns Hopkins University Press, 1993.

"From Views of the Campaign of the North-Western Army, Etc.: Character of Tecumseh." *American Weekly Messenger; or, Register of State Papers, History and Politics, Vol. II: for 1814–15* (26 March 1814): 8.

Gilbert, Bil. "The Dying Tecumseh." *Smithsonian*, July 1995. Http://www.smithsonianmag.com/history-archaeology/object_0795.html.

———. *God Gave Us This Country: Tekamthi and the First American Civil War*. New York: Atheneum, 1989.

"The Infant Tecumseh," *New-York Mirror: A Weekly Gazette of Literature and the Fine Arts*, 15 May 1824, 332–333.

Konkle, Maureen. *Writing Indian Nations: Native Intellectuals and the Politics of Historiography, 1827–1863*. Chapel Hill: University of North Carolina Press, 2004.

Laxer, James. *Tecumseh and Brock: The War of 1812*. Toronto, ON: House of Anansi Press, 2012.

McAfee, Robert B. *History of the Late War in the Western Country*. 1816. Reprint, Bowling Green, OH: Historical Publishing, 1919.

O'Sullivan, John L. "Annexation." *United States Magazine and Democratic Review* 17 (July–August 1845): 5–10.

Rosaldo, Renato. *Culture and Truth: The Remaking of Social Analysis*. New York: Beacon Press, 1989.

Rowland, Thomas. "Copy of a letter from Maj. Tho. Rowland, of the 27th regt. United States infantry, to his friend, Arnold's Mill, River Thames, October 9, 1813." *American Weekly Messenger; or, Register of State Papers, History and Politics, Vol. I: for 1813–14* (13 November 1813): 126.

Sayre, Gordon M. *The Indian Chief as Tragic Hero: Native Resistance and the Literatures of America, from Moctezuma to Tecumseh*. Chapel Hill: University of North Carolina Press, 2005.

"Sketches of Savage Life." *Waldie's Port Folio, & Companion to the Select Circulating Library* (18 June 1836): 203–208.

"Speech of Tecumseh." *Youth's Literary Gazette* 95. Philadelphia: 1832.

Sugden, John. *Tecumseh: A Life*. New York: Henry Holt, 1997.

"Tecumseh." *American Railroad Journal & Advocate of Internal Improvements* (5 July 1834): 414.

"Tecumseh." *National Recorder* (12 May 1821): 299.

"Tecumseh." *The North American, or Weekly Journal of Politics, Science and Literature* (9 June 1827): 28.

Thatcher, Benjamin Bussey. *Indian biography; or, An historical account of those individuals who have been distinguished among the North American Natives as orators, warriors, statesmen, and other remarkable characters*. 2 vols. New York: J. and J. Harper, 1832.

Vizenor, Gerald. "Aesthetics of Survivance: Literary Theory and Practice." In *Survivance: Narratives of Native Presence*, ed. Gerald Vizenor, 1–24. Lincoln: University of Nebraska Press, 2008.

———. *Fugitive Poses: Native American Scenes of Absence and Presence*. Lincoln: University of Nebraska Press, 2000.

———. *Manifest Manners: Narratives on Postindian Survivance*. Lincoln: University of Nebraska Press, 1994.

Warrior, Robert Allen. "The Role of Native American Voices in Rethinking Early American Literary Studies." *Early American Literature* 42.2 (2007): 369–375.

Yagelski, Robert. "A Rhetoric of Contact: Tecumseh and the Native American Confederacy." *Rhetoric Review* 14.1 (1995): 64–77.

"IndiVisible" Identities

Mediating Native American and African American Encounters and Transethnic Identity in A Thrilling Sketch of the Life of Okah Tubbee

SONJA GEORGI

Bringing historical and contemporary interactions between Native Americans and African Americans to the center of public and scholarly attention, the Smithsonian Museum of the American Indian featured the exhibition *IndiVisible: African Native American Lives in the Americas* from November 2009 to March 2010. The exhibition portrayed African American and Native American history as one of shared struggles for liberty and autonomy, and African Native American culture and identity as contested—one could think of the Cherokee-Freedmen debate—but also as thriving.[1] The exhibition brochure pointed to the relevance of presenting to the public this intricate yet often unknown transethnic history of lived familial experiences and creative cultural encounters:

> There still exists a largely invisible story of America—how African and Native peoples came together across space and time to create shared histories, communities, and ways of life. Through centuries of struggle, slavery, and dispossession, then by self-determination and freedom, African American and Native American peoples have become, more often than publicly recognized, indivisible.[2]

As attractive and justified as this concept of affirmative indivisibility is in our postmodern age, autobiographical evidence regarding people of mixed ethnic heritage frequently demonstrates a confirmation of the strict racial divisions of the nineteenth century. Kentuckian Felix L. Lindsey told an interviewer for the Works Progress Administration's Federal Writers' Project in 1937 that he was of mixed African and Native American heritage, but that he was, in his own words, a "nigger" and "proud" of that, having served as a Buffalo Soldier in the nineteenth-century West.[3] He reported meeting Geronimo on the battlefield, who immediately identified him as Native American—but Lindsey told the apparently astonished Apache leader that he (Lindsey) rejected his Native Americanness: "My fatha may been Injun, but my mother's a nigger, an' 'at's the race I chose."[4] His identification as African American rested on presenting Native Americans as the cultural and racial "other." Selecting that "other" ethnicity, Warren McCary, aka Okah Tubbee, probably of mixed black-white heritage, successfully escaped from slavery in the 1840s, claiming to be the son of a Choctaw chief and thus unjustly enslaved. He "documented" his Native American affiliation in his novelistic autobiography. The main common denominator between Lindsey and Tubbee is that they were able to *choose* their ethnic identity in a process of transethnic self-invention. Their accounts do not reflect singular and curious incidents, but—as the "IndiVisible" exhibition would encourage us to assume—are telling examples of the agency possible under the discriminatory social, cultural, and legal circumstances of the nineteenth-century American South.

In the following, I examine Okah Tubbee's autobiography, placing both his life and his book in contexts of mixing and choosing. Tubbee's published work reflects a hybridization of the slave narrative and Native American autobiographical traditions, among others. I first consider the case study, lacing it with current scholarship on transethnicity, and then relate Tubbee's autobiography to transgenre discourse.

A successful nineteenth-century traveling musician of indeterminate ethnic background, a (former) slave, wearing Indian dress, telling tales of being the lost son of a great Choctaw chief, practicing as a medicine man, and aiding poor whites: Okah Tubbee (ca. 1811–after 1854) defied the racial restrictions of his time. Although his life story appears to reinforce the starkly drawn ethnic categories in his choosing to identify as "Indian," in fact he mobilized traditions and lifeways of three ethnicities. No likenesses of Tubbee have survived, but a stereotypical illustration from his autobiography, which shows him cutting firewood in imagined Native dress while a Native woman cooks in the background, stresses his preferred ethnicity.

Figure 1. The stereotypical illustration from Okah Tubbee's autobiography (Laah Tubbee, *A Sketch of the Life of the Okah Tubbee,* 1852) presents him in his preferred ethnicity with his Native American wife. (Courtesy of the University Library, University of North Carolina–Chapel Hill; *Documenting the American South* docsouth.unc.edu/index.html, University Library, University of North Carolina at Chapel Hill)

Okah Tubbee's autobiography, *A Thrilling Sketch of the Life of the Distinguished Chief Okah Tubbee: Alias Wm Chubbee, Son of the Head Chief, Mosholeh Tubbee, of the Choctaw Nation of Indians,* was published by Rev. L. L. Allen in 1848 and as a reedited version by Tubbee's wife, Laah Ceil, in 1852.[5] In *A Thrilling Sketch,* Tubbee tells us that his father was a chief of the Choctaw Nation, that he was presumably stolen while still a little boy by a white man named James McCary and raised by this man's black female slave Franky (or Frances) in Mississippi along with her two children, Robert and Kitty.[6] In Natchez, it was assumed that Franky was his birth mother and McCary his father, which would make Tubbee a mulatto according to racial categories of the time. The narrative revolves around incidents in which Tubbee asserts his Choctaw heritage, trying to achieve this by denying any African American ancestry.

A Thrilling Sketch pursues at least three objectives: First, it tries to renounce Tubbee's legal status as a black slave by asserting his Indian ancestry. Second, it seeks to implement Tubbee as mediator between Native, white, and, by extension, African American cultures. Third, it serves Tubbee's and

Ceil's purported aim of negotiating peace among the Indian nations and of fostering temperance and Christian beliefs. The first section of the narrative focuses on Tubbee's joyless childhood as the alleged son of the slave woman Franky, and he repeatedly presents his readers with chance encounters with Native Americans during which he was identified by them as Indian. The second part then narrates Tubbee's travels and his struggle to be recognized as Native American. To increase the credibility of Tubbee's Native ancestry, the final section of the narrative gives an account of his kidnapping as a toddler from the point of view of Puckshunubbee, who is presented as a friend of Tubbee's supposed Choctaw father, Mosholeh. Puckshunubbee relates his memories of the abduction to Mosholeh's "lost son."[7] Like Felix Lindsey, Tubbee stresses one ethnic identity by demarcating it from the other. Yet opposite to Lindsey, who defended his African American racial and cultural background against Native ancestry, Tubbee tries to set himself apart from his African American heritage whenever possible. Geronimo instantly recognizes Lindsey as a Native, and, similarly, in Tubbee's story a group of Indians that visit his hometown are puzzled when they learn that the white community considers him to be a black slave.[8] Suggesting that ethnic identity is not so much in the blood as in the tongue, in a sentimental account of his first meeting with Indians, Tubbee tells us that he intuitively began to speak Choctaw without having known that he could even speak the language:

> Permit me to describe my feelings the first time I saw Indians. . . . my heart leapt with joy, yet a choking sensation amounting to pain seized me; confused ideas crowded upon in my mind; . . . they came towards me; I was wild with delight, I thought I was their child, . . . I started and held out my hands, tears gushed from my eyes, I addressed them in a language to me unknown before; it was neither English, Spanish or French; astonished, they spoke kind to me, . . . an explanation now took place as one could speak English; he said I had asked in Choctaw for my father, saying he had gone and left me, and I was with bad people.[9]

Tubbee's emotional recollection is part of a larger rhetorical strategy to convince the reader of his ethnic identity as Native American. In the quote above, Tubbee is responding to the nineteenth-century largely triethnic and hypodescent system described by Circe Sturm in a study of Cherokee national identity:

> People with mixed ancestry fell between the cracks of the triracial system of classification that existed in Indian Territory. . . . This system pushed individuals into categories that did not reflect their personal experiences or their familial connections. The rules of hypodescent played out in such a way that people with any degree of African American blood were usually classified exclusively as Black.[10]

Reflecting on and circumventing such legal and cultural classifications of race and multiethnic identity, Tubbee asserts that in order to be a slave, one does not have to be black. Furthermore refuting any claims that he might be black, Tubbee affirms his story of having been abducted from his Choctaw parents whenever he is treated as a black slave, as is the case when he is beaten:

> I underwent a severe course of punishment . . . from the very fact that the woman known as my mother, having been a slave; but as usual I denied her being my mother, told them all I knew of my self before I knew her, which was new to them, and some of my enemies were turned into friends; they said it was not unreasonable to suppose that I was an Indian child, taken when small, for the purpose of making me a slave. Some asserted they had heard of such circumstances, and it was easily done, where there was such a diversity of color as there is in the South.[11]

The rhetorical strategy at work in the two preceding passages from Tubbee's narrative can be interpreted as follows: Tubbee sketches his childhood as the son of Choctaw Chief Mosholeh as an alternative story to his childhood as a black slave in the McCary household. The moments when Indians recognize their lost "son" support his claim. Stressing his Indianness entails that he has to deconstruct any occurrences during which he is treated as African American, whether slave or free black. For this purpose, Tubbee deploys racial stereotypes, pitting black and Indian characteristics against each other, thereby establishing a cultural hierarchy in which he comes out as a cultural mediator between whites and Indians, and in which his blackness retreats further into the background. "Just as African American, Native American, and African-Native American autobiographers drew from multiple traditions in developing their narrative mediating between cultural traditions," Brennan notes, "they also often served as mediators between cultural groups themselves."[12]

Drawing on racial features of the time, Tubbee is careful to point out that he shows those characteristics favorably ascribed to Indians:

> I soon found myself boxing heartily with the boys, both white and black, because they called me nigger, and everything but that which was true, for I could not, and would not, and never will submit to such gross insults without defending myself, which is so characteristic of the Red man.[13]

Yet in Tubbee's case, such incidents during which he shows traits stereotypically associated with Indians could be read as going beyond what Philip Deloria and Shari Huhndorf call "playing Indian" or "going native," respectively.[14] Rather, they serve as a means for self-identification generally denied to transethnic subjects in the antebellum period: "For Tubbee, being an Indian means more than acting in certain ways; specifically it means not being black," writes Paul Gilmore.[15] Accordingly, when Franky suggests that he should buy himself free, Tubbee exclaims that he "would never . . . pay for the freedom with which [he] was born."[16] In another scene where he is punished, stereotypes of submissive blacks and resisting Indians are explicitly articulated:

> for she asked me if I did not know that this was the way the Indians and all wild savages lived, and could not be tamed; that the white people could not make as much service of them, as they could of the blacks, for they would not work for them, but spent their lives in wandering about in the woods, both day and night, living with the wild beasts.[17]

For Franky, the frame of reference on which stereotypically "good" and "bad" ethnic characteristics are mapped is white society, as the phrasing "could not make as much service" indicates. One's place in society is determined by the degree to which one can be of use to that society in racial terms. Hence, in order to secure her position as freedwoman in Tubbee's text, Franky fulfills the role assigned, which in her case is to act as Tubbee's mother, teaching him "his place."

Tubbee seeks to circumvent the social and racial boundaries that mainstream society sets up by positioning himself as cultural mediator between whites and Natives in the multiethnic South, and he seems to move relatively freely between white and Native communities. While he seeks to help poor white townspeople as a physician, he tries to negotiate with Native Americans about relocation. Becoming a physician supposedly trained by both white and Indian medicine men, Tubbee ventures to the poor parts of the towns in order to help those "who had not means to apply a physician of a higher stamp."[18] The pronoun "our" in the conversation between Tubbee and the white doctor Merrill, who says that Tubbee's medical training with Natives would "benefit our race by the knowledge," suggests that Tubbee has asserted himself as mediator between whites and Native Americans; trained by white and Native doctors, he mixes medicines and skills from both cultures to serve those in need of but without the financial means to receive treatment.

> I zealously refused all remuneration, except a keepsake was offered. . . . I could speak several languages, and thereby make myself familiar with the sick emigrant, and many of them have gladly availed themselves of my cheap store, and thus be obliging friends.[19]

We learn that Tubbee sells Indian medicine to his white customers, which could again be another instance of his mediation as well as of his successful quacksalving. The scene of his being of service to poor white immigrants is a story that positions Tubbee as a self-made man within white society, and at the same time it distances himself even further from the black versus red stereotypes that Franky alludes to in the quote above.

A highly publicized anecdote, appearing in newspapers as widespread as Ohio and Vermont, recounting how Okah-Tubbee received his Native identity and name, demonstrates the white appropriation of his agency in choosing his ethnic affiliation. In crass language and with a sense of clever conning, the white manager, Sol Smith, and the treasurer, Mr. Bailey of a theater in Cleveland, plan to "Choctaw" (note the coining of a verb) the musician Warren McCary into a "savage," who is welcome on the stage, whereas an African American would presumably not be acceptable:

> "Make a savage of him," said Sol, "turn him into an Indian." "But how?" "Why," said Sol, "the thing is simple enough—he looks already very much like a Choctaw—all that you have to do is to have him disorder his hair a little, teach him to be a little more doughface in his demeanour, and then change his name. Call him—let me see—(pondering) call him— . . . Oak-Tub." The suggestion was adopted. Mr. Bailey Choctawed the new name into Okah-Tubbee, and on the night of the benefit not an inconsiderable portion of the audience were persons who had come to see the distinguished Chief of the unfortunate aboriginal race who had sought a home on the banks of the Arkansas.[20]

What reads like a curious incident of a spontaneous identity conversion is in fact a more intricate and revealing story about the life of the mixed-race musician, lecturer, and physician Warner McCary, also known as William McCary, Warner Cary, William Chubbee, or Okah Tubbee, who was born around 1811 near Natchez, Mississippi, and whose ethnicity has not definitely been clearly identified.[21] The staging of Native Americans, African Americans, and mixed-race subjects as curiosities in museums and public shows such as P. T. Barnum's "exhibitions" was quite common in the mid-nineteenth century. As Paul Gilmore writes in *The Genuine Article: Race, Mass Culture, and American Literary Manhood*, "although museums represented Indians and blacks in complex, multivalent ways, they tended to make a core distinction between the two races, producing racial distinctions not simply between undifferentiated blacks or Indians and white audience members, but also between Indians and blacks."[22] This circumstance might account for the headline of the *Cleveland Evening Herald* editorial that announced Tubbee—"the Negro Indian"—as a curiosity. The 1843 *New York Herald* newspaper, for example, advertised Tubbee as "the greatest wonder of the age, CHOC-CHU-TUB BEE, an Indian Chief of the Choctaw tribe."[23] This staging of Tubbee as mediator between white and red cultures is taken up again in the final part of the narrative that further serves to ascertain Tubbee's position as a transethnic subject when he speaks in support of Indian affairs during the period of slavery, abolitionism, and Indian removal.

The stories about Native American traditions such as naming practices and burial ceremonies related in the closing chapters of the 1852 edition of *A Thrilling Sketch* credit Tubbee's familiarity with Native cultural practices, which also gives credibility to his stage performances as Indian chief. Visiting the Creeks and Seminoles probably in the early 1840s in the Indian Territory, Tubbee acts as an advocate for Indian affairs. As Laah Ceil writes, "We constantly endeavoured to interest the citizens in behalf of the Indians. Pleading with them that the present home of the civilized tribes should be a permanent location."[24] Daniel Littlefield assumes that the episodes about Indian traditions were originally written as stage recitals and repeated in the narrative:

> If Okah Tubbee visited the Indians of Florida, the date would have been about 1842. However, such a visit was not likely. Instead, he probably saw the Seminoles, if he saw them at all, during his visit to the Indian Territory. The material between this point and the account of his trip to the territory appears to consist of set pieces, probably composed for recitation onstage.[25]

One can note a change in style and tone at this point in the narrative, and the episodes take up the motif of the "vanishing Indian" contained in the two essays that introduced Tubbee's own narrative. While the "simple children of the woods were content with their lot"[26] and holding on to their "hunting-grounds,"[27] the cultural mediator Tubbee predicts the whites' policy of removing the Indians from the territory: "I had had an opportunity of associating with the whites from childhood. I foresaw that they were determined, and would never surrender, or in other words, give up the chase until the Indian was no longer an inhabitant of that soil."[28] Thus, Tubbee sets out to visit the Indians in order to share with them his knowledge about white law and policies:

> As I pondered these things over again and again, a secret desire to visit that tribe soon had grown into a resolute determination, to use my endeavors to show them the hopelessness of their efforts—to impress upon their minds that at the most they would only have blood and revenge, for the blood of their kindred; and in the end, shame and disgrace, and the loss of their lands besides.[29]

The success of Tubbee's endeavors remains unclear in the narrative, yet these passages further establish the narrator as a self-acclaimed mediator in the antebellum multiethnic society of the South. While these anecdotes are sentimental in style, in a later paragraph we find a tentative attempt to deconstruct the myth of the "vanishing Indian" when in an intertextual reference to James Fenimore Cooper's novels, Ceil tells contemporary readers who might consider the Mohicans as having vanished that "there are a few hundred of them still living" in close proximity to the Delawares, her own people, on a "lovely fairy-like land."[30]

In his life as told in his autobiography, Tubbee seems to have been utilizing the public interest in racial confusion and boundary crossings on theatrical stages in order to increase his popularity as well as to secure a status that placed him "publicly to be opposite the slave on the social scale," as Littlefield writes.[31] In *A Thrilling Sketch*, however, it was not the theater manager Smith who spontaneously invented Tubbee's Indian ancestry; rather, Tubbee's stage persona as Choctaw chief is a central part of his earlier identity construction as he relates it in his autobiography. During his travels through the American South and later also to the northern states and Canada, Tubbee assumed various names and personae for artistic as well as legal reasons. When McCary died, unlike Franky and the two older children, Warner/Tubbee was not freed in his will.[32] Assuming that he had gained freedom through an apprenticeship with a blacksmith, Warner/Tubbee was in fact legally still a slave when he left Natchez to start his travels.[33] During a time when the Fugitive Slave Law was in full effect, concealing their ethnic and legal identity was crucial for many African Americans. Thus, for an African American who was known in his county as a runaway slave, the use of various names and identities might not have been as unusual and curious as the *New York Herald* headline suggests.

Tubbee's racial indeterminacy and his legal in-betweenness are also reflected in the generic modes employed in his autobiography, which shares elements with both African American slave narratives and the Native American autobiographies as outlined by Arnold Krupat. Furthermore, the narrative is not only the life story of Tubbee but is also prefaced by two essays, "Indian Character" and "Indian Covenant" ("Biography" in the 1848 edition) as well as a brief account of Laah Ceil's life. Littlefield suggests that the first essay, "Indian Character," might have been written by editor/publisher Allen but that the second one, "Indian Covenant," was probably not written by Allen because of its inaccuracy, which Littlefield sees as uncharacteristic of Allen's writing. Both essays reflect on the following narrative in general and on the sections narrated by Laah Ceil in particular, so they also could have been written by her.[34] Listing Rev. Allen as editor of the autobiography gives it the mandatory credentials common for works written by nonwhites. Like the slave narrative, *A Thrilling Sketch* relates incidents such as the subject's realization of his slave status due to his skin color, of an incident that spurs the wish to escape, the journey to the North, and the arrival in a free state.

While *A Thrilling Sketch* is at times written in the mode of the slave narrative when Tubbee recounts his childhood as a slave of James McCary, its content serves to distance Tubbee from his African American heritage and his status as black slave.[35] Reflecting on political and cultural discourses on race and ethnicity that construe white, black, and red in triangular opposition to each other, Tubbee's account plays with and subverts these racial categories. Thus, his autobiography engages in a form of "mediating Indianness" that serves as an artistic and creative intervention and becomes itself a transethnic identity construction. The act of rhetorically privileging his Native American heritage through the negation of his African American ancestry seems to contradict a claim of transethnic identity; yet my reading focuses on the work's performative confusion of racial and cultural markers that stress the transethnic genealogy of Tubbee as well as of the American South, and it approaches the allegedly invented tale of a runaway slave and charlatan as a narrative of transethnic agency.

Tubbee's "real" ancestry remains unclear. In their respective studies, Gilmore and Brennan discuss the relevance, or rather irrelevance, of Tubbee's real ancestry. In line with current transethnic approaches, Brennan privileges Tubbee's self-chosen ethnic identity as Choctaw over the verification of Tubbee's racial ancestry in terms of the nineteenth-century's monoracial categories:

> Tubbee's identity does not hinge on his "racial" make-up but rather on his cultural affinity. Since he did probably not know who his father was, he was left

> with the task of creating his identity. Since he identified as Choctaw, believed his father to be a Choctaw, was accepted by at least some Choctaws as Choctaw, by other members of Native nations as Choctaw, and by some African Americans as well as many Europeans as Choctaw, Tubbee was for all intents and purposes part Choctaw. Although he was not the same sort of Choctaw as most, the process of identity for many Native Americans (as well as European and other Americans) became irreversibly complex after the colonization by the European settlers. The situation of on-and-off reservation members, mixed-bloods, and federally recognized and nonrecognized Native nations makes it nearly impossible to determine Choctaw lineage with any finality and creates situations in which many Choctaws were not "the same sort as most."[36]

Following Brennan's line of argument, in my reading of *A Thrilling Sketch*, whether Tubbee was really (partly) Native American makes little difference when analyzing his "mediating" of Indian identity through his creative intervention with or even invention of transethnic identity in the antebellum era. Talking repeatedly about memories of his Indian father, Tubbee invents an alternative story about his early childhood that stands in stark contrast to his years as a black slave owned by James McCary and unsettles racial categories of black and Indian.

Having been recognized as Native American on the spot by Geronimo, Felix Lindsey admits that his father was Native American, but he immediately sides with the African American heritage of his mother. That in the nineteenth century the racially and ethnically diverse regions of the South and the West might have led to ethnic "confusions" and "passings" might not seem unusual, yet many African Americans—unlike Lindsey—often referred to Native American ancestors in order to construct an alternative family history outside white-dominated society. In "'African and Cherokee by Choice': Race and Resistance under Legalized Segregation," Laura L. Lovett explains the legal significance of stressing Native American ancestry for African Americans after the abolition of slavery:

> Claiming kinship with Native Americans provided African Americans in the late nineteenth and early twentieth century with a way of rebelling against a system of segregation, discrimination, and "civilization" imposed on them by White society. This can be considered a route of resistance, because White and Black Americans with the aid of cultural images, science, and governmental policy, defined Indians as living outside of White society.[37]

Thus, for African Americans, asserting Native American descent was not only a means of avoiding legal racial categorizations of "white" and "black." Rather, according to Tiya Miles, African Native American family relations were a result of centuries-long complex relationships between Native Americans and African Americans that ranged from "identification" and "interdependence" in the colonial era to "self-segregation [of Native Americans] from black people" in the nineteenth and twentieth centuries and the enslavement of blacks by Natives in the pre-Emancipation period to transethnic African Native American families today.[38]

These historical encounters and cultural and social relationships between African Americans and Native Americans have been researched and analyzed by historians Daniel Littlefield (*Africans and Seminoles*, 1977), Theda Perdue (*Slavery and the Evolution of Cherokee Society*, 1979), Jack D. Forbes (*Black Africans and Native Americans*, 1988), Tiya Miles (*Ties That Bind: The Story of an Afro-Cherokee Family in Slavery and Freedom*, 2005), Celia E. Naylor (*African Cherokees in Indian Territory: From Chattel to Citizens*, 2008), and others. Scholars of literary studies have also worked in this field, of which three anthologies—*Confounding the Color Line*, edited by James F. Brooks in 2002; *When Brer Rabbit Meets Coyote: African-Native American Literature*, edited by Jonathan Brennan in 2003; and *Crossing Waters, Crossing Worlds*, edited by Tiya Miles and Sharon P. Holland in 2006—are key works. With these interdisciplinary anthologies, the editors seek to "expand the conversation about African and Native American interaction and exchange . . . into the fields of . . . American studies," as Miles and Holland write, because Native American and African American relations have primarily been researched by historians.[39]

In the introduction to *When Brer Rabbit Meets Coyote*, Jonathan Brennan calls for a theoretical framework for African Native American literature, claiming that "this literary tradition demands recognition and a critical analysis that acknowledges both the African American and Native American cultural and literary influences and the unique features of mixed-race and African Native American writing."[40] While the slave narrative as the key African American autobiographical mode of the nineteenth century mediates the life experiences of former slaves and their quest for freedom, such as Frederick Douglass's *Narrative of the Life of Frederick Douglass, An American Slave. Written by Himself* (1845)[41] and Harriet Ann Jacobs's *Incidents in the Life of Slave Girl* (1861),[42] Native American life narratives often contain ethnographic elements of tribal history, culture, and customs.[43] Writing about Native American autobiography, Arnold Krupat points out the biraciality of many of the narratives themselves: "[they] are collaborative efforts, jointly produced by some white who translates, transcribes, compiles, edits, interprets, polishes, and ultimately determines the 'form' of the text in writing, and by an Indian who is 'subject' and whose 'life' becomes the 'content' of the 'autobiography' whose title may bear his 'name.'"[44] African Americans who wanted to write about and publish their life experiences in the form of the slave narrative were faced with restrictions to authorship and access to publishers[45] similar to those experienced by Native Americans.[46] Thus, African and Native American literary traditions, which, according to Brennan, evolved separately, coalesce in what he labels the "hybrid text" of the African Native American author.[47] Two nineteenth-century mixed-race writers whose autobiographies Brennan analyzes as key examples of producers of hybrid literary texts are William Apess (presumably African Pequot) and Okah Tubbee (presumably African Choctaw).

Native American and African American personal narratives such as Tubbee's reflect the political, social, and cultural circumstances of black slavery, Indian removal, and white racism, and Tubbee's narrative can be placed between the Indian autobiography as defined by Krupat and the slave narrative since it embodies common denominators of the two genres, such as the as-told-to aspect (or oral testimony), the political cause for abolitionism or sovereignty, the editorial process, and the question of authorship or "authenticity" of the first-person narrator.[48] As Brennan argues, Tubbee's *A Thrilling Sketch* "shares elements of eighteenth- and nineteenth-century African American and Native American literary traditions, drawing from forms that include the Christian conversion narrative, confessional writing, captivity narratives, Indian autobiographies, and slave narratives."[49] It thus mediates hybrid African Native American identity and autobiographical genres in the antebellum era.

A former slave who writes a book and performs as a ventriloquist and stage "savage," who has converted to Mormonism and has several white spouses in addition to a Native American one,[50] who sells fake medicine but loyally supports Native Americans threatened with removal—this indeed sounds like a curiosity who could find a place in Barnum's exhibitions.[51] Although in his annotated edition of *A Thrilling Sketch* Littlefield has filled in many blanks and verified key events and names mentioned in Tubbee's life story, central questions about his ethnic and legal background remain open to speculation, and even less is known about his Native wife, Laah Ceil. In fact, Tubbee might have been a runaway slave who, trying to hide his identity, had found a lucrative way of "fooling" authorities and audiences. However, the anecdotes of intercultural encounters and race relations in mid-nineteenth-century America and the intricate narrative and rhetorical styles employed make *A Thrilling Sketch* a valuable case study that invites new interpretations of "IndiVisible" race relations of African Americans and Native Americans when approached from a comparative ethnic studies perspective. Even if it may be an elaborate hoax, *A Thrilling Sketch* is also a literary work depicting a character who plays with literary genres and subverts racial categories, thereby demonstrating cultural fluidity and individual agency in a time and place usually known for its strict social and racial caste system.

NOTES

1. National Museum of the American Indian, *IndiVisible*, n.p.
2. Gabrielle Tayac, quoted in ibid., n.p.
3. Minges, *Black Indian Slave Narratives*, 145–146. The interviews conducted by the Works Progress Administration's Federal Writers' Project are not unproblematic when used as sources for African American experiences because of the ways in which the interviews were conducted, compiled, and edited. Lovett writes about the racial bias of the interviews: "Although interviewers were often given racist guidelines for representing southern Black dialect, these materials offer a unique glimpse into popular perception of scientific ideas about race and racial inheritance" ("African and Cherokee by Choice," 205). For a detailed analysis of the interviews as literary and historical sources, see Rawick, *From Sundown to Sunup*.
4. Minges, *Black Indian Slave Narratives*, 148.
5. According to Daniel Littlefield, four editions were published in 1848, each slightly revised and reedited. One was edited by Rev. L. L. Allen; the other three versions were edited by Tubbee's wife, Laah Ceil. Further, a fifth revised edition was attributed to Ceil, published in 1852 (Littlefield, *The Life of Okah Tubbee*, xxxix). In my article, I quote from the 1848 New York edition edited by Allen, titled *A Thrilling Sketch of the Life of the Distinguished Chief Okah Tubbee: Alias Wm. Chubbee, Son of the Head Chief, Mosholeh Tubbee, of the Choctaw Nation of Indians. By Rev. L. L. Allen*, and from the annotated reprint of the 1852 Toronto edition published as *The Life of Okah Tubbee* in 1988 and edited by Littlefield.
6. Littlefield, *The Life of Okah Tubbee*, viii.
7. See ibid., 143–144.
8. Ibid., 29.
9. Ibid., 30–31.

10. Sturm, "Blood Politics," 247.
11. Tubbee, *The Life of Okah Tubbee*, 29. In the 1848 edition, the passage is slightly different: "they said it was not reasonable to suppose that I was an Indian child, taken when small, for the purpose of making me a slave. Some asserted they had heard of such circumstances, and it was easily done, where there was such a diversity of color as there is in the South" (22).
12. Brennan, *When Brer Rabbit Meets Coyote*, 181. The quotation comes from Brennan's chapter titled "Speaking Cross Boundaries: A Nineteenth-Century African Native American Autobiography," 168–193.
13. Tubbee, *A Thrilling Sketch*, 16.
14. Deloria, *Playing Indian*; Huhndorf, *Going Native*.
15. Gilmore, *Genuine Article*, 84.
16. Tubbee, *The Life of Okah Tubbee*, 45.
17. Ibid., 23; also quoted in Gilmore, *Genuine Article*, 84.
18. Tubbee, *The Life of Okah Tubbee*, 26.
19. Ibid. Tubbee's remark that he could speak several languages curiously comments on the scene where he claims to have suddenly been able to communicate in Choctaw with visiting Native Americans without having had any previous knowledge of the language.
20. "Okah Tubbee—The Negro Indian"; or the reprint in *The Vermont Journal* (Windsor), 3 October 1851.
21. For a very detailed account of the verified facts around Tubbee's biography see Littlefield's introduction to *The Life of Okah Tubbee*.
22. Gilmore, *Genuine Article*, 67–68.
23. Quoted in ibid., 67.
24. Tubbee, *The Life of Okah Tubbee*, 93.
25. Littlefield, *The Life of Okah Tubbee*, 143.
26. Tubbee, *The Life of Okah Tubbee*, 58.
27. Ibid., 57.
28. Ibid., 58.
29. Ibid.
30. Ibid., 95–96.
31. Littlefield, *The Life of Okah Tubbee*, xiii.
32. Ibid., 134.
33. Ibid., xiv.
34. Ibid., 131.
35. Ibid., x–xi.
36. Brennan, "Speaking Cross Boundaries," 169.
37. Lovett, "'African and Cherokee by Choice,'" 209.
38. Miles, *Ties That Bind*, 28–30.

39. Miles and Holland, *Crossing Waters, Crossing Worlds*, 22.
40. Brennan, *When Brer Rabbit Meets Coyote*, 43.
41. Douglass's subtitle, *Written by Himself*, explicitly rejects an "as-told-to" format, although the preface by the abolitionist William Lloyd Garrison lends the narrative a "white" frame.
42. "The Literature of Slavery and Freedom," 158.
43. Brennan, *When Brer Rabbit Meets Coyote*, 175. Of course the slave narratives also may contain ethnographic material, as in Frederick Douglass's well-known comments on slave songs (chapter 2 of his *Narrative*).
44. Krupat, "Indian Autobiography," 23–24.
45. "The Literature of Slavery and Freedom."
46. Krupat, "Indian Autobiography," 23–24.
47. Brennan, *When Brer Rabbit Meets Coyote*, 168.
48. Ibid.
49. Ibid.
50. See Bringhurst, *Saints, Slaves, and Blacks*, passim.
51. See Cook, *The Colossal P. T. Barnum Reader*.

WORKS CITED

Brennan, Jonathan, ed. *When Brer Rabbit Meets Coyote: African-Native American Literature*. Urbana: University of Illinois Press, 2003.

Bringhurst, Newell G. *Saints, Slaves, and Blacks: The Changing Place of Black People within Mormonism*. Westport, CT: Greenwood Press, 1981.

Brooks, James F., ed. *Confounding the Color Line: The Indian-Black Experience in North America*. Lincoln: University of Nebraska Press, 2002.

Cook, James W., ed. *The Colossal P. T. Barnum Reader*. Urbana: University of Illinois Press, 2005.

Deloria, Philip. *Playing Indian*. New Haven, CT: Yale University Press, 1999.

Forbes, Jack D. *Black Africans and Native Americans*. New York: Basil Blackwell, 1988; second edition titled *Africans and Native Americans: The Language of Race and the Evolution of Red-Black Peoples*. Urbana: University of Illinois Press, 1993.

Gilmore, Paul. *The Genuine Article: Race, Mass Culture, and American Literary Manhood*. Durham, NC: Duke University Press, 2001.

Huhndorf, Shari M. *Going Native: Indians in the American Cultural Imagination*. Ithaca, NY: Cornell University Press, 2001.

Krupat, Arnold. "The Indian Autobiography: Origins, Type, and Function." *American Literature* 53.1 (March 1981): 22–42.

"The Literature of Slavery and Freedom 1746–1865." In *The Norton Anthology of African American Literature*, ed. Henry Louis Gates Jr. and Nelly Y. McKay, 151–162. 2nd ed. New York: Norton, 2004.

Littlefield, Daniel F. *Africans and Seminoles: From Removal to Emancipation*. Jackson: University of Mississippi Press, 1977.

———, ed. *The Life of Okah Tubbee*. Lincoln: University of Nebraska Press, 1988.

Lovett, Laura L. "'African and Cherokee by Choice': Race and Resistance under Legalized Segregation." *American Indian Quarterly* 22.1/2 (1998): 203–229.

Miles, Tiya. *Ties That Bind: The Story of an Afro-Cherokee Family in Slavery and Freedom*. Berkeley: University of California Press, 2005.

Miles, Tiya, and Sharon P. Holland, eds. *Crossing Waters, Crossing Worlds: The African Diaspora in Indian Country*. Durham, NC: Duke University Press, 2006.

Minges, Patrick, ed. *Black Indian Slave Narratives*. Winston-Salem, NC: John F. Blair, 2004.

National Museum of the American Indian. *IndiVisible: African American Lives in the Americas*. Washington, D.C.: Smithsonian Institution, 2009.

Naylor, Celia E. *African Cherokees in Indian Territory: From Chattel to Citizens*. Chapel Hill: University of North Carolina Press, 2008.

"Okah-Tubbee—The Negro Indian." *The Cleveland Evening Herald*, 17 September 1851.

Perdue, Theda. *Slavery and the Evolution of Cherokee Society 1540–1866*. Knoxville: University of Tennessee Press, 1979.

Rawick, George P. *From Sundown to Sunup: The Making of the Black Community*. Vol. 1, *The American Slave: A Composite Autobiography*. 19 vols. Ed. George P. Rawick. Westport, CT: Greenwood Press, 1972.

Sturm, Circe. "Blood Politics, Racial Classification, and Cherokee National Identity." *American Indian Quarterly* 22.1/2 (1998): 230–258.

Tubbee, Laah Ceil Manatoi Elaah. *A Sketch of the Life of Okah Tubbee, (Called) William Chubbee, Son of the Head Chief, Mosholeh Tubbee, of the Choctaw Nation of Indians*. Toronto: Henry Stephens, 1852.

Tubbee, Okah or Laah Ceil Tubbee. "A Sketch of the Life of Okah Tubbee, (Called) William Chubbee, Son of the Head Chief, Moshleh Tubbee, of the Choctaw Nation of Indians." In *The Life of Okah Tubbee*, ed. Daniel Littlefield, 3–128. Lincoln: University of Nebraska Press, 1988.

———. *A Thrilling Sketch of the Life of the Distinguished Chief Okah Tubbee: Alias Wm Chubbee, Son of the Head Chief, Mosholeh Tubbee, of the Choctaw Nation of Indians. By Rev. L. L. Allen*. New York: [s.n.], 1848.

"Buffalo Bill Takes a Scalp"

Mediated Transculturality on Both Sides of the Atlantic with William F. Cody's Wild West, from Show to Hollywood and YouTube

CATHY COVELL WAEGNER

Buffalo Bill's Wild West show[1] achieved unprecedented (inter)national popularity, creating paradigms that deeply influenced the world's image of the encounters on the pre–Wounded Knee American frontier. The powerful film genre of the western arose from the scenes portrayed again and again for more than three decades (1872–1908) on both sides of the Atlantic in the grandiose Wild West show, both billed as and largely perceived as "*authentic*"—whooping and war-painted Indians attacking a settler's home or a stagecoach, for instance.[2] Numerous films and countless books have chosen Buffalo Bill (William F. Cody) and his show as their subjects, but relatively few of them have concerned themselves with the Native American perspective, that of the Indian actors in this spectacle, which included the persevering Native leader Sitting Bull.[3] Although the Wild West Show's format denied any evolving transculturality, freezing itself into ever-repeated confrontations between ethnic groups, the usual climax of the spectacle had a resounding transcultural touch: the reenactment of Custer's Last Stand ending with Cody avenging Custer's death by ostentatiously scalping a Cheyenne warrior "Indian-style." Drawing on theories of transculturality and ethnic performativity, I examine modes of what I call "mediated transculturality," which emerge from the historical Wild West show itself as well as from four works depicting it. "Stop-motion" shots of transculturality are often egregiously offensive, as in Cody's scalping, but are occasionally—when embraced by the Natives themselves through what I call the "transcultural crack"—ingenious and refreshing; archival photos of Native performers in full war-bonnet costume playing lively table tennis matches during intermissions are an example of the latter. On a metalevel, the *reception* of the Wild West show mediation, especially in Internet platforms, also runs a full spectrum, ranging from naively approving to highly critical.

This chapter begins with the two case studies mentioned above—Cody's scalping and the Natives playing Ping-Pong—before presenting relevant theory on transculturality and examining five modes of *mediated transculturality* as pragmatic tools: *experienced*, *experienced once removed*, *redface*, *meta*, and *inverted*. For my purposes, *experienced transculturality* emerges from the posed photographs and reported eyewitness accounts of participants in the Wild West shows. I then develop the notion of *experienced transculturality once removed* through a discussion of James Welch's last novel, *The Heartsong of Charging Elk* (2001), with its Native protagonist, a performer in Buffalo Bill's Wild West, drawn from historical models. Countless Hollywood films notoriously incorporate stereotyped *redface transculturality*, as a consideration of William Wellman's 1944 movie *Buffalo Bill* illustrates. Ironically critical modes serve as a key strategy in works in the protest era of the 1960s and 1970s; Arthur Kopit's theater play *Indians*, first performed in 1968, offers overt and piercing *metatransculturality*, for instance, and Robert Altman's masterful cinematic satire *Buffalo Bill and the Indians, or Sitting Bull's History Lesson* (1976) makes effective satirical use of *inverted transculturality*. Laced throughout my analyses are references to a transcultural crack connected with performativity. This study concludes by investigating the current "new media" reception of Buffalo Bill's Wild West.

The iconographic scene in the Wild West of "Buffalo Bill taking a scalp" was stylized for advertising posters and dime novel covers: a triumphant Cody flaunts the slain Native's bloody scalp and feather headdress in one hand and in the other clutches his long-handled knife, straddling the corpse on the edge of a cliff while admiring soldiers watch from below.[4] The scout William Cody had been staging autobiographical theater melodramas in the East since 1872, but returned to the frontier briefly in 1876. A few weeks after Custer's defeat at the Battle of Little Big Horn on 25/26 June 1876, Cody killed Yellow Hair[5] (whose name has generally been mistranslated as Yellow Hand) at the Battle of Warbonnet Creek on 17 July 1876, gleaning the "first scalp for Custer," as Cody proceeded to proclaim every night from the stage when he resumed his acting career. Supposedly subduing the savages, Buffalo Bill became savage himself—and marketed this transcultural savagery lucratively.[6] He exhibited Yellow Hand's artifacts, including the scalp, in the lobbies of theaters when he performed. Bill supposedly parried criticism of the scalping and his touting of it by claiming that Yellow Hand barbarically had a "woman's scalp at his waist and an American flag for a loincloth"[7] when Cody killed him. One cannot help concluding that the "scalp for Custer" deed was planned with an eye to later staging, since Buffalo Bill even went into the Battle of Warbonnet Creek wearing the fancy velvet pants with silver decoration in which he later reenacted the bloody victory for years in theaters.[8] Thus the "experienced transculturality" reflected in such a historical event as the defeat of Yellow Hand, ostensibly using the Natives' own methods, cannot be viewed without considering a strong lens of "*mediation*," in this case Cody's careful crafting of his public self-image. Ned Buntline and other dime novel authors and illustrators sensationalistically strengthened the mediating lens, dramatically exaggerating Buffalo Bill's scalping feat.[9]

The photos of Buffalo Bill's Wild West Indians gleefully playing Ping-Pong, cheered on by cowboys, cavalrymen, vaqueros or gauchos, and even Cossacks during a rehearsal or show break (probably in 1902 in Bryan, Ohio), are available in the Denver Public Library online collection. The Wild West participants probably picked up this new British sport during their tours throughout Great Britain; table tennis originated in England in the 1880s, and Wild West tours preceding the Ping-Pong photos took place in 1887, 1891, and 1892. The theatrical appearance of the Natives in elaborate headdresses and full-length blanket costumes skillfully wielding table tennis paddles emphasizes this moment of "experienced transculturality," one of many recorded in photo and written accounts during the more than thirty years of the Wild West shows. As the local *Bryan/Ohio Democrat* newspaper put it, with what must have been considered political correctness (despite the unfortunate use of the word "enslaved") just a little more than ten years after Wounded Knee, Ping-Pong provided an interethnic link between the "noble Reds" and "their brethren": "Somebody has taught the Indians of Buffalo Bill's Wild West Show how to play ping pong, and the noble Reds have become as greatly enslaved by the fascination of the game as their brethren, the pale faces."[10] The newspaper article included a photograph similar to the one reproduced below and depicted Black Fox as a sports hero: "It shows Black Fox in the midst of an exciting game. The popular chief is a passionate devotee of the game and has attained great proficiency in its many intricacies." With reference to the notion of "transcultural crack," we can perhaps view the break in the show during which such improvised offstage games could take place as a window for

Figure 1. "Death of Yellow Hand—Cody's First Scalp for Custer," illustration from 1883 publication titled *The Wild West Buffalo Bill and Dr. Carver Rocky Mountain and Prairie Exhibition*. (Courtesy of The William F. Cody Archive, in connection with the Buffalo Bill Center of the West and University of Nebraska–Lincoln)

Figure 2. Wild West Indians enthusiastically playing Ping-Pong during a show break in 1902. (Courtesy of the Denver Public Library, Western History Collection, NS-717)

spontaneous transculturality, a contrast to the staged and confrontational encounters between the Indians and cavalrymen or cowboys in the Wild West arena. The improvised Ping-Pong playing also contrasts tellingly with Cody's theatrical and possibly staged scalping act in his stage clothes during his "break" from the theater.

Wolfgang Welsch's stringent and influential approach to transculturality theory beginning in the 1990s[11] and Günter Lenz's 2011 revision[12] provide a substantial theoretical framework for my comments. In contrast to "bi-," "multi-," and "polyculturality," terms that presuppose homogeneous, single, and distinguishable cultures,[13] Welsch advocates the notion of *transculturality*, which premises permeations, complex mixes, and cultural networkings. His theory stresses the *dynamism* of transcultural processes and the ongoing hybrid transformations in person and cultures. The individual is constantly choosing components of affiliation, although admittedly the choice might not always be one among attractive options. Extending the parameters of Welsch's theory would mean the eventual breakdown of mappable cultural difference, with idiocultures reigning, the philosophical antipode to a (national) cultural "melting pot."

Günter Lenz's recent adjustments to Welsch's approach emphasize a broad form of dialogism that does not undermine the pragmatic notion of different cultures. Lenz admits conflictual and hierarchical forms of interaction, which Welsch viewed as distasteful remnants of the inherited "separate cultures" attitude with its power struggle between distinguishable and unequal cultures. For Lenz, the role of the (new) media in transcultural processes deserves particular attention.

All transculturalists stress the multidirectionality (or at least two-way) and complexity of transcultural impulses, and indeed the political and ethic value of emphasizing them over the monologizing trends fostered by historically "strong" cultures and by globalization with its tendencies to embrace "McDonaldizing" sameness. For our purposes: instead of simple one-way movements of Natives assimilating into white society or whites appropriating Native cultural practices, we can detect more complicated processes at work, involving components of Native strategy, choice, and self-empowerment, often against inordinate odds and with varying modes of mediation.

Other than Cody's revengeful scalping and the joyful Ping-Pong games, further cogent examples of what Welsch and Lenz might agree could be called "experienced transculturality" arise from the Wild West show encounters, especially those taking place during the highly successful tours throughout most European countries.[14] Of course these encounters are mediated, reaching us, for instance, through formal daguerreotypes and on-site accounts. In the first of five selected biographical exempla, John Y. Nelson, an adopted white member of the Sioux Nation who actually rode shotgun for the Wells Fargo "Deadwood stagecoach," was hired by Cody to do the same in his Wild West; in the show, the omnipresent stagecoach was attacked by war-painted Indians uncountable times throughout America and Europe during the thirty years of Cody's Wild West. Nelson traveled as a show member with his Sioux wife and their five mixed children. His daughter Wa-Ka-Cha-Sha, or "Red Rose," when young, was a favorite at performance venues, called the "Pet [or in some cases 'Girl-pet'] of the Sioux" in popular postcards.[15]

One of the leading Show Indians in Europe, Red Shirt, dressed in photo portraits in transcultural grandeur—in one famous picture wearing a Victorian vest and white linen shirt, but also an elaborate Native bone-bead necklace, with rippling long hair, one side braided, holding a Native blanket and a decorated peace pipe[16]—won Queen Victoria's heart. As a widow she had attended practically no public entertainment for a quarter of a century, but she enthusiastically went to the Wild West show in London for her Golden Jubilee in 1887,[17] afterward meeting with Red Shirt and several other Show Indians and commending Red Shirt's "kingly dignity."[18]

Black Elk, the "medicine man" who had joined Cody's Wild West to try to understand the whites' ways in order to help his people,[19] traveled to England with the other performers in 1887; a contemporary daguerreotype shows him as a young man in embroidered loincloth, feathery head decor, earrings, and arm and calf bands.[20] He and several other Show Indians lost their way in Manchester and were left behind. He joined up with Mexican Joe's western show, traveling with that troupe to France and Germany. In Paris, an adoring female fan introduced him to her family and took care of him during a spiritual "illness." He records his intercultural encounters in detail in his classic autobiography (as told to John G. Neidhardt, 1932), *Black Elk Speaks: Being the Life Story of a Holy Man of the Oglala Sioux.*[21] His European experiences were part of what made him, now named Nicholas Black Elk, appear in a photograph taken two decades later (1910) like an Edwardian gentleman, dressed in a suit and tie, in contrast to his Native wife and child in traditional dress. In fact, Black Elk had become a Catholic catechist.

Standing Bear was injured in an arena in Vienna in 1890, and was fortunate enough to be cared for by a daring and clever Austrian nurse, Louise Rieneck, who married him and returned to South Dakota with him. She learned Sioux, and they started several businesses, including combining Native and European medicines, to support their family of mixed ethnicity.[22]

Black Elk and Standing Bear are two prototypes for the Lakota Sioux protagonist in James Welch's 2001 carefully researched novel, *The Heartsong of Charging Elk*,[23] written nearly exclusively from the focalizing third-person point of view of a Native performer in the Wild West shows. It was Native American author James Welch's final book, a gripping protest against the exploitation of the Indians who, faced with the choice between reservation and Wild West show, saw Buffalo Bill's traveling act as the only remaining space for what appeared to be viable action. After an injury, Charging Elk finds himself stranded in Marseille in 1889 with no passport, an utterly alien Other. Relating this to the "experienced transculturality" arising from the historical Wild West show, we can call his painful learning process in this historical novel "experienced transculturality once removed," to appropriate the term "once removed" from New York University's African Americanist Phillip Brian Harper's work.[24] Welch's approach offers a convincing perception of the reasons why the reservation Natives joined Buffalo Bill's Wild West and why their ethnographic showmanship in Europe possibly took on a different quality from the performances in America:

> As Charging Elk rode his painted horse in the procession [in Marseille], he couldn't help but think how fortunate he was. Instead of passing another cold,

> lonely winter at the Stronghold, or being a passive reservation Indian who planted potatoes and held out his hand for the government commodities, he was dressed in his finest clothes, riding a strong horse, preparing himself to thrill the crowds with a display of the old ways. Of course, he knew that it was fake and that some of the elders back home disapproved of the young men going off to participate in the white man's sham, but he no longer felt guilty about singing scalping songs or participating in scalp dances or sneak-up dances. He was proud to display some of the old ways to these French because they appreciated the Indians and seemed genuinely sympathetic. Rocky Bear had once told him, while they were sitting around a fire after the evening show, that these people on this side of the big water called the Indians "the Americans who would vanish," that they thought the defeated Indians would soon disappear and they were very sad about it and wanted to see the Indians before they went up in thin air—unlike the real Americans, who would be only too happy to help the Indians disappear.[25]

The constantly evolving transcultural self with its dynamically changing strands of affiliations from Wolfgang Welsch's theory is exquisitely portrayed as Charging Elk learns French, sceptically enters churches, and reinterprets his understanding of "homeland." When he meets and talks to some Lakota performers at the Buffalo Bill show sixteen years later, in 1905, one of them says—in a statement that could serve as a litmus test for transcultural identity—"I can see you are still one of us, yet you are different."[26] Charging Elk's agonizing choice between returning to his widowed mother on the reservation in South Dakota with these performers or staying in France with his pregnant wife is presented with poetic transcultural landscape as he finally and deliberately turns his back on the show:

> He walked past the sideshows, dark now, and the empty arena. The white, many-pointed awnings over the bleachers looked like distant mountains. He walked away from the show grounds. It was late now and the trolleys wouldn't be running, but he didn't mind. He needed to walk and the Moon of the Falling Leaves would light his way.[27]

Not all of the French "appreciated the Buffalo Bill Indians and seemed genuinely sympathetic" as Rocky Bear had told Charging Elk at the beginning of Elk's time as a Buffalo Bill performer. For Mme Soulas, at least at first, the Wild West Indians are subhuman: "savages," probably "dumb," even "part beast," with their "yipping and yowling, the fierce way they rode their horses" in the show.[28] Her husband, René, reveals the opposite extreme, fascination with the exotic strangers to the extent that he offers his home to Charging Elk as a refuge and evens imitates him during the Wild West show in a reversal of Homi K. Bhabha's "mimicry" of the colonizer by the colonized:[29]

> René had sat on the edge of his seat during the whole of the performance. He had clapped and cheered at the big carriage and the pursuing Indians. He had let out a howl of delight when the Indians rode among the running bison. And he had actually made savage whoops when the Peaux-Rouges had killed the brave soldiers. Madame Soulas had been horrified at his behaviour until she noticed many of the other spectators doing the same thing![30]

This mass imitation of the "savage whoops" that the French audience assumed was Native behavior is a euphemistic version of William Cody's appropriation of Native custom in physically scalping Yellow Hand. In being adopted by the well-intentioned Soulas family, Charging Elk is thus caught up in racist pincers: on the one hand, degradation (Madame Soulas viewing him as a low savage) and, on the other, exoticizing transculturality (Monsieur Soulas actually producing war whoops).[31] The artificiality of René Soulas's appropriation is underlined in the novel as Charging Elk, now working in a French factory, must choose components of French life, such as donning European-style clothing.[32]

The way René and the rest of the Wild West audience immerse themselves in what they see as the "spirit" of the performance in fact misleads Charging Elk in a later, threatening situation. In a brasserie at the port in Marseille, Elk finds himself surrounded by hostile sailors who are yelling at him; he initially associates this with the "sympathetic" and encouraging visitors to the Buffalo Bill show: "Some [of the sailors] were shouting in his direction. Suddenly, he saw the crowds in the stands at the Wild West show with their big eyes and shouting voices as he rode hard after the buffaloes. But this was not a show and these people were not cheering him on."[33] When Charging Elk realizes that with the sailors' discriminatory cries of "goddamn bloody Indian" and "goddamn ignorant blanket-ass" no transcultural mimicry is taking place, he brilliantly selects a component of his Oglala background to assert himself: he begins to sing his tribal and personal "death song," ironically accompanied by the restaurant's French accordion player, who "squeezed his box in a hushed, toneless accompaniment." Through Elk's strategy the potential violence is defused, and Elk is escorted out in dignity by the waiter and the manager. Unfortunately, not all of Elk's encounters as a cultural Other end this felicitously. With a

Figure 3. One of the buffalo dancers in Thomas Edison's 1894 fifteen-second film faces the camera, displaying his knife. (Screenshot from *Buffalo Bill's Wild West: Annie Oakley, Buffalo Dance, Bucking Broncho* [00:00:15])

full range of bewildering, degrading, and self-empowering moments, James Welch succeeds masterfully in (re-)imagining and mediating novelistically the Native protagonist's experienced transculturality.

Before turning to other forms of mediated transculturality, I would like to propose a term offering an instrument for discourse on the performativity of the so-called Buffalo Bill Indians: "transcultural crack." In Charging Elk's thoughts above, we see a fissure in his performance of the "white man's sham" in France: his pride gives an edge to his "scalp dances," an edge that connects him to the "sympathetic" French audience. We see a different form of this "crack" in the fifteen-second Edison Manufacturing Company film of 1894 called *Buffalo Dance*, made in the Edison studio in West Orange, New Jersey, just four years after the massacre at Wounded Knee effectively ended Native resistance to forced acceptance of the reservations. This clip can be considered the ur-link between the Wild West shows and the western film genre.[34] Of the three Sioux buffalo dancers (Hair Coat, Last Horse, and Parts His Hair) in the very short film, one of them in particular looks at the camera/audience and brandishes his knife, cutting through an invisible wall between performers onstage and camera as a substitute for the viewers—a moment of choice, of empowerment, of "giving the crowd a thrill" as Charging Elk has put it. For an ethnic performer playing for a largely white audience, opening up this transcultural crack can permit the entry of enthusiasm, of critique, or irony, of protest. I will be pointing out functions of the opening up or sealing off of this crack. It can fruitfully be compared and contrasted to the "flash of black" in African American blackface performance, brought to light by Ralph Ellison in his "Change the Joke and Slip the Yoke" essay and now a cornerstone of post-1970s research on "black" blackface minstrelsy;[35] later we will consider critical assessments of the recent rebooting of Buffalo Bill's Wild West—these assessments refer to the revival of "Indian minstrel shows." The link to blackface minstrelsy is far from coincidental.

With its standard application of Hollywood "redface transculturality," William Wellman's movie *Buffalo Bill* (1944) offers a double version of this "transcultural crack"—but with a twist. This movie is a "prequel" to the rise of Buffalo Bill's Wild West, which is shown only in telescoped clips in the end, and presents an engagé Buffalo Bill (Joel McCrea) who champions the cause of the Natives to the detriment of his early career. The translation of the German film title "Buffalo Bill, der weiße Indianer," "Buffalo Bill, the White Indian," reflects this in transcultural terms. Blatant Hollywood "redface" makeup is obvious in every scene involving Natives, the film producers ostensibly engaging for a speaking role only one fully Native actor, "Chief" Thundercloud, who played Tonto in the two movie serials of *The Lone Ranger* in the 1930s. The Indian heroine, a schoolteacher who joins the "braves" when they fight the cavalry, is played by the white Hollywood diva Linda Darnell, leading the contemporary audience to a palimpsest viewing of her role: red on white. All of the western stereotypes are stridently employed: English-speaking, screeching Indians raising their hands in the obligatory "How!" gesture, on the warpath, shot right and left off their painted and befeathered horses by brave cavalrymen. Produced near the end of the World War II effort, when the public concept of American nation tended to rally all domestic groups (except Japanese Americans), the film—despite its stereotyping—intends to offer a supportive rendering of Native Americans and self-sacrificial Buffalo Bill's attitude toward them.

The feisty but doomed Cheyenne chief Yellow Hand is played by a young Anthony Quinn, in redface coloring and Hollywood-Native paraphernalia. Cracks in his redface are visible on screen, with, for instance, his at times splotchy facial makeup and artificially darkened eyebrows. I venture to say that most viewers do not realize, however, that Quinn's ethnic background is partially Native:[36] his mother was a Mexican of Aztec heritage. For initiates, this gave him indeed some authority to counter the fake "redface transculturality" otherwise rampant in Hollywood productions up to the 1970s (and even beyond), particularly for leading roles,[37] but then why was the need felt for the copper-color makeup? It is striking that Joel McCrea as Bill Cody also wears dark makeup to contrast with the pale Easterners, including his wife, played by an always perfectly groomed Maureen O'Hara. In a well-known publicity shot, Joel McCrea and Anthony Quinn appear in complementary nakedness, McCrea's bare chest matching Quinn's bare legs, while hefty squaws in color-coordinated leather dresses of beige, light blue, and lavender are lined up to the left and right to watch Buffalo Bill being tied to the stake. Even in the Technicolor version of the photo, no difference in the two protagonists' skin color can be detected. Dare we claim that the red on white of "redface transculturality" fails here and shifts to a visual male versus female split dominating over the white/Native culture clash?

Arthur Kopit's theater play based on Buffalo Bill material, simply called *Indians,* has been continually popular, particularly with university drama groups, ever since the premiere in 1968.[38] It offers sophisticated and overt "metatransculturality" when, for example, an "Indian maiden" in a play-within-the-play in the "White House Ballroom" suddenly foregrounds her performativity, proclaiming, "I'm not an Indian [I'm a Russian] and I'm not a maiden!"[39] The transcultural crack is thus deliberately and largely humorously burst wide open, encouraged by the obvious artificiality of the staging context and calling for poly-ethnicity in the choice of actors.

The humor of Kopit's metatransculturality, however, is often secondary to its function of critique in this engagé play, particularly when the Native voices are heard. Historically, William Cody guided the Grand Duke Alexis of Russia through a highly publicized and profligate buffalo hunt; in Kopit's play the Grand Duke is fascinated by Bill's tall tale of fighting off a large attack group of Comanches, and wants to hunt a Comanche too. Wolfgang Welsch's warning of the dangers of biculturality with hierarchy is pushed to hyperbolic limits when the aristocrat views Natives as subhuman, to be shot for sport. The Grand Duke shoots into the darkness, and Spotted Tail stumbles out onto the stage and dies. In a supernatural moment, dead Spotted Tail rises with dignity and exposes the European's ignorance and, by extension, his arrogance in equating buffalo with Natives as hunting game, by saying, both to the Grand Duke (who understands no English) and, metarhetorically, to the audience: "My name is Spotted Tail. My father was a Sioux; my mother, part Cherokee, part Crow. No matter how you look at it, I'm just not a Comanche."[40] Bill expediently prevents the Grand Duke from comprehending that the lay hunter has shot the wrong game, not a

Figure 4. This promotional poster showing a still from Twentieth Century Fox's *Buffalo Bill* (1944) depicts Buffalo Bill and Yellow Hand—in complementary nakedness—as they face the lines of women in color-coded costumes. (Courtesy of Dickinson Research Center, National Cowboy and Western Heritage Museum, Oklahoma City, Oklahoma, RC2006.067.3.03623)

Comanche, and (anachronistically) a trophaic flash photo is taken of the duke with his human quarry.

Ned Buntline has taken the flash picture; his role in mediating the glorifying image of Buffalo Bill and the degrading ones of the Natives, not only in this play but in history, should not be underestimated. He touted and exaggerated Bill's feats in a plethora of best-selling dime novels, and in Kopit's play he cleverly but demonically instructs Bill, sotto voce, how to act to present the most marketable image. Buntline is not present, however, when, after the Wounded Knee massacre, Bill conducts a dialogue, full of pregnant pauses, with Sitting Bull's ghost about his own motives, the performativity of the Wild West shows, and the near crack in the Natives' participation when they "could almost imagine it was *real*":

> **Buffalo Bill**: Funny. For a while, I actually thought my Wild West Show would *help*. I could give you money. Food. Clothing. And also make people *understand* things . . . better.
>
> *He laughs to himself.*
>
> That was my reasoning. Or, anyway, *part* . . .

> *Pause.*
> of my reasoning.
> **Sitting Bull** (*slight smile*): Your show was very popular.
> *Pause.*
> **Buffalo Bill**: We had . . . fun, though, you and I.
> *Pause.*
> Didn't we?
> **Sitting Bull**: Oh, yes. And that's the terrible thing. We had all surrendered. We were on reservations. We could not fight, or hunt. We could do nothing. Then you came and allowed us to imitate our glory. . . . It was humiliating! For sometimes, we could almost imagine it was *real.*
> **Buffalo Bill**: Guess it wasn't so authentic, was it?
> *He laughs slightly to himself.*
> **Sitting Bull**: How could it have been? You'd have killed all your performers in one afternoon.[41]

For Kopit's Sitting Bull, the "crack" is not empowering and does not link the performers to the audience, as seems to have been the case for Charging Elk in the performances in France, but rather is "humiliating" for the Natives. Buffalo Bill does not grasp Sitting Bull's perspective, and thoughtlessly displays for the theater audience Indian trinkets that he is selling along with his show to "raise [the] spirits [of the remaining Natives]."[42] The audience might "buy" Kopit's mediation, but probably not Buffalo Bill's and certainly not Buntline's.

Robert Altman's ingenious cinematic satire *Buffalo Bill and the Indians, or Sitting Bull's History Lesson* (1976) was inspired by Kopit's irreverent approach to Buffalo Bill's Wild West;[43] with what can be labeled "inverted transculturality," Altman reverses stereotypes, casting an ostensibly weak and foolish Sitting Bull (actor: Frank Kaquitts, a Nakoda First Nations chief), who nonetheless manages to best the whites at their own performance game and to haunt the braggadocio William Cody (played with brilliant irony by Paul Newman).[44] In an initial inversion, the show administrators have mistaken Sitting Bull's physically imposing, self-confidently articulate and obviously transculturally educated translator William Halsey (impressively performed by Will Sampson) for the chief himself.[45] In Günter Lenz's terms, this scene is a cogent embodiment of failed dialogism, in which both sides continue the power struggle and reinforce their prejudices, although opportunities for reassessment present themselves; when Halsey speaks about Sitting Bull's long "incarceration," for instance, using a word Buffalo Bill does not know or understand, Bill's reaction is not respect but a denigrating taunt: "Got a little white blood in you, Halsey?"[46]

When President Cleveland attends the show, Sitting Bull opens a transcultural crack as a master conman to produce his Wild West show triumph: playing the docile, prancing Show Indian, Sitting Bull suddenly speaks in Lakota[47] and points his gun directly at the president; has Sitting Bull cleverly dropped one show persona—the amusing Show Indian—for another, that of the "*warrior* of the western plains who has murdered more white men than any other redskin,"[48] which the announcer bills him as, or even perhaps as the preshow Sitting Bull, who was indeed a chief countering the historical attacks of the cavalry? President Cleveland suffers a moment of intense fear of assassination. Sitting Bull then fires in the air and the show goes on, but not without a feeling of unease for the white politicians and show organizers.

After Sitting Bull's (historically accurate) death in 1890 at the hands of the infamous "Indian police," his silent ghost disturbs Buffalo Bill, who declaims whisky-inspired monologues of self-justification in the ghost's company in the middle of the night. Halsey problematically but perhaps strategically replaces Sitting Bull in Cody's regularly performed triumph over the Natives; Buffalo Bill continues to flourish a scalp to thunderous applause as the highlight of the Wild West show, but his fanatic eyes and wild manner imply his shrill discomfort in the struggle against Sitting Bull's ghost. His initial joy in employing what he sees as "Indian savagery" in triumphing over Yellow Hand back in 1876 has backfired, and by 1890, the zenith of the Buffalo Bill show, this self-serving joy has inverted into internal barbarism.

Current Internet blogs and YouTube uploads relating to Buffalo Bill's instrumentalization of the Natives cast light on all of these forms of mediated transculturality. The number of Google and YouTube links relating to Buffalo Bill's Wild West is vast, ranging from the nostalgic song "Buffalo Bill Is Gone" performed in the 2005 musical *Dust and Dreams*, scenes from the newest productions of Kopit's play *Indians*, sale at exorbitant prices of Wild West show photos, and blogs discussing the ethicality of Wild West show revivals. As one compelling example, the controversy surrounding Thom Ross's traveling exhibition of Wild West figures is being shrilly conducted on the Web. Ross, a Caucasian California artist, has created colorful, life-size plywood cutouts of the Wild West Indians, mounted on horseback, for display on large public spaces, such as Ocean Beach in San Francisco, often with carnival-type face openings for visitors to be photographed as a "wild Indian."[49] The grandiose exhibit is popular in many circles, publicized on the

Figure 5. Paul Newman as Buffalo Bill fanatically reenacts the archetypal "First Scalp for Custer" meme. (Screenshot from *Buffalo Bill and the Indians, or Sitting Bull's History Lesson* [01:55:44])

web by communities that solicit it, with an online vocal Thom Ross loudly defending his project. It is articulately attacked, however, by, for example, an Indian American (that is, a Southeast Asian American, not the expected American Indian), who decries this as a resurrection of Buffalo Bill's stereotypical and degrading "Indian minstrel shows" (pdf flyer).[50] Perhaps in one respect Ross's cutouts should be viewed as even more insidious than the nineteenth-century performances in both red-on-red and black-on-black minstrelsy, since plywood figures cannot open up their own transcultural crack. Furthermore, the photos that Thom Ross has uploaded of himself dressed as General Custer and his comments in Facebook language such as "Custer had a 'bad-hair day' at the Little Bighorn"[51] lessen sympathy for his artwork. Nonetheless, his ratings rise somewhat in connection with one of the strategies in his oeuvre, which is to re-create striking transcultural moments in nineteenth-century history, usually based on original photographs, as with his portrait of "Sitting Bull" signing autographs. His stylized but lively painting of the Show Natives enjoying Ping-Pong [52] deserves special mention here, spiraling our discussion from the newspaper reports and photographs of the Buffalo Bill Indians as skilled table tennis players in their offstage time one hundred years ago to current art interpretation of those nineteenth-century mediations.

The new media thus contributes productively to the complexity of transcultural discourse as well as discourse on transculturality; we should not forget, however, that the heated debate on such performed cultural phenomena as the Wild West is not new. The excitement of the grand show coming to town—for the stop in Barcelona on 20 December 1889, to mention just one European example, an entourage of 1,200 arrived by ship in a flurry of press coverage and word-of-mouth news on Chief Black Heart, medicine man Rocky Bear, warrior Red Shirt, the other Arapaho, Cheyenne, Sioux players, in addition to 200 horses and several bison[53]—and surely Monsieur Soulas's participative excitement during the performance in Marseille was repeated by many spectators in Barcelona.[54] Yet even during the era of the shows, strong and convincing voices objecting to the ethnographic tours were published, like this of a scholar writing in 1914 during the transition from traveling shows to films, for the *Quarterly Journal of the Society of American Indians*; E. H. Gohl, a white adopted member of the Onondaga, eloquently condemns the sham of the road shows and exploitative movies in his article titled "The Effect of Wild Westing":

> A determined stand should be taken by all true friends of our American Indians to discourage and prevent whenever possible Indians making engagements with wild-west shows, theatrical troupes, circuses, and most of the motion-picture firms. . . . From every point of view, touring the country with shows is demoralizing and a menace to the Indian. . . . Both sides lose, the white as well as the red man. The spectator gains no real knowledge of the manners, costumes, and institutions of the Indian. Show managers compel the red man to act the white man's idea of a war dance. All is burlesque. The whole thing is deception. . . . The contrast between the morbid curiosity to see the red man as a savage in war-paint and the desire to see the Indian as a fellow human being [must be maintained].[55]

A colorful description of Buffalo Bill in Barcelona can be found on a *current* tourist website for the city, and a quotation from Gohl's 1914 article appears in the "Indian minstrel show" pdf flyer agitating against Thom Ross's contemporary and politically incorrect, even pernicious Wild West cutouts. The dialectic between eras adds a key axis to the transcultural impulses emerging from the Wild West phenomenon and its mediation. Although simple belief in the Wild West performances as (having been) mimetically "authentic" is no longer possible in our media-savvy times, it is clear that the dispute on the means and effects of ethnographic exhibition is far from over. Sitting Bull and Buffalo Bill continue to haunt and influence each other in transcultural showmanship.

NOTES

1. Officially Buffalo Bill's business, as advertised on promotional posters, was called the "Buffalo Bill's Wild West" without "show or Show," but because of the emphasis on performance in my study and occasionally for clarity and variety, I will often refer to the "Wild West show" or other similar versions.
2. Lurid advertising posters depicting, for instance, Natives attacking settlers were lavishly distributed by Cody's tireless publicist Major John Burke, both in the States and abroad, providing templates for the incipient western movies. Kate Flint describes how "large colored posters were plastered all over London" in 1887 (*The Transatlantic Indian*, 229).
3. These quite recent and fine studies stress the Native perspective: Kate Flint, *The Transatlantic Indian, 1776–1930*, 2009; Sam A. Maddra, *Hostiles? The Lakota Ghost Dance and Buffalo Bill's Wild West*, 2006; L. G. Moses, *Wild West Shows and the Images of American Indians 1883–1933*, 1996. Louis S. Warren's encyclopedic and carefully documented cultural biography of Cody, *Buffalo Bill's America: William Cody and the Wild West Show* (2005) devotes considerable attention to Native concerns, as does Joy Kasson's attractive book *Buffalo Bill's Wild West: Celebrity, Memory, and Popular History* (2000). Dagmar Wernitznig's fine Europe-oriented study (2007) has an excellent chapter called "Indianness Touring Europe: Buffalo Bill's Wild West" (*Europe's Indians*, 70–94). The international documentary film project titled *The Old World and the Old West: Cowboys, Indians and Europeans* by the independent company Riva Productions (New York City), was scheduled for release in 2014. Its international team of advisers, Joy Kasson, Louis Warren, and Don Wilmeth, are all experts on the Wild West material, and surely attempt to do justice to the Native issues. Jace Weaver's 2014 opus, *The Red Atlantic: American Indigenes and the Making of the Modern World, 1000–1927*, provides invaluable historical information and insights with regard to the touring companies, especially chapter 4, "'A Gazing Stocke, Yea Even a Laughing Stocke': Celebrity Indians and Display across the Red Atlantic," 189–215.
4. Many realizations of this iconic scene exist. See www.wyomingtalesandtrails.com/cody.html for this illustration slightly touched up, and for other versions of the scalping incident. For a transcription of a letter by a witness to the scalping, who attests to Cody's egotistical brutality, please see: http://urban-indians.livejournal.com/11558.html.
5. We could speculate that the mistranslation has arisen because Yellow Hair seems to be an inappropriate name for a Native American. A somewhat ironic touch is that Cody was called "Pahuska" by his Show Indians, a Native word for "long hair."

6. Objections to the scalping on stage were voiced in New England, especially in Boston, and thus only lower-class "nativists" (in the sense of chauvinistic Americans) tended to be Cody's spectators; see Warren, *Buffalo Bill's America*, especially 186.
7. Ibid.; Warren gives his sources on 581, n.115.
8. Ibid., 170–171.
9. Some of Ned Buntline's dime westerns featuring Buffalo Bill have been collected in a new publication: R. Clay Reynolds, ed., *The Hero of a Hundred Fights: Collected Stories from the Dime Novel King, from Buffalo Bill to Wild Bill Hickok* (New York: Union Square Press, 2011). Prentiss Ingraham also wrote "penny dreadfuls" idolizing Buffalo Bill in the latter part of the nineteenth century and beginning of the twentieth.
10. The full newspaper article plus published photo is available online: http://news.google.com/newspapers?nid=799&dat=19020828&id=pLxaAAAAIBAJ&sjid=bFIDAAAAIBAJ&pg=7124,2004138.
11. Welsch, "Transculturality."
12. Lenz, "Toward a Politics of American Transcultural Studies." Further recent volumes attest to scholarly energy in transculturality studies, particularly in Europe: Antor et al., *From Interculturalism to Transculturalism*; Arapoglou, et al., *Travel, Migration, and Transculturation*; Raussert et al., *Transcultural Visions of Identities in Images and Texts*; Schulze-Engler, et al., *Transcultural English Studies*. Welsch himself has updated his transculturality theory to include complex forms of commonality, especially deep structures (see Welsch, "On the Acquisition and Possession of Commonalities" in Schulze-Engler, 3–34). Although I am not entirely in agreement with Helmbrecht Breinig and Klaus Lösch's presentation of Wolfgang Welsch's theory, which they limit to his debatable notion of interculturality (see my note 13), in the introduction to a volume titled *Multiculturalism in Contemporary Societies: Perspectives on Difference and Transdifference* (2002), their carefully crafted theory of transdifference promisingly admits a "simultaneity of—often conflicting—positions, loyalties, affiliations and participations" (21).
13. Welsch includes "interculturality" in the list of terms to be avoided in discourse and cultural politics, since for him the concept of *interculturality*, despite the promising and "politically correct" prefix "inter," contains J. G. von Herder's eighteenth-century axiom of "single cultures," including Herder's principle that, left to themselves, separate cultures necessarily lead to "intercultural conflicts" and can "do nothing other than collide with one another" (Welsch, "Transculturality," 196). According to Welsch, *symbiotic influences* of cultures so clearly defined as "different" from each other cannot be included in the interculturality model. See my "Ethnic Transformations at School in

North Rhine-Westphalia, Virginia, Pécs, and Autobiographical Novels, or Can Transcultural Impulses Serve/Save Our Schoolchildren?" in Waegner, Laws, and de Laforcade, *Transculturality and Perceptions of the Immigrant Other*, for further discussion of Welsch's transculturality theory.

14. The list of European countries in which Buffalo Bill's Wild West performed is daunting, including Great Britain, France, Spain, Italy, Belgium, the Netherlands, Germany, Austria, the Balkans, Hungary, Romania, Ukraine, Poland, Bohemia. The first four European tours took place between 1887 and 1892, and the last four were undertaken from 1902 to 1906.
15. The "Girl-pet" postcard is listed on an Internet auction page for the steep price of $400–600: http://www.cowanauctions.com/peek-in-warehouse/item.aspx?ItemId=58000. In an "as-told-to" autobiography, John Nelson describes, not without a dash of (self-directed) irony, how he learned from Canadian trappers to scalp marauding Natives efficiently (*Fifty Years on the Trail: A True Story of Western Life*; *The Adventures of John Young Nelson as described to Harrington O'Reilly* [London: Spottiswoode, 1889; reprint, Norman: University of Oklahoma Press, 1963], 80–81).
16. A high-quality version of this photo can be viewed at http://forums.canadiancontent.net/history/66250-could-british-burial-ground-sioux.html.
17. Queen Victoria attended a private Wild West performance on 11 May 1887 (see Russell, *The Lives and Legends of Buffalo Bill*, 330; Flint, *The Transatlantic Indian*, 229–230); the 20 June 1887 performance for all of the Royal Jubilee guests is described in thrilling detail in Russell, *Lives and Legends of Buffalo Bill*, 331.
18. Russell, *Lives and Legends of Buffalo Bill*, 331; he does not indicate a source for this commendation. No doubt the words are contained in George Earle Buckle, ed., *The Letters of Queen Victoria: A Selection from Her Majesty's Correspondence between the Years 1886 and 1901*, 3 vols. (London: John Murray, 1930).
19. This is Black Elk's own explanation in his 1932 autobiography, as reported to John G. Neihardt (Black Elk, *Black Elk Speaks*, chapter 19).
20. A black-and-white version of this graphic is available at http://masondixonwildwest.blogspot.de/2007_02_01_archive.html.
21. Black Elk, *Black Elk Speaks*, chapters 19 and 20; Black Elk's experiences are the basis for the recent novel by Kate Horsley, *Black Elk in Paris* (2006).
22. See Warren, *Buffalo Bill's America*, 390–396, for a detailed account.
23. *The Heartsong of Charging Elk: A Novel* is the title for the original American publication (Doubleday, 2000); in the United Kingdom, Welch's novel was published by Canongate under the title *Heartsong: A Novel* (2001).

24. Harper's recently completed book manuscript, "Once Removed," considers the "social-critical potential of abstractionist aesthetics in African-American culture." http://english.fas.nyu.edu/object/PhillipHarper.html. I use the epithet "once removed" to indicate another kind of abstraction, i.e., the embedding of imagined but not unlikely transcultural encounters in a work of fiction.
25. Welch, *The Heartsong of Charging Elk*, 51–52.
26. Ibid., 431.
27. Ibid., 438. Kate Flint's reading of the ending interprets Charging Elk's decision to remain in Europe as more conservative than transcultural; she maintains that it is easier for him to keep his culture inviolate as an expatriate in Europe than to move back to what has become a society in which Native-generated Indianness is forbidden (*The Transatlantic Indian*, 294).
28. Welch, *Heartsong of Charging Elk*, 116.
29. Bhabha, *Location of Culture*, chapter 4.
30. Welch, *The Heartsong of Charging Elk*, 112.
31. In an earlier article, I developed a relevant theory of "cultural adulation," an adulation which encodes a racist slant despite the fascination of the "mainstream" admirer for the ethnic culture; see Waegner, "Rap, Rebounds, and Rocawear."
32. It is perhaps not too whimsical to wish that the Soulas family could have had access to the dictum developed in Ella Shohat and Robert Stam's book *Multiculturalism, Postcoloniality, and Transnational Media*: "In our view there are no others and no exotics, there are only processes of otherization and exoticization" (3).
33. Welch, *The Heartsong of Charging Elk*, 200; the further quotes in this paragraph are from 201.
34. One link in this chain has been nearly entirely lost; the movie *The Indian Wars* (1914), starring William Cody, who had started his own film company, reenacts with a largely Sioux cast the final Indian wars, complete with ghost dancing and Wounded Knee, the massacre presented as justifiable and heroic on the part of the 7th Cavalry. Only some clips and stills have survived from this questionable project. A fiery 1914 article by Chauncey Yellow Robe (Sioux; a descendant of Sitting Bull) called "The Menace of the Wild West Show" expresses the Native indignation: "Twenty-three years afterward, on the same field of Wounded Knee, the tragedy was reproduced for 'historical preservation' in moving-picture films and called *The Last Great Battle of the Sioux*. The whole production of the field was misrepresented and yet approved by the Government. This is a disgrace and injustice to the Indian race" (*The Quarterly Journal of the Society of American Indians* 2 [July–September

1914]: 225, http://archive.org/stream/quarterlyjourna001ibrgoog/quarterlyjourna001ibrgoog_djvu.txt).

The Native Irish scholar Jacqueline Kilpatrick offers a critical recapitulation of what is still known about the once influential film in her *Celluloid Indians*, 19–22.

35. Ellison implies that African American blackface minstrels can show a "flash of black," which empowers them while ostensibly adhering to minstrelsy stereotypes. David Krasner supplies support for this by pointing to "signifying" strategies that enable African American performers to undermine the blackface mask of minstrelsy with its "insidious representations": "black performers have negotiated, subverted, incorporated, resisted, challenged, and ultimately 'signified'—the black rhetorical strategy of inversion, parody, and innuendo—on the pervasive minstrel image" ("Afterword," 346). Annemarie Bean describes the twisting of the stereotypes of blackface minstrelsy by African American minstrels: "White minstrelsy came close to defining how the minstrelized black body should sound and appear, but it did not succeed in its latent desire to contain and constrict. This attempt to define the African American staged black Other was thwarted by the nuanced, rebellious, skilled . . . performances of restaging [by African Americans]" ("Black Minstrelsy and Double Inversion," 187).
36. Later viewers probably assume that Quinn is of Greek immigrant background, after his highly acclaimed and familiar performance as the protagonist in *Zorba the Greek* (1964).
37. I recommend the well-informed "red-face.us" website that catalogs and analyzes racist American Indian caricatures and stereotypes, especially in film; the DVD *Reel Injun: On the Trail of the Hollywood Indians*, directed by Neil Diamond (2009) and including interviews with leading Hollywood figures, is an excellent resource. Wellman's *Buffalo Bill* movie still has fans today; here is one glowing web review: "The most incredible thing about this love letter to Buffalo Bill Cody is the surprising sympathetic light afforded the Native Americans, a progressive slant that was not to be seen on the screen for nearly another decade." http://monstermania-batcat31.blogspot.de/2012/07/you-know-indian-cody-dont-you.html [punctuation adjusted].
38. *Indians* premiered at the Aldwych West End Theatre in London, but quickly moved to Broadway (1969), where it ran for nearly 100 performances. The 2008 production at the Theater and Interpretation Center of Northwestern University in Evansville, Illinois, is just one recent example of the interest college students have shown in Kopit's play. It was even performed in 2012 at the British International School of Moscow, with a ten-minute video clip online: http://vimeo.com/39573030.

39. Kopit, *Indians*, scene 7, 47.
40. Ibid., scene 3, 31
41. Ibid., scene 13, 72–73.
42. Ibid., scene 13, 77–78. Kopit presents some of Cody's motives as ambivalent, both self-seeking and well-intentioned. Recent scholars (for example, Carter, Kasson, Maddra, Warren, Flint) have debated the altruism in Cody's reasons for his generosity to the Natives; Louis Warren is puzzled by the Janus-faced but highly successful image that Cody crafted: "The real question thus becomes less how Cody derived his sympathies for Indians than how he fashioned a persona of Buffalo Bill that could denounce Indian conquest at one moment and become its most visible advocate in the next. Of all Cody's characteristics, it is this profound ambivalence about Indians that seems most impenetrable." (*Buffalo Bill's America*, 199).
43. The opening film credits announce that the movie is a loose adaptation: "Suggested by the play *Indians* by Arthur Kopit." In *Indians on Display*, Denzin's experimentally clever accounts of traveling Wild West shows presents largely satirical playlets referencing a variety of historical sources; the chapters focusing on Buffalo Bill's company draw heavily on Altman's 1976 film and thus Kopit's play, featuring Sitting Bull's ghost. The German fascination with a romanticized Native culture is parodied, as when an "adult leader of the German boys" announces, "We have learned how to be Indians by reading Karl May's novels and coming to Buffalo Bill's Wild West show" (156).
44. Sitting Bull was permitted to leave the reservation in 1884 with his wife and some relatives as part of the so-called "Sitting Bull Combination," a touring performance organized by Col. Alveren Allen and billed as educational, before Sitting Bull joined Buffalo Bill's Wild West in June 1885 for four months. Robert Altman carefully studied iconographic photographs for his film, including the well-known one of Cody and Sitting Bull, with Buffalo Bill theatrically posing and Sitting Bull demurely looking downward, taken by W. Notman in 1885; the photo is, along with other pictures of Sitting Bull, displayed on this Swedish website: http://hem.passagen.se/native/photo sittingbull.htm.
45. A posed daguerreotype (http://hem.passagen.se/native/photosittingbull.htm) of the historical interpreter Halsey with Sitting Bull (and several others in the Wild West entourage) shows a short, gentle-looking man with a handlebar mustache wearing a suit with a white kerchief—very unlike the towering Native Will Sampson wrapped in a red blanket in Altman's film.
46. DVD 23:10.
47. Although sources give mixed reports on this, apparently Sitting Bull spoke candidly in Lakota at times when he addressed the non-Native Wild West

audiences, as in Altman's film (1.26:12–1.27:26), presumably using a "private" or "insider" (that is, Native) language to publicly express denigration. In Sitting Bull's performances in the "Sitting Bull Combination" in 1884, before he became one of the Wild West members, his addresses to the audience calling for improvement on the reservations were deliberately mistranslated by agents to make them into lurid descriptions of Custer's death—thus the "secret language" strategy could work both ways. Later, the U.S. government turned the "secrecy" of the Native languages directly to its own benefit by employing Native code-talkers during the two world wars.

48. DVD 1.26:12–1.27:26. I recommend the long analysis of Altman's movie on this "film buff" website: http://theseventhart.info/2011/05/16/buffalo-bill-and-the-indians-an-analysis-part-55/.
49. In his book *Engaged Resistance: American Indian Art, Literature, and Film from Alcatraz to the NMAI* (2011), Dean Rader includes photographs of Thom Ross's installation at Ocean Beach, California, 2008. Rader criticizes Ross's installation, placing it in—drawing on Troy Lynn Yellow Wood's formulation—the category of "public art that misrepresents or misinvents Native Peoples," which "doesn't just summon trauma, it literalizes and memorializes it" (*Engaged Resistance*, 187–190). To my knowledge, Rader's book in the only academic publication that discusses Ross's projects at length.
50. http://ergodicwalk.files.wordpress.com/2008/09/thomross_flyer_pgs1234.pdf; the anti-Ross flyer was apparently composed by Anand Sarwate of the Toyota Technological Institute at Chicago, who authors and manages the blog in which the flyer is nested.
51. Source of Ross quote, which I have slightly revised: http://www.truewestmagazine.com/jcontent/true-westerners/true-westerners/what-history-taught-me/3761-thom-ross-western-artist.
52. http://www.gunnarnordstrom.com/dynamic/artwork_display.asp?ArtworkID=10.
53. http://www.barcelona-tourist-information.info/buffalo-bill-in-barcelona.html; the text tells us that the Spaniards were *not* impressed with the bison, given their familiarity with bull-fighting. Wernitznig assesses the Wild West presence in Barcelona as a failure (*Europe's Indians*, 85).
54. Buffalo Bill's *Wild West* was part of a much larger Amer-European/colonist interest in the late nineteenth century in what were considered exotic ethnic groups, most of which were endangered by industrialization and colonization. Ethnographic shows and exhibits of all types flourished in this era, and they have been receiving considerable scholarly attention since the rise of postcolonial studies. I only mention four books here: one on Carl Hagenbeck, who can be viewed as the German Buffalo Bill: Ames, *Carl Hagenbeck's*

Empire of Entertainments; Kirschenblatt-Gimblett, *Destination Culture: Tourism, Museums, and Heritage*, 1998; and two that emphasize the spectator's responsibility in viewing ethnic shows: Bruner, *Culture on Tour: Ethnographies of Travel*, 2005, as well as Crang and Cook, *Doing Ethnographies*.

55. An adopted member of the Anondagas, E. H. Gohl was a prominent Auburn/New York artist and champion of Indian rights; Gohl's committed article is available in *Quarterly Journal of the Society of American Indians* 2 (1914), http://archive.org/stream/quarterlyjourna001ibrgoog/quarterlyjourna001ibrgoog_djvu.txt. (I have corrected some misspellings in the quote above.)

WORKS CITED

Ames, Eric. *Carl Hagenbeck's Empire of Entertainments*. Seattle: University of Washington Press, 2008.

Antor, Heinz, Matthias Merkl, Klaus Stierstorfer, and Laurenz Volkmann, eds. *From Interculturalism to Transculturalism: Mediating Encounters in Cosmopolitan Contexts*. Heidelberg: Universitätsverlag Winter, 2010.

Arapoglou, Eleftheria, Mónika Fodor, and Jopi Nyman, eds. *Mobile Narratives: Travel, Migration, and Transculturation*. London: Routledge, 2013.

Bak, J. T. J. "'Rewriting' the International Theme: Dislocation and Transformation in James Welch's *Heartsong of Charging Elk*." In *First Nations of North America: Politics and Representations*, ed. Hans Bak, 156–173. Amsterdam: Vrije Universiteit/University Press, 2005.

Bean, Annemarie. "Black Minstrelsy and Double Inversion, Circa 1890." In *African American Performance and Theater History: A Critical Reader*, ed. Harry Elam Jr., and David Krasner, 171–191. New York and Oxford: Oxford University Press, 2001.

Bhabha, Homi K. *The Location of Culture*. New York: Routledge, 1994.

Black Elk. *Black Elk Speaks: Being the Life Story of a Holy Man of the Oglala Sioux* (as told to John G. Neihardt). 1932. Reprint, Winnipeg: Bison Books, 2004.

Breinig, Helmbrecht, and Klaus Lösch. "Introduction: Difference and Transdifference." In *Multiculturalism in Contemporary Societies: Perspectives on Difference and Transdifference*, ed. Helmbrecht Breinig, Jürgen Gebhardt, and Klaus Lösch, 11–36. Erlangen: Universitätsbund Erlangen-Nürnberg, 2002.

Bruner, Edward M. *Culture on Tour: Ethnographies of Travel*. Chicago: University of Chicago Press, 2005.

Buffalo Bill. Directed by William A. Wellman. Twentieth Century Fox, 1944; DVD, Twentieth Century Fox, 2005.

Buffalo Bill and the Indians, or Sitting Bull's History Lesson. Directed by Robert Altman. Dino De Laurentiis Company, 1976; DVD, Metro-Goldwyn-Mayer, 2001.

"Buffalo Bill's *Wild West:* Annie Oakley, Buffalo Dance, Bucking Broncho." In *More Treasures from American Film Archives, 1894–1931* [three short films, directed by W. K. L. Dickson, produced by Edison Manufacturing Company in 1894]; DVD and "Program Notes": "Film Notes" by Scott Simmon and "Music Notes" by Martin Marks released by National Film Preservation Foundation, 2004.

Carter, Robert A. *Buffalo Bill Cody: The Man Behind the Legend.* New York: John Wiley & Sons, 2000.

Crang, Mike, and Ian Cook. *Doing Ethnographies.* Los Angeles: SAGE, 2007.

Denzin, Norman K. *Indians on Display: Global Commodification of Native America in Performance, Art, and Museums.* Walnut Creek, CA: Left Coast Press, 2013.

Elam, Harry J., Jr., and David Krasner. *African American Performance and Theater History: A Critical Reader.* New York: Oxford University Press, 2001.

Ellison, Ralph. "Change the Joke and Slip the Yoke." In *The Shadow and the Act: Essays*, 45–59. New York: Random House, 1964.

Ferguson, Suzanne. "Europe and the Quest for Home in Welch's *The Heartsong of Charging Elk* and Silko's *Gardens in the Dunes.*" *Studies in American Indian Literatures* 18.2 (Summer 2006): 34–53.

Fitz, Karsten. *Negotiating History and Culture: Transculturation in Contemporary Native American Fiction.* Frankfurt am Main: Peter Lang, 2001.

Flint, Kate. *The Transatlantic Indian, 1776–1930.* Princeton, NJ: Princeton University Press, 2009.

Gerteis, Klaus, ed. *Buffalo Bill und die "verfolgte Unschuld": Groschenhefte von 1871 bis ca. 1930.* Ausstellungskataloge Trierer Bibliotheken, No. 31, 1999.

Gohl, E. H. "The Effect of Wild Westing." *Quarterly Journal of the Society of American Indians* 2 (July–September 1914): 226–228.

Griffin, Charles Eldridge. *Four Years in Europe with Buffalo Bill.* Lincoln: University of Nebraska Press, 2010 [originally published in 1908 by Griffin, manager of the Wild West show 1904–1908].

Horsley, Kate. *Black Elk in Paris: A Novel.* Boston: Trumpeter, 2006.

Kasson, Joy S. *Buffalo Bill's Wild West: Celebrity, Memory, and Popular History.* New York: Hill and Wang, 2000.

Kilpatrick, Jacquelyn. *Celluloid Indians: Native Americans and Film.* Lincoln: University of Nebraska Press, 1999.

Kirschenblatt-Gimblett, Barbara. *Destination Culture: Tourism, Museums, and Heritage.* Berkeley: University of California Press, 1998.

Kopit, Arthur. *Indians.* London: Methuen, 1970.

Krasner, David. "Afterword: Change Is Coming." In *African American Performance and Theater History: A Critical Reader*, ed. Harry J. Elam Jr., and David Krasner. New York: Oxford University Press, 2001.

Lenz, Günter H. "Toward a Politics of American Transcultural Studies: Discourses of Diaspora and Cosmopolitanism." In *Reframing the Transnational Turn in American Studies*, ed. Winfried Fluck, Donald E. Pease, and John Carlos Rowe, 391–425. Hanover, NH: Dartmouth College Press, 2011.

Maddra, Sam A. *Hostiles? The Lakota Ghost Dance and Buffalo Bill's Wild West*. Norman: University of Oklahoma Press, 2006.

McMurtry, Larry. *The Colonel and Little Missie: Buffalo Bill, Annie Oakley, and the Beginnings of Superstardom in America*. New York: Simon & Schuster, 2005.

Moses, L. G. *Wild West Shows and the Images of American Indians 1883–1933*. Albuquerque: University of New Mexico Press, 1996.

Opitz, Andrea. "'The Primitive Has Escaped Control': Narrating the Nation in *The Heartsong of Charging Elk*." *Studies in American Indian Literatures* 18.3 (Fall 2006): 98–106.

Rader, Dean. *Engaged Resistance: American Indian Art, Literature, and Film from Alcatraz to the NMAI*. Austin: University of Texas Press, 2011.

Raussert, Wilfried, and Reinhard Isensee, eds. *Transcultural Visions of Identities in Images and Texts*. Heidelberg: Winter, 2008.

Rollins, Peter C., ed. *Hollywood's Indian: The Portrayal of the Native American in Film*. Lexington: University Press of Kentucky, 2005.

Russell, Don. *The Lives and Legends of Buffalo Bill*. Norman: University of Oklahoma Press, 1960.

Sarkowsky, Katja. *AlterNative Spaces: Constructions of Space in Native American and First Nations' Literatures*. Heidelberg: Winter, 2007.

Shohat, Ella, and Robert Stam, eds. *Multiculturalism, Postcoloniality, and Transnational Media*. New Brunswick, NJ: Rutgers University Press, 2003.

Spickard, Paul. *Almost All Aliens: Immigration, Race, and Colonialism in American History and Identity*. New York: Routledge, 2007.

Utley, Robert M. *The Indian Frontier of the American West 1846–1890*. Albuquerque: University of New Mexico Press, 1984.

Waegner, Cathy Covell. "Performing Postmodernist Passing: Nikki S. Lee, Tuff, and Ghost Dog in Yellowface/Blackface." In *AfroAsian Encounters: Culture, History, Politics*, ed. Heike Raphael-Hernandez and Shannon Steen, 223–244. New York: New York University Press, 2006.

———. "Rap, Rebounds, and Rocawear: The 'Darkening' of German Youth Culture." In *Blackening Europe: The African American Presence*, ed. Heike Raphael-Hernandez, 171–185. New York: Routledge, 2004.

Waegner, Cathy Covell, Page R. Laws, and Geoffroy de Laforcade, eds. *Transculturality and Perceptions of the Immigrant Other: "From-Heres" and "Come-Heres" in*

Virginia and North Rhine-Westphalia. Newcastle upon Tyne: Cambridge Scholars Publishing, 2011.

Warren, Louis S. *Buffalo Bill's America: William Cody and the Wild West Show*. New York: Vintage, 2005.

Weaver, Jace. *The Red Atlantic: American Indigenes and the Making of the Modern World, 1000–1927*. Chapel Hill: University of North Carolina Press, 2014.

Welch, James. *The Heartsong of Charging Elk: A Novel*. New York: Doubleday, 2000; published in the United Kingdom as *Heartsong: A Novel*, Edinburgh: Canongate Books, 2001.

Welsch, Wolfgang. "Transculturality—the Puzzling Form of Cultures Today." In *Spaces of Culture: City, Nation, World*, ed. Mike Featherstone and Scott Lash, 194–213. London: Sage, 1999.

Wernitznig, Dagmar. *Europe's Indians, Indians in Europe: European Perceptions and Appropriations of Native American Cultures from Pocahontas to the Present*. Lanham, MD: University Press of America, 2007.

Native Postmodern?

Remediating History in the Fiction of Stephen Graham Jones and D. L. Birchfield

A. ROBERT LEE

I believe we're all invented as Indians.

—GERALD VIZENOR, "INTERVIEW" (1981)

There is a story I know. It's about the earth and how it floats in space on the back of a turtle. I've heard this story many times, and each time someone tells the story, it changes. Sometimes the change is simply in the voice of the storyteller. Sometimes the change is in the details. Sometimes in the order of events. Other times it's the dialogue or the response of the audience. But in all the telling of all the tellers, the world never leaves the turtle. And the turtle never swims away.

—*THOMAS KING, THE TRUTH ABOUT STORIES: A NATIVE NARRATIVE (2003)*

NATIVE POSTMODERN. THE PHRASE RISKS SOUNDING LIKE CONTRIVANCE, an Atlantic fashioning foisted upon Native authorship. The suspicion hovers of a species of fiction too discrepant or modish for the writing-in of Indian Country, its actualities and cultures, its geographies and eras. Well may postmodern hold for a Nabokov or Beckett, or under their penumbra, American metanarratives by, say, Kurt Vonnegut, Thomas Pynchon, William

Gaddis, John Barth, William Gass, David Markham, or Kathy Acker. But can it claim legitimacy in story-work generated from Native lives, Native history and memory? Given the intractably "real" of tribal legacy, each live ongoing cultural tradition, not to mention sovereignty and land issues, governance, American Indian Movement (AIM) legacy, or the emergence of the oil and casino economies, along with the deficits of dispossession, much drift and poverty, school drop-out, and alcoholism and fetal alcohol syndrome (FAS), is this a literary idiom to win credence?

For those who vote yes, then the turn to the postmodern actually does aptest service in holding Native experience to light. Far from some baroque dance, the texts at issue give consequential new bearings, full of transperspective and so willing to reach beyond, even travesty, inherited boundaries of chronology or place. If Native Americans have been made into the silhouettes of noble or demonic savagism, Custer circus or Hollywood screen spectacle, the very nature of the postmodern turn could not better serve as countermand. Reflexivity, the readiness to turn preemptive imagery against itself, the fragmentation and bricolage, and always the polyphonic voicing supply not only means but a situating narrative distance to dismantle what Gerald Vizenor calls in lowercase and italics *the indian.*

Pop culture clichés, from Buntline dime novel to *Dances with Wolves*, Mutual of Omaha war-bonnet to Atlanta Braves replete with tomahawk chop, can be made to segue into their own parody. Chingachgook or Injun Joe, Minnehaha or Tonto can be magicked out of text and time to answer for their impersonations. Edward S. Curtis's twenty or so volumes of Vanishing American photo-images (1907–1930), each posed, sepia, a kind of remnant inertia, can metamorphose back into life. Hallowed clichés, prime among them anthropology's Mother Earth, can be teased. In sum, the *hanoh*, or people, as invoked in Simon Ortiz's "Even 'The Indians' Believed," can assume sway by seeing themselves against how, and to what interpretative effect, they have been played as (or even themselves sometimes played) Indians/*indians*. Contention, almost inevitably, flares.

Were a reminder of the spats needed one has only to turn back to Leslie Marmon Silko's "Here's an Odd Artifact for the Fairy-Tale Shelf," her unyielding 1986 review of Louise Erdrich's *The Beet Queen*. This was fiction as "dazzling and sleek" and "pared lean and then polished" as might be, but damned by Silko for each discontinuity and cross-ply of voice, the supposed all too knowing contra-flows.[1] Under Erdrich's pen her Ojibway-Chippewa world falls short, insufficiently sedimented in historical or specific tribal-community circumstance. Erdrich's own reply was to remind Silko of the kind of novel she was actually writing, one unbeholden to any single template of authenticity or genre. Rather, it sets forth a hugely complex web of mixed-blood border lives, Native and German American, in which the metafictional, and by implication the postmodern, as much bespeaks the actualities at hand as quite any other narrative dispensation. She leaves little doubt, moreover, that on her estimation Native-oral storytelling, in its own right, has always exhibited self-aware fashioning, improvisational plays of indirection or gap. That, throughout her North Dakota dynastic fiction of Pillagers, Kashpaws, and Nanapushes, continues over into script, narrative for good reason to be compared with the workings of Faulkner's Yoknapatawpha cycle.

Whomever can be said to have had the better of the exchange, it provides instructive case-history. How best to give literary telling, or rather a plurality of telling, not only to American and First Nations/Canadian indigenism but, by extension, to all originary Native cultures? Other touchstones add compass. Elizabeth Cook-Lynn's *Why I Can't Read Wallace Stegner and Other Essays*, together with pieces like "American Indian Intellectualism and the New Indian Story" (1996), famously was quick into the fray. Native literary word and art are, in her opinion, to be formulated under realist-representational, not to say tribal-centric, auspices. Mixedblood identity as theme, urban storytelling, the affliction she terms campus-instigated "intellectualism" and assuredly self-referential narrative, all invite short thrift. By way of response Louis Owens's "Blood Trails," a centerpiece of his *Mixedblood Messages*, met fire with fire. Given his own naming in what he terms Cook-Lynn's "mixedblood hall of shame," to include Gerald Vizenor, Wendy Rose, Maurice Kenny, Diane Glancy, Thomas King, Joseph Bruchac, and Michael Dorris, his challenge goes out to almost all her desiderata, but notably the necessity of rez-community domicile and a prescribed, and, as it were, custodial, "tribal realism."[2]

The controversies over "authenticity" go on circling as to texts that do or do not do justice to the Native-real, authors who do or do not pass muster in the way of Native credential. What Native standing a city or suburban story-collection like Michael Dorris's *Working Men* or overseas-sited verse like Jim Barnes's *Paris* and *Visiting Picasso?* Do spy or detective novels meet the prescribed Native bar, Martin Cruz Smith's post-Soviet *Red Square* or Mardi Oakley Medawar's Cherokee-written but Kiowa-centered *Death at Rainy Mountain?* Is yet other mixedblood authorship, William Penn or Betty Louise Bell, Linda Hogan or Eric Gansworth, to be accorded full entry-permits into Native literature? In his well-titled *Who Owns Native Culture?* Michael Brown develops a social science study given over to museum holdings, art, and artifacts.[3] But the implications evidently apply to literary-critical domains.

Debate, inevitably, circles yet further. Arnold Krupat's notion of cosmopolitanism has carried weight, his protocol that modern literary Indigenism inevitably is hybrid, the crosshatch of Native and Euro-American fabling.[4] The discursive flourish of the three Ws—Craig Womack, Jace Weaver, and Robert Warrior—gives the case for coexistence of a Native "redstick" with a "cosmopolitan" aesthetic. Can there not be a "nationalist" call to imaginative arms, with full recognition of discrete tribal codings or trace yet without giving way to essentialism?[5] Paula Gunn Allen's argument for Native-feminism, sacred hoop or woman-engendered sourcing of Native culture and literature, along with two-spirit sexuality and even spirituality, has both persuaded and opened itself to skepticism.[6]

David Treuer's upset of nearly all the applecarts in *Native American Fiction: A User's Manual* takes debate in yet another direction. Argument that decries the corralling of Native texts into the one or another agenda of ethnography, identity, gender, or the requisite authenticity-verisimilitude axis, with judgment dispensed accordingly, was bound to create antibodies. The notion that Native fiction is actually itself a fiction, misassigned category, and Treuer's preference for subjecting the worlds in view to literary-textual lines of scrutiny, the return of emphasis to design, image, voice, rhythm, the sense of an ending, has come to be thought oddly retrograde yet at the same time sharply refreshing.

Enter the debate about the Native postmodern, and its allied formulation, the postindian. Both, conspicuously, have made their entrance in Gerald Vizenor as clarion theorist-practitioner. His edited collection *Narrative Chance: Postmodern Discourse on Native American Indian Literatures*, alongside connecting cultural anatomies like *Manifest Manners: Postindian Warriors of Survivance, Fugitive Poses: Native Scenes of Absence and Presence*, and *Native Liberty, Natural Reason and Cultural Survivance*, bids to open Native life to new regimes of understanding. Under postmodern, and indeed postindian auspices, Native texts have the opportunity to attempt figurations beyond, say, William Bevis's perfectly well-taken "homing in" pattern, or victimhood, or even Coyote.[7] De-essentialization of genre as of tribe becomes all. Trickster, that wily stalwart of Native tradition, is given leave to join at the creative interface with Bakhtinian dialogics, Eco's "open" text, or the semiotics of simulation/dissimulation argued for by Baudrillard.

To a shared end, Vizenor's storytelling, begun with *Bearheart* as irreal pilgrimage to the Fourth World across an America bereft of moral balance as of oil and continued into the plethora of longer and shorter works, unabates in its bid for changed terms of reference. His gallery ranges through Stone Columbus on his Minnesota bingo-barge as radio host descendant of the High Admiral (*The Heirs of Columbus*), Griever de Hocus and Ronin Ainoko Browne as gamester or monkey king in their global reach from White Earth, Minnesota, to China and Japan (*Griever* and *Hiroshima Bugi*), the Browne trickster-family genealogy (*The Trickster of Liberty* and *Hotline Healers*), the survivor-witness to clerical sex abuse and redress on the reservation (*Father Meme*), and a tribal observer-participant in World War I (*Blue Ravens*). Each plot-line somersault, and to immediate point, each wheel of disclosure, works to inscribe truth-to-history yet under the banner of metanarration, the fissures between Native signifier and signified. The notion of the resistant text greatly applies.

Vizenor's forte is to have given trickster new realization, reconstrued authorial fiat. This is to devise discursive argument or force of "story" that undermines, and so takes ownership of, each stereotype and associated cliché that before and since the Columbian discovery myth has been parlayed into *the indian*. The lexicon he creates adds route-markers—*postindian*, to repudiate the reductive monochrome of the term "Indian" or "pan-Indian"; *survivance*, to register a Native America ongoing, culturally oxygenated, as against one of mere survival; or *storier*, to give cagey new display to the oral in the written and to step beyond and overlap novel, story or essay demarcations. His imaginative chutzpah has been rare, often controversial. But however singular, it also supplies a working touchstone for other Native storytelling drawn to the ways and challenge of the postmodern.

Stephen Graham Jones and D. L. Birchfield, respectively of Blackfeet and Choctaw heritage, have yet to win overwhelming recognition. Both regularly are dubbed maverick, the former typically for *Ledfeather* with its dual time-corridors into tribal Montana, and the latter for *Field of Honor* with its canny alternative-reality tribal Oklahoma. Yet a Native literary roster alike in imaginative temper, Vizenorian or otherwise, cannot be said to have gone missing. Sherman Alexie, long-standing *Wunderkind* and rarely better given to the "marvelous real" than in *Reservation Blues*, heads the list not only in sheer gamesomeness but in sales and popularity.[8] The account given by Thomas Builds the Fire, Spokane reservation storyteller, of Victor Joseph and the band Coyote Springs, mirror-voices modern Wellpinit reservation life and the historical "Indian Wars" and Custer, not least as Alexie invokes Robert Johnson devil-myth guitar blues and New York's Cavalry Recording Studio. His virtuosity spans the frequently sardonic but close-observed displacement stories of *The Lone Ranger and Tonto Fistfight in Heaven*, an updated shape-shifter novel like *Flight*, and a metathriller with its Native-white doppelgänger murderer anachronistically acting out historical revenge like *Indian Killer*. Alexie routinely wins favor for his cleansing dark laughter yet rather less so for his postmodern savvy.

"Connectives and disconnectives" is how Diane Glancy speaks to the tease of life and literary genre throughout story-cycles like *Firesticks* and *The Voice That Was in Travel*.[9] It well suits. For her seeming fragments of Cherokee mixedblood history, born-again Bible Christianity, iconographies of road, township, family, and European and Australian travel, reflexively, and with wry contrariety, in fact amount to story-wholes. Gordon Henry makes his *The Light People* into an Anishinaabe Book of Voices, Oskinaway's contemporary reservation quest for his parenting as colloquium-tapestry of story, verse, dialogue, riff, and perhaps above all, parable. A. A. Carr's *Eye Killers* repitches Euro-colonialism in the form of a Navajo-Pueblo New Mexico vampire fable, the Roanhorse dynasty threatened by the Falke coven, and again the one Native history dialogically enwrapped in the other. Thomas King in the 2003 Massey lectures issued as *The Truth About Stories* calls up the multiple ways the Native turtle creation-story, and by implication all Native story, can be told, a plurality of tellers yet ever the one text. From within this plurality postmodern, or at least postmodern-inflected, narration invites its due acknowledgment.

"The truth is never in the facts" observes Stephen Graham Jones in his author's note to *Ledfeather*.[10] Certainly his own prolific output, the dozen-plus novels and over a hundred stories (in journals and on the web, as well as dark-gothic collections like *Bleed into Me* and *The Ones That Got Away*) from a writer barely forty, has acted on that cue. It has held, too, whether he has been writing crypto-westerns saturated in pop culture (his first novel *The Fast Red Road: A Plainsong*), fiction-histories (*Ledfeather* or *Growing Up Dead in Texas*), crime noir that edges toward science fiction (*All The Beautiful Sinners* or *The Bird Is Gone: A Manifesto*), Tex-Mex border absurdist-supernatural (*It Came from Del Rio*), or slasher comedy-horror (*Zombie Bake-Off* or *The Last Final Girl*). Truth, evidently, he indeed takes to operate less through fact than filament and skein, time-fold and overlap of voice.

Nor has Jones been shy in having his fictions signal their own processes of formation. *Demon Theory*, Halloween spook-story, he tells in the format of a film treatment. Director markings, and over four hundred footnotes, underwrite the one storytelling locked inside the other. *The Long Trial of*

Nolan Dugatti edges toward Kafka in the shape of a narrator left in sole charge of customer relations for a long redundant video-game company and whose father's near-absurdist suicide notes cannily inscribe their lost-and-found relationship. The telling might almost be that of a narrator haunted by his own voice. To seize upon only two Jones texts, *Ledfeather* and *Bleed into Me*, thus, is to select from a considerable trove. But both work greatly to purpose, each a metafiction, each a Native focus. Whether or not they win stripes as belonging to the full-fledged postmodern, they clearly inhabit the neighborhood.

"I remember you" (9) reads the opening epigraph in *Ledfeather*. Unglossed, stark almost, and printed as though from an ancient typewriter (the text later implies it was written on a "caligraph"), it might be the very prompt to inquiry into Blackfeet-historical detection. For the novel quickly whirls into complication and alternating shifts of time. Two Blackfeet suicidal boy figures, Doby Saxon and (so-spelled) Lead Feather, and two tribal eras, those of contemporary Browning-Glacier Blackfeet reservation and the Starvation Winter 1880s, parallel each other even as they thread with increasing luminosity into the one continuum. A host of contemporary narrators speak, from on and off reservation, township and school goers, and in the figure of Francis Dalimpere, a federal Indian agent sent to the Blackfeet in 1883, the novel has one of history's ghosts—guilt-stricken at federal insouciance and the 600 winter deaths from hunger of the tribespeople. His ever-more haunted letter-writings to Claire, his actual but ever-more fantasized wife in the East, will pass down time as though messages in a bottle, a capsule to have the Blackfeet past reverberate into the Blackfeet present.

To enter *Ledfeather* is first to hear the voices that give witness to Doby Saxon, Blackfeet-Yellowtail-Piegan intending self-killer as he stands before highway headlights "waiting for another car to come kill him" (45). Son of Malory Sainte as protective but in-and-out of jail mother and Earl Two Jobs (born Piney Saxon) as drifter and elk poacher, snow-frozen, bloodied, displaced, he is ushered like a phantom into the East Glacier convenience store ("This was the Blackfeet Reservation on a Saturday night in late November" [14]). Each witness to Doby—the caring white woman store assistant and her Blackfeet coworker Junior, the hospital nurse, the tourist wife out to buy curios and who witnesses the casino fracas, and the high school circle among whom Doby has been basketball player and oddity—all underline a figure caught short by history. How to account for this rush to self-harm, this descent into self-loss? How to account for the clutch of papers he carries? As the novel unfolds the patterns of causation and effect grow clearer, a formidable Blackfeet tableau of antecedent bearings to include not only

1883–1884 but the brute Marias (or Baker) massacre of 1870 to which James Welch turns with so vivid a narrative command in *Fools Crow*.

"Like them I am starving" (47). Francis Dalimpere's almost first words set the measure, as does his judgment that "the situation is unsalvageable" (49). He calls to mind the white-hunter killing of the buffalo and the Blackfeet dependence on federal rations in their reduced homeland. Most, however, is his near-surreal account of the twelve-year-old boy Lead Feather hurling black stones into the sky in hopes that one will descend and kill him. The one that nearly does, gashing his ear, becomes a virtual stigmata for the agent "in my position as ambassador of the American government" (62), the live embodiment of his anguished call to redemption ("If I can just save one, Claire. . . ." [65]). The horror of Blackfeet hunger and eradication presses ever more into him to the point of phantasmagoria ("In the midst of it, I do not even recognize myself" [79]). To Claire he writes, "you are my confessor" (147).

His bid to discern Blackfeet meaning is mediated through the silent-sharer figure of the tribesman Yellow Tail (however much he is reported as speaking) who, in tacit accusation, bears his own memory of a wife killed alongside all the other Blackfeet at Marias, offers shamanist Elk fables, reveals the story of how he fed his tribe even though it cost the lives of two white trappers, and to whom Dalimpere speaks fur-trader French and thinks he is entrusting his letters to Claire. His trajectory becomes one of transfiguration, the would-be metamorphosis of himself against all spiritual or corporeal appearance into "Indian," none other than a Blackfeet. Given the spectacle of suffering amid what, at one point, he thinks a Montana Eden, he has reason to observe that "Hell for a white man would simply be to be forced to live as one of his subjects" (155). The colonial prism so reverses, subject into object, the hegemonic into the other.

The "gauntlet of the staring dead" (104) possesses Dalimpere (not least as yet another starving Piegan youth makes it his task to keep their eyes open in guardianship of their spirit). His senses are ravaged by the burial area of the Sandhills, in the one perspective hundreds of Blackfeet ghosts rising, or in another, the gas of decomposing Blackfeet bodies. The cruel farce of spoiled federal rations ("the quarterly stipend" [161]), the mockery of a Thanksgiving meal with Sheffield, in charge of the visiting soldiery, Collins, his predecessor as agent, and Marsh the translator, and the contaminating soldier rape of a Blackfeet woman that causes the tribe to forego the remaining provisions, add to the dereliction in which he is embroiled. He, too, moves outside of himself into the third person, notably in imagining the consequence of his well-intended but wholly imperfect effort to feed the tribe:

> the next time the soldiers came up now, they would be leaving with the Agent in chains. Not for killing the six hundred Piegan . . . but for slaughtering the twenty-four government cows. For it was an action that would become legend. (185)

The implications work severally. What moral scale is to be understood? How does a single legalism, the killing of the cattle, stack up against tribal genocide, "the encampment of the dead" (104)?

The only redemption for Dalimpere, however small in scale as he recognizes given the enormity of the enclosing death, lies in saving Lead Feather, to whom he feeds the chewed tongue of the cattle, whom he nurses, and in the wake of whose slow recovery (not unlike Brian Moore's Jesuit, Father Laforgue, from the Huron in *Black Robe*) he can exit into the snows to disappear from history and text. It is this story, or rather the story of the Blackfeet that has become his, that will pass to Doby in the form of the letters ("this sheaf of antique papers" [180]), another Blackfeet both harmed and self-harming. The agent's trauma both shadows and highlights the trauma within the overall history, connecting the Starvation Winter to Doby's contemporary reservation:

> The word coursed through the Indian Agent, finally came to rest at the back of his throat, like a word he could swallow down if only his eyes would close tight enough. (98)

The imagery speaks with eloquence about the unsayable Blackfeet death, the choke of American "Indian" history carried from past to present.

As Lead Feather heads incrementally toward recovery, Doby ("bleeding again" yet seated in a last car scene) holds the hand of a possible lover mimetically called Claire from another reservation. The saga to which Dalimpere has given epistolary form, obliquely, and with a fine sense of proportion on Jones's part, looks to find its final destination, its transhistorical addressee. The one event elides into the other. Images transpose and pair. No single narrative authority has sway. Witness is both past and wholly present-time. Interior self-speech runs alongside community dialogue. A shelf of gain, a saving, against loss is offered. The upshot is a Book of the Dead but also a Book of Life. Jones's novel, polyvocal, heteroglossic, and positioned to move in both parallels and diagonals down corridors of event, memory, language itself—English, French, Blackfeet—so carries all the insignia of postmodern fashioning while remaining at once history, or a version of it, and in William Styron's emblematic term, "a meditation on history."[11]

Each of the sixteen stories that make up *Bleed into Me* can be said to work to similar coordinates. A key inclusion like "Discovering America" deftly turns Columbianism on its head—a reflexive serial of "discovery" by an author writing a play said to have the working title of *The Time That Indian Started Killing Everybody*. The reiteration of "Because I'm Indian in . . . ," with its naming of location and time-stayed, suggests a pattern-poem, almost an incantation. Each contributes to the gathering ironic diary: the Tallahassee shop girl with a medicine pouch around her neck who tells him he should do a rain dance to counter the heat; the Little Rock student partygoers who ask after his animal spirit helper; the Texas oilfield worker who inquires if Montana still runs over its Indians for sport; the warehouse coworker who hits him, racistly, in the face in Clovis in just the manner of the plot-line of his own play; and the Carlsbad agri-crew who think him an animal tracker, a scalper, and call him Chief. It is in this final place that he finishes his play in which each encounter is transmuted, refracted, into text—scalping, heat, rain dance, all the "Indian" paraphernalia the story ironically mimics and subverts.

Other stories do shared duty. "Halloween" aligns peace-pipe ceremony with a modern Native American father who smokes only on the Fourth of July and drinks beer only on New Year's Day. Ceremony has become fuddled, Native parenting a sometimes about-face. Halloween gives proof of one heritage superimposed on the other ("He wore his monster mask every day of the year" [3]). "Captivity Narrative 109" does a clever pastiche of Driving While Indian, the story of Aiche (pronounced H) who in error picks up two young white children en route to school. He deposits the sister, leaving the brother, who sits beside him, to think Aiche turns into a wolf, a clever oddball episode using one cliché of "captivity" to parody another. "Bleed into Me," the title story, offers in the death and funeral of a brother, a mixedblood city son, the portrait of a family to whom pawning things has become habitual. But the thefts, and each resort to the pawnshop, serve in the story as figurations of how displacement has become all. The mother cannot locate the funeral home. The father ends up working in a zoo and fantasizing that had he somehow bled into his son he might have saved him, thereby retrieving generational connection from severance. This is storytelling whose Native implication takes on added, not less, strength from its postmodern styling.

In both *The Oklahoma Basic Intelligence Test: New and Collected Elementary, Epistolary, Autobiographical, and Oratorical Choctologies* and *How Choctaws Invented Civilization and Why Choctaws Will Conquer the World*, D. L. Birchfield puts tribal history into compendious but greatly ingenious format. Both give diligent panorama to Choctaw and related indigenous culture, whole bedrocks of practice, timeline, and geography. But they also carry strings of playfulness, teasing inventions of approach or layout ("Choctology 101" or "Slouching Towards Hillerman"). Much, too, as the contributing chapters confirm an alert eye to scholarship, be it Oklahoma as vintage Indian (and Okie) Country, the role of Andrew Jackson, the frontier, the prairies, oil, Route 66, or Texas and its Rangers, each with due bibliography, there is no lack of recognition of how tribal culture has ancestrally dealt with inheritance ("Indians know that stories are more reliable guides to a people and their past than works of history").[12] That again exhibits itself in *Black Silk Handkerchief*, the first to date of his antic Hom-Astubby Choctaw lawyer mysteries ("Hom Astubby viewed himself as a victim of luck" [6]). *Field of Honor*, however, and without being unduly hoist by category, clearly heads with far greater emphasis into the feints and tactics of postmodern narrative.

"Have You Heard About America?," an early composition in *The Oklahoma Basic Intelligence Test*, gives a sense of Birchfield's flavor overall (19):

> They want to be your friends*
> They want to build a wagon road through where you live†
> Then they want you to move‡
> Then they want you to build a railroad through where they moved you to§
> Then they want to move in with you||
> Then they want you to keep quiet
> and stay out of their way
> while they tell the world
> that ever since then
> your nation has been past tense
>
> * Treaty With The Choctaw, 1786
> † Treaty With The Choctaw, 1801
> ‡ Treaty With The Choctaw, 1830
> § Treaty With The Choctaw And Chickasaw, 1866
> || Oklahoma Statehood, 1907

The "test" stands well enough in its own right. But each footnote to the seeming conversational snippets ("They want . . .") wryly points up shaping truths-to-history. Choctaw encounters with white America are to be understood as a chronology of fake friendship, land-grab, removal, and would-be imposed vanishment.

In this the piece also provides a near perfect point of entry into *Field of Honor*, whose satiric war-and-peace fabling, as ingenious as it is seriocomic, invites comparison with *Slaughterhouse-Five*, *Catch-22*, or *Little Big Man*. As with Stephen Graham Jones's fiction, Birchfield's novel may indeed not qualify as full-bore postmodern but it skirts close, full of prestidigitation and even at times madcap or comic-cuts illogic. For however much a vision of the historical-colonial chain from Indian Removal to LBJ and Vietnam, the techniques in play unmistakably belong to the virtual or self-circling metafictional text. One has only to consider the pattern of run-rabbit, the ironic alternations of realm, or the mock versions of history and place to include Christianity, American Independence (that of a people referred to throughout as German Europeans or, in Choctaw, *Na Hollo*), the Civil War, Mississippi, and Oklahoma itself. Indians, the Choctaw but also the Natchez, à la Vizenor but on the novel's own distinct above-and-below-surface terms, also imitate "Indians"/*indians*. The upshot gives every grounds to be thought a species of trickster postmodern.

For under Birchfield's authorial purview, reversal, and the text made to turn on its own axis, becomes norm. That begins as Lance Corporal Patrick Pushmataha McDaniel, U.S. Marine Corps, mixedblood Choctaw, panics in Vietnam, gets confused in the jungle (an "Indian" cliché turned on its head), is thought captured, and finds his way back to the States to await capture in McGee Valley, southeast Oklahoma. Over a lost decade (it is 1976 yet he supposes the Vietnam War won in weeks with the military engaged to hold down student riots), and as he goes rogue, he takes on the paradoxical role of Marine renegade who uses training in jungle-camouflage, traps, tree-dormitories, and the burglary of military hardware, to await seizure and sentence by his admired fellow Marines for desertion. In his own fantasy "the most dreaded deserter in the history of the Marine Corps" (33), he hopes his honor-code capture will confirm the Corps' "few good men" legend. On being captured, in fact, it leads to his mistakenly being thought a Vietnam hero for having escaped Viet Cong clutches, promotion to major, and the award of huge back-pay. This zigzag, and the Catch-22 runs of plotline in which it is embedded, indicates nothing if not playfield, narrative not only about but itself given shape as board-game as befits the author's own long well-known chess prowess and journalism.

Events are made to turn ever more counter. McDaniel is said to suffer Stockholm Cowardice Syndrome Dysfunction, finds himself accidental sports-hero witness to a vast underground Choctaw world technically advanced and which occasionally sends its people to infiltrate the aboveground world, and becomes embroiled in a Pentagon conspiracy headed by the unhinged Colonel Fay to discover the location of lost oil-reserve sites started in the 1920s under Coolidge. Vietnam, it turns out, was simply a ruse to keep attention focused elsewhere. Yet another of American fiction's truants, when finally, and once again, McDaniel is obliged to light out, it is less for Huck's territories ahead than for those immediately to hand, or in the novel's Oklahoma figuring of locale, those immediately underfoot. For in Choctaw terms, as the text discreetly indicates, he embodies the folk-mythical *chukfi*, or rabbit, of the *Okla Hannali*, one of the tribal branches, trickster yet also the tricked.

Field of Honor, throughout, gives full rein to this counterfactual play. The valley terrain vaunts names like Bugaboo and Wildcat Canyon, Crooked Creek and Chimney Ridge. McDaniel's identity contradictions become a serial: deserter-hero, corporal-major, and once he has fled down through the cave labyrinth into the Choctaw underground, a Lighthorseman super-hero of the Ishtaboli stickball game yet also widely thought a retard (not to mention drugged hospital patient for having run into the wall while scoring the goal that makes him a celebrity). Above ground, Fay's Black Berets use a fake company as mask, yet, in Sergeant Kelley, they themselves have been infiltrated by the actual Kelley, captain in the Choctaw and Ishtaboli ranks. Geological and other survey maps have been changed by Fay and his cohorts to mislead inquirers. Beneath ground, Birchfield has McDaniel, mentored by the boy Little Ejay, learn tribal alter-history, sovereignty discourse, the whir of an advanced technological civilization, in all the Choctaws as might-have-been. Just as it satirizes life above ground, the text also takes any number of genial shies at tribal life—a leadership system that apes university promotion and tenure systems, about-face Choctaw erotica and courtship (in the person of the beauteous Elena), or even comparative spelling and numbers in English and Choctaw (itself broken into Missionary and Standard Choctaw replete with Laurence Sterne–style diagrams) with a riff on the use of colons and semicolons.

The account McDaniel gives Fay on his return to the surface again shadows the deflections of the text in its own right:

> "Sir," McDaniel said, "I got a little bit sidetracked because I thought I'd stumbled into a secret subterranean civilization of Indians, and they got me hooked on some kind of dope that wrung me out pretty good. I mean, it almost caused me to get married. They're right below us, Sir. A huge underground city. Lordy

> mercy, they've got subways and trains and theatres and schools and hospitals and women like you wouldn't believe. And their religion is ball play." (220–221)

In having McDaniel then pretend to think the underground Choctaw both fantasy and "part of the celebration for the two-hundredth anniversary of the Marine Corps" (221), Birchfield engages in well-taken narrative self-reference. Historic roles indeed have reversed, and reversed again, and his novel adjusts its own workings to suit.

It may well be, as in the case of Stephen Graham Jones, that postmodern amounts to a bridge too far. But it comes close, both Jones and Birchfield shrewdest begetters of texts rich in the awareness not only of Native history but a style of textuality that makes engaging new sense of that history. Their re-mediation of past into present, Blackfeet or Choctaw, marks genuine innovation, a fresh way to see but as importantly to hear inerasable tribal presence.

NOTES

1. Silko, "Here's an Odd Artifact," 10–11. For an analysis of the issues involved, see Pérez Castillo, "Postmodernism," 285–294.
2. Owens, *Mixedblood Messages*, 151.
3. Brown, *Who Owns Native Culture?*
4. This argument for cosmopolitanism is notably formulated in Krupat, "Nationalism, Indigenism, Cosmopolitanism," 1–23; and Krupat, "Local, National, Cosmopolitan Literature," 202–232.
5. Each has his well-known critique, but their collective view is helpfully to be found in Weaver, Womack, and Warrior, *American Indian Literary Nationalism*.
6. Her now-classic formulation is to be found in Allen, *The Sacred Hoop*.
7. Bevis, "Native American Novels," 580–620.
8. "Marvelous real"—"lo real maravilloso"—is Alejo Carpentier's celebrated term.
9. Glancy, *The Voice That Was in Travel*, vii.
10. Jones, *Ledfeather*, Author's Note, 215.
11. The phrase is a well-known subtitle: William Styron, *The Confessions of Nat Turner: A Meditation on History*.
12. Birchfield, *Oklahoma Basic Intelligence Test*, 105.

WORKS CITED

Alexie, Sherman. *Flight*. New York: Black Cat, 2007.

———. *Indian Killer*. New York: Warner Books, 1998.

———. *The Lone Ranger and Tonto Fistfight in Heaven*. New York: Atlantic Monthly Press, 1993.

———. *Reservation Blues*. New York: Atlantic Monthly Press, 1995.

Barnes, Jim. *Paris: Poems*. Urbana: University of Illinois Press, 1997.

———. *Visiting Picasso*. Urbana: University of Illinois Press, 2007.

Berger, Thomas. *Little Big Man*. New York: Dial Press, 1964.

Bevis, William. "Native American Novels: Homing In." In *Recovering the Word: Essays in Native American Literature*, ed. Brian Swann and Arnold Krupat, 580–620. Berkeley: University of California Press, 1987.

Birchfield, D. L. *Black Silk Handkerchief: A Hom-Astubby Mystery*. Norman: University of Oklahoma Press, 2006.

———. *Field of Honor*. Norman: University of Oklahoma Press, 2004.

———. *How Choctaws Invented Civilization and Why Choctaws Will Conquer the World*. Albuquerque: University of New Mexico Press, 2007.

———. *The Oklahoma Basic Intelligence Test: New and Collected Elementary, Epistolary, Autobiographical, and Oratorical Choctologies*. Greenfield Center, NY: Greenfield Review Press, 1998.

Bowers, Neal, and Charles L. P. Silet. "An Interview with Gerald Vizenor." *MELUS* 8.1 (1981): 41–49.

Brown, Michael. *Who Owns Native Culture?* Cambridge, MA: Harvard University Press, 2003.

Carr, A. A. *Eye Killers*. Norman: University of Oklahoma Press, 1995.

Cook-Lynn, Elizabeth. *Why I Can't Read Wallace Stegner and Other Essays: A Tribal Voice*. Madison: University of Wisconsin Press, 1996.

Dorris, Michael. *Working Men: Stories*. New York: Henry Holt, 1993.

Erdrich, Louise. *The Beet Queen*. New York: Henry Holt, 1986.

Glancy, Diane. *Firesticks*. Norman: University of Oklahoma Press, 1993.

———. *The Voice That Was in Travel Stories*. Norman: University of Oklahoma Press, 1999.

Gunn Allen, Paula. *The Sacred Hoop: Recovering the Feminine in American Indian Traditions*. Boston: Beacon Press, 1986.

Heller, Joseph. *Catch-22*. New York: Simon and Schuster, 1961.

Henry, Gordon. *The Light People*. Norman: University of Oklahoma Press, 1994.

Jones, Stephen Graham. *All the Beautiful Sinners*. New York: Rugged Land, 2003.

———. *The Bird Is Gone: A Manifesto*. Tuscaloosa: Fiction Collective Two/University of Alabama Press, 2003.

———. *Bleed into Me: A Book of Stories*. Lincoln: University of Nebraska Press, 2005.

———. *Demon Theory: A Work of Fiction*. San Francisco: Mac/Adam Cage, 2006.

———. *The Fast Red Road: A Plainsong*. Tuscaloosa: Fiction Collective Two/University of Alabama Press, 2000.

———. *Growing Up Dead in Texas*. Douglas, Isle of Man: MP Publishing, 2011.

———. *It Came from Del Rio*. Lyons, CO: Trapdoor Books, 2010.

———. *The Last Final Girl*. Portland, OR: Lazy Fascist Press, 2012.

———. *Ledfeather*. Tuscaloosa: Fiction Collective Two/University of Alabama Press, 2008.

———. *The Long Trial of Nolan Dugatti*. Portland, OR: Chiasmus Press, 2008.

———. *The Ones That Got Away*. Gaithersburg, MD: Prime Books, 2010.

———. *Zombie Bake-Off*. Portland, OR: Lazy Fascist Press, 2012.

King, Thomas. *The Truth About Stories: A Native Narrative*. Minneapolis: University of Minnesota Press, 2003.

Krupat, Arnold. "Local, National, Cosmopolitan Literature." In *The Voice in the Margin: Native American Literature and the Canon*, 202–232. Berkeley: University of California Press, 1989.

———. "Nationalism, Indigenism, Cosmopolitanism: Three Perspectives on Native American Literatures." In *Red Matters: Native American Studies*, 1–23. Philadelphia: University of Pennsylvania Press, 2002.

Medawar, Mardi Oakley. *Death at Rainy Mountain*. New York: St. Martin's Press, 1996.

Moore, Brian. *Black Robe*. New York: Dutton, 1985.

Ortiz, Simon. *Out There Somewhere*. Tucson: University of Arizona Press, 2002.

Owens, Louis. *Mixedblood Messages: Literature, Film, Family, Place*. Norman: University of Oklahoma Press 1998.

Pérez Castillo, Susan. "Postmodernism, Native American Literature and the Real." *Massachusetts Review* 32.2 (Summer 1991): 285–294.

Silko, Leslie Marmon. "Here's an Odd Artifact for the Fairy-Tale Shelf." *Impact/Albuquerque Journal Magazine* (7 October 1986): 10–11; reprinted in *Studies in American Indian Literature* 10.4 (1986): 177–184.

Smith, Martin Cruz. *Red Square*. New York: Random House, 1992.

Styron, William. *The Confessions of Nat Turner: A Meditation on History*. New York: Random House, 1967.

Treuer, David. *Native American Fiction: A User's Manual*. Minneapolis: Greywolf Press, 2006.

Vizenor, Gerald. *Blue Ravens: Historical Novel*. Middletown, CT: Wesleyan University Press, 2014.

———. *Darkness in Saint Louis Bearheart*. Minneapolis: Truck Press, 1978; revised and reprinted as *Bearheart: The Heirship Chronicles*. Minneapolis: University of Minnesota Press, 1990.

———. *Father Meme*. Albuquerque: University of New Mexico Press, 2008.

———. *Fugitive Poses: Native Scenes of Absence and Presence*. Lincoln: University of Nebraska Press, 1998.

———. *Griever: An American Monkey King in China*. Normal: Illinois State University/Fiction Collective, 1987. Reprint, Minneapolis: University of Minnesota Press, 1990.

———. *The Heirs of Columbus*. Hanover, NH: Wesleyan University Press/University Press of New England, 1991.

———. *Hiroshima Bugi: Atomu 57*. Lincoln: University of Nebraska Press, 2003.

———. *Hotline Healers: An Almost Browne Novel*. Hanover, NH: Wesleyan University Press/University of New England Press, 1997.

———. *Manifest Manners: Postindian Warriors of Survivance*. Hanover, NH: Wesleyan University Press/University Press of New England, 1994.

———. *Narrative Chance: Postmodern Discourse on Native American Indian Literatures*. Albuquerque: University of New Mexico Press, 1989.

———. *The Trickster of Liberty: Tribal Heirs to a Wild Baronage*. Minneapolis: University of Minnesota Press, 1988.

Vonnegut, Kurt. *Slaughterhouse-Five*. New York: Delacorte Press, 1969.

Weaver, Jace, Craig S. Womack, and Robert Warrior. *American Indian Literary Nationalism*. Albuquerque: University of New Mexico Press, 2006.

Welch, James. *Fools Crow*. New York: Viking, 1986.

Flight Times in Gerald Vizenor's *Blue Ravens*
White Earth Mediating History

A. ROBERT LEE

Blue ravens were the new totem of native motion.

—GERALD VIZENOR, *BLUE RAVENS* (2014)

They said, "You have a blue guitar,
You do not play things as they are."

The man replied, "Things as they are
Are changed upon the blue guitar."

—*WALLACE STEVENS,*
"THE MAN WITH THE BLUE GUITAR"

An Anishinaabe postmodern gamester and, in his own term, *storier*, and a Hartford insurance executive and, at the same time, modernist versifier who made his debut with *Harmonium* in 1923—Gerald Vizenor and Wallace Stevens might not be a pairing that immediately jumps into mind. But given Vizenor's latest novel, with its early twentieth-century setting (the subtitling calls it a "historical novel") and emphasis upon how the painter's coloring or storyteller's flight gives new possession to ground-zero reality, it would be far from out of order. If *Blue Ravens* can be said to have any one overall end in view, and "view" is the operative word, it has to be that visionary powers of creativity are always best called upon to unsettle, and so outflank and transcend, quite all static or either-or prescriptions of "things as they are."

For as the novel has Aloysius Hudon Beaulieu and Basile Hudon Beaulieu, Native brother-twins (though with a twist) and, respectively, visual artist and writer, embark upon their rite of passage from White Earth to the Europe of World War I, it unfolds a world and its era of quite sumptuous artistic breakthrough and yet brutal historical fracture ("the bloody rage of war"). This is to situate the two artist-enlistees, and their Beaulieu-Vizenor dynasty, within a changing but ingeniously linked serial of time and place: Minnesota's turn-of-the-century Chippewa-Ojibway reservation, wartime gas and trench France as American Expeditionary Forces enter the Great War in 1917–1918, and the Europe of transition from belle époque to the 1920s of modernism and Paris. The upshot amounts to hugely ambitious fabling, a magic-real tribute to Native presence, in actuality and art, and within a historic transatlantic, or indeed Red Atlantic, spectrum of war and peace.

"Aloysius Hudon Beaulieu created marvelous blue ravens that stormy summer" reads the opening sentence. It sets up figuration for the whole novel. Aloysius will paint huge, magnificent ravens in Chagall-blue across settings both American and European. Each is totemic, abstract, as though by this avian fantasticality to give new imagining to nothing less than Native and non-Native worlds alike. A later age has Christo wrap buildings and cliffs, Banksy fashion anonymous street graphics, or Jean-Michel Basquiat line-draw his pictograms. But the Aloysius of Vizenor's text paints his ravens as though, virtually, irreally, they have the call to appearance everywhere, whether Twin Cities–Saskatchewan Soo Line rail carriage or Seine River bridge, whether Minneapolis's Orpheum Theatre or the Marne and Vesle battlefields. Only in part will they transfer from outside-world to inside-gallery.

These birds, along with the stories composed by Basile, act as art hieroglyphs fully in their own right. But they also provide filters through which to understand life-affirming liberty, and virtuosity, even as until 1924 the United States denies citizenship and its rights to Native populations, and Europe turns killing-field in the contest for the one or another political ascendancy. Their blueness summons a vast expressive hinterland that includes lapis lazuli, woad, indigo dye, religious stained glass window, Chinese porcelain, Hokusai woodblock, through to the Blue Period and later canvases of Picasso, Matisse, and the recurrent name of Marc Chagall ("Chagall created brilliant scenes that lingered in my dreams and memories"). The effect is exhilarating, a historic novel full, even unsparing, in circumstantial detail, but at the same time imagist tapestry.

Vizenor pitches his date for date novel to work in parallel with the twenty-four-chapter *Odyssey*, with actual citations from Homer's epic. But in having Basile write Aloysius, and their shared Odyssean journey, he equally uses his own style of one narrator for two in a manner to recall *Dead Voices* (1992), *Hiroshima Bugi* (2003), and the ex-journalist to lawyer tactic of *Father Meme* (2008). The White Earth scenes assemble a vintage cast, beginning with extended family ("great storiers"). The father, Honoré Hudon Beaulieu, is both "singer . . . and independent hunter and trapper." The mother, Margaret Beaulieu, "remembers the scent and stories of maple syrup." Augustus Hudon Beaulieu, wiseacre and mentor, takes his place as "cunning and ambitious uncle." Fellow White Earth denizens, besides assorted other Beaulieu-Vizenors who serve in the military, include the trickster savvy trader Odysseus Walker; the healer Missabe; the generous John Leecy of the Leecy Hotel; Patch Zhimagaanish, the valiant railwayman and trumpeter; Father Aloysius Hermeneutz, the Benedictine; and, almost inevitably, a round of Vizenor mongrel dogs. Their world, and the international world beyond, is carried in the White Earth journal, *The Progress*, later *The Tomahawk*, both to be sold at Ogema Station near the reservation but also in Minneapolis and even across the Atlantic.

In France, fact again overlaps with fiction, not unlike E. L. Doctorow's *Ragtime* (1975). Not only do the brothers face combat as scouts ("the war was surreal, faces, forests and enemies"), get captured, escape, and learn first-hand the Hindenburg Line and battles like Montbréhain, they also remember benign heroines like Frances Gulick, the YMCA nurse and welfare worker, and Anna Coleman Ladd, Massachusetts sculptress and pioneer of prosthetic masks and limbs for impaired soldiers. Survivors, *survivancers*, their plunge into Paris as modernist fiefdom after the 1918 Armistice again elides history and art ("the city had become our vision of art and literature, and a chance of recognition as native artists").

Aloysius can continue to paint his ravens fantastically upon the Place de la Concorde, Notre Dame, Gare de l'Est, and the Bastille. His "Thirty Six Views of the Eiffel Tower" again echoes Hokusai. He does so, however, as together with Basile he reads the wholly actual Apollinaire; meets Chagall himself; comes face-to-face with the likes of Modigliani, the cubist Marie Vassilieff, Blaise Cendrars, James Joyce, Sylvia Beach, Gertrude Stein; and displays with great Jewish gallerists like Nathan Crémieux and Daniel-Henri Kahnweiler. The expatriate years they take in France, the returns and re-returns both to White Earth and Paris, their part in Native and French banquet gatherings (Vizenor rarely misses the chance to write up a good menu), leads on to a surge of new ravens from Aloysius and stories from Basile. *Blue Ravens* so works its way to a moment of active rest, Aloysius's undiminishing pigments of blue and Basile's regimes of story—not to mention sharing his body with Maria.

Blue Ravens leaves no doubt of Vizenor's bravura commitment to art's gift of life in the face of death, and for its part, of Native signature as of and for the world.

PART TWO

(Trans)Media Literacy, Youth Cultures, and Nation

ᏣᎳᎩ ᏗᎪᏪᎵ
Cherokee Writing
Mediating Traditions, Codifying Nation

ELLEN CUSHMAN

Commonly found at Cherokee Nation gift shops, a black-on-white license plate reads **ᏣᎳᎩᎯ ᎠᏰᎵ**. At first blush, this might be seen as evidence of Cherokees capitalizing on the symbolic uniqueness of the Cherokee syllabary, the reading and writing system developed by Sequoyah and presented to the tribal council in 1821. Most people who would purchase this plate and put it on the front bumper of their cars probably do not know how to read this. Here is one step:

> **ᏣᎳᎩᎯ ᎠᏰᎵ**
> /tsalagihi ayeli/

This phonetic transliteration allows English readers to be able to pronounce roughly the sounds of the Cherokee characters, but does little to link sound to meaning. A direct translation of the characters is offered in the Direct Translation of License Plate chart. This "literal" translation raises more questions than it answers. Cherokee into the center? Cherokee in the middle? Cherokee in between the capital? So what does this Sequoyan **ᏣᎳᎩᎯ ᎠᏰᏟ** mean?

Direct Translation of License Plate		
ᏣᎳᎩ	**ᏗᏍ**	**ᎠᏰᎵ**
Cherokee	on, in, or into	1. middle, center, between, central 2. half 3. capital

The problem here is not with the translation so much as it is with the approach. If approached from a Western epistemology that presumes an alphabetic bias, this short, clever piece of Sequoyan empties of meaning and import rather quickly. The problem is in dealing with it literally, that is, by the letter, as though these were letters to begin with; as though their meaning would become transparent when parsed this way; as though these can be read the same ways as we might read letters; as though a translation has to work in and on English language readers' terms. "What does it mean?" cannot well be answered through this process of translation, so the questions become: *How does it mean to Cherokees? And what does it do?*

Exploring these questions has been the focus of the last six years of my ethnohistorical research on Cherokee language and identity in which I have demonstrated the instrumental, cultural, and historical logics in the Cherokee syllabary and central to Cherokees' everyday acts of cultural perseverance.[1] In relevant publications, I have pointed to the decolonial rhetoric implicit in every act of reading and writing in Sequoyan, building on a line of thinking begun in Mignolo (1992) and continued in Baca (2008) and Baca and Villanueva (2012)[2] in which the alphabetic lens is taken off to reveal knowledge and subjectivities dehumanized by post-Enlightenment "modern" thinking. This thinking privileges literacy above all other symbolic and graphic systems of representation and has created "tradition" as its own "exteriority," its necessary other, in order to ensure "the inside as the locus of enunciation of knowledge."[3] As Mignolo finds, "Tradition is not a way of life that predated 'modernity' but an invention of the rhetoric of modernity."[4] Cherokee "traditions" have thus always been understood through the alphabetic perspective that seeks a literal translation of words and phrases. To understand Sequoyan in its own right, then, has demanded understanding how the writing system works to codify nonalphabetic Cherokee logics that predate modern thinking.

In this chapter, I explain more fully the decolonial rhetoric of **ᏣᎳᎩ ᏗᎪᏪᎵ** /tsalagi digoweli/ Cherokee writing. First, drawing on Mignolo's work, I discuss the ways in which Sequoyah's invention marked a moment of "epistemic de-linking" in both its instrumentality and in its resistance to the alphabetic influence. Next, I demonstrate how the writing system itself provides for ongoing "acts of epistemic disobedience" found in the "enunciations" of Cherokee knowledge-making in the Cherokee Nation's Four Worlds curriculum.[5] I then return to the license plate to see what might be gathered from it as "an enunciation of decolonial rhetoric." My argument claims that any act of reading and writing in Sequoyan is an act of "epistemic de-linking," an insistence on the currency of Cherokee language and understanding, and a re-placing of Cherokee epistemologies into the "geo- and body politics of knowledge."[6] In understanding how Sequoyan comes to mean and do, we together are engaging in the significant work of epistemic decolonization through a study of the mediated traditions of story and nation.

SEQUOYAH'S INVENTION: AN EPISTEMIC DE-LINKING

The decolonial rhetoric of Cherokee writing began at the moment of its invention. Sequoyah's first de-linking with literacy emerged in the act of creating a uniquely Cherokee writing system. When it was first designed and taught in longhand, the characters bore no resemblance to Roman letters.[7] In 1839 Sequoyah demonstrated the arrangement of the original longhand characters next to their respective eventual shorthand characters, probably for John Howard Payne.[8] A visual analysis of the characters' shapes and arrangement revealed two important findings: first, none of the longhand characters resembled letters. So when it was first learned in script, it was learned without alphabetic influence in its design. Second, this arrangement of characters ordered them according to a visual mnemonic that keyed all eighty-six shapes to the seven forms found in the first column of the chart.[9] In other words, Cherokees were learning seven root forms that organized eighty-six subsequent shapes. The original orthography that Sequoyah developed represented a uniquely Cherokee visual logic.

A linguistic analysis of the characters revealed that the system works both syllabically, matching well the sound system of the language, and morphographically—writing deep levels of meaning with characters.[10]

From the syllabary's inception, Sequoyah ruptured the colonial work of literacy, that is, reading and writing with the letter, by developing a completely unique system of writing that codifies Cherokee language and logics. "One strategy of de-linking is to de-naturalize concepts and conceptual fields that totalize A reality,"[11] Mignolo tells us. Because it was intentionally made without reference to the alphabet, along the instrumental logics of Cherokee designs and language, the invention of the Cherokee syllabary denaturalizes the concept of literacy. Using the basic logic of letter-sound correspondence, Sequoyah invented a system that had absolutely no letters in its original script.[12] This invention, from its very creation, denaturalizes the conceptual fields of civilization, humanity, and knowledge associated with what it means to be literate, even as it appears to be complicit with these forces.

De-linking from the dominant script of advancing civilization, Sequoyah seems to have nonetheless understood the power of writing in the alphabet, for he had seen letters, books, the Bible, and had signed a treaty, all before finalizing his creation and presenting it to the tribal council in 1821. Interviews with Sequoyah and second-hand accounts from relatives reveal that he had tried out a number of symbolic systems before he settled upon the syllabary he created.[13] Mignolo defines epistemic de-linking as central to the work of decolonial thinking and as a counter to critical theory that has no other option but to work within the logics of modernity. As an alternative, "Decolonial thinking . . . is an opening towards another thing, on the march, searching for itself in the difference."[14] Sequoyah seems to have been searching for this "opening towards another thing, on the march," for almost a decade, trying out different writing systems. He alienated himself from family and friends in his "searching for [a writing system] in [its] difference" from the Roman alphabet. His invention was the initial rupture that changed the terms of the conversation about what it meant, indeed what it means, to be literate, thus "civilized" and "fully human."

Today the decolonial rhetoric implicit in the instrumental workings of this writing system continues in the development of Cherokee texts used for educational purposes in Oklahoma and around the country.

SEQUOYAH'S INVENTION: EPISTEMIC DISOBEDIENCE IN "FOUR WORLDS CURRICULUM" AND TWELVE WORDS FOR STORY

For two years, I worked with the Johnson O'Malley program at the Cherokee Nation to help develop the "Four Worlds Curriculum" for their educational programs. This curriculum translates the knowledge presented in a selection of our wampum belts into English and Cherokee and is organized around Cherokee historical time and physical location.

The first unit opens with a consideration of the importance of the Cherokee language and the stories told in this language offered to us by Benny Smith, a former assistant dean at Haskell Indian Nations University and a family member of fire keepers. He finds that "Cherokee storytelling, of course, has always happened in the Cherokee language. The words and phrases in Cherokee carry so much more meaning and subtlety than English alone can possibly capture."[15] Because of the value of storytelling and the profundity of Cherokee language, seven Cherokee language instructors were asked to translate the word "story" for the opening of this section. They produced twelve different Cherokee words for "story."

In the curriculum, we listed all twelve Cherokee words for "story" immediately after the word **ᎠᏂᎦᏴᎵ** "elders," so no mistake could be made about to whom the pronoun "they" refers in the remaining verb phrases. Let me explore just one of these words, "**ᎧᏃᎮᏓ** /kanoheda/," by asking: How does it come to mean? And what does it do?

Story: as it appears in the Cherokee Nation Four Worlds Curriculum:

ᎠᏂᎦᏴᎵ /ANIGAYVLI/ ELDERS

a) **ᎧᏃᎮᏓ** /kanoheda/ also **ᎧᏃᎮᏗ** /kanohedi/ things they have told
Story: the heritage of the word as seen in its action root, below with two conjugations into typical verb phrases:
b) **ᏃᎮᎭ** /hnoheha/ root of the verb: tell somebody, state, talk[16]
c) **ᎧᏃᎮᎭ** /kanoheha/ s/he/it is telling it[17]
d) **ᎧᏃᎮᏍᎪᎢ** /kanohesgoi/ s/he/it habitually tells it[18]
Story: the everyday use of the word as a noun derived from the verb phrases:
e) **ᎧᏃᎮᏓ** /kanoheda/ (story, news, gospel, message)[19]
Story: the Cherokee Bible:
f) **ᎢᏤ ᎧᏃᎮᏓ** /itse kanoheda/ New Testament
Story: The Milky Way Story in Cherokee and Sequoyan (a story from the general curriculum for immersion students)
g) **ᎩᏟ ᎤᏓᏢᏍᏔᏅ**
/gitli udatlvstanv/
dog s/he/it ran (Where the dog ran)

h) **ᎪᎯᏗᏴ ᏥᎨᏒ, ᎠᏂᎦᏒᎵ ᎠᏂᏃᎮᏍᎨᎢᏍ ᎯᎢᎾ ᎧᏃᎮᏓ**
/gohidisv tsigesv, anigasvli aninohesgeis hi'ina kanoheda/
A long time ago, elders they tell this story

The first act of epistemic disobedience in these curricular materials is to privilege Sequoyan over the alphabet, just as Sequoyah seems to have done. Visually and linguistically different from alphabetic text, the script itself presents learners with an initial de-linking from the alphabet, the naturalized mediation of knowledge. "Delinking means to change the terms of the conversation and above all, of the hegemonic ideas of what knowledge and understanding are."[20] The curriculum strives to write Cherokee knowledge in and on Cherokee terms by highlighting Sequoyan at the outset of each unit and story within each unit. The language instructors, Johnson O'Malley program administrators, and Cherokee Nation policies all demand this privileging of Sequoyan. We then situate the entire curriculum around Cherokee understandings of time, philosophy, and organization of our society across history.

The second act of epistemic disobedience rests in treating the genre of story in the first place as heritage in action. Within each of the Cherokee words, continuous and continual action occurs. The twelve words for story have rough translations that show elders giving, speaking, teaching, discussing, knowing, telling, letting go of, picking up, and holding on to in their minds. Story is an ongoing action of knowledge-making that emphasizes the presence of Cherokee heritage in the actions of the elders listening, discussing, receiving, testifying, and telling. The point in keeping these Cherokee words in Cherokee is precisely because they put the doing of knowledge-making within the Cherokees' own paradigm.

The third act of epistemic disobedience rests in the insistence on a social order that privileges elders as keepers of knowledge and understanding. These words for story are verb phrases, words as sentences, that indicate ongoing practices and intentionally point to the noun "elders" to ensure that readers understand the antecedent of the pronoun **ᎤᏂ**/uni/they. "Elder" is not a word taken lightly or applied to all who are older but instead means keeper of knowledge and indicates a position of authority. Every word for story in Cherokee represents the activity of knowledge-making, placing Cherokee elders at the epistemic center of what counts as understanding and knowledge.

The fourth act of epistemic disobedience, then, is in this act of de-linking the word "story" through a temporal/special reading of Cherokee meanings. When I unpack the heritage of the Cherokee word for "story"—**ᎧᏃᎮᏓ**

/kanoheda/, from root, to action, to noun, to Cherokee knowledge—I am moving from the root meanings to common uses and to standardized forms of understanding, adding layers of understanding across time and circularly through cross-reference. Doing so, I wrest the word "story" from the Western geopolitics of knowing in which the "spatial/temporal difference must be seen simultaneously as both imperial and colonial."[21] Now that you understand how "story" comes to mean and what it does for Cherokees, you can no longer understand "story" as quaint, unfactual, anecdotal, unauthorized, primitive, as evidence of the untrustworthy oral tradition—all constructs of modern and imperial difference.

In this unpacking of "**ᎧᏃᎮᏓ** /kanoheda/ story," I have simply followed the decolonial work of Sequoyan by seeking the profundity of meaning in these words and the knowledge that is carried in and through the Cherokee language codified so well with the syllabary.

ᏣᎳᎩᎯ ᎠᏰᏟ: SEQUOYAN—MEDIATING TRADITIONS; CODIFYING NATION

Returning now to the license plate that opens this study: How does it mean to Cherokees? And what does it do? When words such as "**ᏣᎳᎩᎯ ᎠᏰᏟ** /tsalagihi ayeli/" or "Cherokee Nation" are written in Sequoyan, the instrumentality of the writing system itself acts as a decolonial rhetoric. It allows Cherokees to continue to put words such as "Cherokee Nation" into a Cherokee framework, thereby stripping away the alphabetic filter and "Eurocentered paradigm of knowledge." Reading Sequoyan reveals how **ᎧᏃᎮᏓ** mediates tradition with Cherokee understandings of "story" and shows how **ᏣᎳᎩᎯ ᎠᏰᎵ** insists upon the sovereignty of the Cherokee Nation. Mignolo might call any act of writing in Sequoyan an act of enunciation: "the basic apparatus for engaging in institutional and purposive knowledge-making geo-politically oriented."[22] **ᏣᎳᎩᎯ ᎠᏰᎵ**, the Cherokee Nation, is an enunciation of the legal, governmental organization, situating Cherokees geo-politically in the center of our tribe, between the borders of states, in the middle of the country. This word appears on our Nation's seal, the legal license plate, the Nation's headquarters, and all publications by the Cherokee Nation. This license plate, written as it is in Sequoyan, does the work of driving home the presence of Cherokee peoples and knowledge, of enunciating the sovereignty of the tribe, of centering Cherokees in the "geo- and body politics of knowledge."

Even if a Cherokee person cannot read the Sequoyan on this license plate, the mere act of having it on his or her car announces the visible difference of Cherokee understanding. Sequoyah's first act of epistemic disobedience is always present in every use of Sequoyan. Even if viewers mistakenly read the Cherokee characters as alphabet letters, as /G-W-Y-H D-B-P/, the letters make no sense, and so they have to wonder what it means! This epistemic de-linking is activated whenever Sequoyan is consciously employed. No matter how insignificant the use of Sequoyan, such as placing a license plate on the front bumper of a car, each instance presents a unique opportunity to enunciate a Cherokee identity.

Elsewhere I have described the evolutionary moment when Cherokee script moved into print with the casting of the typeset for the first printing of the *Cherokee Phoenix*, our Nation's newspaper and the first Native American newspaper in the United States, in both English and Sequoyan. This moment "reveals a public presentation of Cherokee hybrid identities that at once served to group, protect, and foster the continued survival of the Cherokee language and people as it also grouped, secured, and established the political face of the nation that accepted, indeed demanded, the transfer of political rights from the federal government."[23] The Cherokee writing system helped ensure both the survival of the language for the tribe as it served to codify and symbolize the political profile of the Cherokee Nation as fully legitimate and sovereign. It does so even today with a metal license plate stamped with Sequoyan.

In answering, How does it come to mean? And what does it do?, I've shown four ways in which the Eurocentric paradigm is decolonized by reading Sequoyan on and in its own terms. This epistemic decolonization has worked through two procedures:

One is to show the partiality and limitations of the "theo- and ego-logical"[24] politics of knowledge and understanding. The other is offered by the growth and expansion of the geo- and body politics of knowledge and understanding. Both are de-linking procedures: "Thus, the first step in the grammar of decolonization could be . . . learning to unlearn."[25]

Because you now know that ᎧᏃᎮᏛ is more than just "story," and because you now know that a license plate that reads ᏣᎳᎩᎯ ᎠᏰᎵ is more than just kitsch, you have been engaged in the very de-linking procedure demanded by the epistemic disobedience of Sequoyan. You have begun to understand how Indigenous knowledge is mediated through Sequoyan; and you have moved beyond the "modern" notions of the oral tradition to begin to see the cultural logics imbued in this writing system. You are learning to unlearn your alphabetic bias.

NOTES

1. See, for instance, Cushman, "The Cherokee Syllabary," 2011.
2. Mignolo, "On the Colonization of Amerindian Languages"; Baca, *Mestiz@ Scripts.*
3. Mignolo, "Delinking," 459.
4. Ibid.
5. Mignolo, "Epistemic Disobedience, Independent Thought and De-Colonial Freedom."
6. Mignolo, "De-linking," 462.
7. Cushman, "The Cherokee Syllabary from Script to Print."
8. Walker and Sarbaugh, "The Early History of the Cherokee Syllabary," 79.
9. Cushman, "The Cherokee Syllabary from Script to Print," 626.
10. Cushman, *The Cherokee Syllabary.*
11. Mignolo, "Delinking," 459.
12. Cushman "We're Taking the Genius of Sequoyah into This Century."
13. Ibid.
14. Mignolo, "Epistemic Disobedience and the Decolonial Option," 50.
15. Cherokee Nation, "Four Worlds Curriculum," 12.
16. Http://www.cherokeenationfoundation.org/dictionary/?p=931.
17. Feeling, *Cherokee-English Dictionary*, 141.
18. Ibid., 141, 291.
19. Http://www.cherokeenationfoundation.org/dictionary/?p=932.
20. "Delinking," 459.
21. Ibid., 474.
22. Mignolo, "Epistemic Disobedience, Independent Thought and De-Colonial Freedom," 18.
23. Cushman, "The Cherokee Syllabary from Script to Print," 644.
24. Mignolo, "Delinking," 460.
25. Ibid., 485.

WORKS CITED

Baca, Damián. *Mestiz@ Scripts, Digital Migrations and the Territories of Writing.* New York: Palgrave Macmillian, 2008.

Baca, Damián, and Victor Villanueva. *Rhetorics of the Americas.* New York: Palgrave Macmillan, 2012.

Cherokee Nation. "Four Worlds Curriculum." Unpublished manuscript. Tahlequah, OK, 2011.

———, dir. *Milkyway Story*. 2012. Http://www.cherokee.org/AboutTheNation/Kid'sArea/KidsGames/Default.asp&xgt.

Cushman, Ellen. "The Cherokee Syllabary: A Writing System in Its Own Right." *Written Communication* 28.3 (July 2011): 255–281.

———."The Cherokee Syllabary from Script to Print." *Ethnohistory* 57.4 (2010): 625–649.

———. *The Cherokee Syllabary: Writing the People's Perseverance*. Norman: University of Oklahoma Press, 2011.

———. "'We're Taking the Genius of Sequoyah into This Century': The Cherokee Syllabary, Peoplehood, and Perseverance." *Wicazo Sa Review* 26.2 (2011): 67–83.

Feeling, Durbin. *Cherokee-English Dictionary*. Tahlequah, OK: Cherokee Nation Press, 1975.

Mignolo, Walter D. *The Darker Side of the Renassiance: Literacy, Territoriality, and Colonization*. 2nd ed. Ann Arbor: University of Michigan Press, 2003.

———. "Delinking." *Cultural Studies* 21.2 (2007): 449–514.

———. "Epistemic Disobedience and the Decolonial Option: A Manifesto." *Transmodernity: Journal of Peripheral Cultural Production of the Luso-Hispanic World* 1.2 (2011): 45–66.

———. "Epistemic Disobedience, Independent Thought and De-Colonial Freedom." *Theory, Culture, and Society* 26.7 (2009): 1–23.

———. "On the Colonization of Amerindian Languages and Memories: Renaissance Theories of Writing and the Discontinuity of the Classical Tradition." *Comparative Studies in Society and History* 34.2 (1992): 301–330.

Walker, Willard, and James Sarbaugh. "The Early History of the Cherokee Syllabary." *Ethnohistory* 40.1 (1993): 70–94.

"We Can Tell Our Own History, We Can Tell Our Own Future"

Quese IMC, Culture Shock Camp, and an Indigenous Hip-Hop Movement

CHRIS LaLONDE

NEAR THE END OF THE FILM *DEAD MAN*, AS WILLIAM BLAKE'S EYE wanders through the Makah village and toward the longhouse into which Nobody has entered, Jim Jarmusch's camera lights and lingers upon a sewing machine on the ground. The initial lap dissolve in *Four Sheets to the Wind*, the first feature-length film from Seminole-Creek filmmaker Sterlin Harjo, merges a shot of trees with one of a phonograph, the needle scratching as it rides the final groove of a spinning record. The two machines are telling, and today, at least, we would do well to consider how they are linked. Jarmusch's film is about representation, about film and the film industry, and about the technology or apparatus of the medium. The sewing machine emphasizes the cut, of course, the element of film's grammar that addresses our desire to see more, to see, in the case of Jarmusch's film, Nobody, in all the richly layered meanings of that figure, and a dead man.[1] The camera in *Four Sheets to the Wind* cuts from the record player to the body of Cufe Smallhill's father, who has taken his own life. From its beginning, the phonograph was thought to offer a technology enabling one to communicate with the dead. In the words of Thomas Edison himself, speaking of the capability of his invention, "if we evolve an instrument so delicate as to be affected, or moved or manipulated . . . by our personality as it survives in the next life, such an instrument when made available ought to record something."[2]

Given the dominant society's desire, one might even say need, to link the *indian* and death, it is little wonder that *Four Sheets to the Wind* focuses on the record player in a scene that includes Frankie Smallhill's corpse.[3] More must be said, however, for the sound track of the shot and the scene in which it is a part offer us a traditional trickster story, told in Muscogee Creek. In effect, then, Harjo's film offers the story of rabbit, bear, desire, and a trick as a supplement to whatever had been playing on the turntable, a supplement that, like the film itself, confounds audience expectations and tells an(other) story.

I have opened on *Dead Man* and *Four Sheets to the Wind* to draw our attention both to technologies of representation—technologies of capture and projection, if you will—and to each film's awareness of and concern with those technologies. I have also opened with Harjo's film because if you have seen *Four Sheets to the Wind*, then you have heard the music and lyrics of Pawnee-Seminole hip-hop artist Quese IMC. Cufe's cousin Jimmy listens to "Micco Rebels from the Sun" in his car while talking on his mobile to Cufe about Frankie's funeral. Initially in the background on the audio track, the song increases in volume after the conversation ends; accentuating the cut, "Micco" sutures together the shot in which it is first heard and the three shots that follow to conclude the scene. Here, then, Quese's music is situated to address our desire to hear and know more. A through line materializes: capture technologies, information and communication technologies, movement, death, ceremony, and Native hip-hop.

Before turning to Quese IMC's music and his work with Culture Shock Camp, a word on the startlingly obvious. Anyone surprised by the existence of Native hip-hop could be said to suffer from an understanding of hip-hop as a product of and rooted in urban environments and a misunderstanding of contemporary Native life. Born in the South Bronx in the 1970s, the combination of graffiti art, break dancing, DJing, and rapping known as hip-hop laid claim to the city and announced both the presence of young African Americans and their articulation of the economic and social conditions under which they and members of preceding generations suffered.[4] As Tricia Rose notes in her early, influential study of rap music and African American culture, "hip hop replicates and reimagines the experiences of urban life and symbolically appropriates urban space through sampling, attitude, dance, style, and sound effects." In so doing, "hip hop gives voice to the tensions and contradictions within the public urban landscape . . . and attempts to seize the shifting urban terrain, to make it work on behalf of the dispossessed."[5] More than simply a proclamation, hip-hop is an appropriation that embodies a call to action. Graffiti artists announced their presence on trains that circulated the city, parts of the city abandoned by the dominant society are reclaimed with the music pumping from sound system speakers and with the crowds gathered to listen and move, and technologies of consumption, the turntable and records, are transformed into instruments of creation.

If either unaware of the movement of Natives off reservation to urban centers, especially from the beginning of the relocation period in the second half of the twentieth century onward, or unwilling to imagine the *indian* anywhere save the reservation, no matter what Timothy Taylor describes as the "tolerance of difference, heterogeneity, and . . . cosmopolitan outlook" of those—predominantly urban dwellers—who fancy what the music industry categorizes as world music, one would tend not to think of Natives and hip-hop.[6] Given the subversive and communal nature of hip-hop, however, it makes sense that young Native artists would turn to it as a vehicle for expression and resistance. As a means to, in Quese IMC's own words, "tell our own history and tell our own future,"[7] to get at the history and the future to which he refers, I want to tease out five strands in Quese IMC's three available CDs, link at least two of those strands to his work with his brother DJ Shock B and Culture Shock Camp, and return to technology. The strands are the personal, the political, the cultural, the pan-Indigenous, and what I call being aware.

The fusion of Native and hip-hop cultures is writ large in Marcus Frejo's stage or performance name, Quese IMC. In an interview in the *Hip Hop Herald*, Quese tells George Jackson that Quese is a transcription of the Skiri Pawnee diminutive suffix *kis*;[8] IMC stands for what Quese does: emcee. His discography consists of *The Betty Lena Project* (2006), *Bluelight* (2008), and *Hand Drums for Whiskey Bottles* (2011). Beginning with the first disc and reaching through the third, Quese IMC offers songs that are infused with personal history. In tracks such as "Superbrightstar" from *Betty Lena*, "Little Marcus" from *Bluelight*, and "Best Times of Our Lives" from *Hand Drums*, we hear stories rooted in a childhood in Oklahoma. He begins his rap in "Superbrightstar" by announcing his position as an outsider from Oklahoma City: "Yo, here I am / creeping out the boondocks / to your boombox."[9] From there, Quese traces a trajectory "from killer crossover jumpshots / to crossing over to hip hop / killing MCs every chance I got."[10] Still, he raps that he is "owning every moment / with nostalgic longing."[11] That nostalgia finds articulation in "Best Times of Our Lives," a song about a dear childhood friend no longer present. "Best Times" is haunted by her loss. Quese raps of sharing toys, packs of gum, and childhood Oklahoma streets with his friend. They would stay together late into the night, in no small measure "because your home life was hard and / and you were saddened / so we were just swinging" in the park.[12] Quese's home life at the time was also marked by difficulties, his father and mother divorcing when he was eight, but through the trials, both psychological and economic, he raps "I was there for you / and you were there for me / escaping home life / through music to get free."[13]

Hip-hop is liberating for Quese IMC, then and now. In "House," a song with looped horns and drum tracks that produce and sustain a dance rhythm, Quese proclaims that hip-hop was his parent when his mother and father divorced. He raps in homage to old school hip-hop, from Flavor Flav of Public Enemy to LL Cool J, and for all the b-boys and b-girls and "houses of freestyle" past and present. In a celebration of hip-hop, Quese raps of break-dancing moves, "backspin / head spin / windmill,"[14] includes sustained break beats that create a space for his rap, and verbalizes scratching with his lyrics, "there goes another DJ / thwack, thwack," to complement scratching on the music track.[15] He also celebrates his older brother Brian, whose performance name is DJ Shock B, with a bitingly bright rhyme: "Old school crews bring out all sorts / my brother was a DJ / domestic import."[16]

While songs like "House" and the earlier "Hip Hop 84" celebrate the genre and its connection to personal and social liberation, Quese IMC is aware that not all rap is directed toward positive ends. In "Rebel Music," Quese and fellow rapper 20–20 know that "a lot of MCs don't walk their talk / they remind me of the corrupt politicians."[17] "Empty" goes further, proclaiming that the talk of some artists is, well, empty, taking to task those rappers whose

> style is as dope
> as empty drugs
> you got about as much pull
> as empty gloves
> and your record label is as fat
> as empty pockets.[18]

Contra those artists, Quese IMC offers something dope and fat, but only if one listens, for

> between the lines
> is what
> you missed at first

but
let me tell you
that I'm a poet
story tells
and this is the day
that the music lives.[19]

For Quese IMC, the music lives because it is part of a movement. We hear this in "Mouse" when he announces that "I went from battling with mikes / to battling for rights"[20] and in doing so creates an "opportunity to move and make change / feeling it deep inside / things we fight for our claims."[21] In "The Youth Conference" individual activism is linked to quite specific group activism, for "the youth are a movement" that will be part of a "new revolution."[22] With "The Bird Song" the "I am, I am the movement" gives way to first an address to an unspecified individual, "You are, you are the movement," and then to a statement of solidarity that echoes: "we are, we are the movement / the movement / the movement."[23]

"Mouse" also refers to a number of Native nations, homelands, and sites of activism:

We stood up in Caledonia
manned up in Oka
got sent to Oklahoma
gathered up in Arizona
Big Mountain to Bear Butte
rallied up in South Dakota
Mohawk, Anishinob, Canada to Minnesota
Wounded Knee to California.[24]

In giving his voice to Native nations across North America and to key moments in the history of Native American activism both in Canada and in the United States, Quese IMC is here linking the movement to which he is committed to Native issues and to Native rights.

Quese IMC is well aware that people miss the political, social, and cultural elements of his music, and hence miss the movement, if they are unable or unwilling to see beyond the stereotype of *indian*. Those within the hip-hop world are just as susceptible to this blindness. In "I Am My Ancestors," a song from *The Betty Lena Project* that incorporates the elements of flow, layering, and rupture Tricia Rose identifies as critical to hip-hop and its potential for "social resistance and affirmation,"[25] the strength and power of

Quese IMC's rap are undercut by his competitors in MC battles who trot out the same old tired clichés of *indianness*:

> and it pisses me off
> when I get on a stage and MC battle
> and I am ready with punch lines
> and the guy just babbles
> making fun of my origin, my being
> and my blood's racing
> dissing my culture
> telling me to go back to the reservation
> calling me a drunk savage and everything that's degrading
> dancing around like a cartoon *indian*
> while the crowd's hooraying
> cheering like idiots
> and I'm tired of it being okay for you to make fun of my people.[26]

To counter the cartoon *indian*, Quese IMC turns to one of the primary elements of hip-hop: sampling. Rose contends that "samplers are the quintessential rap production tool;" the computers enable artists and producers to repeat and recontextualize portions of music and lyrics.[27] Rose notes, further, that sampling is a way to "pay homage, [it is] an invocation of another's voice to help you to say what you want to say."[28] There is both an artistic element and a political edge to sampling. Aram Sinnreich's interviews with musicians, producers, software developers, and sound designers revealed that artists move from "taking to making" via their personality and the vision present in the choices they make: "Thus, for configurable musicians, stylistic originality can reside in the selection of source materials, the selection of samples from those materials, the temporal and spatial arrangement of samples, the transformative techniques applied to those samples, or the hermeneutic interplay between samples that characterize the work as a whole."[29] The very act of sampling is also, at least for some, an act of resistance to regulations and industry norms. In the words of DJ Adrian, "you're subverting the dominant cultural paradigm, and turning it into something that you probably personally like. And that's what's really cool."[30]

Quese IMC samples from a wide range of sources. We are offered bits of speeches by and interviews of Malcolm X and Martin Luther King Jr., for instance, along with bits of histories chronicling Native–non-Native relations in the United States and the wrongs done to the First Peoples in the name of progress, the nation, and organized religion. For instance, "Micco

Rebels from the Sun," one of Quese's earliest recordings, begins with two samples: The first recounts an example of the dominant society's desire as it proclaims that "white settlers came to covet the rich Nez Perce land, ignoring their long friendship with the Indian Nation," while the second sounds a note of defiance with Chief Joseph's statement, "the white man has no right to come here and take our country, and we will defend this land as long as a drop of Indian blood warms the hearts of our men."[31] The song closes with the voice of history speaking first underneath the chorus and then standing starkly unaccompanied as it tells us of the promises made to Geronimo in exchange for his surrender, promises that were not kept. In traversing Indian Country from the Pacific Northwest to the Southwest and linking dislocation and imprisonment, "Micco Rebels from the Sun" effectively tells a painful chapter in the history of Native-white relations.[32]

Quese IMC recognizes that those wounds remain, rapping in *The Betty Lena Project*'s "Hey Young World" that

> It was the Spanish and European track that caused damage
> and managed to become a virus in my people who had it
> learning survival skills, but upon being befriended
> that quickly ended, when the gaping wound was opened
> with no bandage but they were candid with the Catholics
> to murder, rape, and molest the Indian people
> on the day they landed[33]

Crucially, we also hear traditional chanting underneath the lyrics of "Hey Young World." That chanting sounds a note of community and cultural practice. Here and in other tracks, then, the chanting stands in opposition to the wishes and desires of the dominant culture. We also hear Houston Tiger speaking in Muscogee Creek and the Eufaula Church Choir singing hymns in the same language on various tracks and the sound of Native drum groups in "The Young Conference" and elsewhere. Such samples correspond to Rose's notion that sampling can pay homage to those who have come before and help the artist say what she or he wants and needs to say.

Sampling can do more than simply mine an archive and use from it that which pays tribute to one's predecessors. It can also call into question the archive and the ideology that underpins it. This, too, is an act of resistance, one that Quese IMC engages in when he samples songs from American popular culture. We hear this, for instance, in "Oklahoma," the fourth track from *The Betty Lena Project*, which in the first six seconds offers the first syllable of the first word of the title song of the popular musical looped and layered to repeat the point of origin; we then hear the chuckle of Quese IMC's co-rapper on the song, as the female voices complete and repeat "Oklahoma," now layered over by other female voices repeating the phrase "we can break it, we can break it, we can make it baby."[34] At the top of this layering the rapper asks, "how you doing Quese, are you ready man?"[35] and then introduces him. In effect, the recognizable first phrase of the musical's title song is invoked not as a point of origin to be paid homage to, but as that which is in need of a supplement that takes the phrase apart. As Quese's fellow artist proclaims, "OKC will be noticed / so we cannot ignore this state."[36] With his hip-hop, Quese IMC is "goin to spark a wildfire / forest / give a culture shock to you tourists."[37]

Similarly, in "Them Country Roads" Quese IMC samples and revises "Take Me Home, Country Roads," John Denver's 1971 hit painting a bucolic and nostalgic picture of West Virginia mountain living. Here the opening follows the chord progression and melody of the pop song, only to have the downbeat of the snare and Quese's singing and revision of Denver's chorus constitute the supplement. "West Virginia" is replaced by "Native America" as "Them Country Roads" becomes a proclamation of Quese's home and a claim for Native land rights. In countering all the voices that have said to him, and to countless other Natives, that he is not going anywhere, that he is destined to be simply a statistic, Quese IMC chooses to "do things kind of different / than you've ever seen" by turning to hip-hop in order to help in the process of "taking it back you all / every song / we sing / is one step to getting our land back."[38] While in "The Bird Song" Quese IMC repeats "the movement" for emphasis, a repetition that one can argue is in keeping with an oral tradition, here both "back" and, later in the song, "a new world" are repeated in order to stress change that is a return and what the change will bring.

The samples at the opening of *Bluelight*'s "Red Zeppelin" add a layer of complexity to Quese IMC's art of the sample. A musical passage from Led Zeppelin's "What Is and What Should Never Be" is remixed to add guitar chords to either side of the sample. Here, the transformation of the sample keeps intact the meaning of the song's title while wresting it from the ahistorical fantasy that Led Zeppelin's lyrics articulate. If, as Quese IMC raps later in the song, "you know my music / you know my intent,"[39] then the audience knows that Quese is keeping before it a fusion of hip-hop, Native concerns, and the lived experiences of those marginalized by the dominant society. Far from the invitation of "What Is and What Should Never Be," where Robert Plant sings "If I were to say to you tomorrow / take my hand child come with me / to a castle I will take you,"[40] Quese IMC brings his listeners to a world where borders are policed and people of color are targeted for interrogation there.

The Led Zeppelin sample is followed by a sample of Xzibit's "Concentrate" where the hip-hop artist announces "I don't drama / I'm just gonna stomp downbeat."[41] While in the context of MC battles "concentrate" can stand, as Brett Esaki states, as an admonition for the artist to maintain her or his focus throughout the battle,[42] Xzibit repeating the word until it becomes a mantra, the lyrics of the song and its music video do not suggest that a rival MC threatens concentration. Rather, "Concentrate" reveals that women can cause one to lose one's focus. And while Xzibit can rhyme "consummate / man was made to procreate,"[43] it is women as objects of sexual desire that comes across loud and clear in both the song and its video: "hypnotized by the way she move / take your time you might arrive too soon" is followed later in the song by "Don't let yo' concentration snap / I love the way she arch her back / like how a mothafucker s'posed to handle that."[44]

Instead of a depiction of women as at least distracting, if not threatening, Quese IMC's "Red Zeppelin" features female rapper Fawksie One and what he calls "female energy / yo, that's what's up."[45] As such, Quese's stomp downbeat here, an effort to "stomp the movement" and help people to "get connected," includes, one might even say needs, females. It is, after all, Fawksie One who has the song's last word. Her rap, delivered with strong line end stops, concludes with the pronouncement that she and Quese are together.

> keeping the balance through hip hop
> masculine and feminine energy alive
> City of Lost Angels
> that's right
> Bluelight[46]

Bluelight is directed at and is from Los Angeles; it is given over to calling out what in the song "California" is described as "artsy-fartsy / art that has no content" and calling for people to join Quese in "spark[ing] the movement" against gentrification, the destruction of neighborhoods in Los Angeles, and antimigration and anti-immigration sentiments and practices.[47] As is true of the rest of Quese's music, *Bluelight* is also from Oklahoma, for, as he announces in "Empty," "I'm rooted deep / with deep roots."[48] With its emphasis on both the male and the female, "Red Zeppelin" makes clear the cultural ground into which Quese IMC is rooted and from which he speaks. According to Duane Champagne, southeastern Native nations such as the Seminoles share "a cosmological view of order in the universe"[49] and recognize that if the universe's forces are in balance, then so too will the human world be in balance.[50] As a consequence, the Seminole, Creek, and other southeastern Nations value order and harmony. As Patricia Wickman writes in *The Tree That Bends: Discourse, Power, and the Survival of the Maskoki People*, "all things exist in complementarity to each other, rather than in opposition. The Giver of Breath and humans, men and women, and humans and nature all function in a symbiosis."[51] "Red Zeppelin" speaks directly from this worldview when it announces that the balance of masculine and feminine are maintained through hip-hop.

Balance, order, and harmony can be maintained through ceremony, of course, and Quese sings in "Them Country Roads" of a ceremony DB, which is to say a ceremony downbeat, that will lead to recovery of land and renewal of tradition. In "Them Country Roads" the ceremony invoked is a sweat; in "Greencorn," the song on *Bluelight* that follows Quese's claim in "Bounce" that he "grabbed a mic and my culture,"[52] Quese IMC references a specific traditional Seminole and Creek ceremony of renewal and healing. The personal and the ceremonial come together in the track's opening narrative when Quese tells the story of his great-great-grandmother, Martha Lena Chubco, who at thirteen was captured by U.S. soldiers during the Seminole Wars of the nineteenth century, was made to walk to Indian Territory, and grew up to be a respected elder and healer. This is the lineage that Quese honors by singing songs that are "culture music / movement music."[53]

The bridge between the story of his great-great-grandmother and Quese IMC's music from the underground, where he and DJ Shock B are "known as the sound chiefs / culture shock / camp / please,"[54] is made with a single word: "*mvto*." Mixed with echo so that the second syllable stretches into the first bars of the music, the Maskoke word meaning "thank you" is an acknowledgment of connection and, potentially at least, community. It also resonates with the centrality of reciprocity in the Maskoke worldview. Wickman notes that in order to understand the importance of reciprocity to the People, one needs to recognize that there is "a reciprocal relationship of the Maskokalgi with all the other elements and forces of the universe."[55] Because medicine "serve[s] as the medium of communication and interaction between seen and unseen forces in the cosmos,"[56] it makes sense that it is in song, itself a medium of communication and interaction, that Quese IMC gives thanks to his maternal kin and continues the cycle of healing of which his great-great-grandmother was a part.

The two "interludes" in *The Betty Lena Project* offering Native voices highlight how the loss of one's language can lead to the loss of self and community for Native peoples. Thus, it makes sense that language and ceremony are linked in "Greencorn" when Quese tells his audience that his great-great-grandmother was a *heles-hayv*, a traditional medicine maker or healer, and the connection is reiterated in the following song, "Herkv, Herkv." There, elder Houston Tiger offers a chant of peace and goodness in Maskoke prior to Quese's painful rendering of impoverished streets and abandoned neighborhoods where children are abused and adults abuse themselves with alcohol and other drugs. Tiger's slow chant or song continues underneath Quese's rap, suggesting that peace and goodness are the counter to the story being told. Quese announces the path to peace and balance when he says that Natives will sweat in order to never forget where they have come from and to pass on that knowledge to future generations.

In the song immediately following the first interlude, "Quese IMC," Quese links who he is both to where he is from and to Culture Shock Camp—the latter is the name he and his brother DJ Shock B use when performing together, the title for the Oklahoma hip-hop summit the two of them held beginning in the mid-1990s, and the name of the outreach to Native youth that they work with. In those endeavors, the brothers combine hip-hop with traditional song and prayer. One is just as likely to see and hear Pawnee and Seminole song and prayer chanted to the beat of hand drums as to see DJ Shock B creating at the turntables, Quese freestyling in the break beats, and Pawnee/Yakama artist Bunky EchoHawk creating a painting onstage. As Quese said in a September 2011 interview, Culture Shock Camp is about "organizing our community . . . [the] movement of our people, empowering our people."[57] Culture Shock Camp gives a shock to the tourists, to be sure, one that opens their eyes and minds to the creative energies and abiding concerns of Native youth.

Given Culture Shock Camp's commitment to tradition and innovation, it is fitting that the song released as a single by Quese IMC and DJ Shock B, along with guest artist Eddika Organista, includes a recognition of the need "to create the balance."[58] This balance is only possible "Because I'm moving with the cosmos / with the message."[59] In Muskoke cosmogony, one moves with the cosmos by recognizing the reciprocal nature of the world and acting accordingly. This "enables equilibrium to be maintained."[60] The message of balance, not stasis, must reach into and inform human-to-human relations as well, for it is only in recognizing, for instance, that social power is relational, that the power is conferred, and that one must wield that power in the name of and for the good of the community that the cosmos remains in balance.[61]

The physical and political movement that Quese IMC calls for through his hip-hop, then, is rooted in Pawnee and Seminole cultures. It is also pan-Indigenous and transnational. Just as he invokes sites of Indigenous activism across Native North America, so too does he turn to the voices and words of guest artists whose roots reach from, for instance, the Big Island of Hawai'i and the land south of the United States–Mexico international border. This helps to make the music a hybrid space or contact zone where sounds and words meet and mingle and are configured in the name of community and change. For example, in "Rebel Music" Quese IMC and Chicano hip-hop artist Cempoalli 20 rap about the importance of making connections over a combination of reggae rhythms and a dance track bass line:

> We are building
> from place to place
> we are building
> from nation to nation
> we are building
> communication
> we are building
> liberation.[62]

Born because "we got new vision," the call to build bridges emanates from Los Angeles, to be sure, but its claim to have "no more / mental prisons / no more / self-inflicted incisions" resonates well beyond Los Angeles as the audience is encouraged to "make a change / build a bridge / fight the power / for all the kids."[63]

Being aware, then, is born of the recognition of one's cultural roots and the connections to be made both within and beyond one's community and nation. In short, one's being is aware, awareness is one's being. More must be said, though, for Quese IMC strikes me as aware of the complex relationship between communication and liberation. To see this, we need to return to sampling.

In *The Betty Lena Project*, Quese IMC samples two very different recorded messages. The first, in "Mad," is a message from his father. In that song and elsewhere, Quese chronicles the hard truth of his father's struggles with alcohol, with the rage that would boil up at times when a twelve pack would not cause everything to "just fade away."[64] Alcohol contributed to his parents' divorce and the beginnings of an alternating pattern of presence and absence as the young Marcus would spend time first at his father's and then at his mother's home. Quese raps about how good it is to see his father get his life back after beating the trap of alcohol, after which we hear the beep of an answering machine followed by his father's voice. The second message, from "Billie Jean Left Hand," is left on Quese's mobile. The song opens with the voice mail system of the phone network giving the day and time, followed by Billie Jean's message. Here, as is not the case with his father's message in "Mad," the sample gets sampled, as portions of the message we first hear at the beginning are repeated midway through the song.

The father's recorded voice in "Mad" needs to be situated as part of the song's foregrounding of and emphasis on media and recording technologies. The song begins in the studio, with Quese checking the microphone and asking for more volume in his headphones. The stress on amplification gives way as the conversation continues to an explanation of the song that Quese, the producer, and the engineer are about to record. However, we only hear Quese's side of the conversation. As such, the opening of "Mad" serves to highlight presence and absence and how technology can mediate both. The crew in the sound booth are present but, because they are silenced on the recording, they are at the same time absent. Quese's father, on the other hand, is absent both from the point of the message—he has to leave a message because he and his son are not together at the same time and in the same place—and from its reception. Nevertheless, the technology enables him to be present even as he is absent. This, then, is the promise of recording technologies.

It is also the pain of recording technologies, a pain sounded with the recorded message to Quese from Billie Jean Left Hand on the day before she took her life. While Quese loops the final word in the phrase "That last message,"[65] and in doing so puts a stress on the recording, the sixteen-year-old's recorded voice echoes as a reminder that the young Standing Rock Native will be forever absent. Here loss is made meaningful, although by no means any less painful, with the sample of "We've Only Just Begun." In *Rhythm Science*, Paul Miller, aka DJ Spooky That Subliminal Kid, notes that the defamiliarization at the heart of the sample effectively links sampling and the uncanny: "Sound and image divorce and reconfigure before they unite in the mix. . . . The samples and fragments speak the unspoken," speak what Freud called the uncanny.[66] The familiar becomes unfamiliar, the canny, uncanny, as we try to make sense of the Carpenters' 1970 hit in Quese's song. It is not enough to say that the song is included for the purpose of irony. What led to Billie Jean Left Hand's suicide calls the vision of "We've Only Just Begun" into question.

At some fundamental and painful level, Billie Jean Left Hand's life was marked by a succession of beginnings that led, I think, to its ultimate end. According to Left Hand's grandmother, Billie Jean's legal custody changed approximately thirty times.[67] In and out of foster homes, Left Hand often had no one to turn to, again according to her grandmother, and over time began to suffer from depression. While Karen Carpenter can croon about a wedding day marked by "white lace and promises" followed by "horizons that are new to us"[68] to be shared by the couple, Billie Jean Left Hand's life was marked by a horizon neither new nor rich with promise. Quese IMC recognizes that Billie Jean's suicide is connected to part of the ongoing "war that has been waged upon our people for far too long."[69] His song honors Billie Jean Left Hand's life and spirit and offers a message of strength and healing for Native youth and their parents as it makes uncanny the Carpenters' song in order to redefine "we" with the Native and their lives at the center, redefine "only just begun" as part of a call for change and action made to Native families, and tacitly posits a new "we," America—one not marked by social injustice, racism, discrimination, and oppression.

The reference to the national game in "That Good Medicine" from *The Betty Lena Project* suggests that the song would have America before the audience.

> I'm a reserve observer, observing the reserve
> ninth inning, bases loaded, full count
> he's throwing the curve.
> One down, let's toss, screw it, let's take the whole thing,
> take my chance on one swing,
> with everything I've got,
> one shot,
> slow motion dream,
> anticipation in my team.[70]

Like Quese, who hits the ball out of the park, "The Good Medicine" handles the curve the nation that is the United States throws with both its initial and final invocation of Sam Cooke's "Chain Gang." With the first invocation, the song indicates how the settler Nation and its ideology imprisons. Underneath the final invocation of Cooke's song, Quese tells his audience what is at stake: "life / yeah, yeah / freedom."[71] Understood within the context of "Chain Gang" and "That Good Medicine," "Life" resonates both as being alive and as doing time in prison. It is only through good medicine, medicine rooted in tribal culture and worldview, that freedom, and therefore life, is possible.[72]

With freedom comes a call to action. Quese recognizes that mass media all too often precludes action, precludes movement, singing in "I Resist":

we're hungry for the knowledge
because we've been misled
misled by the media, misled by the news
update, update, they want you to stay tuned
propaganda on the screens
but the mental breakthrough
will curb the mind control
that keeps you satisfied and glued
to your couch and the screen
that keeps you fat and amused.[73]

Music, as Quese suggests in "Reflection," is a way back to the essence that one can have lost touch with if one is caught up in the small screens containing "text / messages of murder, technology, and mayhem."[74] Quese asks his listeners, "Are you good, you ready, warrior steady?" ("Reflection") while deploying the technology of recording, of representation, and the genre of hip-hop so that he can articulate a warrior stance for himself and others. For the Maskoke people, that stance is ultimately given over to maintaining balance in the cosmos.[75] So it is that, as we have seen, Quese raps with Fawksie One, joins with Watasun on "The Bird Song" to make a plea for the defense of the natural world, and, with Hopi rapper Casper, sings "I Resist." There, in and through song, Quese and Casper call on the audience, Native and non-Native, to join them in resisting authority that does harm to Indigenous peoples, especially, and to the earth. It remains for us, Native and non-Native, to hear Quese IMC's call and "stand with our drums at the protest."[76]

NOTES

1. On film and the audience's desire to see more, see, for instance, Levi, "Crevice and the Stitch," 41–42.
2. Quoted in Rotman, *Becoming Beside Ourselves*, 146, n. 5.
3. I follow Gerald Vizenor's practice of italicizing *indian* lower case here in order to signify the representation created and perpetuated by the dominant society.
4. Rose, *Black Noise*, 2.
5. Ibid., 22.
6. Taylor, "Bad World Music," 93.

7. Radio interview, 23 September 2011, http://www.blogtalkradio.com/nativetrailblazers/2011/09/23/native-hip-hop-artist—quese-imc-on-native-trailblazers.
8. Interview, n.d., http:///www.thehiphopherald.com/Interviews.php.
9. Quese IMC, "Superbrightstar," *The Betty Lena Project.*
10. Ibid.
11. Ibid.
12. Quese IMC, "Best Times of Our Lives," *Hand Drums for Whiskey Bottles.*
13. Ibid.
14. Quese IMC, "House," *Bluelight.*
15. Ibid.
16. Ibid.
17. Quese IMC, "Rebel Music," *Bluelight.*
18. Quese IMC, "Empty," *The Betty Lena Project.*
19. Ibid.
20. Quese IMC, "Mouse," *Bluelight.*
21. Ibid.
22. Quese IMC, "The Youth Conference," *Bluelight.*
23. Quese IMC, "The Bird Song," *Hand Drums for Whiskey Bottles.*
24. Quese IMC, "Mouse."
25. Rose, *Black Noise*, 39.
26. Quese IMC, "I Am My Ancestors," *The Betty Lena Project.*
27. Rose, 73.
28. Ibid., 79.
29. Sinnreich, *Mashed Up*, 126, 127.
30. Quoted in ibid., 185.
31. Quese IMC, "Micco Rebels from the Sun" (single).
32. Carrie Sheffield's 2011 essay on Native hip-hop artists rightly recognizes that hip-hop can be an effective way to address historical trauma and the cycles of abuse it engenders while reaching a youthful, Native audience. However, Sheffield's argument is limited to the extent that it does not attend fully to rap as a genre; nor does it make any reference to cultural specificity in its examination of two Native hip-hop artists. Thus, while she writes that both Maniac: the Siouxpernatural and Night Shade sing of "the contemporary impact of historical trauma [that] can be seen wherever they look on their reservations. Poverty, gang warfare, and substance abuse plague the reservations in their songs" (Sheffield, "Native American Hip-Hop," 104), Sheffield neither identifies the reservations nor the artists' tribal affiliations. Therefore, both historical particularity and, crucially, specific Native worldview(s) and paths toward healing remain unarticulated. See Sheffield, "Native American Hip-Hop."

33. Quese IMC, "Hey Young World," *The Betty Lena Project.*
34. Quese IMC, "Oklahoma," *The Betty Lena Project.*
35. Ibid.
36. Ibid.
37. Ibid.
38. Quese IMC, "Them Country Roads," *The Betty Lena Project.*
39. Quese IMC, "Red Zeppelin," *Bluelight.*
40. Led Zeppelin, "What Is and What Should Never Be," *Led Zeppelin II*, 1969.
41. Xzibit, "Concentrate," *Full Circle*, 2006.
42. Esaki, "Desperately Seeking Silence," 383.
43. Xzibit, "Concentrate."
44. Ibid.
45. Quese IMC, "Red Zeppelin."
46. Ibid.
47. Quese IMC, "California," *Bluelight.*
48. Quese IMC,
49. Champagne, *Social Order and Political Change*, 21.
50. Ibid., 22.
51. Wickman, *The Tree That Bends*, 47.
52. Quese IMC, "Bounce."
53. Quese IMC, "Greencorn," *Bluelight*, 2008.
54. Ibid.
55. Wickman, *The Tree That Bends*, 46.
56. Ibid.
57. Radiointerview,23September2011,http://www.blogtalkradio.com/nativetrailblazers/2011/09/23/native-hip-hop-artist—quese-imc-on-native-trailblazers.
58. Culture Shock Camp with Eddika Organista, "What Is Freedom if We Die?" (single).
59. Ibid.
60. Wickman, *The Tree That Bends*, 47.
61. Ibid., 66.
62. Quese IMC, "Rebel Music."
63. Ibid.
64. Quese IMC, "Mad," *The Betty Lena Project.*
65. Quese IMC, "Billie Jean Left Hand," *The Betty Lena Project.*
66. DJ Spooky That Subliminal Kid / Paul D. Miller, *Rhythm Science*, 25, 28.
67. "Cheyenne River Sioux Working to Curb Teen Suicides," 2002, http://www.indiancountrynews.info/fullstory.cfm-ID=236.htm.
68. The Carpenters, "We've Only Just Begun," *Close to You*, 1970.

69. Interview, *Native Men's Magazine*, n.d., http://www.nativemenmag.com/quese.html.
70. Quese IMC, "That Good Medicine," *The Betty Lena Project.*
71. Ibid.
72. One can compare "That Good Medicine" with Tracie Morris's "Chain Gang" in terms of each song's deconstructive impulse. In Morris's words, "Chain Gang" and some of her other sound poems "usually have a cultural resonance that gives them more currency, more value than the literal meaning as well as a physical premise. I didn't reference the songwriters . . . because I think it's the deconstruction of the version as sung, the particular sound of them even more than the text (in terms of visceral recognition) that determines their value" (Morris, "Poetic Statement," 212). While Quese produces a supplement to "Chain Gang" with his counterpoint to the chorus, Morris opens up that chorus in order to emphasize work, the physicality of labor, and the cultural and historical reality of imprisonment for African Americans. In the words of Christine Hume, "Morris radically unhinges the original," "summons the restiveness and physical toil embedded in Cooke's refrain . . . and adrenalizes it to signify alienation, exhausted patience, anger, and threat" (Hume, "Improvisational Insurrection," 230). Both Morris and Quese IMC, then, take a part in order to take apart the song in the name of liberation. See Hume, "Improvisational Insurrection."
73. Quese IMC, "I Resist," *Hand Drums for Whiskey Bottles.*
74. Quese IMC, "Reflection," *Hand Drums for Whiskey Bottles.*
75. Wickman, *The Tree That Bends*, 95–96.
76. Quese IMC, "I Resist."

WORKS CITED

Browner, Tara. *Heartbeat of the People: Music and Dance of the Northern Pow-wow.* Urbana: University of Illinois Press, 2002.

Champagne, Duane. *Social Order and Political Change: Constitutional Governments among the Cherokee, the Choctaw, the Chickasaw, and the Creek*. Palo Alto, CA: Stanford University Press, 1992.

Connell, John, and Chris Gibson. *Sound Tracks: Popular Music, Identity, and Place.* London: Routledge, 2003.

DJ Spooky That Subliminal Kid / Paul D. Miller. *Rhythm Science*. Cambridge, MA: Mediawork/MIT Press, 2004.

Esaki, Brett. "Desperately Seeking Silence: Youth Culture's Unspoken Need." *Cross Currents* (Fall 2007): 379–390.

Hume, Christine. "Improvisational Insurrection: The Sound Poetry of Tracie Morris." In *American Poets in the 21st Century: The New Poetics*, ed. Claudia Rankine and Lisa Sewell, 215–235. Middletown, CT: Wesleyan University Press, 2007.

Levi, Pavle. "The Crevice and the Stitch." *Critical Quarterly* 51.3 (October 2009): 41–42.

Martin, Jack, and Margaret Mauldin. *A Dictionary of Creek/Muskogee*. Lincoln: University of Nebraska Press, 2000.

Morris, Tracy. "Poetic Statement: Sound Making Notes." In *American Poets in the 21st Century: The New Poetics*, ed. Claudia Rankine and Lisa Sewell, 210–215. Middletown, CT: Wesleyan University Press, 2007.

Native American Rights Fund. *Visions for the Future: A Celebration of Young Native American Artists*. Vol. 1. Golden, CO: Fulcrum Publishing, 2007.

Nielson, Erik. "'We Are Gone': 'Black Steel' and the Technologies of Presence and Absence." *Popular Communication* 8 (2010): 120–131.

Quese IMC. *The Betty Lena Project*. 2006.

———. *Bluelight*. 2008.

———. *Hand Drums for Whiskey Bottles*. 2011.

Rose, Tricia. *Black Noise: Rap Music and Black Culture in Contemporary America*. Hanover, NH: Wesleyan University Press, 1994.

Rotman, Brian. *Becoming Beside Ourselves: The Alphabet, Ghosts, and Distributed Human Being*. Durham, NC: Duke University Press, 2008.

Sheffield, Carrie. "Native American Hip-Hop and Historical Trauma." *Studies in American Indian Literature* 23.2 (Fall 2011): 94–110.

Sinnreich, Aram. *Mashed Up: Music, Technology, and the Rise of Configurable Culture*. Amherst: University of Massachusetts Press, 2010.

Taylor, Timothy. "Bad World Music." In *Bad Music: The Music We Love to Hate*, ed. Chris Washburne and Maiken Derno, 83–103. New York: Routledge, 2004.

Ullestad, Neal. "American Indian Rap and Reggae: Dancing 'to the Beat of a Different Drummer.'" *Popular Music and Society* 23.2 (1999): 63–90.

Weheliye, Alexander. "'Feenin': Posthuman Voices in Contemporary Black Popular Music." *Social Text* 20.2 (Summer 2002): 21–46.

Wickman, Patricia. *The Tree That Bends: Discourse, Power and the Survival of the Maskoki People*. Tuscaloosa: University of Alabama Press, 1999.

Jim Jarmusch's *Dead Man* Revisited

Still Thwarting All Cultural and Cinematic Notions of Alterity

CHRISTINE PLICHT

"The Vision of Christ that thou dost see
Is my Vision's Greatest Enemy"

—"NOBODY" IN DEAD MAN

THESE ARE NOBODY'S WORDS, YET THEY CAN BE QUOTED. Subsequently, somewhere, a certain Nobody must exist. But how can you be somebody and Nobody at the same time? At first glance, this seems to constitute an oxymoron. This contradictoriness introduces the idea of opposition, of difference and antagonism; the evoked "greatest enemy," for instance, is the ultimate opposition. But however adverse, contradictory, or perhaps harmonious any specific relation between two elements might be, what remains is the need to negotiate the terms of the relation.

The quoted words come from a Native American film character in Jim Jarmusch's *Dead Man* (1995). He is called Nobody, which aids in clarifying the quote's origin, but does not entirely do so. Keeping the quoted words and their type of language in mind, one must recognize that they are not what we would typically expect Native American film characters to express. Indeed, Nobody quotes from *The Everlasting Gospel* by English poet William Blake.[1] The Native American quoting an English poet unsettles the seemingly definite oppositions that this quote hints at even more. Nothing is as it seems at first glance, and this is just the beginning of a complex cinematic adventure.

This essay explores how Jim Jarmusch's cinematic approach, although already nearly two decades old, addresses certain processes behind the construction and mediation of alterity, exemplarily focusing on Native American alterity. In contrast to many other films that feature Native American characters, mainstream or otherwise, *Dead Man* stages and mediates the inevitable issue of alterity in an unequaled manner that deeply challenges our concepts of the very subject.[2] A brief overview of the underlying theoretical notions of alterity that *Dead Man* takes on and reworks leads to the analysis of a variety of specific examples from the film. The latter highlights what I suggest is the extraordinary achievement of escaping common representational difficulties by translating the processes behind alterity into an all-encompassing and still novel cinematic mode of destabilization. Thereby, mechanisms are revealed that often remain disguised to a greater public due to simplistic and stereotypical representation even when equality is explicitly suggested and promoted with the best intentions.

Talking about alterity necessarily requires paying attention to Emmanuel Lévinas. The Jewish Lithuanian (later French) philosopher and phenomenologist certainly is among the most influential thinkers contributing to the subject of alterity. He is widely regarded as the first to develop theories on this matter. Nevertheless, even such an eminently respectable mind has to turn to and reference others before him in order to form and present an opinion. In *Alterity and Transcendence* Lévinas explains: "[Martin] Buber says that when I say you, I know that I am saying you to someone who is an *I*, and who says you to me."[3] This statement suggests equality between the I and the You that Lévinas feels the need to question. He challenges the reciprocity of Buber's I-You relation and detects "asymmetry" and what he calls a "radical inequality" in all relations for, initially, the addressed other is the weaker part in the relationship. Before knowledge can be gained and any kind of additional layer can influence the relation, alterity is already there and cannot be avoided. It forces us to deal with difference. Even though the specific nature of the relation between two parties might not be defined yet, it is nevertheless clear that the two are never equal in the direct confrontation with each other.

One must thoroughly pay attention to the contradictory and reflexive nature of alterity in any analysis regarding its representations. Discussing a possible basis for "alterity politics" in addition to "identity politics,"

Jeffrey T. Nealon finds even clearer words as he presents a very similar notion of alterity. He speaks of "constructing an ethical *alterity politics* that considers identity as beholden and responsive first and foremost to the other."[4] The self is not alone in the process; the other has a voice in it, too. Nealon warns of the "tendency to situate others while resisting its own situatedness."[5] The examples in the second part of this essay highlight how *Dead Man* actively prevents us from situating anything without letting it reflect back upon ourselves by immediately thwarting every impression during the course of the movie. It underlines the concept of otherness as a two-way affair rather than a one-way street, where the "I" would have absolute power over all representations.

Dan Zahavi furthers this notion in so far as that although I am internally self-aware while experiencing confrontation with the Other, I am also completely exposed to whatever the Other makes of me. But because this remains somewhat external, Zahavi concludes: "I experience the Other's gaze as an alienation."[6] A twofold power play is evident. Referring back to Sartre, Zahavi also puts emphasis on the role of speech as an important factor in the alienation I undergo and the quest for insight into what the Other takes me to be: "I use *language* and adopt a third-person perspective on myself."[7] We can no longer just be, for we always define ourselves in relation to something else or other. "I am no longer simply 'here,' but next to the door, or on the couch," Zahavi explains.[8]

Language and communication are central to *Dead Man*'s strategy of exposing the processes behind alterity as the examples will also show. Before, however, it is important to consider Michael Taussig's conclusion "that alterity is every inch a relationship, not a thing in itself."[9] He demonstrates that contradictoriness, active participation, and expectations play an extremely important role in the concept of alterity: "Mimetic excess as a form of human capacity potentiated by post-coloniality provides a welcome opportunity to live subjunctively as neither subject nor object of history but as both, at one and the same time."[10] This correlates with the atmosphere in *Dead Man*, which conveys the impression that anything is possible at all times. Because conditions never remain uncommented on or are presented as definite and because the process of negotiation is always stressed, *Dead Man* allows for the constant flexibility of being both at the same time or nothing. Conditions, relations, images, and all impressions the viewer might get are never stable. They must constantly be renegotiated.

Last, criticizing colonial discourse, Homi K. Bhabha connects the idea of ambivalence to discriminatory power. As is well known, ambivalence is central to Bhabha's notion of the stereotype, simultaneously believing "in its recognition of difference and the disavowal of it."[11] He calls for a "shift from the *identification* of images as positive or negative, to an understanding of the *process of subjectification* made possible (and plausible) through stereotypical discourse."[12] The understanding of the background processes by unmasking the modes of their production can be considered the ultimate opportunity in any alterity discourse. Displaying the ability to do so constitutes the exceptional quality of *Dead Man*. What Bhabha calls "the fantasy of origin and identity"[13] becomes exposed in so many ways that the following examples must be considered merely a glimpse into the film's innumerous layers of negotiating seemingly fixed boundaries and oppositions.

Dead Man carefully deconstructs alterity. It takes on and touches upon traditional ways of representation but then adds a twist to them, revealing their lacks and problems of reference while simultaneously offering a new draft. Along the lines of "The journey is the reward" *Dead Man* sketches a notion of unmasking any claim for authenticity, or fixity and stability in general, as a trap, and the alternative is to acknowledge the background processes and the notion that authenticity might not exist. Authenticity is presented as relative to many ever-changing influences and present forms of agency, but never as absolute or stable. *Dead Man* seems to pay the utmost attention to this idea of alterity without clearly defined extremes. This is reflected in nearly all of the film's elements, such as the plot structure, the constellation of characters, the cinematography, and even more specific features like the use of language or music, to name just a few.

In brief, *Dead Man* tells the nineteenth-century story of William Blake (played by Johnny Depp), an accountant from Cleveland who travels to an American frontier town called Machine in order to take up a new job. As early as the opening shots, the film establishes many contrasts. In black and white we see, for example, a journey from east to west as well as the town named Machine that is situated in the middle of the wilderness. Many more extremes emerge, but the film is very quick to add a twist to every single impression. Between the black and white are countless shades of gray. But not only do nuances glimmer in-between; what is presented as dark or light also changes frequently in the cinematography. Machine could be the stronghold of a supposed civilization on the wild frontier, but it appears to be even wilder than the wilderness at second glance. As the viewer learns quickly that what seems to be given and understood is constantly destabilized, Blake must learn in Machine that his job offer is no longer effective. After a series of unfortunate events, the overwhelmed Blake shoots a man

Figure 1. Collage of Blake's changing appearance in the course of *Dead Man*. (Screenshots from *Dead Man*, from top left to bottom right: [00:01:32], [00:38:25], [01:15:50], [01:33:30], [01:36:33], [01:50:30])

in self-defense and runs off to the woods injured, soon chased by bounty hunters. Nobody (played by Gary Farmer), a Native American traveling on his own, finds him and after unsuccessfully trying to remove the bullet from his chest, decides to accompany him to the northwest coast in order to prepare for his death. Several events lead to Blake killing more people and finally steer the two to a Makah village on the Pacific Coast. There, Nobody negotiates with the Makah people and arranges for a ceremony that sends Blake out onto the ocean to drift off in a canoe and reach "the other side." On the shore, the only surviving bounty hunter approaches Nobody, and both immediately shoot at and kill each other.

The personal background of the two protagonists alone illustrates how multifaceted and ambiguous these characters are. The viewer gains certain impressions, just to learn that more is to be discovered. William Blake's character undergoes drastic changes. Being introduced as an innocent accountant and part of western society, he turns into an unpredictable outlaw in the wilderness. Possibly, he is perceived as turning or "playing" Native, yet he does not at all identify as such or even understand what is happening with and around him.

Nobody also reveals several layers to his personality that we would not usually expect from stereotypical Native American film characters, such as his knowledge of English poetry and his status as outsider among other Natives.

Yet even atypical character traits are not left uncommented on, as this would indeed unsettle some traditional conceptions but simply replace them with new one-dimensional representations. Although stereotypes are also employed in *Dead Man*, superiority or preference is never established because of the countless facets and twists. The viewer does not, and I would argue cannot, favor one of the protagonists as both have their flaws and likable features, surprising qualities, and stereotypical traits all at the same time. Furthermore, they change frequently and can be perceived as something else with each new context in which their depiction places them. *Dead Man* challenges the viewer to develop a differentiated assessment of the characters, as it is complicated to define antitheses not knowing for certain what the theses are. The complexity of the characters forces the viewer to reflect on what William Blake and Nobody represent, which is difficult to grasp as conventional images are employed but deconstructed and left for us to rearrange and give meaning to.

Aside from the complex personal background of the characters, their names and the way the film plays with them add to the most ambivalent representation of the seemingly oppositional figures. Nobody calls William Blake a dead man, although he repeatedly claims: "I'm not dead!" Blake does not understand what Nobody is trying to say, and we have to consider that there might not even be a singular, definite meaning to his words. "Then you *are* a dead man," proclaims Nobody after getting to know Blake's real name, taking him for the poet William Blake, whom Blake has never even heard of.

Now the confusion is almost at its peak, but then Nobody himself explains where his name originates from. After returning from England to America, others in his tribe call him He Who Talks Loud Saying Nothing, hinting at the words of the white people that he learned to speak in England. Nobody, however, breaks with the tribe so hostile after his return and prefers to be called Nobody. He refuses to be given a Native name and also dismisses the obvious alternative of adopting an English name. This clearly highlights his in-betweenness and lack of belonging, but it also emphasizes the various possibilities of (self-)identification. Through the active choice of his name, Nobody appropriates, to a certain extent, the process of being named, yet he does so acknowledging the influences of external attributions.

The ambiguity of the name Nobody is also drawn on in the film. When Blake doubtfully asks what would happen if the group they are about to approach killed him, Nobody answers, "Nobody will observe," suggesting both the danger Blake is getting into as well as his loyal help. But this is not an ability exclusive to Nobody. Blake also makes use of the ambiguity, which points out that the limitations of language affect everyone and undermines possible preconceptions about the articulateness of people from any culture. When the trappers ask Blake who he was traveling with, his answer is simple: "I'm with Nobody."

Naming is always a process closely tied to speech. The fact that we have a name for something or somebody does not mean that we have defined and sealed the true nature of the thing or person. The words we use do not carry meaning in themselves, and this becomes evident when we take a look at how communication processes are produced in the film.

Even the seemingly simple case of communication among civilized Westerners is unsettled and nuanced. William Blake, for example, must learn from the illiterate train fireman, whom he meets on his journey to Machine, that some words can be meaningless, although they are written out. When the fireman inquires the reason for Blake's trip, he replies:

> **Blake:** (*silenced for a moment*) Well, I received a letter . . . from Dickinson's Metalworks assuring me of a job there.
> **Fireman:** (*looking at the letter*) Is that so . . .
> **Blake:** Yes, I'm an accountant.
> **Fireman:** I wouldn't know, because I don't read. But I'll tell you one thing for sure. I wouldn't trust no words written down on no piece of paper. Especially from no Dickinson out in the town of Machine. You're just as likely to find your own grave.

On the one hand, language is unmasked as highly unstable and also, in parts, misleading, even among people who all speak the same language. On the other hand, Nobody is not better off considering the communication processes his life involves him in; he descends from two different tribes.[14] This circumstance forces him to acquire a flexible use of language. In addition, he learned to speak English during his time as a captive in England, which puts him in a position that could be described as even more in-between. Then, at the end of his journey with Blake, he negotiates with the Makah, making use of even another language. While speaking several languages surely is a helpful quality, he still is a loner. His path illustrates that the ability to oscillate between extremes and even identification with multiple identities is no true solution either, or that it necessarily enables some kind of belonging. "I was left to wander the earth alone. I am Nobody," he concludes after revealing his life story to Blake.

Considering how Blake and Nobody are both confronted with an extreme unreliability of language among what, at first glance, could be perceived as their people, it could be an option to solve all this by writing a new and unique way of communicating with each other into their story. Jim Jarmusch, however, does not take this easy, misleading way out. He continues to add more layers of uncertainty. Indeed, Blake and Nobody find a way to communicate; yet this leads only to partial understanding. Nobody speaks English, therefore it is easy for Blake to recognize the words he uses. However, by implementing the poetry of William Blake (something Blake is not familiar with) on the one hand and Native sayings (which are all the more enigmatic to Blake) on the other, Blake only understands the words that Nobody speaks, but most of the time he cannot grasp what Nobody wants to say:

> Some of the Blake adages Nobody quotes—such as "The eagle never lost so much time as when he submitted to learn of the crow" . . . from *Proverbs of Hell*—sound like Native American sayings to Blake and to us, and conversely some of Nobody's own pronouncements sound like the poetry of Blake.[15]

The words' meaning remains unclear to Blake, although those words are spoken in his mother tongue.

The following scene addresses many of the significant issues regarding the communication between William Blake and Nobody. The ambiguity of Native beliefs, English poetry, and even conceptions of being dead as well as the nature and qualities of names are taken up in these few sentences:

> **Nobody:** The round stones beneath the earth have spoken through the fire.
> **Blake:** What?
> **Nobody:** Things, which are alike, in nature grow to look alike, and the speaking stones have lain a long time looking at the sun.
> **Blake:** The speaking stones?
> **Nobody:** Some believe they descend with the lightning, but I believe they are on the ground and are projected downward by the bolt. Did you kill the white man who killed you?
> **Blake:** I'm not dead. Am I?
> **Nobody:** What name were you given at birth, stupid white man?
> **Blake:** Blake. William Blake.
> **Nobody:** Is this a lie? Or a white man's trick?
> **Blake:** No, I'm William Blake.
> **Nobody:** Then you *are* a dead man!
> **Blake:** I'm sorry. I don't . . . I don't understand.

> **Nobody:** Is your name really William Blake?
> **Blake:** Yes.
> **Nobody:** Every Night & every Morn / Some to Misery are born. / Every Morn & every Night / Some are Born to sweet delight / Some are Born to sweet delight / Some are Born to Endless Night.[16]
> **Blake:** I don't understand.
> **Nobody:** But I understand William Blake. You were a poet and a painter. And now you are a killer of white men. You must rest now, William Blake. Some are born to sweet delight, some are born to endless night.

Yet again, Jarmusch adds another dimension by not simply leaving us with unsettled stereotypes. He also shows the possibility to actively participate in the process of alterity. When Blake approaches two bounty hunters and is asked whether he is William Blake (meaning the outlaw he has become), he answers: "Yes, I am. Do you know my poetry?" Immediately afterward he starts shooting at the hunters and kills both. Although Blake had to learn that language is highly ambiguous and although he still does not know who the poet William Blake is, he is able to pick up the questions that arise from the use of language and to work with them.

The unreliability of language is also drawn upon in a few other conversations that illustrate quite comically how difficult it is to employ language effectively, even if it is your own. When the trappers sit around the fire, for example, one has to explain the meaning of a word to another. Shortly after, the second trapper comments on a story told by the first one: "That's terrible!" "It's horrible," the first agrees, only to be confronted with the insistence of the supposedly stupider one: "Terrible is what it is!" Thus, we learn that even the white men are not flawless in the use of their language.

The multiple layers of language and its use emphasize how much attention *Dead Man* pays to such issues, neither relying on language itself nor on its application in creating an understanding between two parties, whether they are foreign or known to each other. We have to consider, however, that we can never be certain about Blake's and Nobody's awareness of these issues. It seems that they develop some kind of insight, yet are somewhat stuck, which underlines once again that active negotiation is required at all times.

Turning from the level of storyline and language to imagery, the depiction of nature quickly comes to the fore. Landscapes are often employed as stereotypical elements in films that deal with encounters between Native Americans and the white man. But as *Dead Man* is very much lacking a classical white hero, it is also lacking the stereotypical depiction of Native Americans as comfortably at home in the uncivilized wilderness—for example, the Great Plains or the woods, as the film version of *The Last of the Mohicans* prominently shows. Everything that happens to Blake seems to be written onto a blank sheet of paper. Beginning with the train ride in the very first scenes, nothing he experiences seems to be caused by conscious decisions. On the vision quest that his journey also is, it is difficult to find extensive wide-angle use of nature imagery comparable to, for example, *The Last of the Mohicans* or *Dances with Wolves*. This is due to *Dead Man*'s overall approach of using almost exclusively very narrow shots, thereby emphasizing subjectivity. The equalizing grandeur that we are so familiar with from other films is not evident here. But even though the woods are not captured in their vast extent, they still play an important role in the journey, and the extremely subjective shots demonstrate this at least as beautifully as long shot pictures do. Roman Mauer identifies two significant moments involving the woods in *Dead Man*, which are accompanied by corresponding, distinct camera movements.[17] Both highlight the forest's function as another destabilizing factor.

In the first scene, Blake and Nobody ride through a forest from left to right, as Nobody tells Blake about how he was captured and brought to England. Accordingly, the camera movement can be interpreted as reflecting Nobody's past eastbound journey. I would call this birch forest a light version of a forest in every sense, which matches the early stage of their journey toward the Pacific Ocean and Blake's still barely altered simplemindedness. Later, the two travel from right to left on the screen through a dark virgin forest. Now presented as a dark and all-encompassing element as compared to the light and easily accessible birch forest, the setting also enables more serious dialogue. Here, Nobody explains to Blake how his soul is supposed to enter "the other side" once they arrive at the ocean and Blake can be sent off onto the water. The camera movement again matches the westbound journey that they are talking about and that they are already undertaking. It seems that the dark forest has brought clear focus to Blake's journey, therefore making him as much part of the forestry surrounding as Nobody.

In *Dead Man*, however, the woods are no one's home. Even though Nobody moves easily in them and takes the lead, he is just as much of a passerby as Blake. When we follow Blake's shaky and subjective gaze to the majestic trees, we have the impression that he is not able to grasp his surroundings or what is happening to him. We can only suspect that he has slowly started to develop a sense for his journey on an emotional,

Figure 2. Collage of Blake and Nobody riding through different forests. (Screenshots from *Dead Man*, top to bottom: [00:47:08], [01:26:03])

subconscious level, but his impressions are not addressed, which again leaves us with a very complex picture. Despite his confusion, the forests have also become a temporary home and safe place for Blake; yet he is only able to survive there because of Nobody. The interplay of story and imagery once more emphasizes how all roles are in constant flux.

During the duo's journey to the Pacific Ocean, the water, as another example of imagery, plays a significant role as well. It marks the final destination, which is even ultimate in the darkest sense, as it is the location of Blake's actual physical death. However, this constitutes another misleading perception. Blake has been dead since the very beginning according to the fireman's prediction of his doomed fate. So what does the ocean do, other than being the last stop on his ride? Common interpretations of such imagery often suggest a purifying function, which, although perhaps intended by

Figure 3. Blake shortly before Nobody puts him in the canoe. (Screenshot from *Dead Man* [01:48:48])

Nobody, could lead to a false romanticization of Native traditions. Nobody initiates the journey with his goal in mind of conveying Blake's soul to the other side, but we never gain the impression that the ceremony is staged as something extraordinarily noble. The act seems important, but why exactly remains unclear and is never explained. The ritual does not serve as the solution to everything; it is merely presented as one option in this particular situation from one man's perspective. The Makah people are barely involved in the process, although their village and society are hosting the ceremony and they are the ones making it even possible. The scene certainly does not make Nobody a charitable, immaculate hero. He is shot immediately after Blake's canoe drifts off on the ocean but not without simultaneously shooting his murderer.

The frame right before Nobody places Blake into the canoe very much hints at the ending mainly constituting a challenge to the viewer. Blake lies on the ground barely breathing but turns his head to the camera and looks right at us with dizzy eyes. If any viewer has managed not to question each and every impression the film gives, then this picture on the shore is certainly the moment to start doing so.

Another prominent feature of the last scene is the film's musical score. From beginning to end, in fact, *Dead Man* is accompanied by a most peculiar soundtrack. Usually, films are equipped with a score in order to highlight certain parts or scenes, to create an atmosphere that helps engage the viewer in the story, or to subconsciously trigger the viewer's emotions as he or she is led to grasp the film's intended message. *Dead Man*, however, does not seem to have a message ready and prepared for the viewer to take in. Its music strongly supports the impression of the need to actually think about what is presented on screen and not to simply lean back and enjoy. Canadian rock musician Neil Young created a score that, as I imagine, many people would simply label noise.

Young recorded his music live and alone, using almost exclusively his electric guitars while watching a two-and-a-half-hour rough cut version of the film only three times over. In an interview with Jonathan Rosenbaum, director Jim Jarmusch describes the result of those sessions as Young's "emotional reaction to the movie."[18] He also considers the score an additional character in the movie.[19] It provides a commentating function that does not dictate certain impressions, but rather accompanies the viewer's cinematic experience. It seems as if one was watching the film with somebody in the next seat constantly expressing his reactions to what happens on screen. Such repeated commentary could be annoying, but here is a man with a talent for playing the electric guitar and whose playing (although a little painful to the ear at times) never seems to develop an agenda of its own. This openness is reflected in the score's structure. Instead of songs with an independent and completely finalized melody, we listen to *Dead Man*'s theme, which is repeated and varied over and over again but never gives the impression of completeness. This theme accompanies pictures of Blake's and Nobody's journey, whereas the dialogues are equipped with only fragments of sounds that burst out of Young's guitar. Mauer calls these fragments "musical punctuation marks" and points out that when Blake contradicts Nobody by claiming "I'm not dead," the music seems to resemble a question mark.[20] Such uncertainty corresponds well with the viewer, who is at this point wondering about the strange communication between the two characters. But even if Young's music is not similar to our individual response, it is still merely another person's reaction. Neither true nor false, Young's input adds more dimensions and opens up room for interpretation.

The artificial and electric sounds produced by Young's guitar contrast sharply with the time in which the film is set. This discrepancy attracts our attention and gives food for thought. One could understand it as a reflection on the intruding force of industrialization and supposed civilization. However, because it is never clearly written out fully, it remains, first and foremost, a disrupting force. The music can also be considered a machine that connects with and reflects nature and the state of the protagonist.[21] The sounds often linger as distorted clouds of sound, and sometimes we are hit by what sounds like strokes of lightning and thunderstorms coming out of Young's guitar. Again, the film denies the establishment of clear distinctions or relations between the extremes and instead stresses various interconnections that remain to be negotiated.

Director Terrence Malick takes a strikingly different approach to a soundtrack in *The New World*, for example. Here, the music very much sets a course, highlighting differences to the maximum yet failing to offer any input that could be inspirational to the viewer. The first scenes, showing how Natives and settlers become acquainted with each other shortly after the arrival of the latter, display the wonderment on both sides about habits and ways of the other and at the same time have us listen to very classical European music by Mozart and Wagner. This resembles the huge gap between the two people that encounter each other as those classical melodies seem to scream "Europe" and "high culture" in contrast to the untouched nature we see on screen. This music could be some kind of balancing element, trying to suggest equality between the two people by complementing the images with the opposite kind of music. But because of the simple and, most importantly, unquestioned opposition, we are rather presented with preset conditions. The music suits us as a Western audience, and we are given neither hints at any criticism nor space for ambivalent impressions. The score (though beautifully arranged and mixed with soaring original music by James Horner) does not give us the chance to do anything else but notice inflexible preconditions. It lulls the viewer and reduces any thought-provoking impressions to a minimum by feeding what is sure to be a mainly Western audience very familiar sounds accompanying stunning pictures.

Dances with Wolves upholds an even shallower and more convenient use of music, leading to one of the film's seven Academy Awards in 1991. In this blockbuster, a typical symphonic film score, grand and atmospheric, centers on perfectly finalized key themes. They do not reveal a character of their own in contrast to the music in *Dead Man*, which does that to a great extent. Even *The New World*'s score manages to produce a certain character, but fails to equip it with more than a few set qualities. In *Dances with Wolves*, the theme's sole function is to emphasize what the pictures already suggest, thereby depriving the viewer of any chance for thoughts of his or her own or any contradictory impressions. Without a doubt, the score demonstrates much musical quality, but it merely guarantees the upholding of preconceptions in the display of encounters between Native Americans and settlers on screen.

Neil Young's awareness of topics relating to such encounters is very much proven by one of his earlier songs entitled "Pocahontas." In this song,

Young addresses the approaching wagons, the buffalo massacres, as well as the killings in teepees, and even goes so far as to bring up Pocahontas as an object of sexual exploitation, which must be credited as a quite sophisticated reading of the material. All this and more in the song could develop into a tirade about the white evildoer. But then Young mixes in Marlon Brando and Hollywood, and toward the end of the song he paints a picture of a scene in which the narrating voice, Marlon Brando, and Pocahontas sit together by a fire. Thereby, Young manages to cast just enough doubt on the song's exact point of view so that we are left with a level of uncertainty that makes us listen to the song once again, reflecting on what it might want to communicate.

Similar to Young's approach in the discussed song, the music in *Dead Man* leaves behind some questions. In contrast to *The New World* and *Dances with Wolves*, *Dead Man* engages the music to play an active part without forcing any impressions upon the viewer. It neither simply intensifies the atmosphere nor pampers the viewer or makes him or her feel comfortable. Neil Young adds a level to the film that very much underlines its general thought-provoking approach. The previously mentioned characteristics, as well as the single fact that the variations of the highly ambivalent main theme are used for the joint journey of the white Westerner and the Native American, both extremely multifaceted characters, stress the film's ability to address and reveal matters and questions of alterity.

"If there's anything like a curtain speech, we have to deliver it ourselves, to the strains of Neil Young's music," Rosenbaum notes.[22] The final scene culminates in pictures of the open sky and the vast ocean, leaving the viewer with an empty stage that needs to be actively filled. We are invited to continue the constant negotiation that *Dead Man* has identified as essential in alterity processes. Once again, a moment of intuitive understanding and still simultaneous misunderstanding arises, repeatedly mediating the terms of life and death, voyage, names, sayings, culture, tradition, humor, and more. We are presented with various notions and roles that are interwoven but never blended or assimilated yet always subject to change. Stereotypes are presented and difference is acknowledged, but, most notably, it becomes clear that no ends or absolute references in any alterity process can be expected. The film illustrates the possible deconstruction of all relations and simultaneously asks the viewer to engage in a constant reconstruction. A sign in the trading post where outlaw Blake kills one more person suggests: "Work out your own salvation." It does not promise that this is possible.

NOTES

1. This reference is pointed out by Jonathan Rosenbaum in his extraordinarily insightful and comprehensive general introduction to Jim Jarmusch's film: Rosenbaum, *Dead Man*, 75.
2. In addition to Rosenbaum's comprehensive study, the most prominent analyses of *Dead Man* often comment on and discuss its relevance in relation to the western genre (see, for example, Rickman, "The Western under Erasure" and Szaloky, "A Tale N/nobody Can Tell"). Another focus has been the film's connection to and use of poetry. While Rosenbaum, Rickman, and others also include the film's referencing of and use of poetry in their discussions, Cummings prominently explores how *Dead Man*, among other films, can be viewed as constituting "accessible poetry" in a potentially poetic form of film-making (see Cummings, "'Accessible Poetry'?"). All of the mentioned texts already credit *Dead Man* with the power to question, abolish, or subvert a variety of generic, cinematic, and narrative traditions. In approaching the films she discusses, however, Cummings introduces a certain vocabulary that fits in closely with my analysis of *Dead Man*. She mentions the exploitation and simultaneous inversion of stereotypes, juxtapositions and twists, and speaks of the demolition of unitary notions. In connecting the film's qualities to the issue of alterity, this essay takes up and discusses these methods in order to sketch out how far *Dead Man* can be further exposed as not only novel on many levels but fundamentally unhinging.
3. Lévinas, *Alterity and Transcendence*, 100.
4. Nealon, *Alterity Politics*, 2.
5. Ibid., 3.
6. Zahavi, *Self-Awareness and Alterity*, 163.
7. Ibid.
8. Ibid., 164.
9. Taussig, *Mimesis and Alterity*, 130.
10. Ibid., 255.
11. Bhabha, *The Location of Culture*, 75.
12. Ibid., 67.
13. Ibid.
14. Rosenbaum, *Dead Man*, 19.
15. Ibid., 74.
16. Poem transcribed as quoted in Mauer, *Jim Jarmusch*, 210.
17. Ibid., 200.
18. Rosenbaum, *Dead Man*, 43.
19. Mauer, *Jim Jarmusch*, 231.

20. Ibid.
21. Ibid., 232.
22. Rosenbaum, *Dead Man*, 82.

WORKS CITED

Bhabha, Homi K. *The Location of Culture*. New York: Routledge, 1994.

Cummings, Denise K. "'Accessible Poetry?' Cultural Intersection and Exchange in Contemporary American Indian and American Independent Film." *Studies in American Indian Literatures: The Journal of the Association for the Study of American Indian Literatures* 13.1 (2001): 57–80.

Dances with Wolves. Dir. Kevin Costner. Tig Productions, 1990; DVD, MGM Home Entertainment, 2003.

Dead Man. Dir. Jim Jarmusch. Pandora Film, 1995; DVD, Miramax Home Entertainment, 2000.

The Last of the Mohicans. Dir. Michael Mann. Twentieth Century Fox Film Corporation, 1992; DVD, Twentieth Century Fox Home Entertainment, 1999.

Lévinas, Emmanuel. *Alterity and Transcendence*. London: Athlone Press, 1999.

Mauer, Roman. *Jim Jarmusch: Zum anderen Amerika*. Mainz: Bender Verlag, 2006.

Nealon, Jeffrey T. *Alterity Politics: Ethics and Performative Subjectivity*. Durham, NC: Duke University Press, 1998.

The New World. Dir. Terrence Malick. New Line Productions, 2005; DVD, New Line Home Entertainment, 2006.

Rickman, Gregg. "The Western Under Erasure: Dead Man." In *The Western Reader*, ed. Jim Kitses and Gregg Rickman, 381–404. New York: Limelight Editions, 1998.

Rosenbaum, Jonathan. *Dead Man*. London: British Film Institute, 2000.

Szaloky, Melinda. "A Tale N/nobody Can Tell: The Return of a Repressed Western History in Jim Jarmusch's *Dead Man*." In *Westerns: Films through History*, ed. Janet Walker, 47–69. New York: Routledge, 2001.

Taussig, Michael. *Mimesis and Alterity: A Particular History of the Senses*. New York: Routledge, 1993.

Young, Neil. "Pocahontas." *Rust Never Sleeps*. Warner, 1988, CD; originally released in 1979, Reprise Records.

Zahavi, Dan. *Self-Awareness and Alterity: American Phenomenological Investigations*. Evanston, IL: Northwestern University Press, 1999.

Mediating the Native Gaze
The American Indian Youth's Cinematic Presence in Chris Eyre's Films

LUDMILA MARTANOVSCHI

CHRIS EYRE (CHEYENNE/ARAPAHO) IS THE DIRECTOR OF FILMS THAT have changed the representation of American Indian cultures and have advanced Indigenous viewpoints in the film industry. Three of his most significant works—*Smoke Signals* (1998), based on fiction by Sherman Alexie;[1] *Skins* (2002), an adaptation of Adrian C. Louis's 1995 novel of the same name; and *The Edge of America* (2003), written for television by Willy Holtzman—center on or include young characters whose perspectives on themselves and the world around propose a fresh understanding of Indigenousness on screen. The young people in these three films, Victor and Thomas in *Smoke Signals*, Herbie in *Skins*, Carla and her teammates in *The Edge of America*, are in search of role models since their parents often fail to fulfill this function and contradict their children's expectations. While referring to the harsh reality of growing up with absent or unreliable fathers, the movies also emphasize the resourcefulness of the Native communities that make it possible for others, the teenagers' relatives or teachers, to emerge as guiding figures. In their quest for forging a sense of self, the young protagonists form alliances with peers and sometimes develop a certain group consciousness, relying on shared resistance to outside stereotyping not only of their age but also of their ethnicity. Their finally healthy way of looking at the world and at their own tribal nations is posited as the promise of the Native perspective's continuance into the future.

The current study aims at analyzing, on the one hand, the young protagonists' Native gaze, which is captured on screen, and, on the other hand, filmmaker Eyre's Native gaze, which becomes apparent in the way he modulates his artistic choices and structures his directorial discourse. The three films share characteristics that justify their discussion side by side, Eyre already presenting a recognizable sensibility that sets him apart even within the context of Indigenous cinema, which would allow him to be placed among other auteurs, who, by definition, "possess a compelling vision for their work that emerges from all their films, despite often challenging circumstances of collaboration."[2] Eyre mediates his own and his characters' gaze in as much as he provides a medium for it cinematically and, at the same time, translates or makes it intelligible to mass audiences not familiar with Native cultural practices, worldviews, or ways of perception.

If feminist studies on film theorize the male gaze inscribed in the very creation of early cinema, ethno-critical developments in the field expose a primarily Western gaze, which is similarly problematic throughout the twentieth century. As early as 1975, drawing on psychoanalysis, Laura Mulvey points out patterns of objectification in film:

> The determining male gaze projects its fantasy onto the female figure, which is styled accordingly. In their traditional exhibitionist role women are simultaneously looked at and displayed, with their appearance coded for strong visual and erotic impact so that they can be said to connote *to-be-looked-at-ness*.[3]

When it first appeared, Mulvey's demonstration occasioned a revision in discussing film and contributed to critical writing about the problems of representing the other. The strong visual impact she mentions is also essential for Hollywood films that imply and promote a colonizing gaze meant to turn the Native figure into an object that gratifies the expectations of the mainstream viewer and that have recently been under attack from scholarship concerned with Indigenous issues.

One such endeavor is the documentary *Reel Injun* (2009) by Neil Diamond (Cree), a film particularly relevant for the current analysis since it offers a metacinematic point of view, combating the detrimental effects of cinematic distortions with cinematic tools. In tracing the history of the stereotypes that have permeated Hollywood westerns and later movies about Natives, Diamond presents Eyre as a turning-point director who has inaugurated a new approach to feature filmmaking about Natives, namely a self-empowered one, and who has announced the "Renaissance" of Indigenous cinema. Interspersed throughout the fabric of the documentary, excerpts from an interview with Eyre disclose his insider's views, which are actually theoretical and critical insights on contemporary Native cinema.

A particularly significant intervention included in *Reel Injun* is Eyre's entreaty to all filmmakers involved in representing the Native subject: "You don't always have to make great representations of Native people. We are not asking for that. We are not asking to be nobles or righteous or good all the time. We are asking to be human."[4] These very words could be interpreted as the director's artistic creed since in all of his productions, from *Smoke Signals* to *Skins* and *Edge of America*, he is concerned with departing from the traditional Hollywood depiction of Indigenousness to construct believable and complex portraits of Native characters. Eyre has managed to fulfill his desideratum, according to Jesse Wente, an Ojibway film critic whose expertise features in *Reel Injun*:

> *Smoke Signals* was another film which came right at the end of the 1990s that started the golden age of aboriginal cinema. This was a movie made by a Native guy, Chris Eyre, starring Native people and not about what occurred a hundred and twenty years ago. . . . It was about Nativeness now and that was a big breakthrough.[5]

Whether listed under the label of "aboriginal cinema" as above, or "cinema of sovereignty" in Lee Schweninger's terms,[6] *Smoke Signals* has carved a visible space for itself, reversing the history of objectifying the Native presence on screen. Along with films such as *Whale Rider* (2002) by Niki Caro of New Zealand, for example, *Smoke Signals* is discussed as representative of Fourth Cinema in the context of film studies,[7] thus illustrating a trend that goes beyond the borders of the United States. The very coinage "Fourth Cinema" was initiated by Maori filmmaker Barry Barclay to describe cinematic productions emerging outside the orthodoxy of the modern nation-state.[8]

The importance of offering a fresh vision of the contemporary tribal realities in North America cannot be overemphasized. In her essay "Indians Watching Indians on TV: Native Spectatorship and the Politics of Recognition in *Skins* and *Smoke Signals*," Joanna Hearne acknowledges Eyre's role in the history of Native film and the significance of his focus on Native people's representation by the movie industry:

> Eyre's productions were among the first to offer contemporary speaking roles for Native actors, yet these films simultaneously look back upon the violence of mapping televised Indians onto Native people, of recognizing one's self or relatives in the face and genealogy but not the costumed role of the televised

> Indian, and of the staged encounter between viewers and the Indians on screen as they negotiate the meaning of a media past.[9]

The ways in which the young characters build a sense of "who they are" in connection to their family, friends, educators, and other influences around them include a negotiation with prefabricated media images and often debilitating circumstances. In *Smoke Signals*, Thomas, interpreted by Evan Adams (Salish), seems to defy television stereotypes of Indianness by always wearing a formal black suit, yet he projects himself as a constant storyteller. The role he adopts might be partly extended from his special connection with his heritage and partly acquired from media images of Nativeness. As Dean Rader explains, Thomas is "performing a form of Indianism—that of the storyteller,"[10] his performance having been shaped by the images he grew up with. However, the spectator is unsure of how to assess this geeky young man, who is an outsider in the reservation youth community, but seems gifted in perceiving and relating insights as if from another dimension that surpasses immediately palpable reality.

Thomas has been brought up by his grandmother, as his parents died in a house fire, ironically after a Fourth of July party. In the absence of a father, he transforms Arnold Joseph, the father of a popular and handsome youth, into a father figure. Victor, appropriately interpreted by the highly successful actor Adam Beach (Saulteaux), is dismayed by this, particularly because his own relationship to his father had been quite troubled before Arnold left the family and the reservation, and nonexistent afterward. In Thomas's stories, which create an ongoing flow irritating for Victor, Arnold Joseph took care of and advised the orphan, finding the time to invite the kid to "breakfast at Denny's," which receives the mythical connotations of a feast. If tempted to believe that Thomas artificially creates such an image of Arnold out of his need for a father, the viewer is proven wrong when Suzy Song's testimony reveals that Arnold did feel guilty about having caused the fire after an alcohol-filled party and felt responsible for orphaned Thomas.

The nonathletic Thomas strives to join Victor's group of friends who play basketball, but all his attempts fail since he is perceived as a misfit. In offering Victor his money for the journey to Arizona to retrieve Arnold's ashes, Thomas seizes his chance to travel with Victor, partly since he was in a way Arnold's son and would like to pay his respects, too, and partly since he wants to form a partnership with Victor. Even before they leave the reservation, the two young men are captured in the same frame, thus anticipating the referential mode of filming used by Eyre for the rest of the movie. As they walk toward the border of the reservation and run into two female

Figure 1. Redirecting the Native gaze with an unlikely duo: screenshot from *Smoke Signals* showing Thomas (foreground), the adolescent outsider but master storyteller, with the "cool" but deeply troubled Victor (00:18:36).

"cousins," Victor and Thomas negotiate their roles: the former embodying the disgruntled youth and the latter, the visionary one.

On the way to Arizona, Victor does turn into Thomas's mentor and initiator into the ways of the world. The scene in which Victor urges Thomas to adopt different clothes by telling him, half-mockingly and half-earnestly: "You gotta get rid of that suit [to be a 'warrior']"[11] is emblematic of Victor's capacity to act as a catalyst not only for Thomas's exterior emancipation but also, more importantly, for his interior transformation and embracing of a youthful attitude that would allow him to be recognized as a member of his generation.

Their friendship begins from the very first steps they take on the way from the Coeur D'Alene Indian Reservation in Idaho to the venue of Arnold's decease in Arizona, their literal journey from north to south straight through the United States becoming a journey into maturity, understanding, and mutual support. If on the reservation the two young men situate themselves in opposition, off the reservation they are almost forced to form an alliance against the others' stereotypes about Native people, since they are perceived as similar by outsiders incapable of reading the contrast between their personalities and the contradictions between their attitudes to tradition and Indigenousness. As many scenes show, together, Victor and Thomas learn to return the gaze that often singles them out as undesirable "injuns." One such example is represented by the notable moment when their seats are rudely taken by two white men on the bus, one wearing a cowboy hat and the other a hunter's camouflage cap. Victor and Thomas take deeply satisfying joint revenge by loudly chanting about and satirizing—as the bus travels through breathtakingly beautiful canyon countryside—"John Wayne's teeth" never shown in his countless western movies. Their chant deflates the Indian-fighting movie star's heroic image and, by extension, the superiority of the bus-passenger "cowboys" who degrade them: "John Wayne's teeth: Are they false, are they real; are they plastic, are they steel?"[12]

Upon reaching their destination, the two young men meet Suzy Song (Irene Bedard, Inupiat Inuit), who contributes to Victor's access to and understanding of his father and the way the latter related to his family. Arnold and Suzy had become neighbors and friends before he died. Suzy retells the story she heard from Arnold about a basketball game in which father and son played against two Jesuits, the film inserting the scene as if Arnold's words, echoed after his death, could bring reality into being. The mythical account of the fight between Indians and Christians raises twelve-year-old Victor to the stature of "an indigenous angel," who managed to score points against all odds and secure victory. However, the magical spell woven by the story is dispersed by present-day Victor, who testifies to the fact that he lost the game, which, if the story is metonymically standing for the conversion of Native America to Christianity, would be in keeping with the historical reality of the advancement of the alien religion all across American territory:

Victor: So, he told you I made that shot?
Suzy: Yeah.
Victor: Yeah, well, I missed the shot. I lost the game.
Suzy: You mean your dad lied to me?
Victor: Yeah, a lie that made me look good.[13]

However, Victor himself also admits that his father lied in the story to present him in a favorable light, and this makes him muse endearingly over his father's use of storytelling for strengthening memories of their shared past and projecting a brighter version of a game that could stand for the large-scale encounter between Natives and non-Natives. This might be the very moment that moves Victor toward reconciliation with his dead father and the director's major contribution to illuminating the importance of storytelling for ensuring continuance between generations.

Along the same lines, Simon Ortiz (Acoma Pueblo) emphasizes the propensities of storytelling as a crucial connective between parents and children: "The only way to continue is to tell a story and there is no other way.

Your children will not survive unless you tell something about them—how they were born, how they came to a certain place, how they continued."[14] The very survival of his young son must have been in Arnold's heart and mind; by telling the story over and over again, Arnold hopes to protect his son's memory from fading as much as he hopes to determine his son's growing up and thriving, even if far away. The telling of the story functions as a prayer meant to give Victor strength, energy, and confidence to become everything his father imagines him to be.

The final scene in the film has particular significance in bringing a sense of closure and reconciliation between Victor and his father, as the son completes a ritual of mourning upon his return home. Scattering Arnold's ashes over the river, Victor releases sorrow and anger, which could be interpreted as a step toward a restored sense of continuance between generations and an energetic embrace of the future in transformed circumstances. Eyre effectively creates a multimedia reinforcement of this theme in the texture of the film with poetic voiceover, visual sweep, instrumental music, and vocal song: while the voiceover recites Dick Lourie's poem "Forgiving Our Fathers,"[15] the camera slides over the northwestern landscape, and instrumental sound introduces the relevant song "Wah Jhi Le Yihm,"[16] the dilemma of how we forgive our fathers is projected beyond the boundaries of Victor's situation. LeAnne Howe (Choctaw) interprets the final scene as pan-Indian: "The ending of *Smoke Signals* stands in for all Indians—our ability to release our anger at the American government for its 250 years of abuse directed at tribal peoples."[17] Taking this line of interpretation further, the question is whether present-day survivors, despite and beyond traumatizing practices on the part of the United States, which have affected generations of parents rendered helpless and in no position to nurture their children, can forgive and reconcile themselves to historical circumstances that have stolen their parents away from them.[18] While the culturally specific interpretation may be lost on mainstream or international audiences, the universal father-son tension and negotiation of a meaningful relationship is most definitely retained and recognized. Lourie's poem juxtaposes contradictory movements—"Fathers . . . marrying or not marrying," "speaking . . . or never speaking"—suggesting that intergenerational conflict is inherent to human nature as children will forever reproach their parents for whatever they do or not do, even when the parents' self-effacing and cruel destinies are no fault of their own. The poem implies that the love-hatred relationship into which humans are born cannot be escaped even in the absence of the parent figure, or more so if the parent has deserted his or her offspring. Whether played in Jordan (as testified by LeAnne Howe) or Romania (as testified in my own

Figure 2. Discussing the Wounded Knee Massacre at a family reunion: this screenshot from *Skins* presents Rudy, Mogie, Herbie, and Aunt Helen in a rare moment of togetherness (00:52:00).

setting), the film never fails to elicit an emotional response from student audiences. And building on the impact *Smoke Signals* has on young viewers removed from the U.S. context, the instructor can introduce subtler issues of diachronic and synchronic relevance concerning American Indian sovereignty, and can thus advance reimagining the Native subject internationally.

In many ways more challenging than *Smoke Signals*, *Skins* is also pertinent as far as American Indian youth's cinematic presence in Eyre's films is concerned. Written by a Paiute author, but set on the Pine Ridge reservation in South Dakota, this second film aims at exploring a young man's confrontation with his environment besides claiming to depict a realistic picture of one of the poorest places in the United States. Herbie Yellow Lodge (Noah Watts, Crow) is a seventeen-year-old whose father is unemployed and whose uncle is a tribal policeman. He is first shown asking his uncle, Rudy (Eric Schweig, Inuit), for money. Herbie is forced to turn to his uncle for financial help, given the reality of his own father's failure to fulfill his role as supporter of the family: "As Rudy knows well, at Pine Ridge, dysfunction begets dysfunction, even within (perhaps especially within) families. Mogie, for example, can't even raise his own son."[19] During his brief times of sobriety, Mogie (Graham Greene, Oneida) acknowledges his brother's parenting position for his son.

At a family dinner to celebrate Mogie's release from the hospital,

Mogie mentions American Horse and asks Rudy to tell Herbie the story of Wounded Knee and American Horse's testimony before Congress:

Herbie: So who is American Horse?
Mogie: Your uncle will tell you, so listen up.
Rudy: He testified at the trial of the Wounded Knee massacre. At that time all Indian religious ceremonies were banned by white men, because they were afraid of them. Now up on the western end of the Cheyenne River Sitting Bull resisted, so they shot him. And Big Foot knew that he and his people had to flee the area immediately and so they came to Pine Ridge and when they camped out the Wounded Knee troopers of the Seventh Cavalry . . .
Mogie: That's from Custer's old command. Seventh Cavalry was called in to escort them to the reservation. Then the soldiers disarmed them. Wounded Knee was nothing but a damned massacre of women and children. American Horse testified before Congress.[20]

For Herbie this is a history lesson as much as it is an explanation for his father's bitterness and present decay. Mogie takes over the storytelling, and the camera gives the viewer a close-up, proving that the history of his tribal nation affects him profoundly. He is saddened and infuriated by a recognizable cycle of events that traces the pattern of injustice and dispossession from the earliest dealings with the United States to the most recent ones. Moreover, when Aunt Helen tries to divert attention from the past and historical trauma to Herbie's present-day achievement in sports, the father explodes, showing that he lives in the past and that the history of his people is obsessively present, even more urgent than his own son's needs. Mogie is incapable of focusing on supporting Herbie, the present and future of the community: "Mogie's belittling of his son's achievements stems directly from his overwhelming feelings of anger when remembering Wounded Knee; the story that brings the family together in this scene also furthers their estrangement."[21] The movie also includes a scene in which the viewer witnesses Mogie's inner struggle when he finds out about his son's birthday, but has nothing to offer the boy. The improvisation of a birthday cake, which would serve as gift as well, is a pathetic failure when he trips and it all topples on the floor. It seems that communal trauma, the systematic mistreatment of American Indians on the territory of the United States of which the Wounded Knee Massacre is just one piece of compelling evidence, and individual trauma, both his growing up in a dysfunctional family and his taking part in the Vietnam War, render him incapable of fulfilling his role as a father.

His death does not leave his son stranded, though: "Ironically, as a result of Mogie's death, family ties may well be more tightly established. Mogie's dying wish in a letter to Rudy, which the viewer hears as a voiceover, is that the younger brother look after the nephew."[22] Following evidence already provided on screen, Rudy will fulfill his brother's wish successfully. The task of serving as Herbie's father figure will probably restore a sense of purpose to his own troubled existence: "The viewer has already seen Rudy taking care of Herbie to some extent, and the film gives the viewer no reason to think that he would not continue to do so."[23]

In contrast to Herbie, who is portrayed as a "good kid," having taken Rudy as a role model, a group of young men involved in crime and drugs shows the darker side of tribal reality and how it can affect children on the reservation. The tragic death of Corky Red Tail reveals the potential destructiveness of desperate behavior typical of adventurous but misguided youth, enhanced by the lack of a brighter future and opportunities on the reservation. While on duty, Rudy is asked to check on an abandoned house, a place the local teenagers use as a hangout. Once he arrives, he can see a body covered in blood lying on the floor and surprises two young men making their escape. He tries to capture them, but falls and hits his head on a rock. The only detail that proves to be a helpful hint is the color of one runaway's shoelaces. It is this element that he recognizes days later while breaking up a fight between two apparently random teenagers in a diner. Suspicious of their behavior, he follows them and discovers that their conversation discloses the fact that they are the murderers at the abandoned house. Disguised beyond recognition as the dead kid's ghost, Rudy attacks the two young men with a baseball bat, imparting his own punishment and inflicting such terror in them that the two give themselves up to the police and confess their crime. Even if his actions contribute to the confession and restoration of balance in a way, his approach is highly questionable and stirs remorse when he realizes that his vigilante-style method has serious consequences, both teenagers being hospitalized with broken knees. The violence he inflicted might have saved the two young men from other crimes, but the damage he caused, even if not permanent, is a sight that troubles him deeply as it occasions a glimpse at the vicious circle of destruction and pain he is surrounded by. Doubt and self-questioning make Rudy feel that he should look for guidance, and he talks to the local medicine man, who promises to hold a healing ceremony for him if things do not become better soon.

The two brothers' traumatic youth, which Eyre shows in flashbacks, gives insights into some of the factors that might have contributed to the current situation Mogie and Rudy find themselves in as grown men. A scene from the past introduces them as football players on the field who do not benefit from their family's support since the camera shows their drunk father's attack on their mother and the two teenagers running over to rescue her, rather than concentrating on the game. The shame associated with the episode seems to motivate the two brothers to act in unison and banish their father from their home. Even if drastic, the measure taken demonstrates that, as teenagers, Mogie and Rudy confronted the harsh realities of reservation life and searched for ways of coping with it and solutions to their troubled family life: "Though Eyre is unable to vocalize it, the film connotes a strong bond between the two boys, perhaps as a kind of barrier against their father's alcoholism and their mother's weakness."[24] It is this long-lasting alliance that the viewer witnesses in the present when, despite their superficial arguments, the two brothers can still communicate in the deepest way, confessing the unutterable—for example, Rudy's stating that he had been the arsonist who brought about his brother's injury in the fire at the liquor store. More importantly, Mogie's irreverence for authority and his trickster-style antics inspire Rudy to actually inscribe the Mount Rushmore monument with an Indigenous mark, a bucket of red ink dripping on the iconic stone-carved face of George Washington. Affirmation of survival, statement of resistance to colonization, reappropriation of homelands, symbolic act of agency, invitation to rewrite history from a Native perspective, strategy of coping with unbearable reality, and commemoration of one's brother represent just some of the readings that can be attached to Rudy's gesture right before the end of the film. Eyre's Native gaze also purports circularity, rather than linearity, as the film ends on images with which it had opened, even if now the viewer's perception of Mount Rushmore has been forever modified by the experience of watching the film and the Native reclamation of the site that the film closes with.[25]

The triumphant yet ironically humorous note of the final scene in *Skins* is partially echoed by Eyre's *The Edge of America*, a TV movie based on true events, in which the exposure of racial discrimination is presented in a rather instructive, yet on the whole light-hearted, tone. Kenny Williams (James McDaniel), the new African American teacher who arrives at his post on the Three Nations reservation in Utah, faces uneasiness and suspicion not only on the part of his white interlocutors but also on the part of his new Native acquaintances. The first gesture of including the newcomer in the tribal community and accepting him as adviser and guide for the Native children born and raised on the reservation comes from the school handyman (Wes

Studi, Cherokee). The latter introduces Kenny to two of the girls on the basketball team the new teacher reluctantly agrees to coach as follows: "That's Marissa, my niece, and her best friend, Francie. They are good kids. . . . I tell you what. You look after those girls, I look after your car."[26] With that promise, the girls' uncle-protector transfers some of his responsibility for the education of the young generation to the coach, although the latter is an outsider, and offers to help him in exchange.

However, signs of doubt as to his role in this new environment and his capacity to contribute to the life of the community, which the teacher encounters from the minute he steps on the reservation, continue into the classroom. Carla (Delanna Studi, Wes Studi's real-life niece) seems to be the only one who responds to the task assigned during one of their first English classes, but her story is actually a mock story meant to make the other kids laugh. There is evidence in the film to suggest that Carla is intelligent and talented, but disillusioned with the adult world on which she takes revenge in the classroom. One particular scene shows the fact that she attempts to reach out to her father, who seems to wallow in his own pain over the loss of her mother without paying attention to his daughter's teenage imperatives, but she fails. Her rebelliousness is eventually subordinated by her passion for playing basketball. Initially a reluctant student, Carla strives to obtain good grades for the sake of being selected for the team and metamorphoses into one of the most reliable team members, after learning the lesson of "passing," that is, team solidarity rather than individual performance.

The coach adopts a harsh tone when teaching this lesson, the tone being justified under the circumstances: "Passing. Scoring is a result of passing. Passing is a result of team work. Anyone who holds the ball for themselves is not a team player. From now on, anyone who runs . . . without my say so, sits."[27] The young players definitely filter this through their own worldview and integrate their coach's rule as part of the lesson of interconnectedness intrinsic to their Native culture. They also learn to respect their coach and accept him as part of the community, realizing that he can contribute a great deal to their world rather than alienate them from it.

Gradually and predictably, Kenny wins his colleagues' and students' trust and brings about increasing collaboration among the members of the basketball team, united around the idea of proving their worth and winning the game. The movie conforms to its genre and offers no nuances or innovative solutions to a well-trodden path of cinematic accessibility. As teacher, coach, and individual, Kenny refines his understanding of his host culture and learns how to channel the local energies into constructing

Figure 3. Teaching the lesson of team solidarity: the coach explains the importance of passing to Carla, a talented team member, in a screenshot from *Edge of America* (00:48:42).

positive outcomes and building strength. His guide is his colleague Annie Shorty (Irene Bedard), who has the patience and versatility necessary for cultural mediation. She is aware of the fact that the newcomer has had no previous contact with a Native culture, and rather than tax him for his ignorance, she adopts the role of his teacher. As a matter of fact, she is the one who first mentions the principle of "unity, harmony, all of us together"[28] in one of their first confrontations on matters concerning the contrast in their coaching styles and the difference of approach to their trainees. Once introduced to the key that can actually capture the Native sportswomen's imagination, Kenny is much more successful in promoting team work. A pan-Indian principle, interconnectedness is expanded upon in various tribal contexts with equal poignancy. It has received one of its best definitions in LeAnne Howe's discussion of "tribalography," an original contribution to Native studies:

> Native stories, no matter what form they take (novel, poem, drama, memoir, film, history), seem to pull all the elements together of the storyteller's tribe, meaning, the people, the land, and multiple characters and all their manifestations and revelations, and connect these in past, present, and future milieus (present and future milieus mean non-Indians). I have tried to show that tribalography comes from the Native propensity for bringing things together, for making consensus, and for symbiotically connecting one thing to another.[29]

The symbiosis Howe explains is akin to the view Annie expresses in the film, making the Native worldview coherent to outsiders: to Kenny within the film and to mainstream viewers outside the film. Actually, Eyre himself illustrates tribalography in bringing together different elements: Native actors, long shots of reservation land, effective scripts, intertextuality, sound effects, and music to serve the overall purpose of telling the story of America from an Indigenous perspective.

Even if the movie centers on the girls' efforts to surpass inimical circumstances, unite their forces in sisterhood, and play the game for the sake of weaving a different story than the one they have been condemned to up to that point in their lives, it also includes the interesting case of Franklin, Carla's boyfriend and Kenny's enemy from the beginning. Presented as a teenager with an attitude whose inspiration is of hip-hop descent, Franklin cherishes his solitude and independence. Ironically enough, his adopted construction of rap protest, whose origins reside in African American culture, is easily disrupted by the black teacher who knows how to beat Franklin at his own game. The young man is presented as constantly looking for a chance to escape the confines of the reservation and his condition, and seems to embody the unflinching rebel, but he is eventually helped to see the power of community and interrelatedness. Belonging to the easily recognizable genre featuring an inspirational teacher who creates bonds with his students against all odds—to cite but two examples, John N. Smith's *Dangerous Minds* (1995) and Tony Kaye's *Detachment* (2011), *The Edge of America*'s predictability and didacticism are once more apparent as Kenny manages to break through Franklin's armor in the end.

In his work, Eyre renders the interconnectedness between apparently disparate strands in a tribal community's life, makes use of flashbacks and other devices that allow him to capture the circularity of the Native worldview, and advances a decolonizing perspective by prioritizing storytelling and humor. Irrespective of gender or tribal affiliation, the American Indian youth has a powerful cinematic presence in his films, this very fact constituting the most convincing reason for believing in the Indigenous renaissance that Eyre is portraying and embodying at the same time. The Native adolescents' ways of perceiving their living space, relationships, inherited attitudes, and prospects for the future are diverse and complex. Eyre's film creations support his own plea in *Reel Injun* to media producers to deconstruct received stereotypes and thus contribute to a viable continuation of dynamically changing Native identity: "We are not asking for [noble representations of Native people]. We are asking to be human." His works have undeniably revolutionized viewers' way of looking at Native issues and will doubtless continue to influence future generations of filmmakers.

NOTES

1. The screenplay by Sherman Alexie (Spokane/Coeur D'Alene) draws largely on his short story "This Is What It Means to Say Phoenix, Arizona" from his short story collection *Lone Ranger and Tonto Fistfight in Heaven* (1993). The screenplay also interacts with his novel *Reservation Blues* (1995).
2. Pramaggiore and Wallis, *Film*, 414.
3. Mulvey, "Visual Pleasure," 436.
4. *Reel Injun*, 1:02:39–50.
5. Ibid., 00:53:40–59.
6. Schweninger, *Imagic Moments*, 2–4.
7. Pramaggiore and Wallis, *Film*, 358–359.
8. Ibid., 357.
9. Hearne, "Indians Watching Indians on TV," 65. Similarly, James Cox investigates to what extent Victor and Thomas have been influenced by Hollywood in their self-image and follows intertextual references to *Dances with Wolves* and other productions that surface in the boys' conversation ("This Is What It Means," 81–82).
10. Rader, *Engaged Resistance*, 156.
11. *Smoke Signals*, 00:36:45–50.
12. Ibid., 00:39:30–55.
13. Ibid., 00:54:35–47.
14. Ortiz, *Woven Stone*, 153.
15. *Smoke Signals*, 1:21:11–23:01; a longer version of the poem was originally published in a collection by non-Native Dick Lourie titled *Ghost Radio* (1998).
16. Ulali is a "First Nations Women A Cappella Trio" (www.ulali.com). The title means "I carry you" in Tutelo-Saponi, and the song tells about a young man bringing his father's ashes back to the Native homeland.
17. Howe, "Smoke Signals,"115.
18. In her book-length study of *Smoke Signals*, Joanna Hearne emphasizes that Victor gives Thomas half of the ashes, reading this as a critique of the government's quantification of Indianness, "the bureaucratic fragmentation of bodies in calculations of Indian identity by blood" (*Smoke Signals*, 126). Victor's sharing of his father's ashes is a very different partition that "simultaneously addresses Thomas's need of parental nourishment and Victor's need to take up the values of sharing, taking care of others and forgiveness that he has begun to learn from Thomas's stories" (ibid.)
19. Rader, *Engaged Resistance*, 106.
20. *Skins*, 00:50:32–51:31.

21. Hearne, "Indians Watching Indians on TV," 56.
22. Schweninger, *Imagic Moments*, 171.
23. Ibid.
24. Rader, *Engaged Resistance*, 106.
25. Rader vividly describes Rudy's act in visual terms as the "reddening of America's whitewashing" (ibid., 109).
26. *Edge of America*, 00:12:48-13:19.
27. Ibid., 00:48:41-49:01.
28. Ibid., 00:37:08-10.
29. Howe, "The Story of America," 42.

REFERENCES

Cox, James H. "This Is What It Means to Say Reservation Cinema: Making Cinematic Indians in *Smoke Signals*." In *Sherman Alexie: A Collection of Critical Essays*, ed. Jeff Berglund and Jan Roush, 74–94. Salt Lake City: University of Utah Press, 2010.

Edge of America. Directed by Chris Eyre. Showtime, 2003; DVD, Showtime, 2006.

Hearne, Joanna. "Indians Watching Indians on TV: Native Spectatorship and the Politics of Recognition in *Skins* and *Smoke Signals*." In *Visualities: Perspectives on Contemporary American Indian Film and Art*, ed. Denise K. Cummings, 41–72. East Lansing: Michigan State University Press, 2011.

———. *Smoke Signals: Native Cinema Rising*. Lincoln: University of Nebraska Press, 2012.

Howe, LeAnne. "Smoke Signals." In *Seeing Red—Hollywood's Pixeled Skins: American Indians and Film*, ed. LeAnne Howe, Harvey Markowitz, and Denise K. Cummings, 113–115. East Lansing: Michigan State University Press, 2012.

———. "The Story of America: A Tribalography." In *Clearing a Path: Theorizing the Past in Native American Studies*, ed. Nancy Shoemaker, 29–48. New York: Routledge, 2002.

Mulvey, Laura. "Visual Pleasure and Narrative Cinema." In *Feminisms: An Anthology of Literary Theory and Criticism*, ed. Robyn R. Warhol and Diane Price Herndl, 432–442. New Brunswick, NJ: Rutgers University Press, 1991.

Ortiz, Simon. *Woven Stone*. Tucson: University of Arizona Press, 1992.

Pramaggiore, Maria, and Tom Wallis. *Film: A Critical Introduction*. 3rd ed. Boston: Allyn and Bacon, 2011.

Rader, Dean. *Engaged Resistance: American Indian Art, Literature, and Film from Alcatraz to the NMAI*. Austin: University of Texas Press, 2011.

Reel Injun: On the Trail of the Hollywood Indian. Documentary directed by Neil Diamond et al. National Film Board of Canada and Rezolution Pictures, 2009; DVD, Lorber Films, 2011.

Schweninger, Lee. *Imagic Moments: Indigenous North American Film*. Athens: University of Georgia Press, 2013.

Skins. Directed by Chris Eyre. First Look Media, 2002; DVD, Millennium, 2003.

Smoke Signals. Directed by Chris Eyre. ShadowCatcher Entertainment, 1998; DVD, Miramax Home Entertainment, 1999.

Refraction and Helio-tropes
Native Photography and Visions of Light

KIMBERLY BLAESER

The photographer was thought to be an acute but non-interfering observer—a scribe, not a poet. But as people quickly discovered that nobody takes the same picture of the same thing, the supposition that cameras furnish an impersonal, objective image yielded to the fact that photographs are evidence not only of what's there but of what an individual sees, not just a record, but an evaluation of the world.

—*SUSAN SONTAG, ON PHOTOGRAPHY*

Whatever it grants to vision and whatever its manner, a photograph is always invisible: it is not what we see.

—*ROLAND BARTHES, CAMERA LUCIDA*

WHETHER IN DAGUERREOTYPE, ON GLASS PLATES, IN STEREOSCOPIC images, or in the pictorialist tradition, the majority of the historic images of Native Americans bear the imprimatur of imperialism and Manifest Destiny. When we remember that photographs result from manipulating light and reflection, the problematic nature of the early photographic representation of Native Americans becomes more understandable. Through subject pose, camera position, staging, focus, sepia toning, and other techniques, the subjects were rendered into time-bound, romantic stereotypes of primitive warrior, noble savage, tragic half-breed . . . vanishing Indian. Native filmmaker Beverly Singer comments on the way the photographic documentation works to "foster a categorical public belief in the approaching demise and eventual nonexistence of American Indians."[1]

But understanding the word origins of these art forms—photo from the Greek "phos," for light; "graphe" or "graphein," to write; and "helios," meaning sun—leads us to helio-graph, or sun writing, and photo-graphe, or drawing with light, and also paves the way for understanding the Native re-vision of early colonized representations. Native scholars have chosen to cast new light on older archival images by offering critiques and reinterpretations of photos from the likes of Edward Curtis and A. C. Vroman; they have recontextualized and revitalized the static images by verbally placing them within traditional landscapes, and within tribal and family stories; and they have "remixed" these historic photographs. Sometimes contemporary photographers use archival images in photo collages where their juxtaposition with other photographs might create an enlightening (perhaps ironic) reading; sometimes they highlight supposedly marginal aspects of photographs through zooming and cropping; and sometimes they reproduce modern "takes" of older staged photographs. Contemporary portfolios or collections also often offer "alter-native" photographs made by Indigenous photographers from different time periods (including twentieth- and twenty-first-century artists). These photos, which understandably derive from an "other" focus, often incorporate contemporary cultural spaces, as well as scenes of casual and daily activities, thus humanizing (rather than museumizing) their subjects and, perhaps inadvertently, offering evidence of continuance (rather than disappearance). This Native reflection of tribal life emanates from the work of photographers like Lee Marmon (Laguna) and Victor Masayesva (Hopi).[2]

Indeed, Masayesva has devoted himself to exploring the ideas of a Native or, even more precisely, a Hopi aesthetic related to the visual arts. His far-reaching discussions on the subject have appeared in several commentaries he has written to accompany his photographic work, including the essay "Hopi Photography" in *Hopi Photographers, Hopi Images*, and in the book-length collection of his images and reflections, *Husk of Time: The Photographs of Victor Masayesva*. His complex and still developing understanding of Hopi arts emphasizes, among other things, accountability to clan and tribe, and attentiveness to the sacred. "At Hopi," Masayesva says, "thoughtful action of any sort becomes worship; devoted attentiveness becomes worship."[3] But restraint and sometimes silence also figure in an understanding of artistic engagement, especially when it concerns the sacred. Masayesva asserts, "You cannot violate the silences, just as you would not intrude on ceremony."[4]

As important as the tenets of his visual aesthetic are, they sometimes play out in unexpected ways, such as when Masayesva, formerly resistant to "portrait" photography "in the manner of Edward Curtis," including "photographs that featured Indians posing in native costumes," made his own portrait photos of a Butterfly Dancer. In the process, he discovered the possibility of, as he writes, "releasing a moment that had been resigned to living in the steady current of time."[5] Through a particular engagement with portraiture, he felt he succeeded in reaching "far beyond the moment" and creating a vision of the subject—in this instance, "all the suggestions of butterflyness: lightness, colorfulness, summer"—that helps "release" her "into a future where . . . she is alive on . . . her own terms."[6] Masayesva underscores the idea of liberation, and, although he does not comment specifically on his method, the success of the image arises partly from the visual mutuality it manages to convey. The young girl's face is sprinkled heavily with pollen, her clothing includes a mottled fabric, she is placed before a "mud clay wall covered with rain-streaked kaolin."[7] Various aspects of the photograph suggest an overlapping of being among girl, butterfly, pollen, and clay—an almost symbiotic reality. The photo achieves its effect both through the visual image and through gesture toward an unpictured context or reality, a Hopi understanding of ceremonial relatedness.

Like Masayesva, many contemporary Native photographers, myself included, experiment with ways to disrupt straight representation and employ techniques to engage the viewer in the imagining of photographic meaning or to move the viewer beyond the illusion of status in image. The traditional heliograph involved Morse code–like flashes of sunlight reflected by a tilted mirror. Likewise the art of poetry thrives on "telling it slant."[8] So in my own work I employ symbolic visual cues: refracting image, engaging shadow, suggesting movement, employing juxtaposition, or using gesture to include both presence and absence. Sometimes I incorporate language or bring together images and poetry to create picto-poems. I thus seek to communicate more than the sum of the visual parts and to engage the viewer in a vital sensory experience. Sometimes, like Masayesva's, my work, too, hearkens toward the sacred, toward vision.

Ultimately, the various undertakings in photographic countermanipulation by Native scholars and artists enter into a contemporary struggle for what Channette Romero has called "visual sovereignty"[9] or what Anishinaabe scholar Gerald Vizenor has called "survivance."[10] Lucy Lippard summarizes the inherent quest that stands behind the many theoretical

Figure 1. Symbolic portraiture: *Butterfly Dancer* by Victor Masayesva.

stances and politically informed decisions that have been made with regard to Native, image, autonomy, and truth when she notes: "Perhaps it [a photo] can never tell the whole truth and is often used to tell lies, but there is always at least a grain of truth in a moment that did take place, and it is against that grain that we must test our eyesight."[11] Just as the single grain of sand retrieved from the waters by the mythic *Wazhashk* (muskrat) became our Turtle Island, so too might the small photographic truths we retrieve help us build a life-sustaining Native vision.

In what follows, I examine both the strategies for reclaiming historic images and the creative making of newer works. In each instance, my discussion centers on the attempts to liberate by recontextualization—to view or center "light writing" within a Native or a specific tribal worldview.

COLONIAL SIMULATIONS

Much has been written about the possessive impulse behind the "taking" of Native American photographs, about the distortions of popular colonial representations of American Indian peoples—specifically in the construction of what Vizenor has called "fugitive poses," "poster *indians*," and "interimage simulations."[12] Laguna writer Leslie Silko, for example, speaks of the "intrusive vulgarity of the white men who gazed through the lens,"[13] and Cherokee writer Jimmie Durham claims, "All photographs of American Indians are photographs of dead people, in that their *use* assumes ownership of the subject, which is seen as static."[14]

Like Durham, Choctaw scholar Louis Owens has analyzed the use of these "primitive" images, and noted their appropriation into various colonial cultures' constructions of their master narrative: "Indigenous peoples the world over have been photographed into the archives of the so-called First World. In the process, those people are subsumed into a dominant culture's definition of itself, becoming relevant only as props in the story that culture tells about itself—that is, being contained within the frame of someone else's story."[15] The popular story imperialistic America images and retells involves the tragic but inevitable "vanishment" of anachronistic tribal nations. Indeed, the practice of what Jacob Gruber termed "salvage ethnography" was a purposeful effort to capture the "vanishing" primeval race of the American Indian in a state both pristine and noble, to preserve static image as artifact.[16]

Well-known cultural salvage workers included artists George Catlin and Karl Bodmer in the eighteenth and nineteenth centuries and photographers like Heinrich Voth, Joseph Mora, Timothy O'Sullivan, and Edward Curtis in the nineteenth and twentieth centuries. Of these, Curtis was perhaps the most popular, and his photographic records the more enduring. His extensive work in the pictorialist tradition produced images, sepia-ed and saturated with emotional suggestion, including various photos of tepees, basket-makers from different tribal nations, befeathered Indians, poses of scantily-clothed Native men on cliffs, and the dramatic and purposefully empty landscape. In these representations, the "*indian*" is, to use another Vizenor phrase, a "poselocked fugitive of ethnocentric discoveries."[17]

Scholar Lucy Lippard also suggests, "Many of these images were propaganda—taken not only to record 'vanishing' indigenous cultures, but also to grease the wheels of assimilation."[18] Drawing the pagan-practicing, simple savage, backward blanket-Indian deftly served the mechanisms of Manifest Destiny. Early romantic postcard images were often used to lure tourists and settlers to the mythic West. More important, by photographic arrest, Native peoples are contained in a primitive past and, therefore, in the master narrative, clearly not suited either to oversee proper use of large land holdings or to participate in the industrial future of America. Anthropologist Frederick J. Dockstader recounts an instance when, during a trip to Washington, D.C., Hopi representatives observed "a congressional hearing room plastered with a selection of photographs of [Native] religious ceremonies . . . being used by Bureau officials and missionaries to discredit their religion."[19] According to Owens, "Photographs of Native people taken by non-Natives always participate in the construction of the colonized 'other,' always serve to facilitate dominance, for they can do nothing except subsume the Native subject into the colonizer's discourse."[20] Indeed, the early "documentation" of Native peoples involved various complex, and often unexamined, motivations. For example, the Anne Makepeace film on Curtis's work, *Coming to Light*, takes note of the irony inherent in the funding of his photographic expeditions. The same industrialists responsible for forcing tribes off their lands were among the subscribers supporting Curtis's projects to document the supposedly disappearing "noble" race.[21]

OF REPRESENTATION AND RECLAMATION

Theoretical critiques of early photographic simulations of Native peoples—like those discussions offered by Lippard, Vizenor, and Owens—assist modern viewers in understanding the power dynamics inherent in the othering and voyeuristic commodification of the American Indians, or in what Vizenor also labels "cultural surveillance."[22] These many static representations have constructed the popular image and idea of "*indian*," a construction often unconnected to the everyday lives and survival of contemporary Native people, and one that works counter to mutual understanding and, crucially, counter to just and respectful treatment of tribal peoples today. "Fugitive poses," writes Vizenor, ". . . separated natives from their communities and ancestral land; the simulations of the other as the *indian* turned the real into the unreal with no obvious presence in time or nature."[23]

Now, beyond these academic discussions are activist efforts to reclaim the images and recover the vital presence of Indigenous people as members of complex communities, living engaged with place. In the volume *Partial Recall*, for example, Lucy Lippard gathered essays by Native Americans in which they responded to historic images and in various ways attempted to liberate those captured representations, inviting a new reading of the photos from a familial or tribal context and with an understanding of the project of colonization. In his essay in the book, Paul Chaat Smith, for example, declares, "The last thing these images are about is what really happened in the past. They're fables being told to shape the future."[24] Gerald McMaster reads in the picture of an industrial school football team two stories: he understands the way the "boys represent the colonial experiment" of "transforming the savage into a civilized human being"; and at the same time, he sees "their ambivalence about being photographed, indicated by clenched fists or folded arms" and notes how, through these gestures, "their resistance remains visible."[25] The many readings offered in collections like Lippard's and the volume of commentaries on the Frank A. Rinehart collection, *Beyond the Reach of Time and Change*, edited by Simon Ortiz,[26] enlarge the scope of the historical images by "story-ing" them, expanding the imaginary frame of the photos to include comments on place, time, relationship, historical or cultural context, or, as Lippard writes, "to look *inside* the images."[27]

Of course, not all photographs are taken under the same circumstances, and the degree to which they seem to represent what Lippard has called a "reciprocal" or a "cannibalistic" moment[28] depends upon several factors, such as the identity of the photographer (including whether he or she is Native or non-Native), the relationship between the subject and the photographer, and the number of other "barriers" present or absent in the picture-making. Cultural self-representation does not always involve political intent, of course, but photographs taken by Native American Indian artists may nonetheless embody a kind of resistance to stereotypic representation simply because of intrinsic qualities. Some of the photos or photographic portfolios from the 1980 volume *The South Corner of Time* seem to fall into this category. Certain images, perhaps unself-consciously, offer contemporary correctives to the romantic commercial images, those manipulated, time-bound, sepia-soaked renditions of the stereotype "Indian." They do this through their spontaneity, inclusion of cultural context, or incorporation of modern items and elements demonstrating cultural adaptation. Several recent books, including *Our People, Our Land, Our Images*, also include and discuss historic photos taken by early Native photographers themselves, allowing readers a glimpse at the longer tradition of photographic self-representation.[29]

The process of resisting or lessening the effects of photographic containment can also result from unique creative decisions or maneuvers on the part of the photographer or subject—even when a pose is struck. For example, both Phil Deloria and Jimmie Durham recognize in photos of Geronimo an awareness and a "looking back" or staring down of the colonial gaze.[30] Among other historic images, I have found one in particular that resonates for me as an act of resistance. In 1987 while searching the Western History Collections at the University of Oklahoma, I found an Irwin Brothers photo labeled "Mabel Mahseet, Comanche."[31] The photo shows a young woman, seated in an elaborate white wicker chair with part of a flowered screen visible to her right. She seems to be wearing some form of traditional dress—moccasins, earrings, layered skirts with a fringed layer on top. Her long dark hair falls over her right shoulder and onto her forearm, which rests on the chair. She is somber and unsmiling. The remarkable aspect of the photograph is a frame, placed not around the whole image, but an actual picture frame used within the pose to surround the woman's face. Such an oddity might itself offer an ironic cast to the portrait, but the effect is still more calculated: the woman's right arm and hair spill into another dimension, breaking the illusion of illusion by coming outside the wood frame. This unexpected gesture by the subject or photographer clearly intends to disrupt the boundary between image and reality. It works against Native objectification by seeming to advertise Mabel Mahseet's subjectivity. There is no indication of the origin of this creative decision, no account of who initiated this sign of resistance. Whether we attribute the ironic deconstruction of the romantic representation to Mabel Mahseet or to one of the Irwin Brothers photographers, it is clear someone (perhaps both parties involved in the photograph) has leveled a challenge at the status quo.

Just as the Native essayists in the Lippard volume employed their storytelling to reclaim another understanding of the historic photos they discussed, so I reimagined the Mabel Mahseet portrait, read in the pose her defiance, and offered this poetic reclamation:

"FRAMING"

An Irwin Brothers Indian in a studio photograph. A file number in a Western History collection of classic invented identities. Solemn face, long dark hair, just another sepia memory with reality leeching away like a winding red stream from a cracked inkwell. The irony of American gothic: a lone Comanche women posed on an ornate Victorian chair. But this *ogichidaakwe* breaks out, her wavy waist-length hair, deliberately draped over one corner of a large wood

> frame, reaches beyond the captured image. Hair so full it runs down across her chest, joins the dark of her layered skirt. Together they become the swift pony on which she counts coup, rides her escape from the still-life, the Catlin-Curtis-colonized look-alikes. Mahseet. Warrior woman. *Animwewebatoo.* Run away making noise.

My retelling of this photographic moment brings together both the practice of Indian tourism as manifested in the understood desire for romanticized representation and the act of resistance through ironic commentary that disrupts the possibility of such a consumable construction. Mabel Mahseet becomes a warrior woman in my own native language, and the poem recounts both speaking resistance and symbolic escape.

By serendipity, my Internet search for the proper photo title for the Mabel Mahseet image here discussed led me to another instance of related reclamation. I discovered that a 2007 conference program for the emerging

Figure 2a. "Mabel Mahseet, Comanche." (Courtesy of the Western History Collections, University of Oklahoma Libraries, Irwin Brothers 45)

Figure 2b. *NAISA Re-Mix of Mahseet Photo* featuring Victoria Kidwell, then a University of Oklahoma student. (Courtesy of Victoria Kidwell)

Native American and Indigenous Studies Association (NAISA) also featured this Irwin Brothers image as a cover photo, but more significantly, the back cover of the conference brochure was a contemporary "reenactment" of that framing scene. Featuring Victoria Kidwell, who is identified as a "current OU [University of Oklahoma] student," a closing photo shows a young smiling Indian woman who stands holding a large ornate frame.[32] The symbolic border "frames" Kidwell from her torso up, except for the fingers of her right hand, which wrap around the frame from behind the wood, and her left hand and forearm, which reach over the top and outside of the "picture," just as did Mahseet's own arm two centuries earlier. Clearly, the conference organizers intended a playful act of solidarity and continued resistance.

"COMPOSITIONAL RESISTANCE"

The photographic imitation undertaken by what would become NAISA is a good example of artistic production that moves beyond reclamation through commentary or that employs what Dean Rader calls "compositional resistance." Rader makes the distinction between "contextual resistance," which involves thematic elements, and "compositional resistance," which involves "how a text is composed: the materials the artist uses, the organization or plot structure of a film or novel, or the inversions of Western poetic genres."[33] These elements of material, organization, and structure, and, most especially, inversion, can as readily signal a "compositional resistance" by photographers—as it does in the case of NAISA's satiric replication of the Mahseet image.

Likewise, many of Victor Masayesva's images deliberately take account of composition in order to engage in a visual resistance. For example, Masayesva often inserts strategic, dramatic use of color into an image heavy in earth tones, or he creates intriguing collages bringing together disparate symbols—natural elements like feathers, snakeskins, or owls, with items representative of consumer culture or the nuclear age. Although he often includes items associated with or symbols of Hopi traditional culture and builds the suggestiveness of his photographic collages around issues affecting his tribal nation, Masayesva does not confine his activist stance and compositional resistance to "Native" subjects only. His ironic compositions might as readily be aimed at environmental destruction or at philosophical concepts of time as at the colonization of Native image.

This unapologetic expansion of his photographic vision, of course, simply enacts another resistance, this one leveled against artistic confinement—the limit placed on subjects or approaches considered appropriate or "traditional" enough for the artistic product to be considered "Native." How, for example, might a viewer read "Indian" in Masayesva's digital composite "If Only One," which features a small gray cat and its shadow moving through a literal ocean of beans, with a single bean on its head?[34] The image follows Masayesva's discussion of Indian humor, verbal play, and the role of Hopi clowns. On the page facing the cat image, Masayesva has stated, "Humor, then, is about our best selves sallying out to face the savage world, and sometimes we end up facing ourselves. When we laugh hardest we end up crying, 'Okiw nu! Pitiful me! I laughed so hard I cried!'"[35] The photograph of a cat nearly buried in a sea of beans with one bean precariously balanced on its head might very readily be viewed in the context of Masayesva's statement: like a pitiful human sent into a strange world, laughable in its predicament, or like a cat clown playfully undercutting the "tragic" sense of our nature. Although Masayesva's work may include pieces ranging from this somewhat surreal image to the more straightforward homely photos like "Stacking Corn" or "Weaver" (both casual images showing Native people engaged in common activities),[36] in her discussion of Masayesva's film and

Figure 3. "Green Mobile" by Victor Masayesva, 1997.

photographic work, Romero suggests that, regardless of subject, Masayesva's context is always unerringly Hopi.[37]

Among the artist's many intriguing images, "Green Mobile," from 1997, readily demonstrates Rader's idea of "compositional resistance."[38] The digitally created image brings together a photo of part of a wall in Keet Seel canyon and the sand-colored cliff dwellings that lie at its base at Kawestima, below which sit the frame of an older gray car (perhaps meant to be seen as abandoned or left behind like the ruins) and a bright emerald green convertible, its top down, its backseat filled with corn, and an Indian woman in the passenger seat, posed as if eating from a corncob. The many visual juxtapositions allow for a rich range of intersecting ideas, including several involving "tradition," Native "savagism," and modernity. For example, the collage juxtaposes the ancient and the modern: abandoned ruins or remains of a civilization—a place left behind—together with a sleek symbol of what Phil Deloria calls "automobility."[39] It also recalls the loss and long-unexplained absence of the tribal inhabitants at the same time as it suggests current habitation through the cars and through the abundance of food (here perhaps a symbol of contemporary means for survival).

Deloria's discussion of "expectation" and "anomaly" in *Indians in Unexpected Places* offers a frame helpful for understanding the impact of bringing the ancient and the modern together as Masayesva does here.[40] "There is," he says, "a palpable disconnection between the high-tech automotive world and the primitivism that so often clings to the figure of the Indian."[41] The Indian, he suggests, calls up "nature and nation, violence and colonial conquest, race and race crossing, nostalgia and guilt," whereas the automobile is an "evocative symbol" of "mobility, speed, power, progress."[42] Therefore, stereotypic expectations of Indians can be undercut by images of Native Americans engaged in modern activities.

The title of the image itself, "Green Mobile," also seems to emphasize clashes in expectation. First of all, it admits ambiguity, allowing the possibility of multiple meanings depending upon the pronunciation assigned to "mobile"—mō′ bēl, suggesting the vehicle itself; or mō bīl′, suggesting the ability to move or even motion itself. We might also think of it as alluding by association to "mobile" phone, and thus including the realm of communication. Such a reference could then be read as ironic, given the context of mystery and unknown circumstances (lack of communication) that surround the missing inhabitants of the Kawestima cliff dwellings. The "green" of the title is, of course, also the color of the sleek, modern vehicle pictured; but it might simultaneously call up ideas of the "green" revolution or ecology and the "ecological Native" stereotype. Indeed the image is ripe with suggestiveness, allowing for many layers of meaning.

In *Husk of Time*, Masayesva himself offers one reading of the photo composite in a short commentary entitled "Flash Forward":

> Placing the green automobile (and the wreck in the yard) below the ancestral ruins at Kawestima asserts that we still live here at Kawestima. The seemingly empty, uninhabited ruins are in fact anticipating our return. They are waiting for us when we return by foot, car, wind, cloud, rain, or memory. This is my tribute to the ancestors who have gone before and who await us, looking for the swirling dust that signifies our transport—time.[43]

Continuance. Endurance. Survival. Relatedness. Return. The photo composite, together with Masayesva's commentary, might lead to a fruitful examination of any one of these important ideas. But the last word in the commentary suggests yet another context in which to read the photo: time.

The art of photography is, by its nature, bound up in notions of time. It involves timed exposure, a variable lapse in time between when the image is taken and when viewed, and, for some, an attempt to "capture" or preserve a particular historic moment or period. John Berger declared that "the true content of a photograph is invisible, for it derives from a play, not with form, but with time."[44] The "play" with time involves selecting a moment in which to make a photograph, a decision, Berger claims, resulting in "poles of absence and presence" since "a photograph, whilst recording what has been seen, always and by nature refers to what is not seen" because it "isolates, preserves and presents a moment taken from a continuum."[45] That continuum from which a moment is preserved naturally involves the continuum of time, and many scholars have analyzed photography's peculiar relationship to time. Roland Barthes, for example, noted in *Camera Lucida* the way photographs simultaneously call up past, present, and future; and Susan Sontag, in *On Photography*, made the famous declaration that, "All photographs are memento mori."[46]

In the case of the Masayesva image, part of its power derives from its ability to multiply or intensify allusions to time and factors related to temporality. Through its intriguing composition, the photograph calls up ideas of ancestral time, mythic time, and geologic time. It gestures toward imagined Native past and actual Native past, as well as several historic pasts, including that of the gray car, the era in which corn might figure significantly as foodstuff or ceremonial object, and the past in which the green car might have been relatively new, as in the photo. Layered time periods also include the past in which the cliff dwellings were viable homes, the past in which they were left behind, the past in which they became a tourist attraction. The very idea of age (both timelessness and time passing) is also suggested by the canyon setting, since its weathered appearance seems at once powerful and fragile.

Ultimately then, the image suggests a meaning not pictured, but one created through the juxtaposition of elements or the intersection of ideas. The friction of the incongruous creates a "spark" that inspires a new impression, emotion, thought, or perspective. The revelry thus sparked destabilizes stereotypes and might entail ideas of ancestry and adaptation, endurance or survivance, but the key impact involves entrance into and new creative conjecture in any of the previously mentioned arenas of reference. The innate resistance to "representation" or any singular interpretation we see played out in the "Green Mobile" image characterizes much of Masayesva's work. His symbolic and metaphorical constructions of image undermine simplistic or stereotypic readings of his art, and, as I have noted, often give voice to or enact a certain recontextualization. The images then often tend toward political relevance.

"A GLIMPSE OF THINGS ETERNAL"

The language of "Flash Forward" also suggests a second pattern of allusiveness. Masayesva writes of the "anticipation" of return and of the act of return through common means such as "by foot" or "car," but he also includes the possibility of the reappearance or return of the "us" of the passage by "wind, cloud, rain, or memory." The reciprocal energy noted in the passage may involve a physical form other than human or it may not involve physical being at all. The return might as readily come through "rain" or through "memory." Image and text then allude to participation in another realm of being, here perhaps a natural or even spiritual realm. Masayesva himself has stated, "I believe we would not be far from the mark if we were to take photography as ceremony, as ritual, something that sustains, enriches, and adds to our spiritual well-being."[47] In this particular image, the suggestive acknowledgment of the ancestral connections and tribal continuance may indeed add to an enhanced sense of "spiritual well-being."

The philosophical goals and tenets behind various Native arts often involve a ritualistic or spiritual element. In their volume *The Sacred: Ways of Knowledge, Sources of Life,* Peggy Beck, Nia Francisco, and Anna Lee Walters summarize the Diné storyteller Yellowman's statements about the role of Native creative works, noting they "allow us to envision the possibility of things not ordinarily seen or experienced" and to use "the intangible part of our thinking mind."[48] Often art that seeks a referent beyond itself involves a kind of restraint or an absence in or of the object itself. Masayesva, for example, speaks specifically about "the value of silence" to the Hopi and comments on restraint with regard to cultural objects or ceremony: "Refraining from photographing certain subjects has become a kind of worship."[49] Absence in a photograph can imply a presence outside of the image and imbues the unseen with greater significance. Daisetz Suzuki claims that "every art has its mystery, its spiritual rhythm" and says, "Great works of art embody in them yūgen [unknowability] whereby we attain a glimpse of things eternal in a world of constant changes," again suggesting an experience of knowing or of vision through a withholding or allusiveness.[50]

Suzuki explains the dynamic involved particularly as it pertains to haiku poetry, noting, "Haiku does not express ideas, but . . . it puts forth images reflecting intuitions." These images, says Suzuki, "are not figurative representations," and "the images become transparent."[51] I find important parallels here with the images involved in photography. As photographs resist pictorial representation and work by means of "intuitions," the images too become "transparent." The tension between what Berger calls the "poles of absence and presence" and the reference to what is "not seen" play an important role in creating this transparency, this "glimpse of things eternal" (to use Suzuki's phrase).

Just as Masayesva has employed to his advantage collage together with symbolic and metaphoric objects, I have found particular "compositional" elements helpful in creating photographic images that resist the illusion of static representation. In my own intuitive and self-conscious making of image, I have begun to think about how to picture or imply story, movement, the intersecting borders of being—or even spirit. My experiments in attempting to gesture toward that border existence of being—the verge of vision—involve layering, shadow, double image, reflection and refraction, visual disruption, partial image, and, in the case of what I call picto-poems, the juxtapositions and interactive allusions of language as well.

My photographic focus embraces not only Native American peoples themselves but also images recontextualizing popular public representations, as well as images of Native cultural spaces or places of being, and images engaging with natural and spiritual landscapes. In general, I attempt to create photographs that will disrupt a sense of temporal reality. I try to privilege photographic feeling over fact, spiritual intuition over physical data. One example of a photograph that uses the incongruous to stress the blurred borders of time and experience is "What the Rain Remembers." Obviously, the photo disrupts visual expectation in several ways and requires a re-seeing or new "reading" of the reflected image. The photograph itself is unaltered; only the caption has been added to provide another possible context for engaging with the scene.

When working with natural images specifically, I attempt to insinuate the animate, the cyclical, the eternal—not necessarily motion in the photo, but the sense of possibility suggested through visual vibration or photographic gesture. The image, "Dreams of Water Bodies," has several elements that work to create a sense of movement, perhaps even mythic or ancient journey. These center around correspondence—the similarities of line and color that insinuate an overlapping of being. The vibration of the water ripples appears so like the markings on the cliff wall, which in turn appear like the branching of the tree. The determined forward motion of the beaver, the illusion of an "entrance" at the wall of the cliff, and the reflective repetition in the water world that mirrors the cliff all add to a sense of dream happening. Taken together, these elements work to remove the image from the postcard or commercial reality of forever blue waters with the beauty of resort wildlife outside your door, and instead create a sense of the surreal or mysterious. Ultimately, working in the traditions of the Anishinaabeg dream song and of haiku, both of which use their art to engage a reader/ listener in an experience or spiritual encounter, I too try to create pathways or invite a moment of transcendence or enlightenment similar to that I may have experienced myself in my encounter with the image that gave rise to the photo.

László Moholy-Nagy and Leslie Silko are among those who have seen in photography the potential for these kinds of unexpected perceptions. Avant-garde photographer Moholy-Nagy, who himself pioneered the "photogram," suggested a break from the pictorial use of the camera and believed it possible to use photographic techniques "to make visible existences which cannot be perceived by our optical instrument, the eye."[52] Silko, too, speaks

Figure 4. "What the Rain Remembers" by Kimberly Blaeser.

Figure 5. "Dreams of Water Bodies" by Kimberly Blaeser.

about the unrealized possibilities of photography, suggesting, "Perhaps photographs register ambient bursts of energy in the form of heat or X rays as well as light. Thus photographs reveal more than a mere image of a subject, although it is still too early for us to understand or interpret all the information a photograph may contain."[53] Silko experimented with these possibilities in her own photographic work of flood remains as she attempted to "read" the earth markings. "The photographic images of the stones and wood," she wrote, "reminded me of glyphs. I could imagine there were messages in these delicate arrangements left in the wake of the flash flood."[54] Like other nonverbal symbols, photographic glyphs can carry "messages," can communicate to the viewer something not inked or spoken.

This potentially allusive quality of photographic images parallels other artistic genres or what we might call systems of cultures aesthetics—most significant for me, the dynamics of Anishinaabe dream songs and haiku. In these traditions, the song/poem itself is meant to "disappear" into an imaginative experience beyond words.[55] R. H. Blyth talks about the Japanese haiku:

> A haiku is not a poem, it is not literature; it is a hand beckoning, a door half-opened, a mirror wiped clean. It is a way of returning to nature . . . a way in which the cold winter rain, the swallows of evening, even the very day in its hotness, and the length of the night . . . speak their own silent and expressive language.[56]

Vizenor has often drawn comparisons between the aesthetics of haiku and that of the tribal dream song traditions, noting, for example, how haiku bring about "a moment of enlightenment" and how dream songs achieve a connection "between the conscious and unconscious worlds."[57] The two traditions have other elements in common, but the gesture beyond the embodied art, the referentiality of the forms, is what I see as aligning with the allusive quality of many Native arts, and specifically, with some contemporary Native work in photographic images. Similarly, when Vizenor describes the Anishinaabeg sense of *agawaatese* or shadow, he notes how *agawaatese* carries "the unsaid presence in names, the memories in silence, and the imagination of tribal experience."[58] Key in these traditions is the sense of the embedded, an engagement with or recognition of an-other realm of significance.

Probably yet more helpful in characterizing the potential reach of storied or nonrepresentational photography is Vizenor's sense of what he has called "transmotion." This quality he recognizes as a source of survivance in tribal activists, as a "*sui generis* sovereignty," and as a signifier of the sacred in works like those done by Cheyenne ledger artists.[59] Specifically, Vizenor claims "performative transmotion is an ethical presence of nature, native stories, and natural reason. . . . Native transmotion is an original natural union in the stories of emergence and migration that relate humans to an environment and to the spiritual and political significance of animals and other creations."[60] Through transmotion a story can "reach," Vizenor believes, "to other contexts of action, resistance, dissent, and political controversy."[61] This active engagement with other contexts, the sense of dialogic happening or continuance, suffuses photo art that resists representation.

If by nature photographs derive from play with time and exist as a shimmer between realities, an experience made up of both absence and presence, they then simultaneously involve the material and the immaterial, the known and the unknown; and like other visual arts, they must be "made" and remade at each viewing, imagined into meaning(s) as they are reseen. Thus, they suggestively propel us into the realm of the animate; and like storytelling—what Simon Ortiz has called an "event . . . coming into being"—they can only exist in the multiple inflections and connotations of and the relationships between the various visual elements.[62] When the photographic art involves "compositional resistance" or deliberate engagement with tropes or gestures of some sort, this can heighten its innate referentiality, the complexity of its meaning. And incorporating the realm of language or poetry with the image significantly expands the compositional building blocks and can further disrupt the status of representation.

Of course, story through image is an ancient idea. Petroglyphs and pictographs, for example, employ image and symbol to referentially animate the rock art, to suggestively immerse it in the history, cultural activities, and spiritual beliefs of the tribe. Silko, in talking about "petroglyphs on rock outcroppings," has taken note of that complex referentiality, saying the "ancestors of Pueblos had already begun to make images of spiritual significance."[63] The nineteenth-century works of ledger artists, created through layering images or as palimpsest, likewise actively "come into being" in relationship, not in an isolated representation or time-bound image of the physical world. As Denise Low has noted, "unique Indigenous philosophical concepts emerge from the texts, especially representations of power or 'medicine.' The markings invoke texts of military record, history, natural history, literature, art, and spirituality." She says the images have "multiple layers of simultaneous impact."[64] Vizenor, too, notes the possibilities of these and other images: "Some native pictures are stories, visual memories, the source of directions, and a virtual sense of presence."[65]

"INTO THE MOTTLED WALL": ON PHOTOGRAPHIC ETHICS AND AESTHETICS

Questions will inevitably arise in talking about photographs of scenes or images not specifically or not overtly "Native," just as they do in discussions of literary works by Native American authors on subjects not specifically "Indian" or "Indigenous." I would counter with a simple suggestion that art movements involve not only a subject, but an aesthetic. In addition to the specific techniques and qualities already discussed in relationship to photographic reclamation and compositional resistance, another overarching characteristic often associated with Indigenous art involves the engagement in process.

Years ago, when I was co-teaching a class with a history colleague whose previous career had been as an attorney, we were talking about preparing the students to write their first papers. In discussing how to frame the essay, she said she always tells her students that "a good defense attorney never asks a question for which she doesn't already know the answer." I was momentarily flabbergasted, since my own idea of research and writing always centers on a process of discovery. "A good poet," I countered, "doesn't ask a question for which she does." For me, art is always about questions and gesture. I imagine an Anishinaabe relative who wants you to notice something, who uses first a chin-point and then an eyebrow gesture. Poetry and photography both often ask us to first look *at* something and then to look *through* it. Just as our own creative engagement involves an ongoing process of enlightenment, so too, we invite a viewer/reader into an experience of discovering meaning(s). The ultimate intention, of course, is to engender a way of being in the world: if we are rewarded by looking deeply, it will lead us to pay closer attention, and vice versa—if we pay close attention, we will see more deeply.

As Rader suggests, beyond aesthetic, Native art also involves an ethic. Writing about Jaune Quick-to-See Smith's work in particular, he notes: "The forging of her own artistic language is not simply an aesthetic, but also an ethic. Her work is both a measure and a means of sovereignty."[66] A catalog of the ethics of Native resistance involved in Indigenous artistic expression is beyond the scope of this discussion, and, of course, oversimplification of the tenets or the expectation of strict adherence by all Native visual artists would undermine the very essence of such a set of philosophical values. However, Indigenous scholars and artists alike recognize an ideological grounding around notions of sovereignty, a particular vision that entails everything from justice for oppressed peoples to a biological and spiritual epistemology of autonomous but reciprocal relationships and a foundational understanding of community.

Thus, the application of the term "Native" to photography not involving subjects specifically associated with "Indianness," becomes less problematic. As the Sontag epigraph to this essay attests, each photographer views and records the world uniquely. "Nobody," she notes, "takes the same picture of the same thing," and photos provide not "an impersonal, objective image . . . but an evaluation of the world."[67] Through the photographic process, I believe Native artists suggest a particular way of seeing the world, one that often involves the engagement of many voices—the ironic to the visionary—that involves moments in and out of time, a cultural mapping of place and displacement, and a particular patterning of relatedness.

At their most successful, my own photographs or picto-poems aspire to create or invoke a kind of cultural or transcendent nexus of connections, regardless of the subject. They enact a process of sometimes unexpected associative links. For example, the Brussels image, featured on the cover of this volume in slightly simplified form, was a serendipitous discovery: a flash of intuitive understanding and the necessarily nearly instantaneous following of that "seeing." While walking through the narrow, old city streets at night, I was simply making snapshots, delighted with my surroundings and the fun of being there with my family. I had just snapped a photo of an odd moment of street theater, one involving an optical illusion—three men "joined" together by metal bars. Then, while passing by one shop window, I encountered another visual illusion. I caught a glimpse of my daughter reflected in the window glass and then reflected again in a mirror in the display. Three Ambers. That in itself was a lovely image; but the display in the window (the world into which she was inadvertently cast), replete with toy armies, Old World lace, and figures of "European" caricature, set off multiple vibrations. I lifted my camera. But the wealth of refraction did not end there. The mirror also held the shadow of a parasol, reflection of stained glass and lace, framed photos, not to mention both the face and the silhouette of an innocent passerby—my husband (incidentally, representing nice European stock). History. Class. Representation. Survivance. The more I looked at the image later, the more I discovered.

The "imagic" encounter arose by chance.[68] In that moment, a particular physical angle of vision coalesced with an ironic angle of "seeing" the scene. As Berger has suggested is true in general in photography, what I "saw" in that instant was more than what is visible in the photo itself. I couldn't resist making the photo as a means of remembering the experience, as an invitation to the viewer into such an experience of the strange confluences evoked. To highlight the layers of ironic relationship, I elected to add a "frame" and to suggest, by docking the photo tips, a kind of display of the image (as in a photographic album). I added the language cues of the title, "Indigenous Indices of Refraction, Brussels 2012," to imply one possible context for reading the photo and to enhance the allusive or metaphorical properties of the image. As I continue to "read" the image, throwing it into new associations, it has taken on an animate reality, existing for me in a dimension beyond the temporal reality of the actual photographic moment or the static reality of a simple snapshot.

Among the elements that intrigue me is the strong shadow image of the young woman; she seems to look on or look back, at or from the scene. As Vizenor writes about Native photographic representations in *Fugitive Poses*, "There, in the stare of the shadows, is an elusive native presence."[69] And in another shadow is yet another Native presence—my own. Reflected in the lower corner of the mirror, a viewer can see the hands of the photographer and her camera. Out from that noticing eye and tiny instrument of aperture and mirror opens the entire scene—an interactive image of refracted light, shadows, and imaginative connections. As Vizenor suggests in *Fugitive Poses* and as photographers like Masayesva and Marmon have demonstrated with their work, photographs can bend and refract dominant stories just as the photographic instrument can bend and refract light.

Figure 6. "Ephemeral Habitation at Cavate" by Kimberly Blaeser.

Sometimes to facilitate the "alter-native" reading of an image, I include suggestive poetic language or "story" the moment. As noted, the Brussels image bears a caption or title, while other works might be presented in tandem with a whole poem. "Dreams of Water Bodies," for example, is also the title of a poem reimagining the Earthdiver myth from a contemporary perspective.[70] Still others pieces involve a more intricate collage of language and image. "Ephemeral Habitation at Cavate," for example, is a composite of images and language, or what I call a picto-poem.

Like "Indigenous Indices of Refraction," it began with an intuitive moment of "seeing," a being thrust into a spiral of associative connections. The two photos used were part of a series taken while my daughter and I were hiking in the Bandelier National Park in New Mexico among the canyon trails and cliff dwellings. While we stood looking at the markings that remain on an interior wall, including those left by fire and the anchoring of a loom, the sun came from behind a cloud, and suddenly our shadows also fell on the wall and moved among the ancient dark shapes and memories. I experienced a strange timelessness that coalesced in the vision I had of my daughter peering in to search the colorations of the past, her shadow long and also seeming to lean into another time. That is the photo I made and the one I began with to build the composite. As Suzuki noted about the dynamics of engaging with haiku, for me that image "became transparent."

I elected to continue the experience of layers of time and relatedness, using an image of the cliff walls behind a digitally framed photo of the shadow image reflected on the interior wall of the actual cliff dwelling. I tilt the photo so it appears that the shadow figure faces her past. Lines, holes, shadows, and picto-graphic markings all play a key role in the composition. Then, just as Masayesva used "Flash Forward" to enhance understanding of "Green Mobile," I added language. Here, though, I didn't want to explain the image as much as continue the alliances formed in the ephemera. Therefore, I added two textual layers, the first a pale *Do Not Copy* "copyright" or "intellectual property" embossing behind the image as if it were another of the natural or pictographic elements on the canyon walls. Then I included the suggestive language of poetry, in this instance a "concrete" poem in which part of the effect comes from its visual appearance on the page (or in this case, on the canyon wall).

By stimulating multiple sensory pathways simultaneously as I do here, I hope to create a photographic synesthesia. The various associative techniques intensify and expand the power of the image, can dislocate the viewer/reader in static reality and immerse them in an-other realm, an unpictured place of memory, experience, or vision. My various images may gesture toward cultural context, toward historical incident, or toward the sublime, the inexplicable, the always absent. In each case, my reference point is beyond and invites the viewer to move toward the edge of intersecting understandings and realities. I think about the bringing together of the various elements in my visual work as like the process of starting a fire, initiating the friction in the viewer's own mind that creates combustion—warmth and light.

PHOTOGRAPHY AS SURVIVANCE

If most of the early photographs taken of Native peoples were "salvage ethnography" or works displaying what Renato Rosaldo calls "imperialist nostalgia,"[71] the contemporary work of Native photographers instead self-consciously hearkens after a sense of survivance in Vizenor's sense of "more than survival, more than endurance or mere response," and as "an active repudiation of dominance, tragedy, and victimry."[72] Rader has eloquently demonstrated how within and across various genres of American Indian art, the works are indeed engaged in resistance. "American Indian languages—both visual and verbal," he writes, "respond to and resist American cultural machineries by framing how Native artists, writers, filmmakers participate in engaged resistance that engenders and defends Native identities."[73]

Many early photographs were contrived to render their Native subjects into silent, romantic stereotypes, into visual artifacts of a vanished or vanishing homogenized "Indian" culture. Some of the recent photographic work has self-consciously contested that representation, sometimes with querulous counterimages. Still other art by Native photographers has sought to find a way to work from or within tribal traditions without or with little engagement in the adversarial image/counterimage production. The newest version of artistic survivance might entail simply acting out of rich tribal traditions to offer vibrant and multidimensional pictures of Native reality, rather than reacting to previous stereotypic photographs.

A work like Ojibwe photographer Nikki Isham's "Anty Fixes Cars, 2005" shows the feet of a Native woman amid wrenches, WD40, what appears to be an oil pan, and the handle of a ratchet.[74] Her toenails are painted silver. She wears a silver ankle bracelet. Her lower calf is tattooed with a dreamcatcher image. She is barefoot, and a pair of dusty red flip-flops are abandoned behind her. This delightful photo offers a multifaceted image of a contemporary Native woman. The work can certainly be read as a response to any number of misrepresentations, but it can also exist without reference to

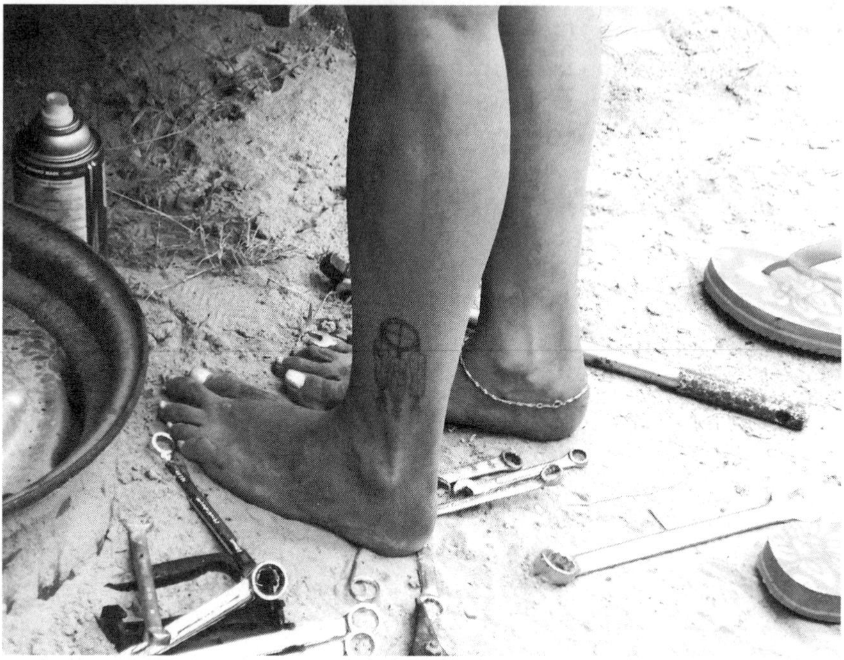

Figure 7. "Anty Fixes Cars, 2005" by Nikki Isham. (Courtesy of the nonprofit arts group In Progress in St. Paul, Minnesota; photographer Phylis Nicole Isham)

colonial depictions of Indigenous peoples. The elements of the image suggest a vibrant, complex reality; the feet of the female subject stand ready to step beyond the frame, fully realized in our imagination.

As many theorists have suggested, photography and particularly artistic photographs involve more than the image placed before us. The meaning of photographs arises from the act of "seeing" the image or beyond the image. The best work assists the viewer in making this imaginative leap. Documentary photographer Dorothea Lange famously claimed, "The camera is an instrument that teaches people how to see without a camera."[75] Working amid a complex history and hive of Indian images, Native photographers choose various paths to liberate Native representation, offering new slants or angles of sight, casting cultural light, inviting vision beyond the frame.

NOTES

1. Singer, "Introduction," ix.
2. Among Lee Marmon's well-known images is "White Man's Moccasins," which pictures tribal elder Jeff Sousea in a headband and wearing several traditional strings of beads, sitting against an adobe wall with his eyes closed. On his feet is a pair of high-topped sneakers. The photo characterizes Marmon's documentation of the contemporary, everyday reality of Native people that incorporates both tradition and change.
3. Masayesva, "Hopi Photography," 11.
4. Ibid., 10.
5. Masayesva, *Husk of Time*, 5–6.
6. Ibid., 6.
7. Ibid.
8. Here I allude to an Emily Dickinson line, "Tell all the Truth but tell it slant." This is the first line in a poem (unnamed, but sometimes referred to by the same title). The phrase "tell it slant" is often invoked in discussions of poetry's methods.
9. Romero, "The Politics of the Camera," 68.
10. Vizenor, *Fugitive Poses*, 15 and passim. In invoking these phrases from Romero and Vizenor as potential goals of Indigenous activists working in the arts, I do not intend to present them as fully equivalent terms. Romero uses the idea of sovereignty in a sense that has become popular in Indigenous studies, intending to allude to the inherent authority of tribal nations to govern themselves, and following in the stead of other Indigenous scholars (most notably Robert Warrior, who popularized the term "intellectual sovereignty" in his book *Tribal Secrets*). The origin of Vizenor's neologism is his blending of the words "survival" and "endurance" or "survival" and "resistance," which does not necessarily entail the same stance as an ideological appeal to "sovereignty." As Michael Wilson has pointed out in his book *Writing Home*, invoking sovereignty actually invokes the sense of "domestic dependent nations," the implications of which may not be the sense of resistance that is generally hoped for (xx). In discussing the "indigenous narratives of resistance" of his title, Wilson himself suggests that what these resistant writers may be vying for is a "different narrative destiny" (161). The play here on Manifest Destiny and the sense of determining destiny of and through literary art has great import for the work of Native photographers. Part of that destiny, as Wilson characterizes it, involves "a viable indigenous presence in America," which, as I suggest in other parts of this essay, also remains a key objective in the contemporary Indigenous photographic movement.

11. Lippard and Benally, *Partial Recall*, 23.
12. Vizenor, *Fugitive Poses*, 145–146, 153, and passim.
13. Silko, *Yellow Woman*, 175.
14. Durham, "Geronimo!," 56.
15. Owens, "Their Shadows Before Them," 191.
16. Gruber, "Ethnographic Salvage," 1298.
17. Vizenor, *Fugitive Poses*, 146.
18. Lippard and Benally, *Partial Recall*, 15.
19. Quoted in ibid., 29.
20. Owens, "Their Shadows Before Them," 192.
21. Makepeace, *Coming to Light*.
22. Vizenor, *Fugitive Poses*, 152.
23. Ibid., 158.
24. Smith, "Every Picture Tells a Story," 99.
25. McMaster, "Experience," 79.
26. *Beyond the Reach of Time and Change* includes essays by descendants of those featured in the Rinehart portraits, some of whom comment on the images as part of their own heritage.
27. Lippard and Benally, *Partial Recall*, 14.
28. Ibid., passim.
29. *Our People, Our Land, Our Images* contains historic photos by photographers Benjamin A. Haldane, Jennie Ross Cobb, Martin Chambi, and Berth Felix Campigli, as well as images by more contemporary photographers, including youth artists.
30. Deloria, *Playing Indian*, passim; Durham, "Geronimo!," passim.
31. Western History Collections, University of Oklahoma Libraries, Irwin Brothers 45, early twentieth century. The Collections estimates the date of this Irwin Brothers photo to be the 1890s or very early 1900s as the Irwin brothers had moved from Oklahoma, where the photograph was taken, to Arizona by 1904.
32. This image appeared on the back cover of the program for an international scholarly meeting titled "What's Next for Native American and Indigenous Studies?" hosted by the Native American Studies Department, University of Oklahoma, May 3–5, 2007; NAISA was founded at this meeting.
33. Rader, *Engaged Resistance*, 5.
34. Masayesva, *Husk of Time*, 83.
35. Ibid., 82.
36. Ibid., 18, 19.
37. Romero quotes Leslie Silko's statement—"In Victor Masayesva's hands, video is made to serve Hopi consciousness and to see with Hopi eyes ("Videomakers," 73, quoted in Romero, "Politics of the Camera," 49)—and she

directly addresses this notion of Hopi consciousness, pointing to Masayesva's films' content, which features traditional basket making, weaving, and the planting, harvesting, and storing of corn, the most sacred essence in Hopi worldview" (ibid., 49). Overall, Romero claims, Masayesva's work depicts "Hopi people within their tribal contexts" (ibid., 52). She also points to the way Masayesva's work reflects the "Hopis' historic suspicion of visual representation" and attempts to "expose the politics of Indian filmmaking" (ibid., 49). Masayesva, she notes, privilege's his Hopi viewers, exercising correct restraint in dealing with ceremonial realities, employing silence rather than explicating certain images and actions in his films, and often refusing to translate for those unfamiliar with Hopi language or culture.

38. Masayesva, *Husk of Time*, 92.
39. Deloria, *Indians in Unexpected Places*, 138. In Deloria's comments on the significance of the automobile as symbol in America, he notes how this symbolism increased the resistance of literally or figuratively "allowing" Indians automobility. He also underscores the irony of linking the modernity of automobiles to the "primitive" Natives as is done in names like "Jeep Cherokees, Pontiac Azteks, Dodge Dakotas, and other 'Indian cars'" (138 and passim).
40. Ibid., passim.
41. Ibid., 138.
42. Ibid., 137–138.
43. Masayesva, *Husk of Time*, 91.
44. Berger, "Understanding a Photograph," 293.
45. Ibid.
46. Barthes, *Camera Lucida*, passim; Sontag, *On Photography*, 15.
47. Masayesva, "Hopi Photography," 11.
48. Beck et al., *The Sacred*, 61.
49. Masayesva, "Hopi Photography," 10.
50. Suzuki, *Zen and Japanese Culture*, 220.
51. Ibid., 240.
52. Moholy-Nagy, "Photography," 166.
53. Silko, *Yellow Woman*, 181.
54. Ibid.
55. For a more thorough discussion of the Anishinaabe dream song, haiku, as well as Vizenor's work in both genres, see Blaeser, *Gerald Vizenor*, esp. 108–135.
56. Blyth, *Haiku*, 1:243.
57. Vizenor, *Matsushima*, 5; Vizenor, *Summer in the Spring*, 11.
58. Vizenor, *Manifest Manners*, 73.
59. Vizenor, *Fugitive Poses*, 15.
60. Ibid., 181–182.

61. Ibid., 182.
62. Ortiz, "What Indians Do," 104.
63. Silko, *Yellow Woman*, 175.
64. Low, "Composite Indigenous Genres," 85.
65. Vizenor, *Fugitive Poses*, 170.
66. Rader, *Engaged Resistance*, 93.
67. Sontag, *On Photography*, 88.
68. Vizenor employs this term as counter to the idea of a static image or "still" photo. See, for example, Vizenor, *Native Liberty*.
69. Vizenor, *Fugitive Poses*, 156.
70. In this instance, the poem (first published in *Verse Wisconsin* 107 [November 2011]: 36 in a slightly different form) is from a suite of poems involving water animals, Anishinaabeg mythic reality, the telling/singing of story or song poems, and the search for *mino-bimaadiziwin*, the good life. In the Anishinaabe Earthdiver Myth, both the beaver of the photo and the muskrat of the poem attempt to bring back sand for Naanabozho, but only the muskrat, Wazhashk, succeeds. The text of the poem that bears the same name as the photo is as follows:

"Dreams of Water Bodies," by Kimberly M. Blaeser

Muskrat—Wazhashk,
small whiskered swimmer,
you, a fluid arrow crossing waterways
with the simple determination
of one who has dived
purple deep into mythic quest.

Belittled or despised
as water rat on land;
hero of our Anishinaabeg people
in animal tales, creation stories
whose tellers open slowly,
magically like within a dream,
your tiny clenched fist
so all water tribes might believe.

See the small grains of sand—
Ah, only those poor few—
but they become

our turtle island
this good and well-dreamed land
where we stand in this moment
on the edge of so many bodies of water
and watch Wazhashk, our brother,
slip through pools and streams and lakes
this marshland earth hallowed by
the memory
the telling
the hope
the dive
of sleek-whiskered-swimmers
who mark a dark path

And sometimes in our water dreams
we pitiful land-dwellers
in longing
recall, and singing
make spirits ready
to follow:
bakobii.

71. Rosaldo, *Culture and Truth*, 68–87.
72. Vizenor, *Fugitive Poses*, 15.
73. Rader, *Engaged Resistance*, 1.
74. Tsinhnahjinnie and Passalacqua, *Our People, Our Land, Our Images*, 61.
75. Dorothea Lange, as quoted in the *Los Angeles Times*, 13 August 1978. In her biography of Lange, *Dorothea Lange: A Life Beyond Limits* (New York: Norton, 2011), Linda Gordon presents this quotation (xiii) and inserts the following endnote (440 n.1): "Lange believed that Max Ernst was the author of the phrase but she was not sure and I was unable to track it down."

WORKS CITED

Barthes, Roland. *Camera Lucida: Reflections on Photography*. Trans. Richard Howard. London: Vintage, 1993.
Beck, Peggy V., Nia Francisco, and Anna Lee Walters. *The Sacred: Ways of Knowledge,*

Sources of Life. Tsaile, AZ: Navajo Community College Press, 1977. Reprint, Flagstaff, AZ: Northland Publishing Co., 1990.

Berger, John. "Understanding a Photograph." In *Classic Essays on Photography*, ed. Alan Trachtenberg, 291–295. New Haven, CT: Leete's Island Books, 1980.

Blaeser, Kimberly M. *Gerald Vizenor: Writing in the Oral Tradition*. Norman: University of Oklahoma Press, 1996.

Blyth, R. H., ed. *Haiku: Eastern Culture*. Vol. 1 of *Haiku*. 4 vols. Tokyo: Hokuseido Press, 1949.

Deloria, Philip J. *Indians in Unexpected Places*. Lawrence: University Press of Kansas, 2004.

———. *Playing Indian*. New Haven, CT: Yale University Press, 1998.

Durham, Jimmie. "Geronimo!" In *Partial Recall: With Essays on Photographs of Native North Americans*, ed. Lucy Lippard and Suzanne Benally, 55–58. New York: New Press, 1992.

Evers, Larry, ed. *The South Corner of Time: Hopi, Navajo, Papago, Yaqui Tribal Literature*. Tucson: University of Arizona Press, 1980.

Gruber, Jacob W. "Ethnographic Salvage and the Shaping of Anthropology." *American Anthropologist, New Series* 72.6 (December 1970): 1289–1299.

Lippard, Lucy, and Suzanne Benally, eds. *Partial Recall: With Essays on Photographs of Native North Americans*. New York: New Press, 1992.

Low, Denise. "Composite Indigenous Genres: Cheyenne Ledger Art as Literature." *Studies in American Indian Literatures* 18.3 (Summer 2006): 83–104.

Makepeace, Anne. *Coming to Light: Edward S. Curtis and the North American Indians* (film). Coproduced by Anne Makepeace Productions, Inc. and ThirteenAVNET, 2001.

Masayesva, Victor, Jr. "Hopi Photography." In *Hopi Photographers, Hopi Images*, ed. Victor Masayesva Jr. and Erin Younger, 10–12. Tucson: University of Arizona Press, 1983.

———. *Husk of Time: The Photographs of Victor Masayesva*. Tucson: University of Arizona Press, 2006.

McMaster, Gerald. "Experience." In *Partial Recall: With Essays on Photographs of Native North Americans*, ed. Lucy Lippard and Suzanne Benally, 77–88. New York: New Press, 1992.

Moholy-Nagy, László. "Photography." In *Classic Essays on Photography*, ed. Alan Trachtenberg, 165–166. New Haven, CT: Leete's Island Books, 1980.

NAISA conference brochure. University of Oklahoma, 2007. Http://naisa.org/sites/default/files/2007%20NAISA%20Program%20U%200f%200klahoma_0.pdf.

Ortiz, Simon, ed. *Beyond the Reach of Time and Change: Native Reflections on the Frank A. Rineheart Photograph Collection*. Tucson: University of Arizona Press, 2004.

———. "What Indians Do." In *Fightin': New and Collected Stories*, 104–111. Chicago: Thunder's Mouth Press, 1983.

Owens, Louis. "Their Shadows Before Them: Photographing Indians." In *Trading Gazes: Euro-American Women Photographers and Native North Americans, 1880–1940*, ed. Susan Bernardin et al., 187–192. Piscataway, NJ: Rutgers University Press, 2003.

Rader, Dean. *Engaged Resistance: American Indian Art, Literature, and Film from Alcatraz to the NMAI.* Austin: University of Texas Press, 2011.

Romero, Channette. "The Politics of the Camera: Visual Storytelling and Sovereignty in Victor Masayesva's *Itam Hakim, Hopiit*." *Studies in American Indian Literatures* 22.1 (Spring 2010): 49–75.

Rosaldo, Renato. *Culture and Truth: The Remaking of Social Analysis.* Boston: Beacon Press, 1989. Reprint, London: Routledge, 1993.

Silko, Leslie Marmon. *Yellow Woman and a Beauty of the Spirit.* New York: Simon & Schuster, 1996.

Singer, Beverly R. "Introduction." In Victor Masayesva, *Husk of Time: The Photographs of Victor Masayesva*, ix–xviii. Tucson: University of Arizona Press, 2006.

Smith, Paul Chaat. "Every Picture Tells a Story." In *Partial Recall: With Essays on Photographs of Native North Americans*, ed. Lucy Lippard and Suzanne Benally, 77–88. New York: New Press, 1992.

Sontag, Susan. *On Photography.* New York: Picador, 1977.

Suzuki, Daisetz Teitarō. *Zen and Japanese Culture.* Princeton, NJ: Princeton University Press, 1959.

Tsinhnahjinnie, Hulleah J., and Veronica Passalacqua, eds. *Our People, Our Land, Our Images: International Indigenous Photographers.* Berkeley, CA: Heyday Books, 2006.

Vizenor, Gerald. *Fugitive Poses: Native American Scenes of Absence and Presence.* Lincoln: University of Nebraska Press, 2000.

———. *Manifest Manners: Narratives on Postindian Survivance.* Lincoln: University of Nebraska Press, 1994; First Bison Books edition, 1999.

———. *Matsushima: Haiku.* Minneapolis: Nodin Press, 1984.

———. *Native Liberty: Natural Reason and Cultural Survivance.* Lincoln: University of Nebraska Press, 2009.

———, ed. *Summer in the Spring: Anishinaabe Lyric Poems and Stories, New Edition.* Norman: University of Oklahoma Press, 1993.

Warrior, Robert. *Tribal Secrets: Recovering American Indian Intellectual Traditions.* Minneapolis: University of Minnesota Press, 1995.

Wilson, Michael. *Writing Home: Indigenous Narratives of Resistance.* East Lansing: Michigan State University Press, 2008.

INTERLUDE

RefleXions
A Creative Essay

EVELINA ZUNI LUCERO

CULTURAL CAPITAL

DURING AND AFTER THE MESEA CONFERENCE IN JUNE 2012, MY THREE companions and I rented an apartment on Passeig de Gracia, 115, located in the posh fashion district of Barcelona. There, I began reading Diné/Laguna Pueblo novelist A. A. Carr's manuscript, "Pleiades Man." Coincidentally, or maybe not, the novel addressed the issues under discussion at the conference: Migration. Transnationalism. Transglobalization. Carr's characters, two Native American cousins/lovers/skinwalkers, have migrated from North America to Europe and are engaged in the business of selling Native American spirituality to gullible Europeans in Bordeaux, France. The protagonist struggles with a sense of displacement he feels as an immigrant and purveyor of culture for self-gain.

Skinwalkers, shapeshifters, breaking of taboos. The subject matter leaped off the pages and into Barcelona, not too unlike the novel's setting in Bordeaux: a port city in an apartment in a building among buildings, a canyon wall of them stretching along narrow eighteenth-century-style streets congested with compact cars.

I read into the night, unable to sleep, my internal clock still ticking to Mountain Daylight Savings Time. Finally, I put the manuscript down and drifted into an uneasy sleep vaguely aware of being in a strange bed in a small, dark, shoebox of a room before I sank into terrifying nightmares intensified by my own sense of displacement. I awoke to a gray dawn. Diffused light filtered in through the curtains from the inner courtyard—a large ventilation shaft, really, where laundry was hung outside windows on drying racks. A garbage truck beeped as it lifted a garbage bin and noisily emptied its contents before lowering it to the street with a thud.

Sitting at the dining room table, still groggy, sipping a strong cup of coffee, I gazed out the large window at the open apartment windows and balconies in the building across, its front awash in the morning sun. Occasionally, feeling like a Peeping Tom, I spied residents moving about a room. Traffic from the street and voices of passersby carried in from the street below. The city was awake. Jane scribbled in her journal while I struggled to recall the night's terror. Something related to Carr's novel. Something about evil lurking out there in narrow, convoluting streets that led nowhere and provided no escape. For the duration of my fourteen days in Barcelona, I was unable to pick up the manuscript again for fear of recurring nightmares.

¿QUE ES?

Me • di • at • ing
Cultural Capital
Buffalo
Bill
Codifies
Lies
Distortions
Confusion
¿Quien?
Cobell vs. Salazar
Identify
Me Llamo
Story Time
Space Place
History
Whose?
Shrinking
Expanding
Signs
Memory vs. Fiction
Myth vs. Truth
Picasso
Fractured

Mosaic
Guadí
Amorphous
S*h*iftS*h*ape
CIB, BIA
M-E-S-E-A
1-1-5
Uno, Uno, Cinco,
Por favor
Cosigns
vs.
Stop signs
Blue Ravens
Crows in Common
Transmedia
Cristóbal Colón
TransAtlantic
Okah Tubbee
Encoding
HipHopping
Okee Dokee
Tricksters
Codetalking
Reel Injuns
HelioTropes
Gone
Viral Communicative
X-ing, TeXting, SeXting,
FaXing
RefraXions
Shape*sHIFTING*
Translations
Blurring
Indian
Ness
Who
me?

TIME, SPACE, PLACE

As my companions and I make our way from Passeig de Gracia down to the Metro, speeding underground, then emerging onto La Rambla, my senses fill to the brim: Buildings shoulder one another down one block to the next, rising sleek and smart, modern and arty, shops and offices on the street level, apartments atop one another, floor after floor; foot, bicycle, motorbike, and automobile traffic crisscross; greenery spills over balcony rails; public art here and there and everywhere; narrow brick passageways; street signs, store signs, graffiti, billboards in Spanish and Catalan. Whiffs of coffee and baked goods from shops. We can feel the ocean in the air.

Hmmm. This is not unlike other European cities—close living, personal and communal space economical and tight, developed and tamed. Every available spot staked and claimed. No wonder Europeans went gaga at the first sight of Native America. All that open space, virgin territory. Empty. Free for the taking. It must have boggled their minds. All the space gone to waste.

Spanish men sporting short beards and mustaches, somehow so distinctly European-looking, gesture animatedly as they converse in clusters in front of shops. Women swing their hips down the street, stepping smartly in high heels, stylish and beautiful in deep-hued fabrics. Families frolic in parks. Corner markets display fresh fruit, vegetables, and flowers in open bins. Bicyclists zip past, toting bread and cheeses in recyclable bags in baskets mounted behind their seat. Viejos sit on benches, enjoying the shade of trees and cool air. The Spanish language fills the air, a refreshing change from English Only.

Inside a trendy women's apparel store, American pop music blares. Michael Jackson. The universal icon. Dead but alive.

TRANSMISSION

The laundry detergent pod eXploded in her hand into her eye the way a narrative line eXplodes and spews fragments of memories onto the page. The way the self-inflicted bullet eXploded out of the barrel at high velocity into his chest. His heart, then our hearts, absorbed the full shock of the expanding bullet. Transmission.

She lifted the pod out of the detergent compartment atop the front-loader in our apartment. The water rushing through the compartment hadn't been enough to break it open and release the detergent. The blue gel packet was wet and intact in her palm when it eXploded, transmission, from one point to the next, spewing the caustic chemicals into her face, burning her eye and reddening the area around it. She yelled in pain, waking us to find her crying in the hallway, her husband comforting her, helping her wash her eye with water to no avail, causing Winnie and Jane to rush her out the door in search of a pharmacy with a green cross (+) medical icon signaling OPEN. Alone in the sudden quiet with the laundry, I gingerly placed an evil eye gel pod into the washer tub atop the clothes, restarted the cycle, watched the soap suds sloshing in the washer window. A doctor's office is nearby, I was told they were told. This time we all went in search of help. Down the stairs into the street. Up the street. Up the stairs. Closed. Too early? Tuesday. 9:30 A.M. No choice but to find a hospital. Cross the street. A flurry of urgent Spanish. Transmission. From one point to the next. The taxi dropped us off at the emergency room of the nearest hospital where her eye was washed with solution—a common injury for niños, they said—then she was directed to an eye specialist. Another taxi, another hospital, a woman's hospital where tired but relieved mámas carried small bundles in their arms and pregnant mujeras, bellies full and taut as the detergent pod, came and went. Find the optometry wing. The doctor brought relief, an eye patch, and a prescription to be filled back at the pharmacy, green cross, near the apartment.

Up the stairs, down the hall. The washing cycle was complete.

CRISTÓBAL COLÓN

On her trip to Spain, my friend Christina from Jemez Pueblo ventured to the pier in Barcelona, past the bronze statue of Cristóbal Colón mounted on a column rising above the city into the clouds, his index finger pointing east to the Mediterranean, not west to the (Old) New World of the Americas. Which way was he going? Christina stood at the ocean's edge, staring across the waters, thinking of Cristobal and how he set off on his voyage, what he started. The waves still lapping almost 510 years later. *This is where it all began.*

In central Italy, in Umbertide, small and provincial, hardly anyone spoke English. I didn't speak Italian, only a rusty, crippled Spanish. All the signs, the menus, the train schedules, the essentials, in Italian. *Italian for Dummies* didn't cover everything. Scusi. Habla inglés? *This is what it's like to be culturally illiterate. It feels like blindness, like helpless, like a Mexican immigrant in an unwelcoming United States, like a traditionalist negotiating mainstream America.*

Like standing, rooted on the pier in Barcelona, staring out over the ocean. Like sailing over the ocean blue toward the edge of the earth where you'll fall into the future. You have to be brave.

RECREATION

> If anyone were to try and copy *Las Meninas*, entirely in complete good faith, and for example got to a certain point—and if I were the copier—would say to myself, "and if I just put this a little more to the right or left?" I would try to do it in my own way, forgetting about Velázquez. The challenge would surely make me modify or change the light, due to having changed the position of a character. In this way, little by little, I would paint *Meninas* who would seem detestable to a pure copyist—they would not be what he thought he saw on Velázquez's canvas, but they would be my *Meninas.*[1]
>
> —PABLO PICASSO

BACK TO THE FUTURE

A historical imagining of 1541 when the Spaniards first entered New Mexico and encountered a Trickster whom the Spaniards called the Turk, not because he was one but because he looked like one. With his words, the Turk spun the mythical dream of The Seven Cities of Gold that he called Quivira. The tale sent the Spaniards on a wild goose chase across the Great Plains:

Sporadic at first, then with regularity, Elsie dreamed of the Turk. At first she watched him from a distance talking avidly to strange, bearded men. The Turk gestured wildly, always pointing east. Then he slowly spread open his arms to indicate an incredible vastness. Excited, the bearded men started talking all at once in Spanish, shouting "Quivira!" The Turk watched them closely, his face impassive. When the men turned away, his eyes went hard, dark and sharp as obsidian.[2]

E=MC^2

What is Me • di • at • ing? Is it the act of going between? The point of transmission, transforming, translating, transference? The = sign in a balanced equation that acts as the catalyst? Is it like Cathy Waegner working tirelessly to bring together the diverse American, Native American, and European presenters at the MESEA conference in Barcelona, Spain, June 2012, to discuss what we do, what we transmit, translate, transform, *mediate* in whatever medium? With patience and persistence like the herder of feral cats, she finally gathers us for lunch in the cafeteria, where we sit at long tables, somehow all of us still in our same groups, talking to the same people we had been talking to since we got there. Separately, we are together like neutrons and protons waiting for the electron to show up so we can eXplode and transmit, transform, translate, transfer energy that is greater than anyone could do alone.

TRANSATLANTIC

At the Barcelona airport, parting ways:

> "Adios, Amiga."
> "Hasta la vista."

I lost my loaner international cell phone at the airport, probably leaving it in a bin at the security checkpoint. I couldn't text home. Couldn't even text mi amiga to tell her I lost my phone. The plane rose up in the air up over the statue of Christopher Columbus. We sailed the blue skies over the Atlantic, transported back home to the United States, long transformed, translated, transfigured from indigenous America.

NOTES

1. Museu Picasso de Barcelona, "The Pigeons."
2. Originally published in Evelina Zuni Lucero, "Prologue: Una Historia," *Oregon Literary Review* 2.2 (Summer/Fall 2007), http://www.oregonlitrev.org/v2n2/OLR-lucero.htm); reprinted as "Historia de Manaña," in Sanchez et al., *White Shell Water Place*. The quotation is from page 73 of the reprinted story.

WORKS CITED

Museu Picasso de Barcelona. "The Pigeons, Highlights from the Collection." Http://www.bcn.cat/museupicasso/en/collection/mpb70–450.html.

Sanchez, F. Richard, with Stephen Wall and Ann Filemyr, eds. *White Shell Water Place: An Anthology on Native American Reflections on the 400 Anniversary of the Founding of Santa Fe, New Mexico.* Santa Fe, NM: Sunstone Press, 2010.

Festa de Sant Joan

June 23, 2012, Barcelona, Spain

JANE HALADAY

This isn't where it started,
but here is where it begins.
Twenty-three juny in the year 2012,
in the rented apartament en
Calle Passeig de Gracia.
Aquí en las calles y espacios
de la ciudad de Barcelona,
after watching Spain conquer France
in soccer in the tapas bar with Evelina,
bellies stretched with papas bravas
y red pimentos stuffed with tuna.

Summer in Barcelona
drops upon us
like a bomb.
Now, the streets throb and echo
with the gunpowder bursts
of the petadores men and children,
mujeres y familias lined up for
en la plaça this afternoon
across the street
from our apartment.
I come to Barcelona
to see Picasso y Miró
to eat cuttlefish in olive oil
to use my California high school Spanish

to buy an all-day ticket for twenty-four Euros
to ride arriba in the double-decker tourist bus
through the shady Parc Montjüic where
brilliant lime green parrots
slice through date palms conversing
as I sit with my friend from Isleta Pueblo
who carries within
the blood de las indígenas
who in 1680 rose up
across this ocean,
against the colonizing forebears
of these beautiful Spanish women
in fabulous leather sandals
the gorgeous men in linen shirts
we two track
while navigating crowded streets
like ancient river trade routes
to lay claim to our possessions in
present-tense non-Catalan Español.

Sí. Verdad. Histories happen just like this.
Compramos cafecitos y comidas Catalan,
my friend the Pueblo writer
and me, the white teacher
from North Carolina.
We mediate together
the streets' tight and ordered beauty
recognizing how too much compression
leads to sinister expansion
to a giddy blind desire
for the spaces and philosophies
long inhabited by others.
New worlds on behalf of ancient saints.
At some point, something has to give.

Now, a breeze floats through my window
from the Balearic Sea over which
Colón still confidently points.
We saw him from the bus
towering bronze beside the bay

atop his sixty-meter pedestal, arm
outstretched in a gesture dooming millions
on the very spot he returned to after
igniting an unsought Taino destiny.

The spangled petadores
light the skies as surely as the stars
must have looked to Colón,
lost navigator desperate to possess
for the glory of queen and king.
Worlds away, a lone dog,
pobrecito, yips and howls
at the chaos en las calles swirling
through this night of celebration.
The Spanish skies pulse
with artificial skylight as
the little dog across the alley
barks on in fear and protest
unilluminated by our brilliance.

PART THREE

Performance, Gender, and Cultural Capital

"The Bear Is Our Protector"

Metaphor and Mediation in the Northern Ute (Nuche) Bear Dance

SALLY McBETH

BASED ON YEARS OF FIELDWORK WITH THE UTES AND ATTENDANCE at numerous annual Bear Dances, this study focuses on the symbolism and mediated meanings of the twenty-first-century Northern Ute Bear Dance. A uniquely Native American spring social dance, the Bear Dance has largely retained its parameters and functions through the ages. Arising from a mythical encounter between a she-bear and a male hunter, the Bear Dance includes music, dance, storytelling, joking, and courting. The Utes say they have been Bear Dancing for millennia, and the dance may indeed be well over 1,000 years old. Gradual developments in language, religious connection, and gender roles can be traced, and strategic accommodations have been made to the twenty-first century—the use of cell phones and Facebook to advertise the dance, for instance, loudspeakers, passing on the tradition through Head Start, alluding to contemporary consumer products; these developments and accommodations have mediated and significantly modified but not erased the original meanings of this traditional dance.

I combine the authority of Ute tribal members through interviews, testimonies delivered at the Bear Dance, and banter by the master of ceremonies (MC) with the theoretical underpinnings of anthropologists who investigate the importance of symbol and metaphor in ritual.[1] From this material, at least four levels of mediation emerge: the deep negotiation between binaries in ritual; the symbolic participation of the bear in Ute lifeways; the mediation in performance as in the MC dialogue; and the effect on the dance of its propagation through "mass" and "viral" media.

The liminality and ambiguity of the most profound point of negotiation in ritual, the intersection between two realms, permit the mediating between ritualistic binaries such as sacred/secular, natural/supernatural, male/female, traditional/modern, and nature/culture, and thus make a variety of understandings and social applications possible.[2] For example, as I demonstrate, the slippage between the sacred and the secular, which was present as early as in the ur-myth establishing the Bear Dance ritual, has developed in various directions, especially since the Christianization of the Utes.

Today the three Ute tribes (who collectively call themselves Nuche, "the people") live on three reservations, two in the four-corners area of Colorado and one in north-eastern Utah; the Northern Ute bands (now officially called the Uintah and Ouray Ute Indian Tribe) were divested of their Colorado homelands and forcibly removed to Utah in 1881. In the past, the Utes practiced a flexible subsistence system sometimes called the seasonal round. Extended family groups (from twenty to one hundred people) moved through known hunting and gathering grounds (several hundred square miles) on a seasonal basis, taking advantage of the plant and animal species available. The image of a group of Indians randomly and endlessly searching for foodstuffs in a semidesert clime is far from the truth. Rather, the seasonal round is a regular circuit in which the group moves from eco-zone to eco-zone, harvesting and hunting the periodic abundance of flora and fauna.[3]

This elegant adaptation required a profound and systematic knowledge of the territory, the plant and animal life, seasonal and annual fluctuations, as well as preservation and storage techniques. Cooperation and communication among and between bands was also indispensable. The speakers of the Ute language did not necessarily think of themselves as a tribe. Folks from different bands intermarried, recognized each other, and traded, but did not otherwise maintain a larger tribal organization. Bands seasonally congregated for communal rabbit or antelope hunts or pine nut harvests, and for the annual spring Bear Dance.

For the Nuche, dance is rooted in communal celebration and is believed to have survival power and cosmic significance critical for the continuation of their culture. The Bear Dance is a socially integrating force that connects Utes with their traditions, their land, their past, and their heritage. It is a celebration of survival and as such is a mnemonic of tradition, history, and cosmology. The twenty-first-century Bear Dance looms large in contemporary Ute practices and traditions, as well as moral instruction, since tribal members are participants rather than passive spectators.

The Bear Dance banter by the MC clearly shows the integration of traditional beliefs with instructive and modernizing tactics, encoded in entertaining humor. The MC (always male in my observations and a member of the all-male singing group) carries on an ongoing monologue or dialogue with the participants in between the songs and dances. This banter draws on ritualistic themes such as the bear as protector, spring and rejuvenation, healing, but not without joking about relationships or dance etiquette with allusions to contemporary consumer products. The repartee—in English rather than Ute—regularly includes elements of freedom and frivolity, which are pervasive in the Bear Dance: "Dance like you're not scared." "Dance like you're single." "Get ready for tomorrow with Bengay and Icy Hot, can't forget the Icy Hot." This diversity, from the sacred (rejuvenation, healing) to the secular (joking), is an important component of the resiliency of the dance. The ritual thus constantly produces social meanings within the mediative performance in correlation with the more serious considerations of the Utes' relationship with the bear who protects them and thus their tribal identity.

There are many versions of how the Bear Dance came to the Utes. In abbreviated format, it is based on an encounter between a she-bear and two male hunters. The hunters, frequently brothers, were hunting in the fall in the mountains and came across a she-bear growling and clawing on a tree, preparing for winter hibernation. Neal Buck Cloud, a Southern Ute tribal elder, tells the story this way:

> There were two brothers who had a habit of going to the mountains; the mountains are high places where you can connect, peacefully, with the spiritual. These brothers were drawn to the high points, the highest mountains they could find. While they sat there for some time, looking down, they could see a bear den located just below where they sat and the bears were basking in the sun.
>
> One day, the younger brother said, "You know, one day I'm going to be down there with them bears. I have fallen in love with the she-bear down there." The older brother thought he was kidding, the bear is a wild animal, but finally one day the younger brother said he would stay, after all, stating, "We are really all the same, we are all created by the maker. But know that our people will accuse you of abandoning me; they will accuse you even of killing me. But wait three days and do not return until the fourth day." So the younger brother stayed, and entered the den, and the older brother returned home. Indeed, he was interrogated and accused of killing his brother. They guarded him in a tipi, and finally after three days, he told the village that he would take them to his brother.

> He came up to the den from the south and called his brother's name as he had been directed. The brother emerged from the den, and he had hair all over his body and he told his people that the she-bear had given the tribe a dance. She told them to build a corral in the spring of the year that would be anchored to the east, since that is the direction that the sun rises. Cut notches in a stick and when you draw another piece of wood over it, it will growl like the bear. The dance also imitates the movements of a bear, moving back and forth and scratching on a tree, after hibernation. This is the Bear Dance. Maybe the younger brother was craving for love, but in return he was given a specific knowledge.[4]

Oral histories such as the above provide common identity, promulgate ethics, reinforce values, and pass from generation to generation. Since the she-bear is a mediating agent, she contributes to the production and reproduction of meaning in Ute society; the performance of the dance is a ritual choreography that passes on not only the dance tradition but also ancient connections between the animal world, the spirit world, and the world of humans. It is both a sacred and secular event maintaining balance in the world of humans and mediating between the natural (human) and spiritual worlds. Throughout Native North America, bears are highly respected and linked with supernatural powers; they are viewed as healers and patron of shamans and herbalists because of the many human-like characteristics they possess. They rummage for roots and plants, are highly intelligent, and are members of a hierarchical and structured group.[5] To the Utes, the bear is one of many "animal people," an anthropomorphic category unfamiliar to most Euro-Americans. In the oral rendition above, the man who fell in love with the she-bear says, "We are really all the same, we are all created by the maker."

Protocol requires that the dance not be undertaken until after the first thunderstorm, which is after bears come out of hibernation. The dance corral varies in size according to the location. A small dance corral is about eighty feet in circumference and is surrounded by a woven brush enclosure with no roof or floor; attendees bring folding chairs to set around the perimeter of the circle. Cedar trees are cut and set up on the two sides of the entrance, which is on the east. While not all do so, one is supposed to bless himself or herself upon entering the dance grounds by touching the cedar and saying a prayer (tobacco, cedar, sage, and sweet grass are believed by many Native peoples to be the four sacred herbs). The dance is open to the public, but generally advertised only locally. Men who want to dance typically sit on the north side; women, children, and families sit on the

Figure 1. Bear Dance corral with brush enclosure; men holding hands, facing east. (Photo by Sally McBeth)

south, although this arrangement is flexible, and visitors can sit in a variety of locations. The dance mediates between the male/female binary, bringing both together in a symbolic circular corral.

The dance is a four-day affair. The steps are simple and imitate a bear walking on its hind legs. The basic step is left foot step forward, right front together; left back, right back together; in Ute it is called *mamakwanika*, the back-and-forth dance. Partners dance across from each other, but not touching each other for the first two days, and then when the Cat Man, the dance leader, approves, they can couple up for the last two days. The couples then move east and west across the dance grounds with a lilting step. When dancers fall (this does not occur at every dance), they are supposed to lie where they have fallen until an elder comes and blesses them. An alternate tradition is that the Bear Dance simply ends when someone falls. Children are warned to be on good behavior and not run around inside the corral as they might trip someone up. These caveats are practical but also remind the adults and children of the mythological origins of the sacred and secular dance, which was gifted to the tribe by the (super)natural bear.

No one seems to know (or will share) the origin of the label "Cat Man."

Figure 2. Bear Dance corral entrance with cedar trees and couples dancing. (Photo by Sally McBeth)

He is present on the third and fourth days of the celebration. It is he who touches a couple, or sometimes a row of couples, with a willow stick, and gives them permission to partner up and dance east and west across the Bear Dance grounds. MC banter includes: "Do what the Cat Man says." "Meow-meow man comes tomorrow. Don't forget to bring some *Meow Mix* for the Cat Man tomorrow." Although the inception of the Cat Man is unclear, the mediation is apparent when the Cat Man enters the dance grounds, allowing males and females to move out of their separate realms into what is clearly a heterosexual domain, at least inside the perimeter of the corral.

The four days of the dance are all female choice. On the first day girls or women select a member of the opposite sex to whom they are not related, walk over to where he is sitting in the dance corral, flick their shawl in his direction, and walk out to the center of the dance ground, facing west. I have been told that in the past, this example of female agency was unusual; today, however, it is seen as a quaint and attractive tradition. Women cannot dance without a shawl. So ubiquitous is the shawl that instead of asking if one intends to dance, the question posed is, "Did you bring your shawl?" The females' partners join them, standing across from them, facing east.

Figure 3. Singers at resonator with wood rasp and bone instrument. (Photo by Sally McBeth)

The females form one line, the men another, with the two lines facing each other. Males hold hands with males, females with females. It does not seem to be a competitive dance. In my years of attending Bear Dances, I have never heard a comment on how well (or poorly) a couple danced. Members of my interview sample have told me the dance is in imitation of the bear as it steps forward and backward at a standing tree, sharpening its claws for the coming hunt. Altogether, they say, this dance creates a rhythm that quickens the flow of blood in the body and renews a zest for life.

The music is made when a bone drawn down across a wooden rasp resonates on a hollow (now corrugated tin) box. The music, accompanied by a group of all-male singers, is supposed to sound like the growling of a bear and a bear clawing on a tree. Most Bear Dance music does not have words (vocables are substituted), but at least one Bear Dance song has words. Translated into English the song says: "The Bear is making a noise. The noise sounds like the lightning. The Bear is traveling a path. And the path is shaped like lightning." The vocables/words of the music are harsh, aggressive, and rhythmic and reflect the dance's vernal significance.

For its participants, the Bear Dance holds many memories of past occurrences of the ritual. One woman in my interview sample echoed many others' views on the significance of the annual repetition of the event:

> When we were little, our parents would go out and buy us new outfits; it is important to look your best, be neat, be traditional. We kids would be all washed and scrubbed. We would pack a picnic lunch and go together as a family. As a young child, I am not sure that I totally understood exactly what the Bear Dance meant, but for us it was a special occasion for dressing up, looking good, getting new clothes.

Many preeminent anthropologists have examined the power and use of symbol and metaphor in ritual including but not limited to Franz Boas, E. E. Evans-Pritchard, Claude Levi-Strauss, Clifford Geertz, and Victor Turner. Combining the theoretical frameworks of Geertz and Turner, I examine the symbol of the bear in the Bear Dance in terms of the emic (insider) and etic (outsider) approach and the dance's effect on social patterns. Clifford Geertz, the "principal architect of symbolic anthropology,"[6] asserts that culture is embodied in public symbols, and is not a cognitive model that resides only in individuals' heads. Members of and outsiders to the culture can discern these outward symbols and better understand the subtleties of the culture's worldview through observing ritual and the like.[7] Victor Turner presents how symbols, particularly symbolic metaphors in ritual and the establishment of antistructures, maintain societal processes.

Many Utes whom I have interviewed have told me that the bear is the Utes' protector, supporting the conclusion that this is a foundational metaphor for Ute identity. Turner reminds us (acknowledging Max Black) that "a metaphorical statement has two distinct subjects—a principal subject [here: bear] and a 'subsidiary' one [here: protector]."[8] The figurative assertion that the bear is the tribal protector is performed publicly in the Bear Dance, showing respect for the bear as "principal subject." The dancers also draw strength from her spirit, an outgrowth of the "protective" function of the "subsidiary" subject.

A 2012 advertisement in the Ute tribal newspaper for the reopening of a grocery store and bowling alley provides a Ute lens on the bear as symbolic metaphor:

> What does the bear mean to the Utes? The Meaning of the Bear Logo: The bear has always had special significance to the Ute Indian People. The Utes originated the "bear dance," an annual dance ceremony signifying the beginning of spring and a new year. The bear is strong, protective, family-oriented,

> and solidly connected and grounded to the land. As with the bear, the Utes are mountain people. The mountains have always been our home, our haven, and our sanctuary. We proudly share this home with the bear and all the other creatures and living things. We are one with them.[9]

In one respect the advertisement equates the bear with the future ideal customers of the grocery store addressed by the entrepreneurs. However, the advertising text's instrumentalization of the Bear Dance and further traditional lore, sense of place, and declaration of difference from non-Native counterparts moves far beyond mere commercial purposes, demonstrating the mediational identity functions of such symbolic rituals as the dance.

As is evident, the bear means many things to the Utes, including the coming of spring and the season of courting and fertility. One of the most common statements made in the Bear Dance grounds by the MC and participants is that the Bear Dance is a celebration of the end of winter. This ritualistic function is linked to social behavior; frequently called the beginning of a new year, many Ute friends have told me that it is a time when old clothing is repaired or new clothing purchased. Extra food is purchased for guests. Advice and instruction are given as to whom not to dance with, what the proper behavior for children in the dance corral is, which side of the corral to sit on, and how to demonstrate the proper demeanor to the Cat Man.

As the protector of the Utes, the spirit of the bear who gifted the dance to the tribe is obligated to support the sustainability of the tribe. For example, she keeps the tribe safe and healthy, helps maintain tribal identity and tribal land, and is responsible for maintaining prescribed social relations and proscribed behaviors. Northern Ute Leah told me that her band members—communicating via text messaging!—combine the ritualistic with health advice in "stretching children":

> When you hear the first thunder and lightning of the season, the first thing that you should think about is the Bear Dance. This spring, when I heard the first audible thunder and lightning here on the reservation, I got a text message from my friend who texted, "Did you stretch your children?" What this means is that it is our tradition that during the spring, the season of fertility and growth, thunder and lightning, the Bear Dance season, you are supposed to take your children outside and stretch their limbs so that they will grow strong and tall and be healthy in their body, their soul, and their spirit.

Tribal members associate the bear with well-being. She comes out of hibernation and as the protector and main symbol of the Utes, is responsible for a vigorous and healthy tribe. Ute language instructor and tribal member Venita describes the healing powers of the Bear Dance and, perhaps surprisingly, how female hormonal processes can hinder this healing:

> I understand that this dance is about healing. This is what I see. There is a healing in this dance that was given to the Ute by the Creator or God or the bear or maybe all of those things combined—whoever or whatever you believe in. Many traditions are included and combined in the Bear Dance.
>
> Women on their menstrual period or women who are pregnant are not even supposed to come to the dance, they are especially not supposed to be inside the arbor. When a woman is on her moon, her blood is very very powerful and a symbol of her fertility. She is so powerful, that her moon time can block the healing.

Here we see that the metaphor of the bear as protector takes on a new mediative meaning. As protector, she is responsible for health and healing, and as a female bear, she is also concerned about the power associated with women's menstruations and pregnancies.

Leo, another tribal member, gave a fairly long speech in Ute. All that I understood were the phrases "high blood pressure" and "depression," which were in English. Afterward we were talking, and he said: "We don't worship no God but the one Jesus Christ. He gave us this dance for our healing. My mom was sick and she danced, and she was miraculously healed. She was entered by the Holy Spirit. That's why I went up there and spoke." This quote not only demonstrates the healing power of the dance but also the variety of religious (and language) traditions that are included in this twenty-first-century celebration. The Bear Dance becomes a platform for the mediation between the Indigenous sacred and the Christian sacred, as many Utes have converted to a variety of Christian sects, yet combine traditional and modern practices and rituals.

Traditional Utes believe that their primal ancestors were bears and that bears are cognizant of this connection.[10] A woman in my interview sample emphasized that the bear and its dance are a powerful source of identity for the Utes: "The Bear Dance started a long time ago, we don't know how far back; its origins are with the Ute people. We didn't borrow it from any other tribe; it is an original dance of the Ute people." Pride in this original Ute dance is clear. It is very different from the more common intertribal pow wow that most Native and non-Native people are familiar with. Metaphorically, the Bear Dance and bear as central figure of the dance are believed to be alive, while moving across reservation and community boundaries.

Nuche cosmology, story, and performance are etched across the landscape of Ute homelands, expressing tribal identity. Tribal member Eva explained it to me this way:

> This Bear Dance travels, it moves! It starts here in April in Randlett [Utah], and then moves in May up to Ft. Duchesne [Utah], then over to Colorado, to Ignacio [Southern Ute Reservation] and then Towoac [Ute Mountain Ute Reservation] in July, and finally ends in Blanden, Utah, at White Mesa [a small Ute community in Utah] in September where we prepare the Bear to go back into hibernation, or at least, that is what I think.

The Utes' strong association with land was noted empathetically by John Wesley Powell well over a century ago. Writing between 1868 and 1880, he observed:

> An Indian will never ask to what nation or tribe or body of people another Indian belongs but to "what land do you belong and how are you land-named?" Thus the very name of the Indian is his title deed to his home and thus it is that these Indians have contended so fiercely for the possession of the soil.[11]

Land and attachment to land require a custodian, a guardian. The Utes and their protector the bear are these stewards.

Petroglyphs (a type of rock art pecked into rock) believed to depict the Bear Dance offer another example of Ute identity through inscribing the dance onto the Ute landscape. For example, near Montrose, Colorado (Ute ancestral territory), at the undated Shavano site, there are bear prints "etched" into the rock, emerging from a natural crack in the stone. They lead to an image of a bear crawling up a tree; a free-standing bear with enlarged paws is also present, in addition to other graphics. Utes and rock art specialists who have visited this site believe not only that these petroglyphs depict the Bear Dance but also that this site may have been a traditional Bear Dance grounds. The dance becomes a part of the landscape, tribal identity, and Ute cosmology as Natives inscribe the memory of the dance on Ute ancestral homelands—the symbol is concretely detailed on stone. This reassertion of the bear's power to reconcile the natural and supernatural worlds as well as ancestral and reservation boundaries is yet another strong indicator of her mediating abilities.

One might think that the Ute Bear Dance offers evidence of female power. After all, it was bestowed on the Utes by a she-bear, and it is a woman's choice dance; men cannot refuse, or they must pay (but they do not sit

Figure 4. Ute Bear petroglyph, Montrose, Colorado. (Photo by Sally McBeth)

inside the dance ground arbor unless they want to dance). I have been told repeatedly that this dance honors women. A simple structural interpretation of the traditional story, however, demonstrates that males are clearly the central and active figures; much more is known about the two brothers than the mysterious she-bear. Additionally, the singers, the MC, and the dance leader (Cat Man) are all male. Males are, however, required to shrug off their masculinity—they must hold hands with each other, wait to be asked to dance, and otherwise take on a more passive role, an antistructural inversion of normative gender roles.

Women's roles are more active, but their dress and demeanor are dictated. Women must wear a shawl, are supposed to wear a skirt or dress, and moccasins. They shake hands with their respective partners at the end of the dance. They are not supposed to be in the dance grounds if they are menstruating or pregnant. Women, not men, are usually the objects of the male MC's banter. For example, "We need security over here—there are two ladies fighting over one guy, and the ugly one's winning." Or, "Lucinda here says that all of her boyfriends have left and married white ladies." Men are also teased, but for different reasons than women. An example of male-directed MC banter is as follows, "If you guys can hear me, honk your horns"—followed by much horn honking in the parking lot. "Why are you guys out there? You should be in here dancing. Tailgating is for football games."

Clearly the MC is trying to lure the males out of their pickup trucks and into the corral. I have regularly prowled the parking lot querying men, "Why are you out here instead of in the dance grounds?" A typical group response is this: "Oh no, all of our ex-wives, ex-girlfriends are in there waiting to pounce on us, and we're too scared of them! We have to pay them if we don't want to dance, and they've already taken all of our money." In this quip we see both male solidarity and the playfulness of this dance, and we might question to what degree the Bear Dance is a reconnection to an important primordial moment. The twenty-first-century humorous, playful, and decidedly postmodern aspects of this ritual serve to reinforce its vitality as an emic, identifying event.

In his book *The Ritual Process: Structure and Anti-Structure*, Victor Turner says that societies are rigorously structured and that people desire escape from this structure.[12] Rituals may provide this escape through antistructure—in the case of the Bear Dance, through a breaking down of gendered social roles. Following Turner, we might also interpret the dance in the light of *communitas* as achieved through antistructure.[13] According to Turner, *communitas* appears where structure does not.[14] Turner uses the term "*communitas*" to convey a stronger unifying human bond than the word "community" implies. In many ways, the Bear Dance provides this antistructure. It establishes a leveling and therefore mediating structure for young and old, male and female, traditional and Christian. Men hold hands; they are passive and must wait to be asked to dance. Women are active. A complex mediation between the powers of the feminine (menstruation and pregnancy) and the powers of the masculine (hunters, providers) is at play in this performance with its at least partial inversion of gender roles. We must also, however, recognize the structure within the antistructure.

A heterosexual norm exists, and the Cat *Man* is the leader of the dance. The singers are all males, and the very important MC (one of the singers) is male. The appropriate etiquette for males and females is equally important, but enforced by the *male* dance leaders. I have been told by men *and* women that "good women know not to gossip, not to be here if they are pregnant or on their moon time, they must dress appropriately; our young people need to learn this." Prescribed Bear Dance etiquette appears to focus more on women than men.

In her seminal essay "Is Female to Male as Nature Is to Culture?" Sherry Ortner sheds light on the bear as mediator between female and male and nature and culture.[15] Since bears are often referred to as "animal people" (I have heard this frequently from Ute elders) and since they possess many human-like characteristics such as high intelligence and the ability to walk

Figure 5. Northern Ute Bear Dance. (Photo by Sally McBeth)

on hind legs, are omnivores, and are very protective of their cubs, they mediate between the natural world of animals and the cultural world of humans. Ortner asserts that human females may be more closely associated with nature and males more closely with culture. Females menstruate, give birth, and lactate, whereas males are associated with culture, which is evidenced by creating tools for the hunt and participating in public political and artistic endeavors. In the contemporary Ute Bear Dance, men are musicians and the Cat *Man* enforces dance corral decorum. Women who are pregnant or menstruating are prohibited from entering the dance grounds, and yet these female procreative body functions are powerful and mysterious, so much so that it is said that women in their moon time may prevent the healing power of the dance if they enter the dance grounds. The female bear mediates between the nature-female/culture-male binary. She accorded a culturally constructed woman's choice dance to the Utes through a Ute *male* who befriended her, and, in the ritual choreography, men are in positions of authority in the public realm of the dance grounds. Women participate in the domestic sphere by fixing food for Bear Dance participants, purchasing and mending clothes, and other preparatory measures. Female agency in a variety of tasks from selecting dance partners to text messaging is certainly present in the Bear Dance event, but as a complicated admixture of traditional, physical, and contemporary Western conventions.

Outside the Bear Dance grounds flirting, drinking, traditional gambling (hand game), and food and merchandise vendors are common. In Foucault's terminology,[16] a counterdiscourse to the antistructured discourse emerges. But this creating of a complex cultural dialogue revalues rather than diminishes the "bear as protector" metaphor.

The Bear Dance includes socializing, courting, teasing, being playful, and not taking the MC banter too seriously. It is above all a sacred and secular dance event containing both ritual and social meanings that are realities of contemporary Ute life. The she-bear mediates between the realms of the natural and supernatural, sacred and secular, nature and culture, male and female as in the double-edged inherited and enacted gender roles. The mythological pasts and current sensibilities merge when old and young embrace the bear and her dance as preservation of Ute tribal identity. An intermediary agent, the bear possesses unique qualities of a liminal dimension and thus has become the ultimate tribal protector occupying a mediating and metaphorical role that might well endure into the next millennium.

NOTES

1. The work of established anthropologists is providing the basis for the emerging academic areas of ritual mediation as well as media and ritual; see, for example, Debrix and Weber, *Rituals of Mediation*; Liebes and Curran, *Media, Ritual, and Identity*; Ling, "Mediation of Ritual Interaction"; Wilmore, "Gatekeepers of Cultural Memory." Although these specific studies are not elaborated on in this essay, they provide unique perspectives relevant for the *Mediating Indianness* volume.
2. See Debrix, "Introduction: Rituals of Mediation" in *Rituals of Mediation*, ed. François Debrix and Cynthia Weber, xxiii. Minneapolis: University of Minnesota Press, 2003.
3. For a more detailed introduction to Ute subsistence patterns, see McBeth, *"Talking About a Sacredness,"* 4–12, which cites Buckles, "The Uncompahgre Complex"; Callaway et al., "Ute"; Greubel, "A Closer Look at Eastern Ute Subsistence"; Jorgensen, "The Ethnohistory and Acculturation of the Northern Ute"; Steward, *Ute Indians*; and others.
4. McBeth, *"Talking About a Sacredness,"* 12.

5. Hallowell, "Bear Ceremonialism in the Northern Hemisphere," 1–175; Miller, "People, Berdaches, and Left-Handed Bears," 274–287.
6. Lett, *The Human Enterprise*, 111.
7. Geertz, *The Interpretation of Cultures*; Geertz, "Making Experiences, Authoring Selves."
8. Turner, "Social Dramas and Ritual Metaphors," 29.
9. "What Does the Bear Mean to the Utes?," 10.
10. Reed, "The Ute Bear Dance," 238.
11. Powell MS 798, as quoted in Fowler and Fowler, *Anthropology of the Numa*, 38.
12. Turner, *The Ritual Process*, 96.
13. Turner, "Metaphors of Anti-Structure in Religious Culture."
14. Turner, *The Ritual Process*, 94–97, 125–130.
15. Ortner, "Is Female to Male as Nature Is to Culture?," 67–88.
16. See Foucault, *The History of Sexuality*.

WORKS CITED

Buckles, William G. "The Uncompahgre Complex: Historic Ute Archaeology and Prehistoric Archaeology on the Uncompahgre Plateau in West Central Colorado." PhD diss., University of Colorado, Boulder, 1971.

Callaway, Donald, Joel Janetski, and Omer Stewart. "Ute." In *Handbook of North American Indians. Great Basin*, vol. 11, ed. Warren D'Azevedo and William G. Sturtevant, 336–367. Washington, D.C.: Smithsonian Institution, 1986.

Debrix, François, and Cynthia Weber, eds. *Rituals of Mediation*. Minneapolis: University of Minnesota Press, 2003.

Foucault, Michel. *The History of Sexuality*. Vol. 1. New York: Pantheon, 1978.

Fowler Don, and Catherine Fowler, eds. *Anthropology of the Numa: John Wesley Powell's Manuscripts on the Numic Peoples of Western North America, 1868–1880*. Smithsonian Contributions to Anthropology No. 14. Washington, D.C.: Smithsonian Institution, 1971.

Geertz, Clifford. *The Interpretation of Cultures*. New York: Basic Books, 1973.

———. "Making Experiences, Authoring Selves." In *The Anthropology of Experience*, ed. Victor Turner and Edward Bruner, 373–380. Urbana: University of Illinois Press, 1986.

Greubel, Randy A. "A Closer Look at Eastern Ute Subsistence." *Southwestern Lore* 68.3 (Fall 2002): 1–16.

Hallowell, A. Irving. "Bear Ceremonialism in the Northern Hemisphere." *American Anthropologist* 28 (1926): 1–175.

Jorgensen, Joseph G. "The Ethnohistory and Acculturation of the Northern Ute." PhD diss., Indiana University, 1964.

Lett, James. *The Human Enterprise: A Critical Introduction to Anthropological Theory*. Boulder, CO: Westview Press, 1987.

Liebes, Tamar, and James Curran, eds. *Media, Ritual, and Identity*. London: Routledge, 1998.

Ling, Richard S. "The Mediation of Ritual Interaction via the Mobile Telephone." In *Handbook of Mobile Communication Studies*, ed. James E. Katz, 165–176. Cambridge, MA: MIT Press, 2008.

McBeth, Sally. *"Talking About a Sacredness": An Ethnographic Overview of Colorado National Monument*. Prepared for the National Park Service, 2010. Http://www.cfc.umt.edu/CESU/Reports/NPS/UNC/2006/06&09McBethh_COLM_ethnography_final%20rpt.pdf, 2010.

Miller, Jay. "People, Berdaches, and Left-Handed Bears: Human Variation in Native America." *Journal of Anthropological Research* 38.3 (1982): 274–287.

Ortner, Sherry. "Is Female to Male as Nature Is to Culture?" In *Woman, Culture and Society*, ed. Michelle Zimbalist Rosaldo and Louise Lamphere, 67–88. Stanford, CA: Stanford University Press, 1974.

Reed, Verner Z. "The Ute Bear Dance." *American Anthropologist* 19.7 (July 1896): 237–244.

Steward, Julian. *Ute Indians I: Aboriginal and Historical Groups of Ute Indians of Utah*. New York: Garland, 1974.

Turner, Victor. "Metaphors of Anti-structure in Religious Culture." In *Dramas, Fields, and Metaphors: Symbolic Action in Human Society*, 272–299. Ithaca, NY: Cornell University Press, 1974.

———. *The Ritual Process: Structure and Anti-Structure*. Chicago: Aldine, 1969.

———. "Social Dramas and Ritual Metaphors." In *Dramas, Fields, and Metaphors: Symbolic Action in Human Society*, 23–59. Ithaca, NY: Cornell University Press, 1974.

"What Does the Bear Mean to the Utes?" *Ute Bulletin*, 19 July 2012.

Wilmore, Michael J. "Gatekeepers of Cultural Memory: Televising Religious Rituals in Tansen, Nepal." *Ethnos* 71.3 (2006): 317–342.

Eric Gansworth's Theatrical Productions

"Indianness" Mediated through the Juxtaposition of Cultural Capital and Performance

NICHOLLE DRAGONE

AS A NOVELIST, POET, PLAYWRIGHT, AND VISUAL ARTIST, ERIC GANSWORTH (Onondaga) is a storyteller. But what exactly does this mean? Does it mean he is a peddler of Native American cultural capital and identity to audiences primarily composed of children? As both the main character in and the playwright of *Re-Creation Story*, Gansworth works through the play to address this very question. In scene 2 of this play, Gansworth discusses with his niece how he plans to fulfill his obligation to talk about the Haudenosaunee Creation story for three hours as a featured lecturer of a literary speakers' series at the small Catholic college where he teaches creative writing and literature. In the middle of this conversation, he bemoans the way the words "storyteller" and/or "Native American," when applied to a speaker, are, more often than not, interpreted as indicating a performance intended for children. As Gansworth argues, very little of his work is appropriate for children. He continues his diatribe by telling his niece that "it is as if the phrase 'Native American Poetry Reading' spontaneously transforms itself, in the space between the page and the eye, or the eye and the brain into the word . . . 'Storyteller!'" and, hence, for children. Furthermore, he says, while "one part of me is delighted that people want to expose their children to multi-cultural literature," the other "part of me is worried that people will have come to see me expecting something like 'How Beaver Got

His Tail' . . . which I can assure you, will never be covered in a presentation of mine."[1] In many ways, this interaction between Gansworth's characters in *Re-Creation Story* defines much of his work as a playwright; his plays, at least in part, address how "Indianness" is mediated through the juxtaposition of the cultural capital and the performance itself. By looking at the way he integrates Haudenosaunee traditional teachings, Indian identification cards, and beadwork with the performances of his plays *Re-Creation Story*, *Patriot Act*, and *Rabbit Dance*, we, as the participating members of his audience, develop a richer understanding of the mediation of Indian identity in Gansworth's performance art.

Re-Creation Story is the dramatization of Gansworth's real-life experience of moving from the comfortable space of storytelling on the written page to the more traditional space of oral storytelling. As indicated in *Re-Creation Story*, this was not a move Gansworth chose to make; rather, he felt compelled to do so because he was "asked" to take on the role of oral storyteller by the very colleague who helped him acquire his present job at a private college in western New York State. The character Gansworth explains his transition this way:

> But, you know, when someone changes your life, you have to acknowledge that. Remember when he showed up at my old job? I was teaching five courses a semester with an advisee load of thirty kids, I was on committees I hated and the administration said publishing was just "okay as long as it doesn't interfere with your real job, teaching." And now? they pay me to think and imagine other possibilities and talk to a small number of students about things that I love. . . .
>
> I have a job . . . I have a pretty good one, and consequently, when Keith asks me to do something, I generally do it with a minimum of resistance, though I wish he would just trust me to do what I do well instead of coming up with something he thinks I should be doing.[2]

As a result, Gansworth finds himself trying to fill three hours with the telling of and/or discussion about the Haudenosaunee Creation story. As this play unfolds, we find Gansworth alternating between telling his staged audience the Creation account; obtaining advice on telling the Creation account; speaking with his niece about this commitment; and dialoguing with both the Sky World beings responsible for Haudenosaunee Creation and the members of his staged audience. This is important because much of his dialogue with other characters in the play involves two issues: one, how little Gansworth feels he knows about the Haudenosaunee Creation account or how little qualified he thinks he is to take on the role of traditional storyteller; and, two, the extent to which Gansworth's perception of himself, his identity as a Haudenosaunee man, is dependent upon his knowledge of and interaction with the Creation story. The irony is that it is only through Gansworth's continuous sharing of the Creation story with his Native and non-Native audiences—the staged audience and the play's audience—that he re-creates his own identity. Thus, it is through the juxtaposition of Gansworth's sharing of the Haudenosaunee Creation story (that is, cultural capital) with the re-creation through this play of his performance as a Haudenosaunee oral storyteller that we can see how Gansworth's own Indianness has been mediated through *Re-Creation Story*.

When *Re-Creation Story* opens, Eric Gansworth the character is struggling with how his lack of knowledge about his own culture's Creation account, together with his lack of skill as an oral storyteller, is undermining his self-identity as a Haudenosaunee man. This becomes obvious within the first few pages of the play, when Gansworth finds himself up in front of a small audience of students, faculty, and members of the Indian Higher Education LISTERV. According to the LISTERV announcements, his scheduled performance is to fill three hours; however, after he finishes telling what he knows about Creation, Gansworth glances at his watch and realizes he has not come close to filling this three-hour chunk of time. Looking at the makeup of his audience, Gansworth's feelings of inadequacy, embarrassment, and resentment reach an all-time high.

> This is all I need to be embarrassed by my inadequacies in public. . . . I have plenty of failings, . . . being a storyteller would be the second thing. . . . But what was I thinking, trying some new thing professionally that I have no business attempting.[3]

Gansworth pictures himself for his audience as a failed storyteller. He feels he has no business telling traditional stories, like Creation, in such a traditional manner. To compound his feelings of failure, Gansworth realizes he does not possess enough knowledge of Creation to give a meaningful telling of this story to any audience:

> I don't really know, easily half the story. There's this whole extended first section that takes place in the Skyworld that I hadn't even heard of until I read this version of it. . . . I kept reading and reading and thinking, who are these people? When Skywoman finally shows up, I didn't even recognize her until she goes through the hole.[4]

This is an important comment for Gansworth to make because Skywoman is one of four main characters in the Haudenosaunee Creation story. In fact, it is she who, with the help of water animals and water fowl, initiates the creation of Turtle Island (or North America) after she falls from Sky World to a water world below.[5]

To complicate Gansworth's belief that he has failed as a Haudenosaunee man because he neither knows his own Creation story nor has the requisite skills to tell this story, much of his interaction with those unnamed Native characters who step out of the shadows in the play indicate that even the Haudenosaunee people who know him do not think he is qualified. In fact, his own niece and two unidentified elders repeatedly ask Gansworth why his colleague thought he was capable of telling this story in this way. This question is repeated a third time by a female elder who continues to emphasize Gansworth's lack of qualifications as a traditional storyteller by asking, "Doesn't he know you at all? All it would take is one look at your whacked out gasoline-pump-hoses-making-love-to-Indian-women paintings to know you're working with different tools than the usual Indian bears, deer, wolves, lightning, etc."[6] These dramatized re-creations of conversations Gansworth had with family and friends about his commitment to give an oral telling of Creation serve one purpose during the performance of the play—to make Gansworth's self-esteem, his understanding of himself as a Haudenosaunee man, spiral deeply into a dark place of self-doubt, of resentment, of anxiety.

However, as the performance continues, Gansworth the playwright weaves five more tellings of Creation into this play, showing how each performance/telling of Creation engages Gansworth with this traditional teaching in a way that enables the re-creation of his self-identity, as a Haudenosaunee man and storyteller. This process begins with Gansworth's second telling of Creation in scene 5. In this scene, he again finds himself at the podium. By this time, Gansworth has learned enough from his elders, his audience, and the story itself to realize not only that several viable versions of this story exist but also that each version has something to offer both the storyteller and his audience. As he describes it, Creation has "very different qualities depending on which version you hear and who you happen to be."[7] Furthermore, Gansworth learned that as the storyteller, the way he tells the story and the way his audience hears the story "are almost never the same thing" because both his performance as the storyteller and the audience's interaction with him mediates which aspects of the story he shares and how he presents it. As he words it, "maybe you know that you've told a story to two different people, two different ways, two minutes apart."[8] By prefacing Creation with this introduction, Gansworth initiates the re-creation of his own identity from novelist/poet/visual artist into traditional oral storyteller/playwright.

As scene 8 opens, Gansworth finds himself at the podium again, sharing yet another telling of his Haudenosaunee culture's Creation story. This time he has perfected his art as a traditional storyteller to include allusions from popular culture, history, and even science to make the story relatable to his audience: "So let's agree that Skywoman looks through the hole, and sees only water below . . . and somehow or another she goes through the hole . . . learning the world's first lesson in gravity . . . eons before Isaac Newton gets hit on the head by an apple."[9]

During his fourth telling of the Creation story, something again shifts for Gansworth. He finds himself performing the telling of this story with Skywoman and her twin grandsons. The twins' interaction with Gansworth furthers his re-creation as a Haudenosaunee oral storyteller by reinforcing their essential lessons—namely, balance and the giving of thanks to the various elements and beings of the natural world that ensure our survival as humans.[10] According to Haudenosaunee Creation, Good Mind, the elder twin, and Bad Mind, the younger twin, are the creators of elements and beings of the natural world, including roses, the thorns on roses, the currents and rapids in the rivers, bears, wolves, deer, flowers, nuts, berries, grains, and humans. For every positive aspect of creation Good Mind provides, Bad Mind attaches something that seems negative. However, the truth is that the brothers ensure the world continues by keeping everything in balance.[11] Furthermore, as Mohawk elder Tom Porter tells us, it is important not to view these brothers as opposites or to prefer one over the other, because that would throw the world, and your place in the world, out of balance.[12] This lesson of Creation is explained in *Re-Creation Story* when Gansworth performs yet another telling of Creation together with Skywoman, Good Mind, and Bad Mind:

> **Eric**: Skywoman has the child she was pregnant with, a daughter, who then rapidly grows up, meets a man and becomes pregnant, herself, with twins. One twin is born the natural way, but the other, obstinate from the start, chooses to leave his mother's body from her armpit, killing her. They're known by various names in different versions, Earth Grasper and Flint, Creator and Warty One. I prefer to call them Good Mind (*backlighting on adult male, standing, stage left*) and the Bad Mind (*backlighting on adult male, standing, stage right*).
> **Elder Adult Male**: I govern the day.
> **Adult Male**: I govern the night.

> **Elder Adult Male**: I make things to satisfy, please and provide for the people I will eventually create.
> **Adult Male**: I teach those same people that they'll have to deal with adversity, and that there are benefits to learning to be tough.
> **Elder Adult Male**: I invent the open admissions college.
> **Adult Male**: And I invent the circumstances that necessitate an open admissions college.[13]

Through this performance, it becomes clear that *Re-Creation Story*, like Creation, is a cyclical process held in balance by the work of the Twin Minds of Creation. This cyclical process catches Gansworth in its spiraling loops, and requires him to join in Creation, to join in the performance of *Re-Creation Story*, telling and retelling the story again in scene 9, and again in scene 11. During the sixth telling, Gansworth weaves into Creation's story the events and experiences from his own life, in particular, his mother's death and his obtaining both his tribal ID card from the Onondaga Nation and his Red Card, which identifies him as a citizen of the Haudenosaunee Confederacy and ensures his rights to freely cross the U.S.-Canadian border. By the end of this telling, the re-creation of Gansworth's own identity as a Haudenosaunee man has been mediated through the overlaying of retellings. He learns, finally, that at the heart of his identity as a Haudenosaunee man are the lessons of Creation: thankfulness for what you have and for those who provided "the opportunity to live a good life on the earth";[14] the realization that the twin minds of Creation are not opposites, nor do they compete with each other, but rather they coexist together in balance; and acceptance of reality.[15]

While *Re-Creation Story* focused on the mediation of Eric Gansworth's own Indianness through the interweaving of his performance as a storyteller and the main character with oral tradition as cultural capital, Gansworth's other plays, including *Patriot Act* and *Rabbit Dance*, mediate Indianness through the juxtaposition of performance with forms of cultural capital extending far beyond the Creation story and the role of the traditional storyteller. Specifically, in *Patriot Act*, Gansworth works through the conflation of neighbor relations and border crossing issues with portrayals of cultural capital in the form of the Haudenosaunee Red Card to mediate Bonnie Door's Indianness.

At first glance, *Patriot Act* seems to focus solely on the impact of the post-9/11 Patriot Act (2001) on the treaty-protected rights of Native North American peoples to freely cross the U.S.-Canadian border; however, these treaty rights are actually a clever trope to discuss the way Indianness is mediated by the very ID card mentioned in *Re-Creation Story*, the Red Card. While Gansworth does not define the Red Card for the audience of *Re-Creation Story*, this card is also known as both the Haudenosaunee Identification Card and the Haudenosaunee Citizenship Card. Until 2008, when the Department of Homeland Security implemented its new passport requirements in response to the 9/11 attacks, the Red Card was sufficient for citizens of the Haudenosaunee Confederacy to cross the U.S.-Canadian border. In the wake of 9/11, however, it has become necessary for the Confederacy to develop new identification cards and passports embedded with the microchip technology now required by the international community for all passports.[16] It is this change from the Red Card to the new ID card and passport that is the linchpin around which the action of *Patriot Act* takes place. In fact, we can say that in both scene 11 of *Re-Creation Story* and the entirety of *Patriot Act*, the Red Card represents Indian identity, Indianness, as cultural capital.

In scene 11 of *Re-Creation Story*, Gansworth the character has a conversation with his mother about the importance of both the Red Card and his Onondaga Nation ID card in mediating Gansworth's identity as an Indian. To set up the re-created performance of this conversation, Gansworth tells his audience that his mother began pestering him in 2003 to apply for these two cards. In response to her repeated requests, he finally tells his mother he has applied for both cards several times and has yet to hear back on either. He reminds his mother he already has a Nation ID card—the one issued to him by the Tuscarora Nation, where he was born and raised. Unimpressed, his mother tells him it is necessary to "go through the right channels and have your ID done right." She cons him into applying "one more time," suggesting he "may get lucky this time."[17] As Gansworth tells his audience, the following year, around the time of his mother's eightieth birthday party, his Red Card arrives "out of the blue."[18] This exchange, embedded in the middle of scene 11, seems to serve no other purpose than to set the stage for Gansworth's mother's death shortly after her eightieth birthday. In fact, these two cards are never mentioned again in this play. As tangential as this conversation seems, however, it is anything but. As a novelist, Eric Gansworth often begins a new novel with seemingly insignificant threads and/or characters from a prior novel. The same is true of his plays. In this case, Gansworth picked up the Red Card thread and wove it into *Patriot Act* as a pivotal storyline and symbol.

Bonnie, the main character, is a citizen of the Tuscarora Nation. However, as she is married to Vernon Ballantine, a non-Native man, she has been living off the reservation in the city of Niagara Falls, New York, for nearly forty years. Niagara Falls, New York, is separated from Niagara Falls, Ontario, only by the Niagara River/U.S.-Canadian border; furthermore, because both cities and the Falls are major tourist destinations, this is one of the few places where people can cross this international border on foot. And it is on this footbridge that much of the action in act 2, scene 1, takes place:

> The bridge between the United States and Canada, Canadian Side, with a sign above: CANADIAN CUSTOMS AND IMMIGRATION. Canadian flags and posters with things like "DISCOVER ONTARIO," pictures of moose, etc. on them. Bilingual signs (English and French), reminding people about proper identification, fruits and vegetables import bans, etc., and a couple of posters in French, as well. At stage right, mist (dry ice) billows in constantly from mid-stage right. At downstage center, VERNON and BONNIE are standing at the counter in the outer office. CANADIAN BORDER GUARDS ONE and TWO are behind the counter, one talking to them, the other at a computer.[19]

In this scene, Bonnie and her husband are on their way into Canada to eat lunch at one of their favorite restaurants, the Jade Garden. Standing in Canadian Customs on the footbridge, Bonnie declares her identity as Native North American and hands over her ID card—"a bright red card made out of construction paper."[20] As she and Vernon clear customs and continue walking across the footbridge, their conversation circles back to the Red Card. Bonnie complains that the border guards often either glare at her or look askance at the Red Card. In reply, Vernon tells her these so-called Haudenosaunee Citizenship Cards almost deserve the negative reactions from the border guards because they are shoddily made. "I'll remind you," he says to his wife, "Red construction paper? Really? And handwritten vital stats?" He continues by maintaining that even Third World countries have real passports. Bonnie tries to justify the design of the Red Card by arguing that these documents are "officially registered documents," administered by the Haudenosaunee Confederacy's government. She ties off the escalating argument by reminding Vernon that he and she "come from different places"; therefore, they should just agree to disagree about the Red Card. It is, after all, the business of the citizens of the Confederacy, not Vernon's.[21]

After having enjoyed their lunch at the Jade Garden, Bonnie and Vernon are walking back across the footbridge toward the U.S. Customs booth, which is draped with the U.S. flag and decorated with posters of the Statue of Liberty and eagles.[22] At first, they are relaxed and enjoying themselves. Their conversation alternates between their different experiences crossing the border—he as non-Native and she as Native—the Haudenosaunee's annual Border Crossing celebration, and Bonnie's stint as the winner of the Maid of the Mist beauty contest. Their conversation shifts, and they find themselves arguing about whether or not Bonnie is racially profiled when she is shopping in the local Niagara Falls stores without Vernon present. He tells her she is paranoid. She, in a fit of anger, storms off, entering the U.S. Customs booth without him.

Rooting around in her "beaded purse" for her Red Card, Bonnie is still unaware that anything out of the ordinary is happening. It is clear that her identity is not only symbolized by but also mediated by this ID card, which has become for her a bargaining chip, the cultural capital that ensures her rights. As she is speaking, however, the Red Card is quickly losing its value. One of the guards finds her Red Card and her New York State driver's license. The Red Card is tossed off to the side as meaningless in this transaction as if it were a mere discount card, while her license is used to enter her vitals into the computer. In response to Bonnie's repeated references to her treaty rights and the Red Card, one of the border guards holds up her Red Card and tells her that in the wake of 9/11, this "little red card" has no meaning. He again tosses the card on the counter:

> You might think this little red card from your purse means something . . . but it really doesn't. If you were in a car, and I thought you were harboring a terrorist in your trunk, I would have you open it or I would open it. You can have your yearly treaty parades, but since September Eleventh, we live in a world full of evil-doers. Your days of crossing unobstructed are over. Do you understand?[23]

The guards firmly explain that circumstances in the world have shifted in a way that makes her treaty rights, her very identity as a Haudenosaunee citizen, as sturdy as the "construction paper" her Red Card is made from. They tell her she is lucky she has a New York State driver's license; the implication is that without her license, she would have been stuck in the no-man's-land between the U.S. and Canadian borders.

Bonnie's husband comes to represent for her all the Euro-Westerners who colonized the Americas since 1492:

> **Vernon**: You could still be living at your mother's place on the reservation, using the outhouse, or in a trailer, get a septic tank and bottled water, but you're not. You're with me, on a prime piece of land in the county. How many people get to live on the river? Less than five miles above the most famous waterfalls in the country . . .

> **Bonnie**: I think you're forgetting this was once all Indian land, including your precious waterfront property.
> **Vernon**: The key word is once.
> **Bonnie**: Once. Yes, I suppose you're right. Why bother claiming anything as my own anymore? If you white people want it bad enough, bam, suddenly it's yours.
> **Vernon**: Babe, you're being unreasonable—.
> **Bonnie**: I am? I had a cat. Someone else wanted it, it's gone. I had a legal ID card. Someone else decided it wasn't good enough anymore, bam, it's gone. What's next, our house? . . . Oh wait, that's happened already. Sorry, reservation, we need some of your land for a water reservoir. What's that? You don't want us to flood your houses? Tough . . . We have to make way for progress.[24]

In dramatizing the way Indian identity via the Red Card is constructed as cultural capital by the very process of negotiating the right to exercise treaty-protected Indigenous rights—such as the right to cross freely the U.S.-Canadian border—Eric Gansworth also directs his audience's attention to other elements of cultural capital that both define Indian identity and highlight ways in which Indian identity has been curtailed and limited. This includes land and water, specifically reservation lands and personal property. In fact, Gansworth's discussion of treaty rights at the border in *Patriot Act* includes at least three borders that intersect through this performance to explore the depths of Bonnie Door's identity as a Tuscarora/Haudenosaunee Indian woman living off-reserve in the twenty-first century. The first of these three borders, as discussed above, is the U.S.-Canadian border. The other two are those separating the Tuscarora Reservation from the surrounding communities of western New York, and the borders delimiting Bonnie Door's property from that of her neighbor's in the city of Niagara Falls, New York. In much the same way that Bonnie's identity is symbolized by her Red Card in the scenes on the bridge, the cat Bonnie refers to above echoes her identity in other scenes.

As *Patriot Act* opens, the stage is set "with two walls, close to center stage, so that we are seeing cutaway views of two different houses' living rooms." The living room windows of the two houses face each other. Bonnie and Vernon's home is decorated tastefully, "with high modern sensibility" and "a number of American Indian motifs."[25] In contrast, the neighbor, Celeste Rigg, has decorated her house in a "prim, baroque" manner with doilies. Also clearly visible to the audience in this opening scene is the strip of grass that separates Bonnie and Vernon's property from that of their detested neighbor,

Celeste. Bonnie describes this strip of land, which Vernon mows although it belongs to Celeste as much as to Bonnie and Vernon, as "no-man's-land," possibly referencing the well-known short story by Cherokee author Thomas King called "Borders," which was dramatized in a short made-for-television movie by the Canadian Broadcasting Company (CBC) in 1995. Set in the early 1990s this story dramatizes the experiences of a Blackfoot woman and her son at the U.S.-Canadian border. Traveling from their home on the Blackfoot Reserve in Canada to Salt Lake City, Utah, to visit family, they find themselves stranded for several days in the strip of "no-man's-land" separating the U.S. and Canadian Customs and Immigration offices at the border. Like Bonnie Door, they seek to exercise their treaty-protected rights to cross this border freely. However, both the U.S. and Canadian border guards refuse to allow them to either enter into the United States or reenter into Canada unless they declare their citizenship as either U.S. or Canadian, rather than as Blackfoot. Unable to leave the "no-man's-land" between the two borders, this Blackfoot woman and her son live in their car for several days until the media becomes aware of their plight.[26] Both King's "Borders" and Gansworth's *Patriot Act* dramatize the way in which "no-man's-land" serves to define Indianness. The contested strip of grass between houses in Gansworth's play is an unsettling no-man's-land just as surely as the land between the two international borders in King's story.

Furthermore, it is in this interstitial space between the two homes that Bonnie Door's identity as a Tuscarora/Haudenosaunee woman is symbolized for the viewing audience by an orange cat, whose ownership is also the subject of heated debate throughout the performance. Alternately known as Copperhead and Lucky Penny, this cat crisscrosses the "no-man's-land" between the two houses at will—a privilege that Bonnie must constantly fight for, usually in vain, with regard to the various borders that surround her. She inconsistently recognizes some (the neighborhood property lines), but rejects or at least regrets others ("this was once all Indian land"). Thus, the performance of Bonnie's recognition or denial of each border in specific situations works to define her identity as an Indian woman. In *Patriot Act*, the renegotiation of Indian identity at each of these boundaries transforms Indianness itself into a form of cultural capital, symbolized by both the Haudenosaunee Red Card and an orange cat.

Again, as a literary artist, Eric Gansworth often picks up seemingly insignificant threads from previous works and weaves them into subsequent books, plays, and poems. In *Rabbit Dance*, a play produced by Ohio Northern University at its ninth annual International Play Festival in 2011, Gansworth adopts not only the image of Indian beadwork (beading in

Rabbit Dance will be discussed at length below) but also two naming motifs from *Patriot Act* to develop the main characters and storyline of *Rabbit Dance*. The first one is the surname "Door," which is the last name of the main characters in both plays, and the second is nicknaming, exemplified in *Patriot Act* by the two nicknames for the nomadic cat. Likewise, in *Rabbit Dance*, Gansworth's main characters—Rhoda and Flossie Door—discuss at length Rhoda's daughter's nickname, Rabbit. This nickname is symbolic of a physical deformity, a harelip. It also links Rabbit to the Tuscarora/Haudenosaunee people because they have adopted the Rabbit Dance into their traditional social dances, and because the Rabbit Dance is connected with the origins of her nickname and her death. Finally, she uses this nickname and her physical deformity to create a new and beautiful design for a Tuscarora art form—the beadwork whimsy. In so doing, *Rabbit Dance* links the presentation of the domestic/spousal abuse of young women with whimsies as a form of cultural capital symbolic of Indianness.

As *Rabbit Dance* opens, we find two Tuscarora women, Rhoda and Flossie Door, setting up vendor tables at Niagara Falls State Park from which they will sell their beadwork to tourists. The location of their vending tables and the beadwork they are vending is critically important because it is symbolic of their identity as citizens of both the Tuscarora Nation and the Haudenosaunee Confederacy. In addition, beadwork, especially Tuscarora raised beadwork, has been a form of cultural and commercial capital in the Niagara Falls State Park since the late nineteenth century. Gansworth, to his credit as a storyteller, takes the time to weave this information into the performance so his audience better understands the importance of both the location of the play and the beadwork.

The stage is set to represent Niagara Falls State Park, which is located on the American side of the Falls in the city of Niagara Falls. The land this park was established on was once a part of the Seneca Nation's lands; however, in the early 1800s, after the Seneca Nation sold the land rights off to land companies and property developers, one of the original founders of Buffalo, New York, Peter Porter, purchased the land. Porter served as an officer in the U.S. Army during the War of 1812. Because the Tuscarora warriors helped protect him from the British, Porter reserved specific rights to the Tuscaroras regarding use of the land he owned near Niagara Falls.[27] These reserved rights are an important aspect of Tuscarora identity in the twenty-first century. In fact, it is because Tuscarora women have continuously exercised these reserved rights to sell Indian crafts at Niagara Falls that tourists visiting the Falls often come home with souvenirs crafted by Haudenosaunee Indians.

Consequently, since the early nineteenth century the Indian has been "a symbol of the Falls and an icon of this untamed wilderness."[28] In 1906, one of Porter's descendants stated that the prior generations of tourists would remember seeing Indian women "at various points along the route of the tourist on the steep banks of the road leading up to the rapids, on Luna Island, to old Terrapin Tower, and at various points around the Ferry House, and what is now Prospect Park, offering for sale . . . beadwork, pin cushions, moccasins, etc."[29] Not only were the Tuscaroras selling beadwork at the Falls, but also tourists often made side trips from the Falls to the Tuscarora Reservation, which, according to an 1839 guidebook written by S. DeVeaux, had been listed as one of the places to visit while touring Niagara Falls: "Our party having arrived at the [Tuscarora] village, look into their wigwams; make such observations, take such notes of the customs and manners of the inhabitants, as a short and hasty visit affords; purchase some articles of Indian manufacture."[30]

When New York State purchased the lands now comprising Niagara Falls State Park from the Porter family in 1885, it purchased these lands subject to the Tuscaroras' reserved rights. One of these is the right to sell whimsies and other souvenirs to tourists at Niagara Falls. As Gansworth points out in *Rabbit Dance*, Tuscarora people continue to exercise these reserved rights every summer.[31]

The whimsies sold at the Falls form the backdrop of Gansworth's *Rabbit Dance*. The original whimsies were made of velvet and took many forms, including but not limited to the following: strawberry, heart, bird, and Victorian boot-shaped pincushions; purses; velvet-covered picture frames; boxes; pillows; and wall-hangings.[32] The whimsies were further decorated with raised beadwork, usually floral and animal motifs.[33] While many different designs have been incorporated over the years, as Gansworth's main character, Rhoda Door, tells the young woman who came to interview her, most bead workers still make these old-style souvenir designs because the people who buy them today seem to "like [them] for [their] historical connection"; consequently,

> most of the things we make now are pretty much what the first ladies from home made when Niagara Falls was turned officially into a state park instead of what the old private owners used to do with it. That was over a century ago. Our women used to sell beadwork down here, when you had [to] pay to look at the water falls through a peep hole in a wood fence.[34]

Given the history of selling souvenirs at Niagara Falls, and the history of the whimsies, both the whimsy and the reserved right to sell whimsy souvenirs at Niagara Falls State Park are forms of cultural capital; perhaps more importantly, however, both are symbolic of Rhoda, Flossie, and Crystal Door's identities as Tuscarora/Haudenosaunee women working to carry a historic tradition or right into the future.

We meet Flossie and her daughter, Rhoda, early in the play when Myna shows up at their vending tables. After reading a newspaper article about Rhoda Door, a Tuscarora woman seeking "to get a monument erected to document the beadworking legacy at the park" in honor of her late daughter, Myna decided Rhoda was the perfect interviewee for a project for one of her high school classes. In fact, she skipped some of her other classes to go to the Falls and interview Rhoda. While she is talking to the Doors, it becomes clear to them that this young girl is being physically and emotionally abused by her boyfriend. As Rhoda's daughter Crystal was murdered by her abusive boyfriend, both women quickly become protective of Myna. Through their efforts to protect Myna from her boyfriend, Gansworth's *Rabbit Dance* overlays the historical and Native gender significance of beadwork with a captivating performance about domestic abuse.

Crystal Door specialized in creating souvenir rabbits. First crafted from a gift her boyfriend had intended as a cruel joke—a stuffed white rabbit—Crystal decorated it with red velvet and beadwork until it was quite literally the most beautiful piece of beadwork her mother had ever seen. According to Rhoda, what made this piece particularly beautiful was Crystal's use of a strawberry/heart pin cushion as an exterior heart-shaped pocket:

> She covered [the rabbit] in velvet and then highlighted it in her best beads. She took one of her pincushion strawberries, divided it up to look like a split heart, and re-sewed it to where it had inner borders, secret pockets revealed only when you opened it. The rabbit became her signature piece. She made little versions of it, by request. Graduation gifts from mothers to daughters, usually.[35]

The backstory of the original stuffed white rabbit is as important as the rabbit whimsy with its secret borders. Crystal was born with a cleft lip, which as Rhoda explained to Myna, is also called a "harelip" because, like a rabbit's upper lip, it is split. Some harelips are so grave that the person's entire upper mouth is divided. According to the reservation doctor, however, Crystal was lucky; only her upper lip was cleft, the cleft so "minor" he refused to approve surgery. He told Rhoda if she wanted it fixed, she could pay for it herself. However, as selling beadwork is Rhoda's primary source of income, she was unable to pay for an "unnecessary" cosmetic surgery:

> **Rhoda**: This is our primary source of income. Surgery's an awful lot of German tourists. We kept thinking maybe one day, she'd be in the circumstance where she could have plastic surgery. It wasn't *that* noticeable, but when you're fifteen, I'm sure all she could see in the mirror was—.
> **Myna**: The name. All she could see was a rabbit.
> **Rhoda**: Through the looking glass.[36]

As Rhoda and Flossie tell her story, Crystal's poor self-esteem was soon compounded by the way her boyfriend, Cameron, used her harelip to make her feel small and ugly. He called her "Gwaa-(rh)oot," the Tuscarora word for rabbit.[37] He tried to say he chose that nickname because it reminded him of the Haudenosaunee Rabbit Dance, a social dance in which the female chooses her dance partner. Eventually, Crystal internalized and adopted the nickname. Similarly, she turned the stuffed white rabbit her boyfriend gave her into a beautiful representation of Tuscarora artwork and history, and capitalized off the desirability of its tragic beauty.

Rhoda describes this process as "learning to live with your scars." This idea of learning to live with scars by making something beautiful out of them is a recurring theme in Eric Gansworth's literary works. The novel *Mending Skins* juxtaposes Tuscarora women crafting quilts and pillowcases out of their families' old, worn-out clothing with the idea of learning to mend one's own "skin," after the emotional and mental trauma of losses. In *Smoke Dancing*, narrator Fiction Tunny—who, like Gansworth, is an Onondaga citizen living at Tuscarora—beads one of the most beautiful and horrifying traditional dresses anyone can imagine. The design of the dress was born the night Fiction's father beat her to the point where she had to be hospitalized. While at the hospital, pictures were taken of the bruises his fists left. At some point, it occurred to Fiction that these bruises blooming into a rose-like design on her body could be transformed into purple raised-beadwork roses. She took the pictures, photocopied enlargements of the bruises, and then used them to trace macabre roses onto the black velvet that would become her dance regalia:

> The [raised-beadwork purple] roses clearly took shape in the proper places along the bodice of the light-absorbing black material. They were a hardy sort, blooming again in the middle of winter. My father's rose garden was of a perennial variety. It would keep coming back.[38]

Fiction wears the dress for the first time at the New Yah Feast. As she says, her father, who had refused to acknowledge her as his child, "want[s] me to wear them on the inside, in secret, like he wants me to wear my identity" as his daughter, "but, I can't do that."[39] Later that night, the clan mother who taught her to bead tells Fiction that she would have offered Fiction a coat to wear home, "but I suspect you are not ready to bury your roses yet."[40]

Smoke Dancing, *Mending Skins*, and *Rabbit Dance* all highlight characters who survive abusive relationships and terrific losses, and who somehow manage to live through the scars and create beauty out of their pain, grief, and loss. In all three works, the characters' identities are symbolized by the very beauty they create, a beauty that can also be manipulated as cultural capital. However, it must be noted here that only in Gansworth's *Rabbit Dance* does the character in question eventually die at the hands of her abuser. In the two novels, the women subjected to spousal/domestic violence and/or loss survive the trauma and tell their own stories. This is an important distinction, because it is only through the narration of Myna's abuse at the hands of her boyfriend, and Rhoda and Flossie's attempts to protect Myna, that we, the viewing audience, hear Crystal's story. And it is only because Crystal dies as a result of domestic abuse that Rhoda and Flossie seek to intervene on Myna's behalf, and teach her the lesson of the Haudenosaunee Rabbit Dance, the lesson of choosing a partner wisely.

Thus, it is in performance about domestic violence, neighbor relations, and border crossing, and his own personal experience of being transformed into a traditional storyteller, that Eric Gansworth not only addresses how "Indianness" is mediated through performative forums, but also how it is problematized when cultural capital becomes part of the performance itself. By looking at the way Haudenosaunee traditional teachings, the Haudenosaunee Red Card, and beadwork whimsies serve as symbols and content in his plays *Re-Creation Story*, *Patriot Act*, and *Rabbit Dance*, we have become privy to the way Eric Gansworth opens up complex Indian identities in interstitial spaces.

NOTES

1. Gansworth, *Re-Creation Story*, 24–25.
2. Ibid., 13–14.
3. Ibid., 9–10.
4. Ibid., 11–12.
5. Mohawk, *Iroquois Creation Story*, 10–14; Porter, *And Grandma Said*, 40–53; Mitchell, *Traditional Teachings*, 5–8.

6. Ibid., 29.
7. Ibid., 47.
8. Ibid., 39.
9. Ibid., 49–50.
10. Wojcik, "Why No Iroquois Fiction?," 211; Mohawk, "Foreword," xiii.
11. Mohawk, "Foreword," xiii; Williams, "Creation," 3–7.
12. Wojcik, "Why No Iroquois Fiction?," 211.
13. Gansworth, *Re-Creation Story*, 52–53.
14. Ibid., 74; see also 9, 55.
15. Ibid., 74; See also Wojcik, "Why No Iroquois Fiction?," 211.
16. Horn, "Haudenosaunee Inks Deal"; Onondaga Nation, "Haudenosaunee Documentation Committee"; "Canadian Human Rights."
17. Gansworth, *The Re-Creation Story*, 59.
18. Ibid., 60.
19. Gansworth, *Patriot Act*, 6.
20. Ibid, 30.
21. Ibid., 33.
22. Ibid., 36.
23. Ibid., 48.
24. Ibid., 52–53.
25. Ibid., 3.
26. King, "Borders," 133–147.
27. Gansworth, *Rabbit Dance*, 5–6, 8, 12–13, 20.
28. "Niagara Falls."
29. Peter Porter qtd. in "Niagara Falls."
30. *Falls of Niagara*, 110.
31. Gansworth, *Rabbit Dance*, 8, 12–13, 20, 30, 36; see also Elliott, "Iroquois Beadwork," 38, 43–45.
32. Gordon, *Niagara Falls Whimsey*, passim; Elliott, "Iroquois Beadwork," 38–42; Gansworth, *Rabbit Dance*, 8, 11.
33. Gordon, *Niagara Falls Whimsey*, passim; "Niagara Falls"; Gansworth, *Rabbit Dance*, 11.
34. Gansworth, *Rabbit Dance*, 12.
35. Ibid., 34.
36. Ibid., 27.
37. Ibid., 25, 26.
38. Gansworth, *Smoke Dancing*, 128.
39. Ibid., 132.
40. Ibid., 134.

WORKS CITED

Borders. Directed by Gil Cardinal. Canadian Broadcasting Corporation, Toronto, 1995. Television.

"Canadian Human Rights Commission Recommends MCA Complaints for Mediation." *Indian Time*, 10 May 2012. Http://www.indiantime.net/story/2012/05/10/news/canadian-human-rights-commission-recommends-mca-complaints-for-mediation/229.html.

DeVeaux, S. *The Falls of Niagara or Tourist's Guide to this Wonder of Nature*. Buffalo, NY: The Press of Thomas & Co., 1839.

Elliott, Dolores. "Iroquois Beadwork: A Haudenosaunee Tradition as Art." In *Preserving Tradition and Understanding the Past: Papers from the Conference on Iroquois Research, 2001–2005*, ed. Christine Steinberg Patrick. Albany: New York State Education Department, 2010.

Gansworth, Eric. *Mending Skins*. East Lansing: Michigan State University Press, 2005.

———. *Patriot Act*. Identity Play Series, State University of New York at Oneonta. Oneonta, NY. February 2011. Performance.

———. *Rabbit Dance: A Play*. International Play Festival, Ohio Northern University. Ada, OH. April 2011. Performance.

———. *Re-Creation Story: A Play*. Second Native Theater Festival, The Public Theater. New York City. November 2008. Performance.

———. *Smoke Dancing*. East Lansing: Michigan State University Press, 2004.

Gordon, Beverly. "The Niagara Falls Whimsey: The Object as a Symbol of Cultural Interface." Vols. 1 and 2, PhD diss. Madison: University of Wisconsin, 1984.

Horn, Greg. "Haudenosaunee Inks Deal to Produce New Cards, Passports." *IORI: WASE KahnawakeNews.com*, 9 March 2009. Http://kahnawakenews.com/haudenosaunee-inks-deal-to-produce-new-id-cards-passports-p208-1.htm.

King, Thomas. "Borders." In *One Good Story, That One*. Toronto: Harper Perennial Canada, 1993, 133–147.

Mitchell, Michael, ed. *Traditional Teachings*. Cornwall Island, Ontario: North American Indian Traveling College, 1984.

Mohawk, John. *Iroquois Creation Story: John Arthur Gibson and J. N. B. Hewitt's Myth of the Earth Grasper*. Buffalo: Mohawk Publications, 2005.

"Niagara Falls and Tuscarora Beadwork." *Historic Iroquois and Wabanaki Beadwork*, 31 May 2011. Http://iroquoisbeadwork.blogspot.de/2011/05/niagara-falls-and-tuscarora-beadwork.html.

Onondaga Nation. "Haudenosaunee Documentation Committee." *Indian Time*, 7 February 2008. Http://www.indiantime.net/story/2008/02/07/letters-to-the-editor/haudenosaunee-documentation-committee/031220121410929355171.html.

Porter, Tom. *And Grandma Said . . . : Iroquois Teachings as Passed Down through the Oral Tradition*. Bloomington, IN: Xlibris Corp., 2008.
Williams, Paul. "Creation." In *Words Before All Else*, 3–7. Cornwall Island: Native North American Traveling College, 1995.
Wojcik, Jan. "Why No Iroquois Fiction?" *Wicazo Sa Review* 12.1 (1997): 205–215.

Eric Gansworth's *Re-Creation Story*
Mediation and Remediation

JOHN PURDY

IN HIS RECENT BOOK *IMAGINE: HOW CREATIVITY WORKS*, JONAH Lehrer attempts to identify exactly what happens when the human mind produces something new and remarkable for our world. He draws upon the work of scientists who combined the use of magnetic resonance imaging (MRI) and electroencephalography to try to pinpoint the activities that take place when creativity happens, and his argument is that when confronted with seemingly unresolvable dilemmas, the human mind will first try to reason a way through complex problems to discover a solution. When this does not work, and the frustration builds accordingly, the dilemma will then be diverted to the right hemisphere of the brain and the anterior superior temporal gyrus (ASTG), in particular, where brain cells will reconfigure and the epiphany will materialize, the new way will be revealed, the problem solved.

Lehrer's research fits my considerations here in several ways, some more odd than others. First, the ASTG is also where the brain processes figurative language—metaphors and similes, for example—but also interprets jokes, so this is the sphere where Gansworth not only creates text but also where we interact with his texts. The odd part? As he tells us in *Re-Creation Story*, when he first went to college he "didn't know there was such a thing as an English Major. So, for reasons I can not explain, I got a degree in Electroencephalography, the study of brain waves."[1]

I would argue that Gansworth's growing frustration with the ways America has mediated and re-mediated Indians, including him, provides an impetus for his art, but so does his frustration with publishing his work, "getting it out there" to reshape an audience's thinking. The attempt to "make it new" and thereby have impact places him in the perfect position for the ASTG to do its wondrous work as he creates multiple re-mediations. Over time, his dramatic presentations have become not only more inventive but also more personal. His work contributes to the larger discourse on literature and other media, including the literature of Native Americans. I will add personally that I think he is a genius, one who inhabits the convergence point of myriad strands of contemporary life. His ASTG is on full overdrive.

Gansworth is a novelist, poet, critic, professor, artist, and, most recently, dramatist; he is also a member of the Onondaga Nation who was raised on the Tuscarora Reservation near Niagara Falls, New York. He has always been a media shifter whose visual art plays the chorus to his verbal arts. With his paintings and writings, Gansworth creates two forms of *mediation* as he situates between his vision and his audience: one mediation is visual and thus visceral and immediate; the other is verbal and thus cerebral and long-lived. However, while in the act of creating and performing, he may be engaged in a re-mediation: a reclamation of older narratives—personal and communal—that becomes a retelling of self, a re-creation story.

In an interview my colleague Oliver de la Paz and I conducted with Gansworth, he shared the early genesis of his written canon:

> I would have to say that I am definitely a product of reservation culture and its obsession with popular culture. I learned: storytelling technique from Stephen King and from a couple of young adult novels (*The Outsiders*, *The Pigman*); subtext from horror movies (most notably, *Dawn of the Dead*, *The Texas Chain Saw Massacre*, *Videodrome*, *Last House on the Left*, all straight-on horror with relatively sophisticated culture critique imbedded and integral). I learned poetic devices (leitmotif, careful turn of phrase, repetition and variation, whole work cohesion among all smaller movements within a piece) and the ultimate lesson of being moved by words from rock music, specifically the bands Rush, Pink Floyd, Queen, and naturally, The Beatles. These all prepared me and made me a better reader for when I was finally introduced to more formally recognized poets and fiction writers.[2]

What these media share is the ability to bring image into sharp relief for audiences raised on the visual and aural and provoke an emotive response. Then, as Gansworth noted about his paintings:

> Visual art can really be the same story arc, as it were. I *loved* commercial art from a very young age, was always attracted to the graphics on toy packaging and was dedicated to a few specific comic book artists, even in an era before

> they had their own kind of marginal celebrity. . . . I knew I wanted to paint the unusual in the same kind of strange "Hudson Valley River School meets pulp fiction images" style. As I got to be an adult, I realized, again courtesy in part of *Blue Velvet,* where David Lynch embraced and transformed the things he knew, what a rich set of icons and images and stories I had from my own cultural history, and I have been exploring those ideas ever since.[3]

Certain icons and images form central points of reference for the stories he tells. I explore several of these from his literary works, although there are many, and tie them to a few from his visual and dramatic texts. But first, his overall agenda.

As I have noted elsewhere, Gansworth draws very clearly defined lines—political, ideological, physical—yet blurs these with his novels' overriding imperative, which is community survivance for the next seven generations. Characters who act equitably with this desire guiding them are much better off than those who do not, and this applies to Natives and non-Natives alike. Unlike some writers whose works create a world in which "white people" comprise the "dominant culture," Gansworth's novels operate in the reverse; they dramatize a clearly demarked community in which white people are the exotic, the curiosity, the "Other." They are referred to not as the dominant, but the "outside" culture. Consider this configuration in his first novel, *Indian Summers* (1998), in light of the idea of pop culture as an alternative to mainstream culture, one that is resistant and, as a reviewer of his play *Re-Creation Story* calls it, "sassy."[4]

In the written narrative, Floyd's family is grouped around his mother, listening to music (Billie Holiday) and a police scanner (somewhat a high-tech "moccasin telegraph" window into the movements of "the Other") and telling stories in her gazebo, depicted illuminatingly in the background of the cover illustration. In one scene, a professor visits the family, and his ethnocentric assumptions—perhaps symbolized in the stereotypical plastic toy Indian in the foreground of the novel's cover—do not work here; his frustration ultimately leads him to replicate the police department's racial profiling of the reservation community at large:

> "It's the way you live. I'm sorry to say so, but it's true," he surmised. "It's all the junk laying around, making everything look cluttered. That's a sign of no self-respect. . . . Instead of buying colored televisions and VCRs and stereos, you could put in plumbing. There aren't supposed to be outhouses in twentieth century America. . . . And that fuckin' gazebo, why did you build that fucking gazebo when the house needs so much work?"[5]

Figure 1. Cover of *Indian Summers*, artwork by Eric Gansworth. (Courtesy of Michigan State University Press)

For the readers, the professor's rant is—strategically on Gansworth's part—annoying because we know the genesis, the back stories, of the gazebo, the lack of plumbing, and the racial profiling so central to the characters' lives, so the patronizing professor becomes a stooge of a Western ideology that does not recognize—cannot "see"—the residual and resilient acts of communal culture inherent in the scene: its family values and sense of belonging.

Eric commented upon the element of the novel that places the uncle with a guitar at the center of a family's cohesion: "I remember initially thinking about the loss of my uncle's guitar-playing for the family's children when we were all growing up, and how subsequent generations of my family would not have that benefit, because none of us had bothered to learn from him, before he had passed on. It seemed like a perfect manifestation of cultural loss in the personal."[6]

This cultural in the personal and contemporary is central to his canon. His uncle lives again in his books and plays, so it is not that traditions are dead or dying, but evolving and transforming while they maintain the core values that have always adhered in them, and sometimes they are not immediately recognizable or visually outlined. Gansworth makes them visible.

The need to make informed choices about the future—individual and/or communal—is given metaphoric presence throughout Gansworth's fiction, and one recurrent motif deployed to do this is, once again, a visual one: his use of vehicles' rearview mirrors as an imagistic cue and visual metaphor. These small, framed images—much like a living painting or movie—operate in several ways. In one way, they signify a simultaneous look backward and forward, as characters move away from an event, person, or scene and into a new, often uncertain future that requires reaction. Seeing what is "behind" can help one make informed decisions when confronting what is up ahead. Seeing what is behind helps Gansworth construct his art.

Interestingly, it is the Clan Mother Ruby who chooses Bud as Chief in the novel *Smoke Dancing*, although she witnessed the loss of his ghost when he was young and being baptized. That he had one at all is one deciding factor for her, the hereditary nature of the choice another. Ruby knows his "father had not been a total convert—attending the Protestant church but still sneaking off to Longhouse ceremonies as well, taking me with him in his old Indian car, where I served as his rear-view mirror, looking back and letting him know when it was safe to pass."[7] The knowledge of what is behind—the community's history both personal and public—guides the lives of several characters who, in turn, provide a center for the community and its respective generations. Given the matriarchal tradition Gansworth describes, it makes sense that women fulfill this central role, and this becomes a central issue of *Re-Creation Story*.

Throughout his writings Gansworth employs a multimedia, performative methodology, complete with sound, even in his novels:

> Early drafts of my fiction always have to be weeded of "stage direction" sentences. I am constantly writing these overly elaborate passages where characters walk around rooms, lift items from tables, lean in doorways, etc.—moments that really do not add to the narrative, but that describe the way I see the scenes playing out in my imagination. I tend to see the stories in edited form: action/reaction shots; establishing shot, crane shot, closing in; dolly tracking shots. I would love to include a soundtrack CD with every book, music you are required to play as you read. It is of course nearly impossible to translate that visual style into traditional narratives, so I often accept that I have to strip the work of its visual style, and perhaps that is how the paintings came to be parallel narratives within the novels, and within the other books as well. They are kind of like "establishing shots," trying to deliver tone in one image.[8]

Re-Creation Story was produced at The Public Theater in New York in November 2008, with an actor playing the character of "Eric Gansworth."[9] As one reviewer, Tom Pearson, notes, this strongly autobiographical play "stands as an example of a work that deals with Native issues in the present tense, issues about preservation but also issues that center on readying tradition for the future, all filtered through the individual experience of the telling of the stories."[10] In fact, the play is *about* telling stories and how stories come to shape us as individuals, much as Tom King reminds us in his wonderful book *The Truth About Stories*: "The truth about stories is that that's all we are."[11]

Pearson describes the intermedial setting:

> Standing at a podium, an actor playing Gansworth tells his story. Additionally, slide projections behind the podium where Merasty [the actor playing Gansworth] speaks often support his postulations by incorporating Gansworth paintings. More frequently though, the slides layer an additional voice onto the narrative with written comments becoming a kind of two dimensional character that speaks sassily back to the character of Eric and the audience. The fragmented narrative begins with an effort to tell the Creation Story of the Haudenosaunee and is quickly complicated by the enormity of the task and the self-realization on the author's part that he is not a storyteller. A misstep, involving an inadvertent reply to an email list-serv, suddenly elicits a multitude of advice from the wider population and quickly shows us the complications of ownership and variation within the telling of this tale.[12]

Here, email and PowerPoint, visual art, dramatic movements, and literary utterance combine to produce a new mediation. But Pearson misses the point: Gansworth—actor *and* playwright—contextualizes the telling of the Skywoman story in several ways, only one of which is concerned about his ability to tell it; another is about how the story works in the world of a professor, in an academic setting. What he ultimately reveals is that the story operates on so many levels and in so many telling contexts that no one can tell it fully, completely, even though there are those who attempt to provide the "authoritative text."

However, he keeps in front of us (pun intended) the fact that this is a lecture, one that is to last three hours, so he is implicated in that academic, authoritative enterprise, while the other actors on stage perform both as chorus and heckler, conscience and editor. The "X, Y, and W" on the slides refer to the authorities—the ethnologists and anthropologists—who have published collections of Haudenosaunee stories: their tellings. Letters are replaced by actual names as the lecture presentation progresses.[13]

The play is all about how audience and situation shape telling. It makes sense then that as the phrases and names and past experiences emerge, the persona Eric Gansworth funnels down to the second telling of the Skywoman story through a series of dramatized scenes, personalized experiences/stories, some involving family members. We finally understand that he has wrapped the old story into the life of the teller to help us see what in it speaks intimately to him but also how it has shaped his life and ways of perceiving.

This is yet one more iteration of the rearview mirror, with images/stories of the past embedded in the scenes we see before us as we try to reconcile the two and make meaning. The twin characters from the story—the Good Mind and the Bad Mind—factor prominently here, and one lesson offered about them focuses on the way the universe, the world, is a place of balance and accommodation.

Many other words, stories, images in the play resonate with Gansworth's visual art and his books. This dramatic work's concluding scenes, which number thirteen, are all visualized in the opening with his art work. In scene 10, when asked by a Latina writer, "What do you write about?" Eric replies: "Reservation life. Family. Memory, loss, recovery. Family." And the final scenes describe his mother's death, where he weaves Skywoman through stories of his mother, including the events leading up to his second-row seats at a Tears for Fears concert in Cleveland when he receives a cell call about her stroke. He tells of her in the hospital and the story of becoming an EEG operator who performed tests on people like his mom. When she dies, he turns to the Skywoman story to "find a way" to survive and cope but also to transcend, and this is what the Skywoman story offers him.

Near the conclusion of *Re-Creation Story*, the character Eric articulates the lesson learned about how stories like that of Skywoman can help us "recover" and maintain a delicate balance with all that contemporary times can throw at us: "If you are Haudenosaunee, like me, and you know what that means, like me, even on your worst day, you are thankful. Even on your worst day, you are still here, walking around on the back of a turtle that has sacrificed itself for you, and that alone is worth being thankful."

For the New York production of *Re-Creation Story*, ironically, Gansworth did not have the opportunity to "play" himself. However, a few years later he extended its concept in a new play, *Home Fires and Reservation Roads*, and in its first production, he finally found himself on stage, providing a personal immediacy and relevance lost in New York. This drama also brings together so many of the strands of story that weave throughout his work. As the play concludes, Gansworth riffs off the chords his uncle used to play in songs like "Amazing Grace" on his guitar, the "tradition" Gansworth once thought lost, emphasizing two primary ones, "D and A . . . DNA." As the PowerPoint projection above the stage cycles through a gallery of images, on multiple screens, including family photos but also images that morph into others, one screen offers a shape strongly evocative of a human fetus. This is followed by a story about Gansworth buying a guitar, the one that has been sitting on stage all along waiting for its part. This he picks up, noting as he does that it is not his uncle's guitar or his uncle's canon he plays, but his own, built from the past but also responding to changes as each generation finds its own song to sing, its own identity, the past extending into the future. Then he plays and sings, and the song? Pink Floyd's "Wish You Were Here."[14]

A refrain, "Keep it simple. Stick to the basics," which resounds late in *Re-Creation Story*, can only be understood ironically; Gansworth's performative (re)mediations are anything but simple. He certainly stimulates the spectator's ASTG and evokes epiphanies about the startling interconnections among reservation and family life, pop culture, and a plethora of layered media, both traditional and innovative.

NOTES

1. Gansworth, *Re-Creation Story*, n.p.
2. de la Paz and Purdy, "Border Crossings," 163.
3. Ibid.
4. Tom Pearson uses the adverb form "sassily" ("Circuitry and Storytelling," n.p.).

5. Gansworth, *Indian Summers*, 96.
6. de la Paz and Purdy, "Border Crossings," 173.
7. Gansworth, *Smoke Dancing*, 208.
8. Ibid., 164.
9. I am working from the original script of the play. Initially, Gansworth was to play himself, but during the direction—the negotiations that took place to bring it to the stage—he was replaced and some of the scenes altered, but the general outline and central issues remain.
10. Pearson, "Circuitry and Storytelling," n.p.
11. King, *The Truth about Stories*, 2.
12. Pearson, "Circuitry and Storytelling," n.p.
13. Academics become a recurrent motif in his canon, including Indian professors such as Dr. Annie Boans (bones?) in his fourth novel, *Extra Indians* (2010), but also Gansworth himself.
14. Interestingly, Gansworth learned to play the guitar for this performance, an ironic mirror to the issues he has explored with the play. Sometimes, the "next" generation does, indeed, pick up the instruments of the past and make new music.

WORKS CITED

de la Paz, Oliver, and John Purdy. "Border Crossings: An Interview with Eric Gansworth." In *A Usable Past: Tradition in Native American Arts and Literature*, ed. Simone Pellerin, 161–176. Bordeaux: Presses Universitaires de Bordeaux, 2010.

Gansworth, Eric. *Home Fires and Reservation Roads: A Performance*. Goodrich Theater, State University of New York at Oneonta. Oneonta, NY. April 2011.

———. *Indian Summers*. East Lansing: Michigan State University Press, 1998.

———. *Re-Creation Story: A Play*. Second Native Theater Festival, The Public Theater. New York City. November 2008. Performance.

King, Thomas. *The Truth about Stories: A Native Narrative*. Minneapolis: University of Minnesota Press, 2008.

Lehrer, Jonah. *Imagine: How Creativity Works*. Boston: Houghton Mifflin Harcourt, 2012.

Pearson, Tom. "Circuitry and Storytelling." *The Online Journal of the Public Theater's Native Theater Festival*, 26 January 2009. Http://thenativetheaterfestival.blogspot.de/2009/01/review-eric-gansworths-re-creation.html.

Mobile Indians

Capitalism, the Performance of Mobility, and the Mediation of Place in Minda Martin's Documentary Free Land

KERSTIN SCHMIDT

In the opening credits of Minda Martin's documentary *Free Land*,[1] her father assures his daughter—and us as the viewers—that "there hasn't been any free land here for decades."[2] The promise of "free land" has been crucial for the self-perception of the United States and has been a vital part of the promising lure that continues to attract immigrants by the millions. The American West has especially lived off the—deceitful—idea of an abundance of space available for building a life that can support a newcomer with family. Martin's film explores the complex relationship between space/place, ideas of mobility, especially forced mobility, and a precarious logic of capitalism in her own family, particularly with regard to its female members but also on a larger, national scope. She has developed an experimental visual language that, as I argue, challenges established ways of seeing and expresses a sense of filmic resistance, allowing her to control mediated images of Native Americans and finally to achieve what Michelle Raheja has expounded on as "visual sovereignty."[3]

Landscape shots are the dominant images of Martin's film. The semiarid landscapes of the American West, the Arizona desert area, stretch out before the viewer, in their vastness and immensity, with only a highway cutting across. In the beginning, the camera is effectively placed on a sort of traffic island in the middle of the highway, which leaves us with fast-moving cars and trucks both to the left and right of the viewer position. Cars are coming toward the camera from the left, passing the viewer, but there is also an endless trail of vehicles to the right, heading steadily toward the limitless horizon. Only the camera, that is, the viewer, remains immobile and in place. Landscape and especially place, as well as mobility, are thus established, already in the opening credits, as the main images and themes of Martin's filmic quest.

The film's narrating voice is a questioning one, and it starts with Martin's eponymous question to her father about the availability of free land. The narrator's voice quickly establishes the gist of the film: "I looked into it, and he was right [that no land was vacant and procurable for him]." Martin's film traces her family's Native American history, trying to uncover the roots of their continuous poverty and the concomitant reasons for the family's constant moving in search of a home. Her film tells the story of the family's compelled mobility as a condition that defined both her childhood and her adolescence perhaps more than anything else. The film shows how the family moves from one decrepit housing situation to another, never being able to stay in one place for long, and from one badly paid job to another short-term low-income employment. It is the story of a permanent state of homelessness. And the film leaves no doubt that poverty and homelessness mutually reinforce one another, a vicious circle with hardly any chance for escape. Whenever Martin's family finds a place, they see themselves confronted with the same series of questions by prospective landlords: Do they own another car? Do they have a TV? A savings account? Who do they know?[4] Her father's dream, to be able to raise and support a family, is contingent on land ownership, which proves to be so difficult to attain. In hard labor, Martin's father is shown attempting to rake the stony soil by hand. It is arid, hot, inimical land that demands great effort and toil from those trying to subsist on it.

Martin has chosen to trace the family history through her mother's paternal American Indian heritage, which starts in Georgia and Tennessee. She tells the story of the family's involuntary journey to the West and her parents' zigzagging movements across western states. Her family has been constantly "on the move," never being able to settle for a longer period of time. Martin's film is thus a documentation of Native displacement, revealing constant migration from one temporary home to the next as a dominant theme. Her film then becomes a powerful deconstruction of the myth of America as "free land," and her primary means to achieve this is a challenging autobiographical filmic discourse.

Martin's film is at its best when it comes to *how* the story of displacement is told, how it is mediated in a documentary that in itself uses many different modes and strategies of showing and telling the story. *Free Land* is a very suggestive feature, artful and experimental, convincing especially in its deviance from established documentary modes. There are good reasons for Martin to experiment with the form of the mediation. Her film creatively and progressively engages with the history of the tragic manipulations of Native images. Her formal experiments problematize the ways in which Native history has been made and presented by a given power distribution and hence how the meaning of the "real Indian" has been (mis) constructed. The crucial issue, for contemporary Native filmmakers, is how to mediate an image that has so often been mediated, mostly violently and derogatively, and to achieve a resisting and independent, self-determined mediation. For *Free Land*, Martin has used a variety of visual representations, including historical matcrial, maps, photographs, and films, but she also includes parts of official census data, inserts quotations from historical figures on screens, and quotes from personal notebooks, private letters or telegrams, and so many more.

MOVE IT: SEARCHING FOR A PLACE IN THE WORLD

The film's cover image (figure 1) shows a close-up of a piece of land, shot from a very low angle, almost as if the camera were sitting on the very ground itself. The mailboxes are curiously put in the center of the image; they are larger than life-size due to the particular shooting angle. Their visual arrangement suggests that they are the objects of desire, reminding us that once you have mailbox, you have a place to stay, a piece of land you can call your own, and thus you have a home. The pictorial arrangement alone expresses the importance of owning a piece of land on which one can build a home. Having an address, permanently if possible, is epitomized by the dominant placement of the mailbox as the central object in the picture, and in Martin's family's, the object of their lifelong struggle (see figure 1).

The opening credits end with a rather psychedelic comic sequence that provides a fast-forward of national U.S. and Indian history as well as Martin's personal family story. The focus in this sequence is placed on important dates and events for the nation, especially for Native Americans and for the Martin family. For instance, 1976 marks the bicentennial of the United States, with abundant official celebrations, but it also happens to be the

Figure 1. *Free Land* DVD cover. (Screenshot from *Free Land* [00:49:44])

year in which her family was once again looking for a place to live. Also in 1976, President Ford passed the federal Land Policy and Management Act, which officially ended homesteading. The rapidly cut comic sequence presents, first and foremost, the image of the U.S. flag as a powerful emblem as well as the number 200 in huge flashing digits. The stars and stripes–motif of the flag is presented in an animated way, the stripes, for instance, developing into fast-moving avenues that make the viewer feel as if on a roller coaster ride; the stripes, or avenues, however, end in space, apparently leading nowhere. The film's key motif, mobility, is hence taken up and connected to the flag when, once again, in another sequence, the flag transforms into an acorn that cracks open and releases a bird. This bird is shown as flying across the United States, from west to east, passing a series of well-known geographical and cultural landmarks. Among those is a candy-colored version of the painting *American Gothic*, defamiliarized in pop cultural terms and resembling an Andy Warhol–treatment of cultural icons. The language of pop culture, this comic strip version of American History (with a capital "H"), in its irreverence at once liberates Native history from its overpowering national symbols and takes up the motif of forced mobility that characterizes so much of Native history, turning it upside down by the inverse direction from west toward east as well as by resorting to the comic idiom. This particular rendering of history also seems to say that it may be necessary to look for answers by changing the direction, that is, by countering the history of the involuntary westward removal that has resulted in hopeless situations for families such as Minda Martin's.

Figure 2. The rearview mirror, showing both a reflection of Minda Martin as well as her ancestor Mary Taylor. (Screenshot from *Free Land* [00:06:47])

THE REARVIEW MIRROR: A WOMAN'S STORY OF DISPLACEMENT, POVERTY, AND HOMELESSNESS

Minda Martin looks back in her film, trying to uncover and document the sources of her family's chronic poverty and forced itinerancy. Her filmic tool to express the gesture of looking back, while at the same time connecting the backward glance to the present, is the rearview mirror. This massive mirror is placed in the middle of the typical southwestern landscape. The doubling of the landscape image in the mirror once more underscores the importance of land for Martin's family. But the mirror also gradually shapes into a collage that shows her female ancestor Mary Taylor as well as Martin herself (figure 2). Martin thus connects landscape, family history, especially the matrilineal ancestry that she investigates, to her own story and living situation.

In this way of looking back, Martin does not seem content with simply unearthing historical material, records, letters, data, photographs, and the like, which she would then neatly fit into the story of her family. What is more, she presents historical footage, only to distort it and defamiliarize it in her idiosyncratic way of telling the story. There are only three more or less consecutive narratives in her film: those of her female ancestors Mary Taylor and Cordelia Taylor Freeland as well as the story of her father, but they, too, are told in a blatantly nonlinear fashion. When parts of these personal stories are told, they are juxtaposed with images from a variety of contexts—for instance, large-scale political events and decisions or footage of industrial labor and economic developments. Thus, bits and pieces of different story lines collide and are intertwined in the film with other related, but actually different events and contexts, as if she wanted to approach her topic in other ways than that of linear progressive narration. As a reviewer has it, the film and its voices are arranged "as if concentric circles are created around one's own story."[5]

Later in the film, Martin admits that she had originally planned to tell only her mother's story, but then she found so few documents, so little her mother had left behind, that this project was not feasible in the end.[6] Her mother, we learn, committed suicide when Minda was still very young. In the movie, one of Minda's aunts, Mary Dee, reveals alcoholism as the chief motive for the suicide, but Mary Dee also talks about the grandparents' refusal to help their destitute daughter, who suffered immensely from the hopeless financial situation of her family. Minda admits in the film that it was precisely the relative abundance of records left behind by both Mary and Cordelia that she found so fascinating, stimulating her determination to dig into the family's history.

Given the characteristic search for roots and lineage, the ancestral material Martin discovers is indeed of great significance and personal value. In short, her ancestors' stories lay bare the same compulsory mobility and the same struggles for survival that still define her and her father's late twentieth-century experience: Mary Taylor was born in 1802 in Tennessee, married a white man, David, and had thirteen children, as we hear from a transcript of an 1851 census roll. Without her husband, she and the children were forced to move westward in order to make a living, continually searching for a permanent home. We also hear about Cordelia Taylor Freeland from a partial transcript of an interview with the Dawes Commission in 1905. Cordelia, born in 1865 in North Carolina, moved at least forty-three times after the Cherokee removal of 1830. Martin presents these stories of mobility with quite effective, provocative filmic means. For instance, she constructs a sequence of shots of her father, each indicating matter-of-factly a period of time and the respective occupation that he held at that time. In a similar sequence, the film shows a series of business cards that her father has had over the years (00:33:30). All in all, his jobs add up to thirty-two, which involves a total of twenty-seven times that the family had to move (from 00:34:27 on). Since 1999, her father has been unemployed and has been living in Tucson, Arizona. If one moves so much and continues to be so poor, part of the lineage, part of the heritage, can easily be lost. This happened in the case of the Martin family. In her mission to look into the issue of poverty and homelessness, Minda Martin had to dig up and rediscover the bits and pieces from a variety of sources, adding up the fragments to virtually reassemble and reconstruct family history and make connections to her own life. In this respect, the rearview mirror that she uses is an adequate metaphor, reminding us of the safety warning that is obligatorily engraved on passenger side mirrors of vehicles in the United States: it prompts us to pay attention, as "Objects in mirror are closer than they appear."

A PLACE-BASED IMAGINATION AS THE OTHER OF THE LOGIC OF CAPITALISM

Mobility and poverty also define the stories around Minda's birthdays from her early childhood. On birthdays, her grandfather would take her to the junkyard in his pickup truck. There, she tells us in a tender and caring voice, they would look for things they could still use, reassemble parts, and, more often than not, she would be given "homemade" presents, mostly from pieces found in the junkyard. We see close-ups of moving tires and pictures of seemingly endless heaps of junk, reminding us of the by-products of a so-called civilized way of life. The capitalist logic of constant consumption, which means consuming, concretely, buying new things and not recycling waste items, is lost on those lacking the financial resources to participate in it. Another sequence of the film shows Minda's father pushing an empty shopping cart across the street as he tells the story of his failed business ventures (00:34:20). He had no success in business, he explains, because he himself simply lacked the capital necessary for a propitious start and had nobody to turn to for a financial boost. The family failed in terms of capitalist success, and economic failure has a long family history. We hear the story of Minda's ancestor Cordelia, whose husband, Henry, works in a coal mine. Henry suffers from lung disease as a consequence of his hard labor in the mines. Cordelia, fully aware of the eventual futility of the taxing industrial labor, sees opportunity in the open road and urges him to move away, believing that they could make it elsewhere. Henry, however, dutifully goes to the mine every day, even if his health deteriorates and the labor becomes harder day by day. Quite poignantly, Cordelia sums up the oxymoronic capitalist paradigm and her family's inversion of it (00:31:37 on): "We've been scraping by every month. . . . We're making less this year than last year even though we're working longer hours. I don't understand this life.

We spend so much for today, thinking we'll earn more tomorrow to pay off what we had taken in yesterday."

A more recent case of family history connects economic failure to issues of gender. Minda's family had found yet another rundown place to live, being determined to succeed this time in working the land and living off it. Minda's brother tells his little sister that if she only works industriously and cleverly, she is surely going to make it in the world. Her brother reiterates the quintessential founding myth of the United States in which, as it seems, he still firmly believes. Minda's mother, by contrast, is more cautious and contends that, as a woman, one can work as hard as possible, and yet "you will never get as far as you hope because you are a woman in a man's world" (00:26:45).

In the United States, economic failure is generally seen as individual, not as systemic. In other words, if someone fails, it is always attributed to personal failure, and the causes for it are not necessarily seen as consequences of inequalities of political and social conditions. Thus, Martin's filmic project is needed even more urgently since her film establishes economic failure as structural, referencing her family's long social history of economic shortcomings. Sadly, not that much seems to have changed for her people over the course of roughly a century.

In opposition to capitalism's power to dislocate, Martin's film posits a place-based imagination as the "other" of the logic of capitalism. She uses powerful landscape shots, often almost landscape stills that are held for a longer stretch of time, but she also directly connects the human body to the land. In a notable sequence at the beginning of the film, the narrating voice explains that Minda and her mother used to tread the dirt road leading up to the mountains, and Martin employs an image of a bare foot walking the road to accompany this part of the story. The film shows the foot in motion, as actively walking and thus moving forward on the land (figure 3).

The visual assertion of place is strong and dominates Martin's documentary. "I come from somewhere other than nowhere," says Mary Taylor in the beginning in the film. "Somewhere" designates a concrete place of origin, which becomes even more significant in light of the constant, often mandatory relocation of Native Americans in general and Minda's family in particular. "Somewhere" as opposed to "nowhere" postulates a sense of place and of belonging, thus counteracting a history of homelessness, both literally and figuratively, and geographic dispersal. The importance of place and the problems arising from lack of it are expressed in Cordelia's moving story of her husband Henry's burial. Henry ultimately died of lung disease, and Cordelia talks about their searching for a place in the mountains to

Figure 3. Close-up of bare foot walking the land. (Screenshot from *Free Land* [00:04:01])

bury him. When they find a suitable spot for Henry's burial, Cordelia starts musing on the intricacies of place and landscape. Her family never owned a piece of land, and, given her family's history of relocation, she claims that she had always known her directions, always knew which way to go, but "I have never been able to get to that place called here" (00:42:52). "Here" posits a specific place of belonging that she has never been able to find; by contrast, Cordelia is aware of her admirable skills of direction on which she could always rely on the continual journey across the U.S. continent—but the desired place called "here" remained perennially out of reach.

THE VANISHING VERSUS THE MOVING INDIAN: NATIVE PRESENCE, TECHNOLOGY, AND FORMAL REVOLTS

As a child, Minda tells us, she did not have glasses despite considerable ametropia. Her parents had wanted to buy glasses for her, but other more pressing expenses often kept them from doing so. This meant that her life, she says, was strangely "out of focus" (00:05:20). This lack of focus was later doubly cured by acquiring glasses as well as by operating a camera. Lenses, in both senses, provided a clarity that, as the narrator continues to tell us, "made poverty hard to look at."

What was true for glasses at a fairly young age seems to echo in her use of the camera lens later in life. The camera, for Martin, seems a helpful contraption to shift focus and to see things more clearly. However, the clarity that her filmmaking provides clashes with the history of Native image-making. Not just since the publication of W. J. T. Mitchell's epochal work on the importance of visual material and the "pictorial turn" do we know that images are a powerful way of knowing the past as well as the present of a given culture. More particularly, Mitchell accounts for the anxiety over visual representations precisely because we do not yet fully know "how they operate on observers and on the world."[7] Critical analysis of visual representations, hence, is of paramount importance because of the meaning-making power of visuality and "visual construction of the social" that Mitchell sees operative.[8] A visual culture studies approach and, accordingly, the analysis of strategies of mediation are of particular relevance for Native Americans. "The Indian," Gerald Vizenor reminds us, "is an imprinted picture, the pose of a continental fugitive"; photographs, especially, are "poselocked in silence." Due to the immense "possessory" power of visual representations, they rule the past and to a large degree determine the present.[9] Vizenor, Baudrillard, and others have so often laid bare the simulated and commodified nature of dominant representations that are, however, taken to be the real. If these representations cater much less to their referent, but rather to desire and commodification, it means that much more work must be done to offer new ways of knowing the referent—in Martin's case, of learning about her family in its respective historical context. Knowing about the simulated nature of representations can hence also have a liberating effect, creating the need as well as the possibility for new images reflecting different perspectives as well as new modes of telling and knowing. Minda Martin offers a variety of formal tools and technological possibilities in order to challenge the "dead" representations on the film reel or on the photographic plate.

For one, her documentary mixes historical documentation, such as census polls, letters, and interviews with the Dawes Commission, with contemporary material, including personal family shots and interviews as well as creative writing. Parts of the story are imagined, or they are only inspired by real-life events. Literary critics might be quick to read this strategy as postmodern, but it surely expresses that the available historical material is biased as important perspectives are left out or altered by the given power dynamics of historical discourse. As a filmmaker, Martin "fills in" parts of the story, adding and/or imagining missing links. After all, this is what any reader or writer does, but not necessarily a documentary filmmaker. Deliberately integrating creative writing into a documentary calls into question the very possibility of (objective) documentation. Traditionally viewed as antithetical to the documentary mode, creative writing expands the borders of the genre as it casts doubts on the genre's founding principles.

In her father's story, Martin juxtaposes recent footage of him that is accompanied by flashing text-bits announcing every job he has held and every place in which he has lived. The seemingly endless repetition of this structural pattern powerfully conveys the trying and demanding life he has led. Cordelia's story is, then, told over images of industry, as Henry dies of black lung disease. Thus, the cause for Henry's trouble and, later on, for his death is expressed both by the voice of Cordelia as well as by photographs and short films of the mining business that blatantly expose the power and danger involved in this kind of labor. The images of the mining industry are additionally fractured and colored to a nightmarish effect, presenting mines and factories in greenish, dark lighting as if mirroring the murky dark atmosphere in which miners actually carried out their work.

More important, perhaps, the mediated images are reframed in Martin's picture. She uses images, adapts or even defamiliarizes them by using effects of posterization, solarized images, colored negatives, racking focus (changing focus of lens during a shot), slow focus, or double exposure shots; dynamic montage; sepia-coloring; and many more techniques. The resulting *Verfremdung* effects serve to disorient the viewer from established interpretive patterns, thus creating space for their (creative) rethinking. At times, photographs are shown as negatives; well-known pictures of the U.S. Army or western movies in particular are extracted from their all too familiar context and changed in color and focus to render recognition extremely difficult. Martin challenges the viewers to make reconnections between visual representations that are part and parcel of the cultural heritage, but by estranging them and putting them into new contexts, she resists established reading patterns and fosters the possibility for new meaning to emerge.

The maps that Martin extensively uses in her filmic collage are a striking case of abstract visual representation. Naturally, maps have been paramount to the colonization and settlement of the West as well as the concomitant forced relocations of Native people. Martin includes sequences in her film that show how maps are actually drawn, how borders are created, are virtually performed, on the abstract space of a piece of parchment. Territory and ownership of land are not givens, but are processed and finalized on the page. The illustration in figure 4 demonstrates the performance of boundary-making. The index finger in the sequence glosses over territories, claiming and appropriating them in the process. The scene is a collage with yet another medium: the section on the left, where the hand is dimly visible, shows a scene from a movie that is gradually shifted into focus. It shows

Figure 4. Collage of a map with index finger and historical film sequence. (Screenshot from *Free Land* [00:08:27])

laborers working hard to build the railroad in the western United States. The map is rendered with a greenish coloring, and the multimedia collage of finger, historical movie, and the defamiliarized abstract representation of space, that is, the map, puts center stage the uneven relationship between (Indian) labor and national politics, between the actual colonization of space in real life and the powerful abstract representations.

Martin's film has rightfully been called a "dreamscape,"[10] although the expression "nightmare-scape" would be quite fitting as well. Reminiscent of the conventions of surrealist montage, Martin includes the posterized image of a train moving toward the viewer. White smoke gradually occupies more and the more of the picture space, leading to a visceral affective response by the viewers. The collage also features negatives of photographs of dead buffalo, corroborating the alienating effect of this particular distorted representation of Indian history (figure 5).

This montage formally expresses the connection between the railroad and colonization of the West and the extinction of the Native way of life. Using effects of gradual posterization and solarization, Martin eventually makes it impossible to differentiate between the two different images, revealing both as highly disturbing traumatic experiences that are conveyed here most effectively by exaggerated coloring and distorting shapes. Martin thus renders the story of Native Americans in general and her own family in particular in terms of a cinematic retelling resisting the frozen images of the past and turning these representations into refractured and mobile mosaics of

Figure 5. Railroad with steam (in soft pink color) with photographs of dying buffalo. (Screenshot from *Free Land* [00:30:56])

the present. Her original documentary thus lays bare a particular politics of the camera that is resistant and performative. Martin's approach to history corresponds to what Dean Rader has termed "engaged resistance" in his analysis of Indian art, literature, and film.[11]

Technology not only plays a crucial role in Martin's documentary in terms of the possibilities for formal experiments with cinematic material. The film itself takes up technology as a powerful and active force in the history that the film tells. Hence, railroads and factories play important roles, as do films, telegraphs, and photographs. Multiple reframings take place when Martin, for instance, shoots a scene showing historical footage of a movie theater audience that, in turn, watches a film titled *How We Got What We Have* (00:23:15). In the manner of opening a Russian doll, she unwinds the layers and contingencies that, as a matter of fact, explain how Native Americans and her own family "got what they have."

Free Land also features interesting soundwork. The transcript testimonies from 1851 and 1905, which so vividly prove that homelessness is not new in Martin's family, are delivered by voice actors in the film. Since there were no sound records of the testimonials at the time, viewers have reported a "haunting" effect when hearing a live voice telling the stories, while at the same time knowing it cannot be the authentic voice.[12] What is at stake is thus not so much credibility—as one may think with regard to a documentary—but a theatrical performance that lends presence to the silent textual material. The live voices are an attempt to subvert the dead and silent representation of the Indian, substituting a present and performative model that lures us by the live voice and its capacity to effect a sense of presence.

THE POWER GEOMETRY OF MOBILITY AND THE POLITICS OF THE CAMERA

> *Natives must create their own stories; otherwise, the sources of their identities are not their own . . . ; [they] create stories of survivance, a sense of presence and distinctive identities in the midst of . . . many contradictions and contingencies.*
>
> —GERALD VIZENOR, *NATIVE LIBERTY*

Martin's *Free Land* is a painful testimonial of the destruction of the basis for subsistence and survival for American Native peoples. The documentary is a filmic essay using a variety of memory fragments. Her family's failures in business and the resulting disorientation lay bare the continuing dominance of capitalism. Despite tackling big issues such as poverty, unemployment, and homelessness among Native Americans, the film remains very local, tied to particular places, as Martin reads her family's history into a bigger, national context. She extends biographical inquiry, as her film freely mixes diary, historical text, cultural anthropology, creative writing, soundwork, and visual experiments, reading the resulting collage not only in a local, place-bound and personal context but also in a larger historical and political frame. The end product, *Free Land*, in many ways corresponds to what Joanne Hearne refers to as "intertextual cinema" in her essay on documentary filmmaking, orality, and Indigenous identity.[13] There is also conceptual overlap with Barry Barclay's "Fourth Cinema," which has elsewhere been described as exhibiting "the indigenous world insofar as it creates something the West can look at, namely the film itself; however it seeks to create a representation of indigeneity that is free from the debilitating gaze of the outsider."[14]

Martin's film is no reactionary, naive recovery of landscape, no glib reiterated assertion of the sacredness of the land for Native Americans; she refrains from making an attempt to seek or re-create ways of expressing "ethnic purity."[15] Place, rather, is presented as a complex site for agency to develop. In many ways, the sense of place as presented in Martin's documentary is reminiscent of Doreen Massey's conceptual elaboration on place.

Figure 6. Close-up of Bob Martin, Minda Martin's father. (Screenshot from *Free Land* [00:53:59])

In her influential work, Massey calls for a "global sense of place," place seen as progressive space defined not as "self-enclosing and defensive," but as outward-looking, interactive, and, most importantly, productive.[16]

Despite their constant forced mobility over more than a century, it is blatantly clear that the Martin family has not been in control of movement. Rather, they are imprisoned by it. Their failure in mastering the capitalist system has turned mobility into a condition for survival. What is important, however, in Martin's picture is that she has achieved control of the images that have been constructed of Native Americans. She has uncovered them, adapted and defamiliarized them, making them her own in the formal process. Her film is a sovereign act "on the move," one that eschews the pitfalls of tragic Indian representations, the poses fixed on the photographic plate, which have been models for how we conceive of Indians for too long. Gaining control of visual representations and creating an idiosyncratic aesthetic language is thus one of many achievements of Martin's work.[17]

That the role of capitalism, poverty, race, and gender is still salient and that the film's narrative is also valid in the present is clear when, at the end of her film, Minda Martin traces her own history, which has also been defined by poverty, placelessness, and the struggle for survival. After high school, her plans to go to college put her in serious financial troubles. Obtaining an education proved to be difficult for her, reminding us of the many (broken) educational promises to Native people. To make ends meet, she worked several jobs, none of which paid enough to make a living. Lacking a home, she slept in her car, which created ever more problems. Without an address, she learned, it seemed impossible for her to obtain work and make a living in present-day California.

Martin's documentary, however, does not rest at pointing out systemic inequalities that everyone with only a superficial interest in the matter would have known long ago. She establishes a challenging visual language that exposes the blatant disconnect between the official rhetoric and the painful experience of her family and herself as well. The traces of the historical and actual living conditions are perhaps best seen in a close-up of her father's lined face. By telling his story, even in its purportedly most trivial yet important and revealing details, she achieves a remarkable personalization of the abstract story of mobility and economic hardship. Her father's face clearly expresses the body's destruction from hard labor and thus contrasts with the U.S. American insistence on and appraisal of the motif of economic profit. Toward the end of the film (figure 6), she shows a close-up of her father's face, etiolated by economic struggle and hardship, a visual map of his family's convoluted paths.

NOTES

1. *Free Land*; for production details, refer to www.mindamartin.com. The film is available as a DVD via this website. To my knowledge, no full essays or secondary criticism on this film have been published to date; for a list of reviews and past/future screenings, see Martin's webpage.
2. Ibid., 00:00:33.
3. See Raheja, *Reservation Reelism*, especially chapters 2 and 5.
4. For example, 00:25:40.
5. Review of Minda Martin, *Free Land*. The original reads: "als ob sich konzentrische Kreise um die persönliche Geschichte ausbreiten würden."
6. Minda Martin has produced a short documentary video on her mother called *Mother's Heritage* (1995; 11 min.)
7. Mitchell, *Picture Theory*, 14.
8. Mitchell, "Showing Seeing," 100.
9. Vizenor, *Fugitive Poses*, 145, 147, 154.
10. Review by Robert Koehler, http://variety.com/2011/film/reviews/free-land-1117945099.
11. Rader, "Engaged Resistance," 179. Rader expanded his argument and material from this 2003 article into a book: *Engaged Resistance: American Indian*

Art, Literature, and Film from Alcatraz to the NMAI (Austin: University of Texas Press, 2011).

12. Anderson, "ImaginaNative," n.p.
13. Hearne, "Telling and Retelling in the 'Ink of Light,'" 320.
14. For Barclay's definition of "Fourth Cinema," see "Celebrating Fourth Cinema." For the explication, see Bennett, "Fourth Cinema," 19. A critical discussion of the concept can be found in Schweninger, *Imagic Moments*, 4–7.
15. "Sacredness" has been pointed out as a basis for the development of a distinct Native aesthetics by acclaimed filmmaker and photographer Victor Masayesva. For a discussion of Masayesva's claim, see Steven Leuthold, "Native American Documentary: An Emerging Genre?" *Film Criticism* 22.1 (1997): 82.
16. Massey, *Space, Place, and Gender*, 156, 147.
17. On the concept of Native aesthetics, see, for example, Steven Leuthold's work, especially his monograph *Indigenous Aesthetics: Native Art, Media, and Identity* (Austin: University of Texas Press, 1998).

WORKS CITED

Anderson, Samantha. "ImagineNATIVE 2010: Free Land." Http://www.cbc.ca/news/arts/things-that-go-pop-blog/2010/10/imaginenative-2010-free-land.html.

Barclay, Barry. "Celebrating Fourth Cinema." *Illusions* 35 (Winter 2003): 7–11.

Bennett, Kirsty. "Fourth Cinema and the Politics of Staring." *Illusions* 38 (Winter 2006): 19–23.

Free Land. Written, photographed, directed, and edited by Minda Martin. Produced and distributed by Martin, 2010.

Hearne, Joanna. "Telling and Retelling in the 'Ink of Light': Documentary Cinema, Oral Narratives, and Indigenous Identities." *Screen* 47.3 (Fall 2006): 307–326.

Koehler, Robert. Review of Minda Martin, *Free Land.* Http://variety.com/2011/film/reviews/free-land-1117945099.

Massey, Doreen. *Space, Place, and Gender*. Cambridge: Polity Press, 1994.

Mitchell, W. J. T. *Picture Theory*. Chicago: University of Chicago Press, 1994.

———. "Showing Seeing: A Critique of Visual Culture." In *The Visual Culture Reader*, 2nd ed., ed. Nicholas Mirzoeff, 86–101. New York: Routledge, 2002.

Rader, Dean. "Engaged Resistance in American Indian Art, Literature, and Film." *Peace Review* 15.2 (2003): 179–186.

Raheja, Michelle H. *Reservation Reelism: Redfacing, Visual Sovereignty, and*

Representations of Native Americans in Film. Lincoln: University of Nebraska Press, 2011.

Review of Minda Martin, *Free Land*. Http://www.viennale.at/de/film/free-land.

Schweninger, Lee. *Imagic Moments: Indigenous North American Film*. Athens: University of Georgia Press, 2013.

Vizenor, Gerald. *Fugitive Poses: Native American Indian Scenes of Absence and Presence*. Lincoln: University of Nebraska Press, 1998.

———. *Native Liberty: Natural Reason and Cultural Survivance*. Lincoln: University of Nebraska Press, 2009.

PART FOUR

"Crow Commons": Creative Correspondences and Virtual Affiliations

An Exposition of Virtual Exchanges

KIMBERLY BLAESER
JANE HALADAY
GORDON HENRY JR.
MOLLY MCGLENNEN
JESSE PETERS
IN ABSENTIA, GERALD VIZENOR

A TWO-YEAR CREATIVE ROUNDTABLE DISCUSSION, PRESENTED AT THE 2012 MESEA conference in Barcelona

Gordon: sings *Four Directions Song*

Bindiigin, welcome to the Crow Commons. *Indishneekaws* Dr. Gaween,[1] *Anishinaabe endao, endao, endao, endao* a practitioner of postmortem Western theory, a songmaker, an artist—I know some of you will disagree—of adjacent possibility, a grandfather in the Great Anishinaabe Commung.

Kim: Demonstrating our ongoing conversations over the past four years, our roundtable discussion today will center on the continuous ways in which we understand connective imagery in Anishinaabe poetry, and the connections made between us—members of the Crow Commons—because of the literature. In doing so, we hope to articulate what Gordon calls affiliate relationships—not just among the poets themselves but also through affiliations across notions such as place, myth, song, historical and cultural beings, forms, and other authors outside of the Anishinaabe cultural commons.

Molly: We will show how this doubling of affiliation inside of and outside of the Anishinaabe cultural commons leads to literary innovation or "adjacent possibilities" in the work of Anishinaabe writers.
Jane: With this roundtable, we intend to rework methods that normally define conference panels by delivering an exposition of our exchanges leading up to the conference and our creative responses to these conversations; we foresee our roundtable as an evolving engagement with Anishinaabe poets in culturally specific formations of knowledge-building.

At this time the Crow Commons is an expressive commons—a place where voices meet, ideas gather, and we as people join together to work through a common(s) purpose to begin again.

THOUGHTS ON METHODS

Molly: Perhaps we can begin by briefly articulating our methodology, which we intend to be a departure from traditional conference presentations. As Native people and Native studies scholars we continue to engage in and look to ways of "Indigenizing" writing, teaching, and theorizing, so we believe that there might be a way to bring a similarly creative alternative, dare we say Indigenous, form of conferencing. We imagine the theory of the cultural commons and literary/personal filiations/affiliations to be our vision for a new kind of conferencing that is dynamic, collaborative, ongoing, teasing, personal, intellectual, and resonant with the patterns in and the motion of the natural world.
Gordon: Edward Said claims:

> The contemporary critical consciousness stands between the temptations represented by two formidable and related powers engaging critical attention. One is the culture to which critics are bound filiatively (by birth, nationality, profession); the other is a method or system acquired affiliatively (by social and political conviction, economic and historical circumstances, voluntary effort and willed deliberation).[2]

Molly: Our hope is that the delivery of our thoughts at the roundtable itself demonstrates the consensus building we both struggled with and thrived on along the way leading up to the conference. We also envision that our presentation of our research is one that invokes cyclical (rather than linear) constructions of voice. For instance, we hope listeners can pick up the recurring threads of story throughout and across the roundtable members' blocks of connective narratives. We also hope that this structure (much like storytellings themselves) allows for associative (rather than "reasoned") accruals of knowledge-building as well as the creative affiliations that are often absent from "traditional" academic papers.

Gordon: To be sure the commons is not a monoculture, even though the idea of the commons has roots in traditions related to shared use of grazing lands, prior to the issuance of private property. In this sense the commons defied enclosures.

In contemporary usage, the commons relates to culture, including literature, music, radio and television, film and video, arts, design, information and software, and particularly sites of heritage.

We would like to approach very carefully, with a few circles and arrows and illustrations, the introduction of the Anishinaabe commung as transcendent and immanent; so as the material production and conditions of Anishinaabe people or the commons may transcend material form, physical space, human place, physical body and so forth, the transcendental formless may take form in the Anishinaabe commung. Further we believe the elements of the Anishinaabe commung will transcend the commung and create new possibilities for adding to it by interacting with elements outside of the Anishinaabe commung through adjacent possibility and exaptation, to innovate and to find extended uses of cultural features that existed in the commons before we encountered those forces, people, and systems which may have attempted to remove those features from our cultural commons.

THE CORRESPONDENCE COMMONS

Gordon: from *Dead Letters: The Unsent Letters to Relatives*

"Manito Giizhiisons—Little Spirit Moon"

Dear Joe V2:

Shall I tell you my story, the one of grief, the one of deception, the one of travel, the one of the talk over a wooden table after a funeral, the one of the glass draining rum into a face just beyond reach in the dark? Should I tell you the story of the one I wanted to shoot, the one I wanted to love, the white feather falling from the sky, the search on the other side of the river for the lost child, the Uncle who wanted to kill your mother, the North Dakota prayers ties, on the tree we gave tea to, before we cut it. Shall I tell you the one about the ugly fights over missing articles, ownership of clothes and

> cars and the heart attack regalia your father wore, at the grand entry where he died? Shall I tell of the one, following the old man to a yellow house in winter where he ate with other women and woke up one Sunday to find you sleeping in a snowed over driveway, as he made his way to mass. Shall I tell you the one about the altar boy latin I could not memorize, not the words you've seen like e pluribus unum, or semper fi, or vedi, vici veni, but a whole fucking confiteor, the complete god damned lords prayer, all the litanies, the hymns, the gospels, the Friday rules. Shall I tell that one?[3]

Molly: January 11
Happy New Year, crow riders!

I am just back from Mpls where I spent almost 2 weeks with lots of family. And, yes, there were some Crow stories (and one fox story). I'm really looking forward to seeing you all in New Mex!

Here's a Vizenor poem I've been reading this morning (from *Almost Ashore*):

> **"Crow Nests"**
>
> crows return
> by words
> bold messages
> perched high
> in the october
> white pine
>
> crows strut
> on country roads
> parapets
> cemetery stones
> past the dead
> homesteads
>
> crows preen
> feathers clean
> cold rain
> brightens
> precious stones
> stolen beads[4]

My auntie told me this story when I was back home. After she cooked a pheasant around Christmas time, she put the bones outside her house late in the evening. She could see them in the snow from a large window in the front of her house. My cousin (her twenty-year-old son) was out late that night (as twenty-year-olds often are) and she was worried about him and couldn't sleep. So when she heard the door she got up out of bed. She didn't see her son, but when she looked outside the large window the moon was full and very bright and it lit up the whole yard. There was a fox stepping around the bones, sniffing, it was almost like he was dancing she said. The next morning she saw all the fox's footprints in the snow and the bones were gone. Then she added, of course the crows were there, talking.

I really liked her story, and I couldn't say why at the time. I thought she was telling me about how she worried about her son, my cousin, how he's dropped out of school and running with some "not so great" crowds . . . and now I'm not so sure.

anyway, wanted to share that with you.
write back if you have time, crow crew
Molly

Jane: February 4

Affiliates in Motion: We take wing. We fly in. From Wisconsin, from New York, from Michigan, from North Carolina. Crow Riders. Our migratory paths stretching back even farther: to California, to Minnesota, to Georgia. To White Earth, to Anishinaabe homelands, to Tongva homelands suburbia superimposed; to rural south Georgia, Cherokee homelands, with murders of crows raising cain in pecan trees. We take flight and land in New Mexico, Pueblo homelands. We roost here these few days, confabulating. Weaving together with language the nest we've been building across glowing digital spaces during the months apart. This woven nest where our breath warms ideas til they hatch. We share this feast with friends.

The E/motion of the Center

"We are searching for interpretive ground, a critical center," Kimberly Blaeser writes in "'Like Reeds through the Ribs of a Basket': Native Women Weaving Stories." "It doesn't take long to realize that the center inhabits shifting ground, borderland in motion. Mixedblood, margins, cross-blood, mixed culture, frontier space."[5]—affiliates moving together to meet in the cultural commons. We're winging it and we know it.

"This center (or these centers) are always dynamic, never static," Blaeser notes. "This mobile center of consciousness might be a place, a person, or an event; it might reflect the motion of the landscape, of people, of the seasons, or of families or communities."[6] This mobile center of consciousness might be the text message your fingers are working to send right now during this session as we speak. This mobile center of consciousness is the blissful shimmer atop the circle of hot black coffee in the cup you cling to listening to me as we speak. This mobile center of consciousness is each one of us sitting and standing here cloaking our stories in our beautiful scarred bodies, and radiating them outward within and beyond the Anishinaabe cultural commons where the crows meet to consider and confer.

Molly: "Some Kind of Likeness," by Kimberly Blaeser:

> Again today it happened. At my feet I saw the grey bird wing, just one severed from the bird. Slight and curved in the remembered form. With my backward glance the texture unmasks itself, becomes a small fallen segment from a tree. The weathered wood surfaces from feathers. I stand before them—wing, wood, wing, wood, wing—back and forth. The grey shape drawn, erased, redrawn, hovering like bird or bark on the edge of realities. Holding the air-thin space between sight and vision.[7]

Jesse: "Sleeping in Rain" by Gordon Henry Jr.:

> September sun in the old church. Smoke of sweetgrass in stained glass light. Red, blue and yellow light. Prisms of thought behind every eye. Chippewa prayers stumbling through my ears. Old Ojibwe chants fading away in the walk to the cemetery. I look at the hole in the ground. I look at the casket beside it. I look at the hole. I look at the casket. At the hole, at the casket, at the hole, at the casket, at the hole.
>
> The clock glows red across the room; a digital 2:37. My cousin lies in darkness. Another figure covered up in sleep.[8]

Jane: I know this story. The center won't hold, or the hole is the center, and so is the wing, the bark, the casket. All story centers opening and shutting onto something, like valves of the heart. It happens for me most in summer when I see the spotted brown Carolina toad masquerading as a dry leaf on my walks, or the dark little frogs pretending to be stones. When I get closer, the toad does not hop away and remains a leaf for protection, or the frog a stone. The toads who want to be revealed will hop away, showing me their beautiful plunking bodies, their motion of spring and sprint. But I often do a double-take—leaf, toad, leaf, toad, leaf again. All of us within the seasonal motion of a North Carolina summer.

Kim: February 5

Happy Winter, Crow Riders!

Hope your snow is piled like Jack's beanstalk—right up to an-other world, a world of bigness and mystery. Thanks, Jane, for starting out the discussion. I like the links you made. The permeability of all that we call reality is one of my great preoccupations. I've written a bit about it in an essay that I think only came out in France. There are allusions to things that pass earlier in the essay, but I think the essence is accessible:

> What is it about similarity, about the recognition of repetition in our environment, that pulses with the knowing of the great unknown? Late this spring I stood looking at a pine on which patches of bright rust marked the branches. These frayed ovals of color that dotted the green pines at first I took for the fruits of that tree. They *looked* like pinecones forming. But when I came close enough to see the pale pastel candles growing at the tips of the branches, close enough to see the still small, still green cones just beginning to develop, I realized the nests of rust lay at the *base* of the green needles, that they were themselves needles burnished just now in some seasonal cycle. And then I saw another feathered rust oval, a twin in shape, as bright in color, but at trunk level, close to the ground. And it saw me. It waited a long moment, until I could untangle it from the tree world and recognize it whole and part: a spring robin, fat breast the color of fall pine cones, of the rust needle patches marking this pine. A chameleon could not have camouflaged itself more aptly. Finally it flew, and unaccountably, my spirit, too, soared. A slight moment of beauty, multiplied to the third power. I felt alive with some unspeakable discovery.
>
> Does correspondence mark some tiny crack in this shell of mortality through which spills the reviving waters of grace? Can the simple overlapping of being spell our ransom from the illusion of human separation? Native nations for centuries have believed and lived within this wisdom—the ultimate unity of all times and realms of being. The dream songs of my Anishinaabe culture, for example, arise from the transformational moments of knowing these connections. Frances Densmore, early twentieth century translator of Ojibwe oral songs, describes dream songs as arising from a moment of "direct communication with the supernatural," when the dreamer "contemplates nature in a certain aspect so long and so steadily that he gradually loses his own personality and identifies himself with it."[9] A near equivalent in the Yaqui tradition, *maso bwikam* or deer songs, verbally enact what scholars Larry Evers and Felipe Molina describe as "equivalencies" with "that mythic, primeval place," a "double world."[10] We are all heir in own our ways to the recognition of a timeless, dimensionless reality of spirit. Perhaps we rejoice at the smallest encounter of relatedness because it signals the greater. We

feel reassured knowing that this season continues a familiar cycle; we feel empowered knowing that one acquaintance of being links us to another.[11]

The longing that we live out in our day to day compels us sometimes toward paths that promise a tiny breach in the impalpable. Among crow riders that compulsion sometimes leads us to the language of writers we think have marked a trail. Perhaps they are "relatives of light people," "men and women of gifts and vision."[12] I think simultaneously we search the natural world, listen to crow talk and follow track, paddle out with dawn light to see preened feathers on the morning waters, take ourselves always to the edge of what we now know and then inch forward bit by bit into the unknown. That unknown, our ecstasy. We affiliate with teachers—stories, cranes, crows, songmakers, images of ancestors—all teachers in the cultural commons whose vision brings the gift of another small light.

Gordon: from *Dead Letters: The Unsent Letters to Relatives*

"Namebini Giizhis—Sucker Moon"

Dear Marie:
You must forget strawberries, even if
you happen to hear the meadowlark
calling you toward sunned streams;
you must forget the yards of grandchildren
summers hollering sundown
as you must forget the moonlight,
as you brushed your hair on the iron
bed while the old man listened to the
narration of the Twins playing
through the static on the radio

Don't try to go to grandmother's land, or back into the house
to turn out bread for strangers again.
The water basin remains half-buried
Rusting next to the old stove mouthing
Weeds and yellow flowers

The memory of your shaking hands will be enough
To light a cigarette for me, though
I often showed up after years overseas, years and travels
beyond the last address you saw under my name,
I was never a stranger.[13]

Jesse: February 6
Hello all,

After reading Kim's thoughts, I found myself thinking about my place and my childhood. We moved to south Georgia when I was about two years old. My parents had grown up in sharecropping families, picking cotton by hand, plowing with mules, going to town in wagons. They wanted their children to grow up in a rural area and on a farm, so they bought a large piece of land after years of working various jobs in and around Atlanta. The place had been part of a larger plantation in the late nineteenth and early twentieth centuries. It was not a big white columned plantation type situation when we arrived. The buildings were all old barns and slave/sharecropper cabins. My father re-did one of those cabins, and that's where we lived for about six years. No underpinning, no heat, no indoor plumbing (yes, an outhouse). It was painted barn red and had a tin roof. The road was red Georgia clay.

As you can imagine, everything I did until I went to college was linked with the landscape. I hunted, fished, walked the swamps, collected jars of tadpoles and lightning bugs, played in the dirt. I guess maybe in some ways the place and the self were indistinguishable.

So why am I telling you this? I'm not sure exactly. But when Kim talks about dream songs and Densmore's point about how one might lose his own personality in a contemplation of nature, it really made me think of how I grew up. Could it be a filiation/affiliation with the natural world? I don't know.

I have no dream songs, but I have had a few strange dreams in my life, ones I have told few people about. I do not have a cultural tradition to explain such things, and it is always dangerous to be pegged as "trying to be Indian" if you ever have dreams about animals. But I'll share the CliffsNotes version.

Once when camping by a lake in NM, I dreamed that a bear came to my tent and pressed its nose into my cheek through the tent. I could feel its breath on my face.

Once I dreamed I was in one of the areas of our farm, near the beaver pond. It was during the day, and I was playing with four black panthers.

Once I dreamed that I was holding a rattlesnake with no fear.

Once I dreamed that I was talking to a blue eagle.

And once I dreamed that a raven came to visit me, sending me greetings from a friend.

Kim: What Jesse's words strum for me is the honest motion of our existence. For one, it voices the physical—the embodied manifestations of *searching* affiliations—our constant whether we consciously understand this or not—as we try to locate ourselves in our positionings (edge, inside, outside, observer, center, shadow, margin, behind, within, etc.). Think of the physical language of crows, wolves, small children, and yes, that special species—poetic conference attendees! The poem weaves stance, gesture, ritual in a timelessness we understand. The meeting of eyes, voicing, or stopping down the voice, handshakes, passing of food and drink—these exist, are interwoven, OVER time or in ALL time. Just so the multivoiced present includes actual external spoken but also the interior voice of the poet, that is populated with a history of voices here including Louis's, Gordie's, my own, and Jesse's, too. Remember somewhere Joe Bruchac talked about how a language could not exist with only one speaker, without someone to hear and understand? The poem is speaking a message that can only be understood in an intersection of being, in a crow commons amid a complex shared knowledge encompassing history, literature, land-knowledge, story, past associations of affiliations as well as present, and I would venture that it gestures into the future because it assumes a listening, responding, on the other end. Maybe that seems too simplistic, but when I think of what we must supply in our reading of poetry the stretch is timeless and also not confined by the dimensions of a single way of understanding experience—not merely literary, documentary, or critical, but always a web of related comprehensions: personal, historical, mythic, place-based, embodied, spiritual, ceremonial—adjunct in many ways. When I wrote *Apprenticed to Justice*, I wanted to suggest those various elements of community—like the list of elements of the commons Gordie identified earlier—all those realities to which we are inevitably linked, to which we live apprenticed. That ongoing relatedness is what Jesse speaks so wonderfully, what I love about the litanies that characterize Gordie's poems, why I challenge myself to follow the tangles of juxtaposition and intraconversational links of Vizenor's writing.

Molly: February 15

A Vizenor poem from *Almost Ashore* and then a Blaeser poem from *Apprenticed to Justice* for you:

"Crow Stories" by Gerry

three crows
blue in the night
winter sun
trickster poses
in the birch

bloody sumac
buried overnight
in the hard
crusted snow

deer crack
the bony crests
treacherous
river ice

crow stories
tease memories
cruel seasons
of rusted plows
barbed wire
and lonesome
timber traders
at city docks
suddenly
out of breath[14]

"Haiku Journey: iv. Winter" by Kim

ground painted in frost
thirsty morning sun drinks white
leaves rust golds return

winter bare branches
hold tattered cups of summer
empty nests trail twigs

lace edges of ice
manna against darkened sky
words turn with weather

now one to seven
deer or haiku syllables
weave through winter trees

Northern follows jig
body flashes with strike, dive:
broken line floats up.[15]

I really love these two poems next to one another; they are speaking to one another (as are Kim and Gerry, it seems). While in Vizenor's poem the crows enact the story of the timber traders at city docks within the wintery Ojibwe landscape, it is the Northern that activates the winter story in Blaeser's poem. Both the crows and Northerns survive this harsh (but incredibly active and beautiful) landscape; and it is the timber traders who are left "suddenly out of breath" and the absent-referent ice fisherman/woman left with a "broken line."

More thoughts, crow riders??

Love,

Molly

Jane: March 7

Kim writes that Vizenor "understands 'filiation' . . . as 'eternal return' with 'difference.' In Vizenor the 'received traditions' mentioned as part of filiation are not static, but part of the 'transmotion' of stories. . . . My own take on this is that we inherit or are storied in filiations; we intuit, elect, or pursue affiliations."

Jesse is reminded in what Kim writes about Densmore's Anishinaabe dream song descriptions—in which "the dreamer 'contemplates nature in a certain aspect so long and so steadily that he gradually loses his own personality and identifies himself with it'"—of his own growing up in south Georgia and wonders, "Could it be a filiation/affiliation with the natural world?"

Yes. I think it must clearly be true that earth is our original filiation, the one that we all share. We are her children, both lost and found.

And if earth is our shared filiation, dreaming about a bear's snout and conversation with a blue eagle doesn't mean you must be an Indian, any more than dreaming about the Leaning Tower of Pisa means you must be Italian, or dreaming about windmills means you're Dutch. Does it? Our dreams arise from many places, and one of the most significant is the locations we move through and inhabit, the intimacy of the lands we have studied and embraced, and have been embraced by, folded into. We eternally return to these places, perhaps in body, perhaps in dream. We eternally return, with difference. Dreams and earth places, memories and stories, become part of our autobiography, of our transmotional poetics of self.

In an autobiographical essay on the making of autobiography and the creation of our storied selves, Vizenor quotes from Georges Gusdorf's article "Conditions and Limits of Autobiography":

> This conscious awareness of the singularity of each individual life is the late product of a specific civilization. Through most of human history, the individual does not oppose himself to all others; he does not feel himself to exist outside of others, and still less against others, but very much *with* others in an interdependent existence that asserts its rhythms everywhere in the community.[16]

Gordon:

"Leaving Smoke's"

To Gogisgi and Claudia

Black
wings sun glanced
green, crows
circle and half circle
snowfields before scattering
over old barns falling
slowly paintless
against the sky

across the road.

Your car shivers
to start, windshield
trembling, Sky, Blue
barked breath floating
white through
fences behind his
back and the door
opening she waves from.

At the stop sign,

the prism hanging
between door curtains
sun colors

still turns
on the kitchen floor.

On M-66

something or the wind
moves outside
and turns his head to
windowed dusk's sun

leaving behind barns
with glazed empty
snowfield
beyond the prism
still.[17]

Kim:

"Out of Order" (by Gerald Vizenor)

crows on the wire
whole moons
bounce back
on the wet black
mission road
north of white earth

birch leaves
shudder
near the cold
windy
lakeshore
of bad medicine

engines moan
surrender
to the haze
that october
morning
near beaulieu
cities declared
out of order
for the season[18]

Molly: March 8

I only wanted to add that each of these writers (Gerald, Gordon, and Kim) have taught me a great deal, as a poet, as a scholar, and as a human being. For example, when I first came across Kim's poetry oh so many years ago, it was like "going home." What she writes in her preface to *Trailing You* allowed me to begin to articulate my own thoughts about poetry's ability to signal filial languages and unearth the encoded messages of our ancestors we find in our home landscapes. I thought, wow, poetry that affirms my then tentative, unsure belief in the power of creativity and the notion that family stories matter—poems operating as give-a-ways, memorials, paths of continuance. Poems as regenerative passageways, a gesture toward feeding networks of connection. Like Kim's preface says, poems can be places in which "we are visited by people, places, stories, and events that shadow and shape my present."[19] This has taught me how Ojibwe storytelling not only is alive in real and varied ways (a space where living things commune) but also takes on transformative and adaptive shapes. Twenty-first-century verse as a continuation of my grandma's stories. Like Kim's poem, "Speaking Those Names": "aloud / speaking those names / you have given me / calling myself by those names / in just that voice that you have spoken / hearing myself in those names / each time / I become myself again."[20]

Jesse: March 9

It is true Molly; we must become ourselves. And that is probably the most difficult thing for us to do. It seems the story is the becoming, the call of the crow is the life of the crow. Gordon wrote, "So under another discourse model we turn to a story, a narrative that illustrates a trail of affiliation that engenders shifting contexts of experiences and language. In this case the narrative, story, establishes intercultural affiliations in the ongoing life of the intergenerational, multiple context transmissions of narrative. That is, the story, initially transmitted through filiations, continues through affiliations."[21] So my affiliations with each of you have created the concept of self that I carry. I think of the long nights filled with conversation and wine that I have shared with each of you and how much they have shaped how I see life. Our experiences before we met were so vastly different, but the connections seemed so natural. Some could see that as odd, I'm sure, but then again, the filiations of our lives enabled the strong affiliations we now share.

I never knew my grandfathers. My mother tells us how her father, Jesse Bayron Guthrie, would sometimes lie down at the edge of the field for a long, long time. He said that he liked to watch the plants grow. I've often thought of that story, and my discussions with all of you over the years have helped me see why the carrying of that story is important. I now imagine crows watching him from trees, calling to each other, and perhaps even to him.

I now understand that lying on the earth, looking for the almost imperceptible changes in the life around us, is the most important scholarship we could ever undertake. On one hand survival, the need to survive draws us into the adjacent possible. In this case, the old man goes into an adjacent domain, or landscape or biosphere, and he connects with another possibility for survival, as given to him by the natural world through the voice of the eagle, in a form of a nest which transcends its usage, in one world by the Eagle, and portends a new usage of the next in the Anishinaabe community. Further the nest moves on through the Anishinaabe cultural commung through story and ceremony.

Jane: June 5

Hola, Crow Riders!

Another year has flown by, and soon we will be gathering again, this time to roost in Barcelona. Touching down on the home terrain of the royal couple who six centuries ago funded the voyage of that ultimate mediator of Indianness, Cristobal Colón, Indigenous exterminator and master "[simulator] of the absence of the tribal real,"[22] the presence of absence of Native existence in a world that was not new but ancient, rich, vibrant, and alive. And remains so within and beyond the Great Anishinaabe Commung, our common ground, the Crow Commons.

The following ruminations extend the Anishinaabe Commung geographically west, into overlapping homelands with the Dakota and Lakota peoples. Indulge me if I shift focus here, friends, and let me know if I'm flying too far afield. The motions of mediation, filiation, and affiliation fill my thoughts as I write to you on this moving Amtrak train, sweeping me from Southern Pines, North Carolina, to Alexandria, Virginia, to visit a friend who has flown in for a meeting from Sapulpa, Oklahoma. The crows wisecracked by the tracks as I stood waiting in the early morning cool for the Silver Service/Palmetto line, which originates in Miami and terminates in New York City. I am thinking about our many sites of shared affiliation and filiation, the beautiful lands we move through and that move through us. And the painful histories in blood and earth that eternally connect our spirits to one another. The motions of death and life, these sacred concentricities, as Gordon has so aptly named them.

My affiliations with all of you, and with Ed from Rosebud and Richard from Sapulpa, are through the strange terrain of the Academic Commons. And so I am turning my portion of our discussion in this direction today, toward that complex meeting place, space, and concept: Education. Indigenous and otherwise, instructive and invasive.

I'm just back from Rosebud Reservation two days ago, where I spent six days in the Lakota Nation with my friend Ed Valandra, my affiliate from my UC Davis days and now, eight years later, still my friend. I had never been to South Dakota, never been to Rosebud, which is next door to Pine Ridge, the place a *New York Times* editorial the week before I left dubbed "The Poster Child for Poverty."[23] A narrow and disrespectful mediation of Indianness, a skewed and partial tag line for the Media Nation to present to a global readership, most of whom know nothing about the realities of American

Indian life. Amerigo Vespucci is alive and well, translating and disseminating mediations of Native peoples to serve the perceptions of others.

Kim: June 7

Ah, Jane. That place of statistics. Statistics about poverty and suicide and joblessness and life expectancy. That's a place, metaphorical to be sure, but real, too, and hard. When the *Minneapolis Tribune* "featured" White Earth Reservation many years ago as the poorest county in Minnesota and proffered all the usual depressing statistics about high school dropout rates and teen pregnancy and blah and blah and blah, I remember feeling troubled, now I might say it was by the intrinsic labeling, I only know I struggled to reconcile the elements of my life, a vibrant and human mix of experiences—yes, some tough to handle, but others joyful—struggled to reconcile my sense of family and community with the statistical evaluation.

Let me share two excerpts from longer works that weave in and out of the complications of the kind of romantic "gaze" that will lament the poor conditions of Native people while denying them respect and justice, and the intellectual "gaze" that wants to deny the reality of Indigenous "difference" by labeling it essentialism. This first excerpt is from an essay, "A Very Specific Nostalgia." This section, my talking back to the essentialism witch-hunters by cataloguing the actual, humanizes the community at this moment in time in a way that the accumulated social science measurements fail to achieve:

> The big intellectual brotherhood may charge me with a romantic nostalgia, may find in my work an insidious, infectious ubi sunt motif. I reject this charge. I scoff with the best at the romantic tragic garbage peddled to invented-Indian loving consumers. If I voice nostalgia, it is not for the invented Indian past of popular film or fiction, not for the broadly conceived lost past. I long specifically for White Earth Reservation, summer 1983.
>
> In May 1983 I am twenty-something, a newly awarded M.A. recipient, have recently ended a relationship, and am working as a waitress at Cedar Crest Resort for the summer. In 1983 my mother is still alive with no warning signs of cancer, my father can still read with no signs of macular degeneration, and I can still run with no back injuries to slow me down. The sewing factory is still operating and my auntie works there, my cousin Tami still lives only 36 miles away, my old best friend has moved back to Mahnomen, and my uncle Bill who never drove in his life has just purchased a used pickup truck. Most mornings I get up, run along the silo road, then come home and eat an ice cream bar and drink coffee for breakfast while I play cribbage with my parents. My mother keeps a neat record of our wins, losses, 28-hands and skunks. We have lots of drop-in visitors, fill our days just as we choose depending on weather and the ripeness of various berries. I play on a

local softball team and I am still limber and lunatic enough to change from my waitress uniform to my softball outfit one Saturday while driving to a tournament. This is the summer I have a private conversation with Johnny Cash at a country music festival, learn about leeching and the night crawler business, and go on a fishing trip to Ontario with my new boyfriend and an Alaskan bush cook. I try waterskiing for the first time, sew a jingle dress with my mother, and spar with the courthouse about Grandma Antell's allotment which was taken for back taxes.

No, I am not longing for some imagined time when vaguely outlined Indian children sat around quietly listening to elders tell stories. I am longing for paydays when relatives dropped in for coffee and gossip while they were in town, for wonder-if-I-could-borrow-twenty-until-next-week days when everyone was busted and we played cards for match sticks. I don't long for some long ago time where Indians spoke great truths, I just liked the times when Laurie and Marge Brown used to come with my Uncle Bill that summer and tell stories about hunting by Bass Lake, or when Quig and Doyle got together to tell the story of how Von wanted to clean gophers for her old cat Beasty and thought putting them through the wringer of the washer might work. I don't care how many times I remember that story, the way they shout when they say *Run!*, or the putrid image of exploding gophers, it always makes me laugh out loud. No, I am not hooked on someone's crazy vision of wise Indian elders with profound philosophical sayings. Where I come from, when someone says something like *Be careful where you cast your shadow*, they are probably giving you very practical advice. Maybe about catching frogs for fishing—you had better be careful not to scare them away by letting your shadow fall on them. Of course, levels of meaning multiply, and once you know how to catch frogs you might hear the same thing again referring to something else. But, more than likely, catching frogs probably gave you enough time to pay attention and figure other things out for yourself so the same end is served.

But if I am scared off of my own past because I fear the label of essentialism or romanticism, I become Indian on someone else's terms. Because the mysterious teacher Indian is just another film type doesn't mean Indian people don't sometimes teach in round-about ways or through humor. Because Hollywood has capitalized on American Indian tragedies, does not mean the tragedies themselves are invented or inauthentic. In that summer of 1983, the son of one of my close cousins committed suicide. I remember driving after a few hours of sleep, along unfamiliar country roads, to the place where a traditional wake was being held. I remember standing in a small graveyard in the early morning, amid the scent of wet pine, immense sadness, and young men who threw shovels of dirt upon the body of their lost comrade. The summer is not an idyll filled with unrelenting happiness. It had alcohol incidents and relatives feuding, the usual amount of trouble and loss. Yet it stands as an example of a very specific time when the

> many circumstances of life among a small Indian community create a kind of life that against all theory does distinguish itself from life outside that community. I could pick another season and year to inhabit in memory. The results would be the same. I would remember it lovingly. Not because it is past, not because it is perfect, but because I honor the everyday lives of the people in that community. I could pick yesterday, today, tomorrow. I am not rooted to a lost past, but to a present lived with the knowledge of and respect for the past.[24]

This second piece is one of the shorter poems from my Inez Hilger series (Sr. Hilger being an anthropologist who descended on White Earth 1938 to "study" housing and families conditions there). The poem contrasts the accumulation of statistical detail (which was Hilger's method) with other more intrinsic kinds of cultural markers.

"Summary Tabulations Descriptive of One Hundred and Fifty Chippewa Indian Families on the White Earth Reservation"[25]

1938.
An anthropologist in Ojibwe country
black-robed and wimpled,
Mary Inez, you cast yourself among tribal clans.
Summer and fall you study count collect and tally,
in appendices and tables you set your faith.
Housing conditions, retention of the Chippewa language,
religious affiliations, the liquor problem,
household equipment, unmarried mothers.
Size and use of rooms.
Outside White Earth lakes lap mildly
amidst tamaracks and the graceful bow of white birch,
close among the call of checker-backed loons
whose vowel song ripples the blue edges of eternity.
Methodically, you collect data on doors:
find *inside doors* absent in *44 homes.*
Find *99 homes* with *unscreened outside doors.*
Carefully you accumulate details of floor coverings:
count *8 traditional bulrush mats,*
79 braided rag rugs of six or eight ply.
Sister, with pink Lady Slippers opening at your feet
how can you march booted and laced among the columns
and lead-pencil precision of mathematical statistics?
Smallest tar-paper shack, 630 total cubic feet of airspace,

Largest tar-paper shack, 5940 total cubic feet of airspace.
And if you do not count each tinkling silver cone
worn on the dream-born jingle dress in June,
and if you do not stay to weigh block ice
cut with chainsaw from Sugarbush Lake in winter,
can you believe you calculate culture?

Jane: Of course the crows on Rosebud were talking. So were the people, unmediated. Lakota filiations fuel Sicangu life, just as they do life on White Earth in the summer of 1983, Kim, as you so beautifully describe it. We are all relations: I met five of Ed's siblings, two nieces and a nephew, one cousin in four days. On Memorial Day, in Ed's home community of St. Francis, Lakota families brought flowers, pinwheels, plates of food, wind chimes, ribbons, to the Catholic cemetery by St. Francis Mission, where they set up lawn chairs at family grave sites and camped for the day, feasting their departed forebears and visiting with other families, sharing stories, remembering. A web of filiation and remembrance. I saw no other *wasicus* there.

"It's an intimate gathering," Ed told me as he parked the car along the dirt road by the cemetery. I understood and stayed in the car. We Are All Relations, but sometimes, in some spaces, some of us more than others. In some spaces, filiations hold sway: "an example of a very specific time when the many circumstances of life among a small Indian community create a kind of life that against all theory does distinguish itself from life outside that community," as Kim writes of White Earth. As I watched people walk past carrying their colorful decorations to the graves, I heard the drum and singers honoring the deceased. As if on cue, the mission bells of St. Francis began to clang the time, strident and domineering, drowning out the Lakota voices. As usual. Still. Always.

But the people still sang, if out of my hearing. Still sang, and have been singing since long before the intrusion of mission bells. As usual. Always.

I went to Rosebud to visit Ed and to give a presentation on Indigenous narratives from the U.S. boarding school and Canadian residential school course I created and taught at UNC Pembroke, to share my curriculum with interested Lakota educators and community members. Six or seven of Ed's siblings went to boarding school at St. Francis, I learned while I was there. On the night of my presentation at Sinte Gleska University, the Rosebud tribal university, Ed's sister Judy Beth told the story of Sister Cowboy, one of the nuns at St. Francis when they were kids. Their older sister Patsy Ann stood up to "Sister Cowboy"—so named because of her bow-legged walk—and her cruel treatment of the littler girls at the school. Patsy would stand up for the little girls, and so "I was always in trouble," said Patsy. "I was a 'bad' girl. 'Go weed another row of wheat!' they'd tell me." Everyone laughed. Judy remembers Patsy telling her later on, after they'd all left St. Francis, "If I ever meet Sister Cowboy on Main Street, I'll beat the fuck out of her!" Everyone laughed. Hard laughter, Ed said later. Laughter that covers pain and helps hold up the heart. Patsy was a "bad" girl because she would not conform to cruelty.

These experiences have been too widely shared within the colonizing educational commons.

I think of the poem by Anishinaabe poet Linda LeGarde Grover from the collection Kim edited, *Traces in Blood, Bone, and Stone: Contemporary Ojibwe Poetry*:

"Everything You Need to Know in Life
You'll Learn at Boarding School"

Speak English. Forget the language of your
grandparents. It is dead. Forget their teachings.
They are unGodly and ignorant. Cleanliness is
next to Godliness. Indians are not clean. Your
parents did not teach you proper hygiene. Stay
in line. This is a toothbrush. Hang it on the hook
next to the others. Do not allow the bristles to
touch. This spreads the disease that you bring
to school from your families. Make your bed with
mitered corners. A bed not properly made will be
torn apart. Start over. Remember and be grateful
that the boarding school feeds and clothes you. Say
grace before meals. In English. Don't cry. Crying
never solved anything. Write home once every
month. In English. Tell your parents that you are
doing very well. You'll never amount to anything.
Make the most of your opportunities. You'll never
amount to anything. Answer when the teacher
addresses you. In English. If your family insists on
and can provide transportation for you to visit home
in the summer, report to the matron's office immediately
upon your return. You will be allowed into the
dormitory after you have been sanitized and de-loused.
Busy hands are happy hands. Keep yourself occupied.
You'll never amount to anything. Books are our friends.
Reading is your key to the world. Forget the language
of your grandparents. It is dead. If you are heard speaking

it you will kneel on a navy bean for one hour. We will ask
if you have learned your lesson. You will answer. In English.
Spare the rod and spoil the child. We will not spare the rod.
We will cut your hair. We will shame you. We will lock you
in the basement. Learn from that. Improve yourself.
You'll never amount to anything. Speak English.[26]

At K. L. Carver Elementary School in San Marino, California, as a good and obedient and English-speaking and unquestioning little middle-class white girl, I learned the following rhyme:

"In fourteen hundred and ninety-two, Columbus sailed the ocean blue."

He "discovered" a "New World" and in the New World he discovered "Indians." Then Europe and then America discovered them, much to their profound dismay.

Ever since then, my people the Whites have been putting the mediated presences of Columbus's Indians in movies while putting real Natives in prisons, in graves, in reservations, in boarding schools, in their place. In English.

But the center doesn't hold, and there are multiple centers, and the Indians get around. In English. In Lakota. In Anishinaabemowin.

I am thinking of these things. My filiations and affiliations, both the ones I want and the ones I have to face regardless of what I want. Mediations in the cultural commons.

Time for me to stop, friends. I look forward to your thoughts.

Gigawaabamin,

Jane

Molly: June 6

By this time, I should not be surprised to find out that we crow commoners are moving in overlapping circles of thought. I am really heartened by your words, Jane, because you are mapping very clearly the directions I've been moving toward as well recently. I am just back from the Mohegan Reservation, and more specifically the Mohegans' giant casino, Mohegan Sun, where the NAISA conference took place. There, a day filled with Shinobs chattering about the commons, Niigon Sinclair, Jill Doerfer, Heidi Stark, Dale Turner, and I speak about the shape of the Anishinaabe as a nation, a series of concentric circles ("forever connected and forever expanding outward" says Niigon) that start with the dodom, with relationships, and the protocols for behavior toward nurturing and sustaining those relationships. Later in the day, I listen to Heid Erdrich read her poetry in English, Meg Noori read Heid's work in Anishinaabemowin, and find myself transported to Minnesota, walking around the city lake with the speaker, witnessing a mink track across the frozen ice. I think, Niigon is right, the commons forever expands.

Then, my mind moves again. I'm reminded of sitting at a table eating dinner a couple years ago with Gordon, Niigon, and Jill. Niigon looks at me and asks, "how do you find living in New York?" And I reply quickly, "lonely." Niigon looks at Gordon and then at me, and proceeds to tell a story about how I might be able to see the sacred miigis shell in the landscape around me if I look for it. "After all," he says, "that's where we came from."

Funny, now some two years later, I find evidence of it everywhere, especially as I drive the 140 miles from Vassar College in New York to Mohegan and back. I'm consoled by the direction it provides me throughout the day. I try not to have any plans for the conference, just let other people and other things lead. That's when I find myself laughing and telling stories in Heid's hotel room with a number of other writers, as if we're all trying to catch up on each other's lives and our lives' stories in these meaningful (although brief) moments. Heid says casually, "You gonna be back home in the end of June by any chance?" "Yes," I reply surprised. "Want to read your poetry with me at Garrison Keillor's bookstore on the 28th?" My Google-map directions lost somewhere along the way, I drive back to Poughkeepsie from memory.

Over the past two weeks, I've been re-reading Louise Erdrich's collection of poems *Baptism of Desire*, so when you brought Linda's poetry on boarding schools into the commoners' mix, Jane, it was like hearing echoes out on the lake.

"Fooling God"
—Louise Erdrich

I must become small and hide where he cannot reach.
I must become dull and heavy as an iron pot . . .[27]

A history of Indian people mediating colonialism, negotiating the dark halls of boarding schools and the even darker nights. We tell stories to make sense of that historical legacy, to find ways to map our direction back toward connection. Though experiences at boarding schools were extremely varied and cannot be reduced to a single narrative, at its base, the colonial project was about disconnection—from nation, from family, from culture, from land. This is antithetical to Anishinaabe lifeways, to Indigenous ways of being Anishinaabe writers "evince the scars" (I say in my poem "To Do List")[28] and "return" the mnemonic markers so to provide our own mappings of those "ways."

More soon, crow crew.
Molly

Kim: June 7
Dear Crow Riders,

Boarding schools—this is a rough topic to ride. It permeates the work of many Anishinaabe writers and scholars. I remember teaching Louise Erdrich's "Indian Boarding School: The Runaways," having my voice break in class, and how an older Native student stepped in and continued reading that poem to the end. It was a powerful moment, one many in that room will remember, symbolic as it was of loss, the legacy of loss, survival, and even a kind of triumph.

My own feelings about education can never finally be extracted from the boarding school legacy, the stories that were told in my family, and the silences that marked us perhaps even more deeply. In "Family Tree," I have this stanza:

> Two uncles who ran away
> from Pipestone
> Indian boarding school
> and an auntie who stayed
> who lost her fingers
> saw them caught mangled
> in the laundry press
> who beaded kneaded quilted and braided
> her way through four children
> just the same.[29]

What stands behind this single stanza: the details of those boarding school years; my uncles' story of running away, traveling more than 300 miles on foot to return to Nay-tah-waush; my Auntie's life-long determination to live as if the phantom fingers were not lost in some colonial territory where education has been confused with cultural genocide; and the imprint of these experiences on the lives of their descendants—the reasons I simultaneously teach and undermine the standard pedagogical approaches to teaching. What stands behind this single stanza and Louise Erdrich's poems, and Linda LaGarde Grover's boarding school poetry, and Jim Northrup's, and Gordie's "Prisoner of Haiku" is the need to remember and, as Paula Gunn Allen has it, to "re-member" by retelling.

Gordon: A few weeks ago, I read with the jazz master from Greal Galaxy, a Muslim sax man. I read and he entered through an interval of stops and valves, notes and half notes, feathered and quartered into space which I had just left at the end of a string of names and text. He passed on a week later. As in the midst of that jazz . . .

We just keep on connecting things. In that regard I still think of the Deleuze we cut, the edited out, the suicidal, transfenestrator; it figures the guy we cut from the last Crow Commons goes through a window and doesn't survive the open (w)hole. There must be some justice in treating Deleuze like an abstract Indian; he's almost understandable, like Vizenor, in bits and pieces, in slices of neologism, while our parts fly at us from all over the world, Connecticut crow in Pequod commons, Rosebud crow, Sacramento crow, the filiated crow, the sets, seemingly closed, communicating with the outside through invisible processes, matrices, and algorithmic, encrypted identities

HEY YA YA HEY YA YA *becomes a bear song*

like a song with its own personality coming into your life and going out of your mouth. And what happened to all the other crows, the road crows, the funeral day crows, the drum face crows, the black and white crows, the captured crows, the golf course crow, the Johnny Depp crow headpiece, the mimetic crow who thinks poetry takes on the personality of the imitated, the Jesus Christ I almost killed that crow with a Buick, the crow unfinished, stuck in the tattoo stylus, the crows who won't let us see, the morning voice crows, beating the rooster to dawn, the master crow who remixes, engineers the whole crow caw-cough phonic orchestration, the murder organization, cycling particles and waves of crow through sky, and the five thief crows who always bring us back to our reasons for trying to see something in crow, the in-common crow, reclassified crow on the crow website on Mac, or pc crow screen, as crow started a nest from a bundle of sticks.

Gordon drums on a Santa Fe tourist shop hand drum, and starts to sing:

Ground control to Major Tom

Gordon stops drumming.

Gordon: No that's not it

Gordon drums on a Santa Fe tourist shop hand drum, starts singing again:

Half of what I say is meaningless, but I will say it
just to reach you . . .

Gordon stops drumming.

Gordon: No that's not it

Gordon drums on a Santa Fe tourist shop hand drum and chants.

NOTES

1. Dr. Gaween is a persona Gordon Henry alludes to in his creative publication *The Failure of Certain Charms and Other Disparate Signs of Life*. An epigraph to Henry's prose poem "Entries into the Autobiographical I" (22–24) reads "Autobiography is the subject of personal logistics of knowable selves. How does one put I where one is or was? One needs a center, around which to build. The center is rarely an I" and is attributed to the *Uncollected Writings of Dr. Gaween*.
2. Said, *The World, the Text*, 24–25.
3. Gordon Henry, unpublished poem.
4. Vizenor, *Almost Ashore*, 94.
5. Blaeser, "Like 'Reeds Through the Ribs of a Basket,'" 265.
6. Ibid., 268.
7. Blaeser, *Apprenticed to Justice*, 26.
8. Henry, *Failure of Certain Charms*, 6.
9. Densmore, *Chippewa Music*, 118, 126.
10. Evers and Molina, *Yaqui Deer Songs*, 7.
11. Blaeser, "Waxing Traditional," 80.
12. Henry, *The Light People*, 15.
13. Gordon Henry Jr., unpublished poem.
14. Vizenor, *Almost Ashore*, 94.
15. Blaeser, *Apprenticed to Justice*, 49–50.
16. Georges Gusdorf, "Autobiography and the Cultural Moment: A Thematic, Historical and Bibliographic Introduction," in *Autobiography: Essays Theoretical and Critical*, ed. James Olney (Princeton, NJ: Princeton University Press, 1980): 28–48, quoted by Gerald Vizenor, "Crows Written on the Poplars," 107.
17. Henry, *Failure of Certain Charms*, 12–13.
18. Vizenor, *Almost Ashore*, 89.
19. Blaeser, *Trailing You: Poems*, xi.
20. Ibid., 3.
21. Henry, "The Eagleheart Narratives," 300.
22. Vizenor, *Manifest Manners*, 4.
23. Kristof, "Poverty's Poster Child."
24. Kimberly Blaeser, "A Very Specific Nostalgia"; this became part of "Waxing Traditional," 77–78.
25. All italicized words in the poem are taken from Sister M. Inez Hilger's *Chippewa Families: A Social Study of White Earth Reservation, 1938*.
26. Grover, *Traces in Blood, Bone, and Stone*, 87–88.

27. Erdrich, *Baptism of Desire*, 3.
28. McGlennen, *Fried Fish and Flour Biscuits*, 5.
29. Blaeser, *Apprenticed to Justice*, 4.

WORKS CITED

Blaeser, Kimberly. *Apprenticed to Justice*, Earthworks Series. Cambridge, UK: Salt Publishing, 2007.

———. "Like 'Reeds Through the Ribs of a Basket': Native Women Weaving Stories." In *Other Sisterhoods: Literary Theory and U.S. Women of Color*, ed. Sandra Kumamoto Stanley, 265–276. Urbana: University of Illinois Press, 1998.

———. *Trailing You: Poems*. Greenfield Center, NY: Greenfield Review Press, 1994.

———. "Waxing Traditional: Navigating the Aesthetic Landmines of Nostalgia and Essentialism in Native America." In *A Usable Past: Tradition in Native American Arts and Literature*, ed. Simone Pellerin, 73–82. Bordeaux: Presses Universitaires de Bordeaux, 2010.

Densmore, Frances. *Chippewa Music, Vol. I*. Bureau of American Ethnology, Bulletin no. 45. Washington, D.C.: Smithsonian Institution, 1910. Reprint, New York: Da Capo Press, 1972.

Erdrich, Louise. *Baptism of Desire: Poems*. New York: Harper & Row, 1989.

Evers, Larry, and Felipe S. Molina, *Yaqui Deer Songs/Maso Bwikam: A Native American Poetry*. Tucson: University of Arizona Press, 1987.

Grover, Linda LeGarde. "Everything You Need to Know in Life You'll Learn at Boarding School." In *Traces in Blood, Bone, and Stone: Contemporary Ojibwe Poetry*, ed. Kimberly Blaeser, 87–88. Bemidji, MN: Loonfeather Press, 2006.

Henry, Gordon, Jr., "The Eagleheart Narratives: Contexts, Process, Representation, and Ceremony in Making Texts." In *Stories through Theories/Theories through Stories: North American Indian Writing, Storytelling, and Critique*, ed. Gordon D. Henry Jr., Nieves Pascual Soler, and Silvia Martínez-Falquina, 291–306. East Lansing: Michigan University Press, 2009.

———. *The Failure of Certain Charms and Other Disparate Signs of Life*. Earthworks Series. Cambridge, UK: Salt Publishing, 2008.

———. *The Light People*. East Lansing: Michigan State University Press, 2003.

Hilger, Sister Mary Inez. *Chippewa Families: A Social Study of White Earth Reservation, 1938*. St. Paul: Minnesota Historical Society, 1939.

Kristof, Nicholas D., "Poverty's Poster Child," *New York Times*, 9 May 2012. Http://www.nytimes.com/2012/05/10/opinion/kristof-povertys-poster-child.html.

McGlennen, Molly. *Fried Fish and Flour Biscuits*, Earthworks Series. Cambridge, UK: Salt Publishing, 2010.

Said, Edward W. *The World, the Text, and the Critic*. Cambridge, MA: Harvard University Press, 1983.

Vizenor, Gerald. *Almost Ashore*, Earthwork Series. Cambridge, UK: Salt Publishing, 2006.

———. "Crows Written on the Poplars: Autocritical Autobiographies," in *I Tell You Now: Autobiographical Essays by Native American Writers*, ed. Arnold Krupat and Brian Swann, 99–110. Lincoln: University of Nebraska Press, 1987.

———. *Manifest Manners: Narratives on Postindian Survivance*. Lincoln: University of Nebraska Press/Bison Books, 1999.

Envoy
Response to "Crow Commons"

GERALD VIZENOR

Crow Commonage

common crows
tease the seasons
winter rain
summer thunder
night flight neologisms
outside of praise
sentiments
courtesy of traditions

common crows
boast on the road
forever blued
by sundowns
great shadow shows
under the cottonwoods

common crows
convene overnight
stay in poems
crease the wonder
tease the smoke
trace and transience
slights of ancestors
caught on stage

common crows
arouse dream songs
shoulder the beat
mock rehearsals
translations
touch the distance
linger on a porch
roosts and faces
change on the wing
score and treasure
beaded crowns
overturned in play
against the wind

common crows
caw and sway
anishinaabe poets
caw and sway
crows bounce
anishinaabe bounce
crows strut
anishinaabe strut
crows soar
anishinaabe soar
creative scenes
poems and stories
by kimberly
gordon
molly
jane and jesse
teased in motion
blue shimmers
alight in the white pine
crow commonage

Frances Densmore recorded and translated "The Song of the Crows," a dream song restored by Henry Selkirk, in the early 1900s at the White Earth Reservation. Selkirk told the translator that a "young man heard the crows in the trees and imagined that he learned this song from them." The crow became his *manidoo,* the presence of a native spirit or totemic favor of the crows, because the boy "understood the language of the crows."

> The first to come
> I am called
> Among the birds
> I bring the rain
> Crow is my name[1]

My introduction to haiku and imagistic poetry, by chance of the military, made it easier for me to understand natural reason, court the favor of crows and ravens, and the sense of presence and survivance in native dream songs and literature. How ironic that my service as a soldier would lead to a literary association of haiku, and an overture to the natural motion of *anishinaabe* dream songs. Truly, haiku and imagistic poetry enhanced my perception and experience of *anishinaabe* dream songs, and my consideration of natural reason, comparative philosophies, and native survivance.

NOTE

1. Frances Densmore, *Chippewa Music*, Smithsonian Institution, Bureau of American Ethnology, Bulletin 45 (1910; reprint, Minneapolis: Ross & Haines, 1973), 133, 134.

Notes on Contributors

Kimberly Blaeser is a poet, critic, essayist, playwright, and fiction writer. Her poetry collections include *Apprenticed to Justice*, *Absentee Indians and Other Poems*, and *Trailing You*. Her critical study *Gerald Vizenor: Writing in the Oral Tradition* was the first Native-authored book-length study of an Indigenous author. Blaeser edited the volumes *Traces in Blood, Bone & Stone: Contemporary Ojibwe Poetry* and *Stories Migrating Home: A Collection of Anishinaabe Prose*. Her own writing is widely anthologized, including in *The Heath Anthology of American Literature*, and her poetry has been translated into several languages, including Spanish, Norwegian, Indonesian, and French. Anishinaabe and an enrolled member of the Minnesota Chippewa Tribe, Blaeser grew up on White Earth Reservation in northwestern Minnesota. She is currently a professor of English at the University of Wisconsin–Milwaukee, where she teaches creative writing, Native American literature, and literature of place and the environment.

Ellen Cushman, Cherokee Nation citizen, is a professor of writing, rhetoric, and American cultures at Michigan State University (MSU) and has served as a Cherokee Nation Sequoyah commissioner. Her book *The Cherokee Syllabary: Writing the People's Perseverance* (2011) is based on six years of ethnohistorical research with her tribe and explores the evolution and historical importance of the Cherokee writing system. Recent essays from this research demonstrate the cultural, linguistic, and historic importance of the Cherokee syllabary and can be found in *Ethnohistory*, *College English*, *Wicazo Sa Review*, and *Written Communication*. She earned her PhD from Rensselaer Polytechnic Institute in rhetoric and communication. She currently serves as codirector of the Center for Applied Inclusive Teaching and Learning in Arts and Humanities at MSU, and is coeditor of the National Council of Teachers of English's flagship journal *Research in the Teaching of English*.

Nicholle Dragone, an Indigenous scholar of Lakota/Dakota descent, is faculty in both the American Indian studies and English departments at Black Hills State University. Dragone completed her doctoral degree in American studies and a law degree at the University at Buffalo. She has published articles and book chapters on

Haudenosaunee literature and film. Dragone is currently editing a critical anthology on Onondaga writer Eric Gansworth's literary and visual art. She is also revising for publication *Haudenosaunee Literature: A View from Outside the Culture*, which presents a critical model for allied scholars and Native literary scholars studying the literatures of cultures other than their own.

Sonja Georgi is lecturer in American studies at Johannes Gutenberg University Mainz, Germany. She received a master of arts degree in American studies, applied linguistics, and economics and a PhD degree in American studies from the University of Siegen. Her dissertation, "Bodies and/as Technology: Counter-Discourses on Ethnicity and Globalization in the Works of Alejandro Morales, Larissa Lai and Nalo Hopkinson," was completed in 2010 and published by Universitätsverlag Winter in 2011. Her current postdoctoral research project focuses on Native American and African American encounters in literature and culture in the nineteenth and twentieth centuries. She has taught courses on American science fiction literature, science fiction film, African American literature, and the American Renaissance as well as introductory courses to literary and cultural studies and to academic writing.

Jane Haladay is associate professor of American Indian studies at the University of North Carolina at Pembroke. She holds a PhD from the University of California, Davis, in Native American studies with a designated emphasis in feminist theory and research and an MA from the University of Arizona's American Indian Studies Program. Her publications and research areas emphasize collaborative pedagogy, cultural models of Indigenous literary theories, issues around violence and healing for Native women and communities, humor in Native literature, ecological literacy, and social justice.

Gordon Henry Jr., an Anishinaabe poet and novelist, is an enrolled member of the White Earth Chippewa Tribe of Minnesota. His poetry has been published in anthologies such as *Songs from This Earth on Turtle's Back: Contemporary American Indian Poetry* (1983) and *Returning the Gift: Poetry and Prose from the First Native American Writers* (1994). His novel *The Light People* (1994) was awarded the American Book Award in 1995. He has also coauthored the textbook *The Ojibway* (2004), to which he contributed a number of essays on Native American culture. In 2007 Henry published *The Failure of Certain Charms*, a collection of poetry. In 2010, he coedited *Stories Through Theory/Theory through Stories* with Silvia Martínez Falquina and Nieves Pascual Soler. From 2010 to 2013, Henry served as the director of the Native American Institute at Michigan State University. He teaches courses in American literature, creative writing, and American Indian literature.

Chris LaLonde is the author of a book on the early fiction of William Faulkner, a book on the novels of Choctaw-Cherokee-Irish writer and scholar Louis Owens, and numerous essays on Native American literatures and, more generally, twentieth-century American literature. His most recent publication is an essay on the literary activism of White Earth Anishinaabe Gerald Vizenor. LaLonde is a professor of English and director of American studies at the State University of New York, College at Oswego.

A. Robert Lee, a Britisher formerly of the University of Kent at Canterbury (1967–1996), from 1997 to 2011 was professor of American literature at Nihon University, Tokyo. He has held visiting U.S. appointments at Princeton, the University of Virginia, Bryn Mawr College, Northwestern University, the University of Colorado, the University of New Mexico, and the University of California, Berkeley. His book publications include *Multicultural American Literature: Comparative Black, Native, Latino/a and Asian American Fictions* (2003), which won the 2004 American Book Award; with Gerald Vizenor, *Postindian Conversations* (1999); editor *Loosening the Seams: Interpretations of Gerald Vizenor* (2000); editor with Deborah Madsen, *Gerald Vizenor: Texts and Contexts* (2010); editor of *The Salt Companion to Jim Barnes* (2010); *Native American Writing*, 4 vols. (2011); editor with Alan Velie, *The Native American Renaissance: Literary Imagination and Achievement* (2013); and essays on Carter Revard, Simon Ortiz, Louis Owens, Leslie Marmon Silko, and Native autobiography.

Evelina Zuni Lucero is Isleta/Ohkay Owingeh Pueblo. She is associate professor in the creative writing program at the Institute of American Indian Arts in Santa Fe, New Mexico. She is author of *Night Star, Morning Star*, which won the 1999 First Book Award for Fiction from the Native Writers Circle of the Americas. She also coedited *Simon J. Ortiz: A Poetic Legacy of Indigenous Continuance*, a collection of interviews, creative pieces, and critical essays focusing on the life and work of Acoma Pueblo poet Simon J. Ortiz. Her fiction has been published in various publications, including *White Shell Water Place, Kenyon Review, ekleksographia 4.0, Oregon Literary Review*, and others. She is working on a second novel set in New Mexico.

Ludmila Martanovschi obtained her doctoral degree from the University of Bucharest, Romania, in 2008. She teaches twentieth-century American literature and ethnic studies as an associate professor at Ovidius University, Constanta, Romania. She is the author of *Decolonizing the Self: Memory, Language and Cultural Experience in Contemporary American Indian Poetry* (2009). As a Fulbright grantee, she conducted research on American Indian literatures at the University of Nevada,

Las Vegas (2003–2004) and on American drama at the Graduate Center, City University of New York (2011). She is an active member of the Association for the Study of American Indian Literatures (ASAIL), the Society for Multi-Ethnic Studies: Europe and the Americas (MESEA), and the European Association for American Studies (EAAS).

Sally McBeth is professor of anthropology and department chair at the University of Northern Colorado (UNC). Her areas of expertise include Native American studies, multicultural and women's studies, folklore/oral history/life history, field methods in cultural anthropology, religion, and cultural interpretation. She earned her PhD in anthropology from Washington State University in 1982. Her most recent research is working with the U.S. Forest Service, Bureau of Land Management, and the National Park Service to integrate Ute perspectives into the cultural interpretation of these government agencies' lands. McBeth has authored two books, *Ethnic Identity and the Boarding School Experience* (1984) and *Essie's Story: The Life and Legacy of a Shoshone Teacher* (1998), and three online publications: *Native American Oral History and Cultural Interpretation in Rocky Mountain National Park* (2007), *Ute Ethnobotany Project* (2008), and *"Talking About a Sacredness": An Ethnographic Overview of Colorado National Monument* (2010), in addition to numerous journal articles and encyclopedia entries.

Molly McGlennen was born and raised in Minneapolis, Minnesota, and is of Anishinaabe and European descent. Currently, she is an associate professor of English and Native American studies at Vassar College. She holds a PhD in Native American studies from the University of California, Davis and an MFA in creative writing from Mills College. Her scholarship and poetry have been published widely. McGlennen's first poetry collection, *Fried Fish and Flour Biscuits*, was published in November 2010 by Salt, and is part of its award-winning Earthworks series. Her scholarly book *Creative Alliances: The Transnational Designs of Indigenous Women's Poetry* was published in 2014.

Jesse Peters was raised in rural Georgia. He is currently professor of English and American Indian studies at the University of North Carolina at Pembroke. He holds a PhD in English with a focus on Native American literature from the University of New Mexico. His main area of research focuses on the ways Native American writers use syncretisms in their work. He enjoys fly-fishing and riding BMW motorcycles.

Christine Plicht received a BA in the Literary, Cultural and Media Studies and Economics Program at the University of Siegen, Germany, in 2010, completing it with research on cinematic deconstructions of Native American alterity. During her studies, she spent a semester abroad at the University of Otago in Dunedin, New Zealand. In 2012, she finished the American studies MA program at the University of Mainz, Germany, with a thesis on indigeneity and commodification in a global age, focusing on the Maori warrior image. She is currently working and preparing her PhD research at the Center for Comparative Native and Indigenous Studies in Mainz with Mita Banerjee.

John Purdy is professor of English at Western Washington University. His most recent books include *Writing Indian, Native Conversations; Nothing But the Truth: An Anthology of Native American Literatures;* and a novel, *Riding Shotgun into the Promised Land.* A former editor of *Studies in American Indian Literatures* and *American Review of Canadian Studies,* he is the founder and first editor of the online literary quarterly *Native Literatures: Generations.*

Kerstin Schmidt is professor of American studies at the University of Eichstätt in Germany. She is the author of *The Theater of Transformation: Postmodernism in American Drama* (2005) and has published on modern American drama, ethnic literatures in the United States and Canada, the Harlem Renaissance, theories and cultures of diaspora, as well as on media theory and visual culture studies, especially on documentary photography. She coedited the essay collection *America and the Sea* (2004) and has edited and contributed to *Space in America: Theory History Culture* (2005) and *McLuhan neu lesen: Kritische Analysen zu Medien und Kultur im 21. Jahrhundert* (2008). She is also a founding member of the women's studies journal *Freiburger FrauenStudien.* Her current research focuses on "Negative Space and the Making of Modern America: Concepts of Space in American Literature, Architecture, and Photography" as well as on "The Literature of Relation: Reconceptualizations of the Black Atlantic and Diasporic Writing."

Billy J. Stratton earned a PhD in American Indian studies from the University of Arizona in 2008 and currently serves as assistant professor and director of undergraduate studies in the Department of English at the University of Denver, where he teaches courses on twentieth- and twenty-first-century Native American and American literature. His scholarly work on captivity narratives, Native literature, and American writers including Cormac McCarthy have appeared in journals such as *Wícazo Sa Review, Weber: The Contemporary West, Arizona Quarterly,* and *Rhizomes.* His book on the influence and legacy of the Indian captivity narrative, *Buried in Shades of Night,* was published in 2013. In 2013 Stratton was a Fulbright Senior Lecturer in American studies at Julius-Maximilians-Universität Würzburg, Germany.

Cathy Covell Waegner teaches American studies at the University of Siegen in Germany. She obtained degrees from the College of William & Mary (BA) and the University of Virginia (MA, PhD). In addition to her work on William Faulkner and Toni Morrison, she has published on transculturality in the ethnic bildungsroman, minstrelsy, AfroAsian "postmodernist passing," 400 years after Jamestown, "hybrid tropes" in film, and the interaction between American and European cultural phenomena. Waegner coedited a project volume with Norfolk State University scholars, *Transculturality and Perceptions of the Immigrant Other: "From-Heres" and "Come-Heres" in Virginia and North Rhine-Westphalia* (2011), as well as *Literature on the Move: Comparing Diasporic Ethnicities in Europe and the Americas* (2002). She served as MESEA (Multi-Ethnic Studies: Europe and the Americas) treasurer for four years. Her current research focuses on new forms of cultural diaspora.

Guest Contributor: Gerald Vizenor is Distinguished Professor of American Studies at the University of New Mexico and professor emeritus of American studies at the University of California, Berkeley. He is a citizen of the White Earth Nation, and has published more than thirty books, including *Native Liberty: Natural Reason and Cultural Survivance*, *Survivance: Narratives of Native Presence*, *Native Storiers*, *Father Meme*, *Fugitive Poses: Native American Indian Scenes of Absence and Presence*, *Hiroshima Bugi: Atomu 57*, *Shrouds of White Earth*, *The White Earth Nation: Ratification of a Native Democratic Constitution*, *Blue Ravens: Historical Novel*, and *Favor of Crows: New and Collected Haiku*. Vizenor received an American Book Award for *Griever: An American Monkey King in China*, and recently a second award for *Chair of Tears*, the Western Literature Association Distinguished Achievement Award, and the Lifetime Literary Achievement Award from the Native Writers' Circle of the Americas.